Gender in Contemporary Education Research

Gender in Contemporary Education Research

Edited

Ratna M. Sudarshan
and J.B.G. Tilak

KALPAZ

ISBN : 978-81-212-1362-2

First Published, 2017

Published by

Gyan Publishing House
5, Ansari Road
Daryaganj, New Delhi-110002
Phone: 9811692060
E-mail: books@gyanbooks.com

Printed at: G. Print Process, Delhi.

CONTENTS

INTRODUCTION

RATNA M. SUDARSHAN AND J.B.G. TILAK

Gender in Contemporary Education Research: an overview

This volume presents a selection of papers on gender and education, briefly reviewed in this introduction. Achieving 'gender equality' is a frequently reiterated objective of education policy. At the outset, the understanding of 'gender equality' that frames this review is briefly presented here. Gender is a concept that refers to socially constructed roles and relationships, generating gender differentiated responsibilities. The implication of these differences is a starting point for gendered analysis. Within the sphere of education, barriers in the access to schooling can be created by the socialization of boys and girls into gender specific roles and responsibilities which starts at home and much before children start school. Similarly drop out in response to household crisis may be influenced by domestic and other roles of boys and girls. School systems and within-school processes can either reinforce, or question, the socialization of the family and community. There are implicit as well as explicit messages contained within educational texts in regard to gendered norms and expectations. Gendered practices may be seen in classroom practices, such as sex segregation in classrooms, or a gendered allocation of routine tasks. Subject choices have been noted as being gendered, in that girls and boys may be guided towards a different set of optional choices, influenced by prevalent understanding of what would be 'useful' in the future; if girls are to be home makers in the future, their educational needs are defined accordingly. There may be gendered aspects to achievement and under achievement in academic work, as well as different levels of participation by boys and girls in cultural and sports activities. The outcomes of education are likely to be influenced by completed level of study, the economic and political environment, the social and cultural expectations from boys and girls, and are reflected in work choices. Prevalent gender norms and biases influence the environment beyond the educational system - mobility and safety, gender wage gaps and labour market discrimination for example.

In practice, 'undoing gender', or practices that try and change prevalent gendered social norms towards more equitable roles, has become understood within education as first and foremost ensuring girls have equal access to and are retained in schools. This concern stems from measurable indicators such as enrolment, drop out and transition rates that historically showed large gender gaps in favour of boys. Internationally, the better educational performance of girls in certain contexts has drawn attention. In India too, over the years these gaps have considerably narrowed, and drop out of boys is in some contexts higher than that of girls; moreover it is increasingly recognized that to capture prevalent inequalities data needs to be disaggregated along multiple axes, including gender, caste, class, location.

While parity or equality of treatment of all children is desirable and important as an objective, it is clearly distinct from substantive equality and the concern with equality of opportunity and outcomes. Commonly used indicators of gender parity include enrolment, survival (or drop out), attendance, average years of schooling, transitions between levels, number of male and female teachers (or parity in the supply of teaching), literacy levels (See Subrahmanya 2003, page 10). These indicators tell us little about whether or not underlying patterns of discrimination and disadvantage are changing. These patterns are rooted in socio-cultural norms and reinforced by choices made in regard to education, health, work and so on. Indicators focusing on parity tell us little about quality and experience of schooling. They do not tell us whether, in each particular context, education is enabling agency. Gender equality, which is closely connected to processes of social change, can be hard to capture or define precisely and unlike parity, is difficult to measure. It is not an easy goal to reach, requiring as it does the dismantling of inherited social structures and uprooting of deeply entrenched ideologies and norms: 'empowerment is a complex process of negotiation, rather than a linear sequence of inputs and outcomes' (Cornwall and Edwards 2014: 27). A concern with equality leads to an effort to understand the ways in which girls and boys from disadvantaged groups and locations can be enabled to exercise initiative, take responsibility, negotiate their preferred choices and in this way, exercise agency.

More recently, there is recognition that if gender equality is to be defined in relational terms, there needs to be an engagement with men and boys, and that deconstructing and reconstructing gendered norms requires equal effort from both genders. But while such deconstruction opens up new opportunities for girls, it is less clear what it offers to boys: and very little effort has gone into developing a shared vision of a better society that provides the motivation for working towards change.

Recognising the complexity of the gender question has certain methodological implications. One is that in the formulation of research questions, equality needs to be made explicit to ensure that the analysis goes beyond parity. Mixed methods of analysis are needed, at the least, and for some issues detailed ethnographic methods might give the best understanding. Qualitative information is necessary not only to fully interpret the quantitative data, but to go beyond that and understand the context, the processes of change that are on-going (or not), and how education is enabling (or not) wider changes reflected in changing gender roles and aspirations and outcomes of schooling. Situating education within an equality discourse (rather than one about parity) also means taking a holistic perspective, exploring and recognizing the connections between the home, the workplace, the community and the educational system.

A focus on equality is also a focus on transformative change; equality outcomes cannot be predicted and do not follow pre-determined routes. Perhaps an underlying reason for the dominance of parity indicators is the search for linear and predictable patterns of change. Within a stipulated development trajectory, education becomes an instrument for change and an investment that helps to reach stated targets in education and through education. It is expected for example, that literate, skilled and educated people would have higher productivity and contribute to higher rates of economic growth. A clearly stated and resource backed development agenda is conducive to an emphasis on parity and instrumentality; there are non-linearities in the equality and empowerment discourse that are at odds with this.[1]

With this broad understanding of gender equality, we would like to examine the extent to which gender issues in education have been noted, researched and highlighted by education researchers in India, and what these issues are. This would allow usto identify the issues that have been well researched and the issues that have not received much attention. Are there any theoretical or empirical contributions to understanding gender equality 'in, within and through' education in India?

Forthis particular purpose, we focused on the *Journal of Educational Planning and Administration*, a quarterly journal published by the National University of Educational Planning and Administration, New Delhi. The JOURNAL published since 1987 has an international editorial advisory board and it covers all areas relating to educational policy, planning, administration and development. It provides useful perspectives on a range of issues around education. It not only covers all levels of education, but is also international in its coverage. It is regarded as a leading journal in education in India offering a broad social science perspective on several research and policy issues in education. The present volume represents mainly a collection of articles published in the journal over the last three decades. The objective is also to see whether there have been any noticeable changes in the understanding of gender in education over this period. The articles selected are those that have tried to make theoretical or empirical contributions to understanding gender equality 'in, within and through' education in India. Limiting the selection to this one journal would not, it is anticipated, unduly curtail an assessment of the range of the research done by education researchers in India, although there may be considerable literature on education and gender that is located within other disciplines.

* * *

Stephen Brint, in his insightful analysis of the collective mind in the sociology of education in the USA, has used the term 'collective mind' as one that can be described by 'a pluralistic and fragmented image, based on counting each specific piece of work in the field'. As he put it, 'the collective mind of U.S. sociology of education is only one part of a much larger collective mind defined by the intellectual field of education studies. This larger collective mind can be conceived as the aggregate of all journals and book publication related to education and educational systems from all countries in the world and on all topics, from cognition to pedagogy to classroom and school organization'. (Brint 2013: 273). Borrowing the language from Brint, an attempt is made here to articulate the 'collective mind' of gender and education research in India, as expressed through JEPA, and presented below.

JEPA publishes 4 journals in the year, and each issue has 3 or 4 research papers. The methodology followed in reviewing and selecting articles is as follows. Out of all research papers published between 1987 and 2015 a shortlist was made of those that have addressed gender issues. Only research papers have been included, that is, research notes published in JEPA are excluded, and articles based on empirical studies in countries other than India have also been excluded (with one exception). An initial list of approximately forty articles was classified into three groups. The first is those that develop a theoretical framework or analytical concept with an explicit gender lens, the second consisting of girl/women-focused articles that examine outcomes of female literacy/ education, such as empowerment and decision making, and the third, and largest group, consisting of papers that use gender disaggregated data in their analysis. However, it was seen that gender disaggregated data has been used by many JEPA authors who may not have an interest in exploring gender issues per se, but who are concerned with the achievement of gender parity. Many of these articles focus on the social background of boys and girls (caste, mother/ father education, location etc.) to explain the influence of different factors on enrolment and drop out in particular. A further selection has therefore been made, essentially with the aim of including only those papers that seek to push the gender analysis beyond description of difference. Fourteen articles have been finally selected from JEPA. Two additional articles have been included written by NUEPA faculty and based on recent research.

A picture of the 'collective mind' of JEPA authors on gender issues is suggested below by identifying the main themes that inform the research.

(a) *The story of girls education*

Because 'gender'is often interpreted as a focus on 'girls' education', for reasons to do with deep-rooted discriminations,three articles are included here that spell out different concerns in girls' schooling. At the outset, it is to be noted that prevalent views about appropriate gender roles and responsibilities have shaped the ways in which women have acquired an education as much as the content of that education and its outcomes.

Writing in 1987, in the second issue of JEPA, and soon after the National Policy of Education 1986, Chiplunkar writes that women's education 'is possibly the foremost challenge for educational planners and administrators in the country' (173). The paper discusses the project Maher, initiated in 1985 in Satara district of Maharashtra. With 35 per cent girls in the age group 6-14 out of school at the time, it is a good reminder of the slow processes through which girls education could spread. Shushmita Chatterjee Dutt in reviewing the history of girls' education makes the important point that an exclusive focus on actual enrolment numbers understates the numbers of educated women, given that many women acquired learning through informal methods and systems, especially in the 19th century and earlier. 'To condemn Indian social arrangements completely, and state that very few girls were educated because very few were 'enrolled' at school, fails to capture the true conditions or arrangements made by Indian society, both public and private, for the education of girls and women' (Dutt 2001: 208). In 1920, less than a third of educational expenditure came from public sources; and the colonial government argued that girls' schooling was not 'cost effective'. Added to limited funds was the widely held perception that girls needed to be educated for future roles as wife/ mother. Consequently there has been little policy support for educating girls as equal citizens and partners.Gurminder Singh (2011) points to government efforts towards girls education as well as persisting disparities by gender, caste, class. Singh emphasizes that 'Education is the means towards empowerment of women, and the empowerment of girls'. (227). Any programme for eliminating gender discrimination within educational institutions needs to be complemented by changes within families and communities – the equal treatment promoted in schools 'ought to be able to transform the thinking within families'. Importantly, noting that freedom and equality have to be seen in relation to culture and structure of specific societies, while on-going interventions are all based on a fixed social construction of appropriate behaviours for girls, suggested ways forward include setting disaggregated targets; encouraging new initiatives; incorporating gender perspective in all aspects of planning; and learning from strategies followed by Tamil Nadu and Kerala, which have had early success in girls enrolment.

(b) *Framing gender in education: equity concerns*

Substantive equality, or the need to address pre-existing inequalities in order to create a level playing field, is a powerful argument for special measures to be taken; without this, in a context where groups start from unequal positions, equal treatment could enhance inequality and will not reduce it. The presence of intersecting inequalities due to gender, caste, location, etc. makes a strong argument for special measures or equity provisions. Frameworks and approaches that link gender to other forms of disadvantage have been strongly advocated in two JEPA papers included here.

Padma Velaskar argues that 'In India educational issues as related to caste, class, gender, ethnicity and region, are by and large separately examined. Educational analysis does not take into account the interactive influences of these structural variables and tends therefore to homogenize, simplify or distort a complex and highly differentiated educational reality.' (Velaskar 2005: 459) She examines the implications of the interactions between caste, class and patriarchy for educational access of dalit girls in Maharashtra. The dual impact of caste movements and the women's movement has led to the emergence of a dalit women's movement, for whom the education of dalit girls is a key agenda. Between 1979-80 and 1998-99, the growth rate in enrolment at primary and upper primary levels of dalit girls exceeded that of general category girls, and that of girls was greater than that of boys. The gender inequality reduced at all levels over this period, however, literacy and education remains lower among dalit women as compared to non-dalit women and dalit men. Overall greater gender than caste disparity in education indicators points to persistent gendered structural barriers; but the influence of caste has not disappeared, and class creates further exclusions.

Dhanwanti Nayak (2007) discusses equity in education, and its significance in a context of poverty and deeply rooted gender and social group inequalities. Equity is to be understood as 'all the means or approaches to achieve the goal of equality' and in that sense equity is what enables substantive equality. It follows from this that in education 'an approach focusing on equality would be limited to equality of status while an approach focusing on equity would be more inclusive and bring in the equality of opportunity' (Nayak 2007: 260, 263). Gender equity and social equity are the two main types of equity considered in this paper, as these identify groups that have been historically/ traditionally discriminated against, and where membership is not a matter of individual choice. Nayak suggests that in relation to gender equity, 'we mean to focus on those differences that exist between men and women as two groups rather than as individuals; that have their origins outside the context of individual agency; focus on those mechanisms, policies and practices which remove systemic barriers to their access to opportunities within society to develop themselves fully; and those mechanisms which allow for differential treatment for them as a group to create opportunities which they would otherwise not have access to, such as free education for the girl child in government schools' (ibid 266). The paper makes a strong case for educational equity (that is group focused) as essential to equitable education (individual focused) with education for an equitable society being the ultimate aspiration.

Madhumita Bandopadhyay uses data from a study conducted under the CREATE[2]-NUEPA project to examine the gendered nature of educational exclusion. The zones of exclusion model, developed by the CREATE project has been adapted to the Indian education system. Six zones of exclusion have been identified: children not entering primary school (Zone 1); children who drop out from primary school (Zone 2); children at risk of silent exclusion i.e. enrolled but not learning (Zone 3); children who complete primary school but do not enter upper primary (Zone 4); children who drop out from upper primary (Zone 5); and children who do not transit to secondary level of education (Zone 6). Field survey data from selected schools and villages in Chhattisgarh and Madhya Pradesh is used to illustrate the gender aspects of these different types of exclusion as also possible strategies to address them.

Vimala Ramachandran in her paper, which draws upon a mid-term assessment done at NUEPA in 2007 ofEducation for All, and other recent research, emphasizes the heterogeneity of gendered realities within education. Through a mapping of socio-economic factors (including being in abject poverty, above poverty line, based in rural, urban or tribal areas, belonging to SC, ST, Muslim or other groups, engaged in home based or outside wage labour, affected by seasonal migration, or by displacement and conflict, affected by violence at home or in school, gender attitudes, disability and health) against aspects of the prevailing school system (including physical access, teachers and teaching, learning, monitoring and supervision, accountability and transition to the next level), the different realities faced by girls is articulated. She recommends a focus on three areasas non-negotiable principles in order to move forward and address some of these observable inequalities, meaningful access to education, non-discrimination, and foregrounding gender in the construction of knowledge.

Nelly Stromquist (2015) uses the concepts of 'structure' and 'agency' in her analysis of why women faculty continue to be in a disadvantaged position as academics. Stromquist suggests that structures or 'the set of principles that shape social practices as well as the set of the institutions that officially sanction and enforce those practices' in general act as a constraint to change, although there is a dynamic process of change resulting from the interplay between structure and agency . Agency, or 'action taken by individuals in response to their environment' can take the form of conformity or resistance. It could be individual or collective. Stromquist suggests that women academics exercise considerable individual agency but less so as a collective force to address gender issues within academia. The paper is based on data from the USA, however the ways in which there is a persistence of gendered behaviours within universities resonates with the situation in India and probably elsewhere.

(c) *Culture vs economic opportunity*

The role of culture in creating gender differences in the experience and the aims of education is well recognized, although less research is available on the changing relative balance of culture and economic opportunity.

Satinderjit Thind and Sushma Jaswal discuss the gender bias in education among rural Sikhs in three cultural zones of the Punjab, and find cultural values, sex discriminatory practices to set constraints on girls' education. The study finds among families from southern Malwa a higher value on acquisition of land, to investing in education particularly for girls. In all zones, very few girls went outside the village for education; and girls did not assert themselves for seeking higher levels of education. 'The sensitization of girls that they shall be appreciated most by the members of the family and the community for learning household tasks well kills their motivation for studies'. Denial of education to the rural girl child means that 'education, which could have been a major instrument of women's equality, change and empowerment, is unable to play its due role in this regard' (Thind and Jaswal 2004: 54).

T. Lakshamanasamy (2006) uses data from Tamil Nadu for married and unmarried women and shows that pre-marital investments on women in the form of education and dowry provide labour market and marriage gains: not only does women's education improve own earnings, but it also has a positive effect on the husband's earnings. Assortative marriage prevails, and this means that better educated women can marry better educated men. However the analysis also suggests that education does not improve women's position within the family, and their bargaining power and role in household decisions remains weak.

Educational participation is influenced by 'culture' but exclusive focus on culture would miss the influence of economic change and opportunity. That 'girls' do not constitute a homogenous population is well understood. It becomes important then to explore the relevant factors behind weak educational participation for girls within larger social groupings. Zakir Husain, using NSS data, examines enrolment and drop out of Muslims in West Bengal. He points out that there is a perception that barriers to educational progress among Muslims, especially girls, are religious and socio-cultural, and hence it has been felt that state intervention could not have major impact. The data show that parents of only 4.6 per cent of Muslim children aged 6-12 do not value education, and only about 11-12 per cent of Muslim boys and girls are not enrolled. Other explanatory factors behind low enrolment include limited labour market opportunities, prevalent unemployment, and poor quality of schools. Only in the case of girls in urban areas, the perception that education is not important is a major reason for non-enrolment. Drop out is higher for Muslim boys than girls, and reasons could include job related discouragement. Within the community there is a perception that educated girls can better manage household accounts, fend for herself in case of desertion, and also unlike other communities it is acceptable for a girl to marry a less educated boy (26 per cent of educated Muslim women have illiterate husbands, as cited from Hasan and Menon 2004). This means that girls are left to continue studying until marriage, while boys are under pressure to start earning. The paper argues that there is little support for the view that Muslims do not value education; and the role of economic factors in the high dropout rates needs to be assessed. Affirmative action is recommended, and avoiding the anomaly that 'despite the fact that only 4 per cent of Muslim children in West Bengal are enrolled in Madrasas, the West Bengal government has tended to focus on Madrasas as the panacea for educational deprivation' (Husain 2009: 364).

Karuna Chanana (2013) discusses the ways in which even higher education continues to play only a limited role in social change because of slowly changing views on socially acceptable female work roles. Globalization and the knowledge society affect education – 'For example, formation of intellectual capital, as a market commodity, is being viewed or projected as an indispensable instrument for a high-skills economy' (143). While there is a greater presence of women in higher education, Chanana points out the ways in which horizontal segregation is replacing vertical segregation: thus in agriculture women are seen concentrated in agro-chemistry, agro-engineering and technology and agro-social sciences, while being much less present in the sub-fields of animal studies, plant studies and agriculture. Similarly in the natural sciences women are seen much more in life sciences, zoology, botany, and biology, and much less in geology. And so on with other disciplines. In this way 'disparities across subjects are being replaced by disparities within specialization through the process of simultaneous inclusion and exclusion' (151). Thus 'layers of disadvantage' can be seen with data disaggregated by gender, caste, ethnicity and other categories reflecting social or economic disadvantage.

(d) The wider impacts of literacy/ education: education/ decision making/ empowerment

The reproduction of societal inequality within schools is well established. More is known about the society-to-school influences than is known about school-to-society. The wider impacts of education have been discussed in a few papers, although cross-sectoral studies are largely absent.

Private returns to education are an immediate 'wider impact' and Jeemol Unni (1996) uses NSSO data to compute private returns to education for urban wage workers, males and females in the 15-64 age group, in Madhya Pradesh and Tamil Nadu. She finds the returns to education to rise with level of education for both men and women; a decline in wage inequality as educational levels increase, and higher rates of return to education for women as compared with men (except among graduates in Madhya Pradesh, which might reflect small numbers of women in the sample for this group).

Usha Jayachandran (2001) examines school attendance and work participation to make the important point that school attendance and child labour need not be 'two faces of the same coin'. There is a complementarity between poor school attendance and 'unaccounted children' – neither at work nor in school. Overall, while 50 per cent of the child population (5-14) is in school, 45 per cent are 'unaccounted children', and the highest per centages are in states with poor school attendance - UP, Bihar and Rajasthan. Analysis of the data shows that female adult literacy is positively associated with school attendance overall and girl child attendance. Child work participation on the other hand is influenced by availability of work opportunities; male child work participation (based on 1991 Census data) is seen to be higher than that of female children in urban areas across all states, perhaps pointing to higher migration levels of boys. Data also show a positive relationship between adult female work force participation rate and female child work force participation rate. Thus higher levels of adult female education are correlated with higher girl child enrolment and school attendance, but not necessarily with lower levels of child work.[3]

Rakhee Banerjee, Pradip Kumar Sahu and Santiranjan Pal (2010) examine the correlation between an empowerment measure (which measures the intensity of involvement in a range of decisions including work) and an education index (based on literacy and enrollment) calculated separately for men and women, for 2 villages in each of six soil-agro-climatic zones of West Bengal. They find that higher education and higher levels of empowerment are correlated, although pathways may be different. In the hill and terai zones for example, there are greater work opportunities, such as in the tea gardens. The study points to the regional disparities, and to the combined positive impact of education and work.

Madhusudan Raj (2011) using data on 300 women over the age of 25 in Surat city, Gujarat, through different regression methods shows that women's education is positively correlated with some variables including knowledge of family planning methods, education of child, having a bank account, saving, being in the labour market. But being educated did not give women greater overall economic freedom, ability to go out for social events without taking permission, having more charitable activity, lower dowry or lower marriage expenditure, different religious beliefs or level of voting.

It is hoped that this overview and the sixteen papers that follow present a rich base for an understanding of the nature and kind of attention given by contemporary scholars to issues relating to gender in education.

References

Bandopadhyay, 2015, Gender, Educational Deprivation and Exclusion: A Case Study of Madhya Pradesh and Chhattisgarh, this volume.

Banerjee, Rakhee, Pradip Kumar Saha, Santiranjan Pal, 2010, Women's education and empowerment in rural areas- a case study of West Bengal, India, JEPA Vol XXIV: 1, 23-52.

Banerji, Rukmini, 2000, Poverty and Primary Schooling, Economic and Political Weekly, Vol XXXV no 10.

Brint, Steven, 2013, 'The "collective mind" at work: a decade in the life of US sociology of education', Sociology of Education 86 (4) 273-279.

Chanana, Karuna, 2013, Higher education in a changing world, JEPA XXVII: 2, 141-155.

Chiplunkar, V.V., 1987, Education and empowerment of women: project Maher, JEPA Vol 1(2) 173-190.

Cornwall, Andrea and Jenny Edwards, 2014, Introduction: negotiating empowerment, in Andrea Cornwall and Jenny Edwards (ed) Feminisms, Empowerment and Development, Zed Books: London pp 1-31.

Dutt, Shushmita Chatterji, 2001, De-constructing of the interaction of colonial rule with the education of Indian girls, JEPA Vol XV: 2, 197-224.

Husain, Zakir, 2009, Enrolment and dropouts of Muslims in West Bengal: evidence from NSS 61st round, JEPA Vol XXIII: 4, 347-367.

Jayachandran, Usha, 2001, Understanding school attendance and children's work participation in India, JEPA Vol VX: 1, 5-47.

Lakshamanasamy, T., 2006, Women's education, dowry, bargaining and gains to marriage, JEPA Vol XX: 1, 27-51.

Mukherjee, Dipa, 2005, Educational attainment in India: trends, patterns and policy issues, JEPA Vol XIX (4), 523-541.

Mukhopadhyay, Rabindranath, 2005, Literacy and participatory Human Development: an illustrative Indian exercise, JEPA Vol XIX: 3, 313-333.

Nayak, Dhanwanti, 2007, Equity and education, JEPA Vol XXI: 3, 257-273.

Raj, Madhusudan, 2011, Non-market benefits of women's education, JEPA Vol XXV: 2, 123-140.

Ramachandran, Vimala, 2015, Heterogeneous gendered realities and multiple disadvantages: Issues that frame women and girls education in India, this volume

Singh, Gurminder, 2011, Elementary education for girls in India, JEPA vol XXV (3), 223-234.

Sinha, Shantha, 1996, Child Labour and Education Policy in India, The Administrator Vol XLI, July- September 1996, pp 17-29.

Stromquist, Nelly, 2015, Women in Higher Education Today: Structure and Agency from a Gender Perspective.

Subrahmanian, Ramya, n.d, Gender Equality in Education: Definitions and Measurements, *Background paper for UNESCO GMR 2003-04*.

Thind, Satinderjit; Sushma Jaswal, 2004, Gender bias in education among the rural Sikhs of Punjab, JEPA Vol XVIII:1, 49-56.

Unni, Jeemol, 1996, Returns to education by gender among wage employees in urban India, JEPA vol X (2) 153-172.

Velaskar, Padma, 2005, Education, Caste, Gender: Dalit girls access to schooling in Maharashtra, JEPA Vol XIX:4, 459-4.

Notes

1. The achievement of education goals appears to have been most successful when aligned with development goals and 'gender equality' is one of the goals that has not been so successfully aligned, or met – Aaron Benovot at NUEPA, Jan 15, 2015.
2. Consortium for Research on Educational Access, Transitions and Equity.
3. Although Shantha Sinha (1996) has said that 'all non school going children are child workers in one form or the other', other research also finds that not being in school does not necessarily imply being at work, even when 'work' includes house work and sibling care (Banerji 2000).

PART – I

THE STORY OF GIRLS EDUCATION

1

EDUCATION AND EMPOWERMENT OF WDMEN PROJECT MAHER

— *V. V. CHIPLUNKAR*

Women's education is possibly the foremost challenge for the educational planners and administrators in this country. Although it is true that there is substantial awakening in this regard as a result of several programmes and activities initiated for accomplishing the twin target of universalisation of elementary education and adult education, the alarming figures of school drop-outs and consequent rising numbers of female illiterates in *the* country call for urgent attention and concerted action. Women unmistakably assume a very significant position in the process of total development of human resources. "For full development of our human resources, the improvement of homes and for moulding the character of children during the most impressionable years of infancy, the education of women is of even greater importance *than* that of men... The education of women can assist greatly in reducing the fertility rate. In the modern world the role of the woman goes much beyond the home and the bringing up of children. She is now adopting a career of her own and sharing equally with man, the responsibility for the development of society in all its aspects... This equal partnership will have to continue in the fight against hunger, poverty, ignorance and ill health."[1]

2. The National Policy on Education, 1986, it is worthy to note, holds out a promise that education will be used as an agent of basic change in the status of women and envisages the interventionist role on the part of the National Educational System in the empowerment of *women*.[2] While delineating concrete operational guidelines, the Programme of Action published by the Ministry of Human Resource Development, (Education Department),

Government of India, mentions gearing the entire education system to plan such a role, to create dynamic manegerial structure to cope with the targets envisaged and to encourage educational institutions to take up programmes which directly benefit the community and bring about the empowerment of *women*.[3]

3. The task is indeed stupendous and it needs a multipronged attack and an integrated approach at different levels of educational planning and administration. It essentially calls for measures like generating a climate for the promotion of women's education, increasing facilities of formal as well as non-formal instruction, instituting a variety of support- programmes and expanding the existing ones, preparing supplementary courses to meet actual needs of the target groups and initiating appropriate changes in planning, administration and monitoring strategy. With about 35% girls in the age group 6-14 still out of orbit and about adult women in the country still illiterate, it is imperative, that possibility of launching a mass movement is fully explored and an all-out effort is made to build up an army of voluntary workers gifted with missionary zeal to combat the cause on a war footing. It is high time that the prevailing infrastructure with a network of educational institutions at all levels of the system, with organised man-power at its command, gets sensitized and activized towards this singular target.

4. The Project Maher is a move in this direction.

II. Basic Assumptions

The following are some of the basic assumptions that prompted formulation of this project:

1. There is a growing awareness on the part of the community even in difficult areas to send girls to school, as is revealed from the .rising trend of enrolment.
2. The prevailing formal system has, by and large, failed to retain the majority of girls belonging to weaker sections till the completion of the school stage. This calls for immediate improvement.
3. Their economic condition prevents them from availing of the facility of full-time instruction, which necessitates opening avenues of part-time and own-time instruction as a supplementary measure.
4. The prevailing course-context falls short of the practical requirements of the vast majority of the early school-leavers, which points to the need to introduce supplementary courses of shorter duration to be completed conveniently out of school hours.
5. Girls' enrolment and retention improve with increasing participation of women in teaching, planning and administration in schools.
6. The present support programmes are short of actual requirement in many cases and need further strengthening.

7. The majority of women seldom get an opportunity for rest, recreation and personal development, confined as they get to the household duties throughout life.
8. A large resource of educated and effectively literate men and women still remains untapped, which could be otherwise harnessed to the cause of women's education with a special effort.
9. Voluntary organisations, though very few in number, are doing some innovative work in this field which deserves appropriate recognition and adequate support.
10. The network of educational institutions and administrative set up possessing rich potential for undertaking developmental programmes is engaged in maintenance-oriented activities and need to be geared to development needs with thrust on linkages with community.
11. The system is already badly hit by monetary constraints and there is urgent need to step up monetary inputs. However, there is enough scope for non-monetary inputs as well, which if tapped, may help to mitigate the situation to same extent.

III. Objectives

The Project Maher aims at:

1. Mobilising human resources, especially woman resources for promotion of women's education, providing necessary climate for unfolding of their qualities of leadership,
2. Reaching out the benefits of education to out-of- school girls and illiterate women,
3. Providing occasional facilities for rest, recreation and development to women,
4. Encouraging women to participate in planning, organising and monitoring of educational development of girls in the given locality, and
5. Attempting a change in the role and functions of the established infrastructure of educational insti-tutions and administration.

IV. Coverage

The Project was initiated in October, 1985 first at Naigaon. Naigaon is the birth-place of the Late Savitribai Phule, a great social reformer and pioneer of women's education in the middle of the 19th Century and the wife of Mahatama Jyotiba Phule, a well-known champion of the cause of the down-trodden and a great reformist. Naigaon is a small village with population of 2500 in Khandala Block, District Satara, in the State of Maharashtra. There is a full-fledged elementary school run by Zilla Parishad, Satara and private aided full- fledged secondary school with enrolment of 410 and 153 pupils respectively. Out of 19 teachers, seven are women. A school complex is formed with the secondary school as *the* Lead School with four feeder primary schools for the purpose of planning, organisation, professional development of teachers as well as for strengthening curricular and co-curricular activities including participation in programmes of community development.

The Project Maher is now extended to other five villages in the Khandala Block, which in fact is a typically droughtprone area with total rural character. It is expected to cover the entire Block with the population of 83000 spread out in 61 villages, having a contingent of 87 elementary schools, 15 secondary schools and a college. Out of about 650 teachers in the Block, 170 are women teachers - 122 working in elementary schools and 48 in secondary schools. 6044*girls are on rolls of the elementary schools and 2354 in *the* secondary schools. About 300 girls in the age-group 6-14 are out of school and about 2500 women in the age-group 15 to 35 still illiterate.

V. Tasks

The following tasks have been envisaged in the Project:

1. To enrol all children, girls in particular, to school at 6.
2. To muster community support in cash and kind to facilitate their retention.
3. To run Balwadis for children in the age group 4-6.
4. To conduct creches and child-health and care centres for children below 4.
5. To arrange for non-formal education of out-of-school girls in the age group 9-14.
6. To arrange for education of illiterate adult women in the age-group 15 to 35.
7. To conduct continuation education activities for neo-literate and literate adult women.
8. To arrange excursions, cultural activities and social camps for school going girls and adult women.
9. To avail of the benefits of the national programmes like Family Planning, Small Savings, Social Forestry, etc.
10. To organise a variety of activities for the development of girls and adult women including imparting of vocational skills.
11. To arouse popular will and secure expertise from the field, etc.

VI. Strategy

The following strategy was finalised as a result of initial discussions with teachers, headmasters, officers and non-official members of the Panchayat Samiti and Zilla Parishad including women representatives:

1. Survey of educational and developmental needs of girls and adult women upto the age of 35.
2. Identification of and building up a team of workers, viz., teachers, headmasters, social workers, officers, non-officials - both men and women - as well as senior pupils ready to volunteer for this cause.
3. Orientation and training of workers.
4. Planning of programmes and activities at the grassroot level, school complex level and block level.
5. Enlisting wider community-support.
6. Implementing programmes and activities.
7. Monitoring and evaluation.
8. Changing the role and functions of existing educational institutions, and
9. Making *the* best possible use of the infrastructure - material and human resources - obtaining with them.

VII. Operational Details

The following operational details were worked out for effective planning and implementation of the Project:

1. To institute -tiie village Project Advisory Committee with adequate number of women representatives (preferably couples - one per hundred families). Members of the Village Panchayat and representatives of past students (particularly girls, if any) should be included in the Committee.
2. To prepare lists of villagers - both men and women who will be able to give help and assistance to the project. The kind of help/assistance they would like to render should be mentioned against their names.
3. To prepare lists of children at 6+ and admit them to school.
4. To prepare a list of villagers willing to pay in cash/kind to pupils to help their retention at school, this programme is being implemented under a different name, viz., Mahatma Phule Chhatraseva and to form a local committee for this purpose.
5. (i) To prepare ward/mohalla-wise lists of children in the age group 4 to 6.

   (ii) To conduct as many Balwadis for them as needed.

   (iii) To prepare lists of women-volunteers for this work and arrange for their orientation.

   (iv) To collect equipment for Balwadis, and

   (v) To form Balwadi Committee, distribute responsibilities and initiate action.

6 (i) To prepare lists of women and children in need of creche facility.

(ii) To prepare a list of women-volunteers to run the creche, and

(iii) To select places and start the creche accordingly.

7. To start a child-health and Care Centre with the help of a local physician, if any (or in the vicinity).
8. To prepare lists of out-of-school boys and girls in the age-group 9-14 and start non-formal education programme for them with the help of willing retired and working teachers and women workers, using the materials produced by the SCERT.
9. To prepare lists of illiterate adult women in the age-group 15-35 and start adult education programme for them, using the materials produced by the State Adult Education Institute.
10. To start reading-rooms and classes for neo-literate omen; to prepare lists of such women and those willing to conduct this activity.
11. To prepare lists of women in the age-group 18-40 who have not passed the SSC Exam., but who are effectively literate, to prepare a variety of courses of small duration for them, to identify persons able to handle them and start the programme with their help.
12. To prepare a programme of recreation, excursions and special camps for girls and adult women and organise it as per schedule.
13. To take active part in the national programmes like Family Planning, Small Savings, Social Forestry, Bio-gas, etc.
14. To under take, programmes for total development of girls and adult women, including skills which may earn them self-employment.
15. To prepare lists of experts (particularly ladies in different fields) who could be invited on different occasions for conducting different programmes and activities.
16. To form programme-wise sub-committees of two or three women workers (preferably couples).
17. To prepare time-schedule for different programmes.
18. To convene monthly meetings (as far as possible on a specific date) of Village Project Committee and Sub-committees to take stock of the situation and monitor progress, and to maintain proper record thereof, and
19. To get the 'Declaration Form' duly filled in from those willing to work for the Project Maher and enter the 'women's education service' (specially instituted to enlist workers with missionary zeal for the cause of women's education).

VIII. Monitoring and Evaluation

The Block level Project Advisory Committee is constituted under the Chairmanship of the Chairman, Panchayat Samiti of the Khandala Block with Block Education Officer as Member-Secretary, with adequate representation to heads of schools, teachers, women-workers, officers and non-officials.

The School Complex level Advisory Committees will be headed by the Head of the Lead School with a woman-teacher as a member-secretary and adequate representation to other functionaries.

The Village-level Project Advisory Committees will function as mentioned earlier.

Thus, there would be three-tier mechanism for planning, managing, monitoring and evaluation. Presently, the Project is initiated in six selected villages only. The Advisory Committees at the School Complex level would be constituted as the Project is extended to cover the whole Block in a phased manner. It is also envisaged that effort would be made to involve as many women as possible in planning, organisation and management of the Project, thereby encouraging their leadership.

IX. Progress Achieved - A Glimpse

As stated the Project has been initiated at Naigaon in October, 1985 and is extended to other five villages, namely, Khandala, Bavada, Jawale, Guthale and Mariaichi Wadi with effect from August, 1986.

A social camp for adult women was conducted at Naigaon in the last week of December, 1985, which was attended by 30 women.

Village Project Advisory Committees have been constituted in all the six villages and proceedings of the meetings are maintained.

Village-wise lists of persons willing to work for the Project have been prepared, indicating the kind of help and assistance he/she would like to give. The village-wise number registered so far is as follows :

Table 1: Persons Willing to Offer Help/Assistance

S.No.	*Village*	*Male*	*Female*	*Total*
1.	Bavada	21	16	37
2.	Guthale	25	00	25
3.	Jawale	32	32	64
4.	Khandala	35	44	79
5.	Mariaichi Wadi	11	01	12
6.	Naigaon	55	10	65
	Total	**179**	**103**	**282**

There appears comparatively low response from women in Guthale, M. Wadi and Naigaon. However, the work is in progress as the Project is just introduced in those villages. The position is likely to improve in course of time. The response, on the whole, is quite encouraging.

Census of children of 5+ is completed in all the six villages. In Maharashtra children are allowed admission to Std. I even at 5+. The general tendency is, therefore, to admit children at 5+ in places where there is greater awakening. Table 2 gives th picture of work done in this respect.

Table 2: No. of Children at 5+

S.No.	*Village*	*Male*	*Female*	*Total*
1.	Bavada	31	36	67
2.	Guthale	10	11	21
3.	Jawale	19	26	45
4.	Khandala	61	34	95
5.	Mariaichi Wadi	11	7	18
6.	Naigaon	22	22	44
	Total	**154**	**136**	**290**

Mahatma Phule Chhatra Seva Saraitis are also formed in all the six villages for enlisting community support in cash and kind to help pupils' retention at school. Table 3 indicates the progress made so far in this respect.

Table 3: Community Support in Cash and Kind

S.No.	*Village*	*Amount in Rs.*
1.	Bavada	180.00
2.	Guthale	50.00
3.	Jawale	200.00
4.	Khandala	365.00
5.	Mariaichi Wadi	50.00
6.	Naigaon	755.70
	Total	**1600.70**

Census of children in *the* age group 3-5 is completed in all *the* six villages and Balwadis are conducted with the enrolment as shown in the Table 4.

Table 4: Enrolment in Balwadis

S.No.	*Village*	*Boys*	*Girls*	*Total*
1.	Bavada	15+25	15+25	30+50 (Two Balwadis)
2.	Guthale	12	15	27
3.	Jawale	22	18	40
4.	Khandala	30	20	50
5.	Mariaichi Wadi	13	17	30
6.	Naigaon	28	18	46
	Total	**145**	**128**	**273**

In every village, a committee is formed to solve "Hie day-to- day difficulties in the conduct of the Balwadi.

A survey of mothers and children needing the arrangement y of creche is made. Lists of women willing to work for running the creche are also prepared. Creches are expected to start functioning before 14th of November, 1986, i.e., Children's Day.

Child-Health and Care Centres have been started with the help of local physicians.

Survey of illiterate adult women is completed and literacy classes are conducted for them. Post-literacy classes for neo-literate adult women have been started at Bavada and Naigaon.

Women's rallies were organised at Bavada, Jawale and Naigaon.

Women take active part in the programmes of Family Planning, Small Savings, Social Forestry and Bio-gas programmes of national significance, along with men. The progress of Small Savings Scheme is given in Table 5.

Table 5: Collection in Small Savings

S.No.	*Village*	*Saving in Rs from 1.4.86*
1.	Bavada	42,000
2.	Guthale	7,000
3.	Jawale	25,000
4.	Khandala	60,000
5.	M. Wadi	5,000
6.	Naigaon	60,000
	Total	**1,99,000**

Sewing class has been started at Jawale and Yogasana class is conducted at Naigaon of which about 40 and 30 women are taking benefit respectively.

Lists of men and women willing to work for the cause of women*s education and declaring the commitment are also in progress.

Other programmes and activities are being taken up as per operational guidelines and it is expected that with growing enthusiasm and willing support and active involvement of teachers at all levels, heads of educational institutions, officers, non-official members of the Village Panchayats, Panchayat Samiti and Zilla Parishad, social workers - both men and women - common village folk and pupils, the project will pick up gradually and take a shape of Mass Movement for the promotion of women's education in the near future. It is gratifying to note that the age-old educational infrastructure given to maintenance administration is now showing signs of change over to the developmental type as a result of which optimum utilisation of the facilities obtaining in educational institutions for the promotion of community development in general and for women's education in particular is proving to be a practical proposition. The kind of enthusiasm, dedication and spirit of service seen generated in all sections of the community - both men and women, young and old, teachers and pupils, officers and non-officials, farmers and land labourers - holds a promise for a better future. Women's voluntary support to the Project and their active participation amply speaks of the potent success of the process of their empowerment as contemplated in the National Policy on Education, 1986. The Policy is likely to fetch expected results if success is achieved in spotting at least one woman (preferably a couple) per 100 families in every village and urban localities, in training them and backing up with administrative support with the recognition to his or her service rendered with missionary zeal.

X. Educational Institutions - March Towards a Change

A change is often beset with a challenge. When the total education system is undergoing a radical change, it is in the fitness of things *that* every educational institution from top to bottom transforms itself in consonance with the overall objectives, methods of working and priorities. For meeting the challenge of women's education, the Project envisages the following changes in *the* prevailing system:

1. Persons and institutions whether schools or colleges at the top within the operational area taka initiative in breaking new grounds and establishing horizontal as well as vertical linkages within and outside the system. They seek cooperation from the teaching and administrative fraternity working with them, as well as from other agencies within the overall developmental framework including teachers' organisations, voluntary agencies like Youth Clubs, Mahila Mandals, etc.

2. They identify persons capable of delivering the goods, organise them into teams and orient them towards the intended change.
3. They break isolation and bring various institutions and agencies closer *to* form small clusters to function, as effective organisational, planning and action units.
4. Educational Institutions change their traditional dominant role of preparing pupils for examinations and focus their attention on *the* total development of the pupils in the context of the community development and attempt establishing closer relationship for the mutual benefit of both the institutions and the community which in fact are inseparable.
5. Educational institutions assume the role of agents of change within the broad framework of national perspective and undertake the function of extension in addition to its normal curricular and co- curricular functions. They thus attempt breaking barriers created by the four walls and employ their human and material resources in the service to the community with persuation rather than with force.
6. They tap hidden human resources, mobilise them and utilise them for this purpose. Especially, in relation to women's education they motivate women teachers, wives of male teachers and other members on the staff and educated women in the locality to spare some of their time and energy for attending to the needs of the target groups.
7. Educational institutions also utilise the holidays, long vacations and out-of-school hours for arranging non-formal education courses or continuation education classes for out-of-school girls and adult women, treating time as an important input for a developing community which is forced to work under compulsions imposed by money constraints. A substantial progress is achieved if persons within the system and outside offer at least an hour a day to this solemn cause.
8. Planners and administrators in educational institutions at various levels make a concerted effort at planning for the change with due attention to training of workers engaged in different tasks in reaching out to the target groups and employ the mass media for that purpose.
9. They also set their own example by playing a leading role in actual field operations and work with their fellow colleagues and other workers. When modern planning and management theories expect workers in the field to plan their work even at the micro level, it is high time, that planners in their turn set an example of working out the plans. The process of change, like charity, has to begin 'at home'.

XI. Limitations

1. All said and done, education system, helpless under the stranglehold of examinations, takes time to change.
2. Administrative set-up whether in the public or private management is still stuck up to the 'Top-down' approach.
3. As a result, the organised formal educational structure lacks initiative in breaking new grounds.
4. There is often acute shortage of material and monetary resources.
5. There is lack of expertise needed, particularly in difficult and distant rural areas.
6. Those who have earned the benefits of education, by and large, tend to be self-centered and are seldom sensitive to the needs of the deprived ones, of women in particular.
7. Those who possess scientific knowledge and techniques seldom evince capabilities and the spirit of actual service, whereas those who work in good spirit, seldom display an attitude to learn new techniques of planning and working. It is seldom realised that science without spirit is futile and spirit without science is sterile.

XII. The Title

In spite of a few 'Limitations' (it is doubtful whether they could be styled 'problems'), enumerated above, the Project Maher is picking up gradually as an institutionalized effort. Its leadership is provided by the Panohayat Samiti, which, is a well-established institution in the set up of democratic decentralisation. Besides, the title 'Maher' itself is catching not merely because it is the birth-place (and 'mother's place' too) of the Late Savitribai Phule, champion of the cause of women's education in Maharashtra, but it has also a direct appeal to the women-folk in general. Women, it is seen, enjoy a climate of affinity and freedom at the 'mother's place'. It is generally taken as a rightful place of rest, recreation and free access (so essential for development). The Project Maher attempts to create that kind of climate of affinity and freedom for the development of women which, it is experienced, helps in sustaining in them not only a sense of belongingness, but security as well.

References

1. Education and National Development - Report of the Education Commission (1964-66), Ministry of Education, Government of India, pp. 238-39.
2. National Policy on Education, 1986, Ministry of Human Resource Development, (Department of Education), Government of India, p. 6.
3. Programme of Action, National Policy on Education, 1986, Ministry of Human Resource Development, (Department of Education), Government of India, p. 108.

2

De-constructing of the Interaction of Colonial Rule with the Education of Indian Girls

— *Shushmita Chatterji Dutt*

Abstract

Contrary to the popular belief that historically the Indian system did not support the education of women and girls, the traditional systems were not uniformly inclusive: women and girls from some selected families and groups in society always had access to education. This selective support continued even after the arrival of the western colonizers; and eventually, the Indian agency supported the efforts of the colonial administration. The little activity for girls' education that took place during the colonial period was possible only with active Indian contribution, in terms of advocacy for girls' education, collaboration with money or other academic support. The paper examines how colonial rule impacted girls' education in the twentieth century. Some scholars have argued that colonial administration co-opted the elite among the colonized through their education policy in order to sustain and secure their rule. The obvious nervousness about the wisdom of educating a subject people and suspicions regarding the loyalty of the elite groups resulted in the strong tendency to control and the resistance to building up a truly inclusive, modern and science/technology based education system. Instead the system put in place was entangled with interweaving chains of control and an educational content that excluded Indians from partaking of the scientific and technological gains being made in the west.

Misconceptions regarding Girls' Education (upto 1900)

Girls' Education in Ancient and Medieval India

The environment for the education of females in ancient India was supportive within certain classes and castes. Women appear to have been eligible for studying Vedic literature and performing sacrifices till about 200 B.C. The 'upananyan' ceremony might also have been performed for girls as the Vedic prayers could not be recited without this. At a later stage the 'upananyan' ceremony for girls was explicitly prohibited by Yagnavalkya as incomplete education and incorrect pronunciation of the Vedic Mantras would lead to negative results. Women are said to have composed Vedic mantras and hymns. The main institutions for girls' education were perhaps the family and the home. Panini refers to boarding houses for girls but no clear evidence of these institutions can be cited.

Jaiswal contends that society in the Rig-vedic period was still predominantly pastoral and nomadic, not producing enough surplus to allow any section of society to be completely subordinated or withdrawn from the process of production. Desai and Krishnaraj discuss that this perhaps explains the comparatively better situation of women in the Vedic period in terms of access to education, religious rights, freedom of movement etc. "Education of women, which was an accepted norm during the Vedic period, slowly began to be neglected and later on girls were totally denied any access to education."

The growth of classes in society, which manifested itself as varnas, the rise of private property and the decline of the position of women appear to have occurred simultaneously in the post-Vedic period. Patriarchal' values relating to sexuality, the regulation of female movement and early marriage, thus controlling her 'purity', get entrenched during this phase. The overall changing social mores affected the different classes in varying ways. "Girls in the ruling class families did receive some training in military administration and fine arts. There were a few outstanding scholarly women like Gargi, Maitreyee, Atreyi who provided an alternative style of female existence."

During the Buddhist period, monastic orders included nuns or **Bhikkhunis** who received some instruction in the Buddhist doctrines and also perhaps in reading and writing. But few nunneries, unlike monasteries, grew to be centres of education for lay women. The **Sangam** works of Southern India refer to the writings of women like Nappashalai, Vennikuyuthi, Avvai, Adi Mandi and Gangadevi. Rajyashri, Harshvardhan's sister, was taught Buddhist philosophy. Vijaya Bhattarika of the Chalukyas (7th century), Sugandha and Didda of Kashmir (10th century) were trained to manage their own states. But the spread of education among a wider cross-section of women and girls effectively curtailed popular culture that associated female education with prostitutes. Keay quotes Abbe Dubois, "These prostitutes are the only females in India who may learn to read, sing and dance. Such accomplishments belong to them exclusively and are, for that reason, held by the rest of the sex in such abhorrence that every virtuous woman would consider a mention of them an affront." Subsequently, the Devadasis became the custodians of many classical treatises on mythology, dance and music.

Although during the medieval period women's and girls' education was much restricted due to the 'pardah', yet, as proved by the example of Razia Sultan, girls from the nobility and royalty were educated through arrangements within private homes. Throughout the period, the occasional woman from royal families is referred to as writing letters and composing poems. Akbar arranged for lessons in his harem at Fatehpur Sikri, as did Ghiyas-ud-din, ruler of Malwa (1469-1500). Women also funded, opened and looked after institutions of learning. There were poetesses like Meerabai in the 15th century and Bibi Ratan Kaur of the 18th century, who wrote poems in Hindi or linked dialects.

Women of royal households also took part in administration throughout the period. The Chalukyan princess Akkadevi and Sovaladevi (1174 AD) took part in administration. Marco Polo mentions the rule of two women, Rudramba or Ganapamba in Warangal around 1262 AD. A number of women, such as Nur Jahan, from the royalty, were associated with administration during the Mughal period. Chand Bibi of Ahmadnagar, Rani Durgawati Tarabai in the 16th and 17th century, and Ahalyabai of Indore in the 18th century ruled in their own right. These women were probably all iterate, but even if they were not so, they had an understanding and appreciation of the skills required for administration and state-craft. It is argued that the meaning of education and its links with literacy needs to be revisited, specially in light of the fact that Akbar was supposed to have been illiterate.

The examples quoted above are those that indicate that some exceptions to the general situation did exist but that does not provide an insight into the status of the average woman in India. Although some amount of information is available on the education afforded to women of the royal households and nobility, there is very little information on education of females from among the common people. Ibn Batuta (1333-45 AD) records having seen schools as against education within the home. "I saw in Hanaur thirteen schools for the instruction of girls and twenty-three for boys." These may have been for the common people. Pietro Della Valle (1623 AD), an Italian traveller left a vivid account of village schools mentioning rote learning and the use of fine sand spread on the floor for writing.

The social system that existed in India made for the exclusion of many on the basis of caste and also on the basis of gender. It is doubtful if, even at the most liberal of times, girls from ordinary families and lower castes had any access to education or even literacy. The general environment in such families would usually not be a literate one, with little opportunity for girls to gain acquaintance with literacy.

By the time of the advent of the Europeans, the position of women had further deteriorated. Sati was widely prevalent; child marriage had spread to some sections of Muslims. Purdah was strictly enforced on Muslims and on some sections of Hindus. Finally, female education was often regarded "as a source of moral danger since only dancing girls could normally read and write."

Indigenous Arrangements for Girls' Education at the Arrival of the Europeans

Indian education systems existed[2] prior to the arrival of the East India Company traders. Most villages had their own educational arrangements such as tols, pathshalas and madrasas, though there existed no uniform or systematic organization of such schools and the syllabus studied therein. Evidence of education of girls among certain families and classes in the medieval period has already been quoted. That some women during the Mughal period were accomplished poets points to the possibility of the content of their education being wider than just what was necessary to keep household accounts and carry out religious duties.

The colonial administration for the 19th century documented mainly the enrollment of girls at missionary schools and those aided or managed by the British administration. The Indian social usage was more supportive of girls being educated at home. Indian families who educated their girls did not do so for public approbation and would have no interest in sharing this fact with outsiders. The western forms of documentation and enumeration[3] were not able to capture accurately and in detail the informal or non-formal nature of education provided to Indian women and girls within their homes. Sometimes a hint of the correct picture is available by comparing the school enrollment data and the literacy data from the census. As Raman has rightly argued, popular western impression of female education in India during the colonial period was based on missionary[4] reports and as these missionaries "had little access to upper caste and upper class homes, their impressions of elite Hindus were often clearly prejudiced and exaggerated." Unfortunately this impression has gained greater currency than the more accurate picture which emerges from Indian literature or oral history of the period.[5]

Gradually formal girls' schools came into wider existence and were both under private Indian as well as colonial government management. Indian efforts for girls' formal education (connoting a school or institutional arrangement for education) included the philanthropic efforts of the royal houses and of religious or social trusts. The ruling house of Tanjavur founded twenty religious charities or Chhatrams near Rameswaram temple between 1743-1837. The Raja of Vizianagram financially supported a Caste Girls' School at Vishakhapatnam and started others between 1867-77. In Bhaunagar (Bhavnagar, Saurashtra) there were 16 schools for girls with a total of 1468 students. The State had appointed Miss Brooke, a lady teacher from the Female

Training College at Ahmedabad, as Inspectress of schools. The Mahajiraj School in Bhaunagar city had 283 girls from the wealthy and influential Jain, Brahmin, Rajput, Parsi and Mohammeden families. The Wadhwa school opened in 1868 was meant for working class families (gardeners, fruit-sellers, artisans, basket-weavers, agricultural labourers) and had about 150 girls on its rolls. The annual report of the Maharani's Caste Girls' School, Mysore, 1884, notes the efforts for enrolling girls thus: "The first is by persuading intelligent relations of the children to permit them to stay longer in the school, and the second by providing the means of home education to those unwilling to attend school." There had been substantial effort at organizing a special curriculum and courses to keep girls in school for longer periods.... On the basis of our curriculum we have drawn up schemes for examination of our girls of standards corresponding to the Middle School and Matriculation Examination of the Madras University — necessary on account of the existing prejudice in sending girls to the examinations for boys.....

The great problem with us has been, as has already been stated, how to carry on their education after leaving school. The zenana system,....we believe,....is the best course.... It has been found that books published- for use of boys' schools scarcely answer the needs of girls' schools. Various books have, therefore, been undertaken and published by duly qualified gentlemen and many more are under preparation, for example, Nitichintamani brought out under the joint authorship of Messrs. B. Sriniwasiengar, B.A. and M.S. Puttanna, B.A. and a translation of the well known Pandita Ramabaiji's Sri Dharmniti in Marathi." The Goculdas Tejpal Free School for Girls run by the Goculdas Tejpal Trust in Bombay city, was flourishing in 1893- 94. At this time there were also some 20 Koran schools for girls with an average of 15 scholars each in the Bombay Presidency. Most schools for Parsi girls were managed without grant or aid from the Government, and therefore, were exempt from official inspection. Mary F. Billington, a correspondent for the **Daily Telegraph and Graphic** in England, who toured India in 1893-94, describes a Parsi school started in 1885 where the kindergarten was as good as any in Europe. There was evidently a concern for quality for girls' education in Indian efforts. Billington concluded that Indian women were "not altogether in such pitiful plight as some of their so-called friends come and tell us...."

Besides setting up their own institutions and arranging for domestic instruction, Indians donated generously for the so-called 'Government' efforts. Rajah Boidonath Roy Bahadur of Calcutta and Rao Bahadur Mughanbhai Karramchand of Ahmedabad donated Rs.20,000 each to the foundation of several female schools for Indians. J.E.D. Bethune wrote regarding the Bethune Girls' School, Calcutta.

"...Baboo Dukkina Runjin Mookerjea, a Zamindar, who was previously unknown to me, but who, as soon as my design was published, introduced himself to me for the purpose of offering me the gift of a site for the school, or five beeghas of land valued at 10,000 Rupees, in the Native quarter of the town and Pundit Madan Mohan Tarkalunkar, one of the pundits of the Sanskrit College, who not only sent two daughters to the school, but has continued to attend it daily, to give gratuitous instruction to the children in Bengali, and has employed his leisure time in the compilation of a series of elementary Bengali books expressly for their use." In 1849 Baboos Joykissen and Rajkissen Mookerjee petitioned the Governor-General regarding the establishment of a female school at Ooterparah near Howrah. However, this and a number of similar initiatives by Indians were thwarted by officials of the colonial administration ostensibly fearful of going against popular native sentiment.

In 1865-66, the Director of Public Instruction, Punjab, writes: "But, besides all these, there are the very important, though as yet elementary. Female Schools in the cities of Lahore and Umritsar, numbering no less than 223, and containing 3,841 scholars. These schools are entirely under the management of Committees of Native gentlemen at the two chief cities of the Punjab." There was in 1893 no Inspectress of Schools in the Bombay Presidency, but some ladies of the National Indian Association had started to carry out these duties. Therefore, all effort for the education of girls in India at this period was substantially supported by Indian agency, though at times this was in conjunction with British officials. To attempt to restrict an analysis or understanding of Indian effort and involvement to only those arrangements and institutions which were initiated and managed solely by Indians is to project only part of the picture. Indian effort and involvement existed on a much wider canvas and included even those institutions under the artificial categorization of 'official or Government Schools.'

Girls' Education under the Colonial Administration

The East India Company initially showed little interest in the education of the natives. The Company Directors observed, prior to the Charter Act of] 793, that "they had just lost America from the folly of allowing the establishment of schools and colleges and it would not do for them to repeat the folly." Finally in 1813, the Board of Directors of the East India Company sanctioned a sum of 1 lac of rupees in each year for the education of Indians. Wood's Despatch of 1854 introduced the principle of sanctioning Grant-in-aid to private efforts and brought to India the idea of State controlled education, an idea alien to India. It introduced supervision by the Government agency, establishment of "Normal" schools and vernacular medium for general education.

The official apathy towards female education was strong. "Prior to the Despatch of 1854, female education was not recognized as a branch of the official system of education in India under the British..... This is evident from the fact that in none of the despatches received from or submitted to the Court of Directors during the first half of the 19th century, is there any reference to the education of women and girls" The Despatch of 1854 noted "....that the Government ought to give to the native female education in India its frank and cordial support" The first Indian Education Commission under W.W. Hunter (1882) reiterated the need to foster women and girls' education.

Missionary Activities

The earliest efforts to introduce any form of female education beyond the purely indigenous system emanated from missionaries and foreign private societies and individuals (whether officials or others); but not the official administration. Christian Missionaries followed the traders and set up educational institutions from the middle of the 18th Century. One Miss Cooke (later the redoubtable Mrs. Wilson) arrived in Calcutta in 1821 and arrangements were made for her to work with the Corresponding Committee of the Church Missionary Society. Adams notes "... she gradually extended her labours until she had in 1824, twenty-four schools under her superintendence, attended on an average by 400 pupils. In that year the Corresponding Committee relinquished the entire management and direction of their female schools to a committee of Ladies who formed themselves into a society called the Ladies' Society for Native Female Education in Calcutta and its vicinity..... and a Central School was built for that purpose and occupied in 1828." The missionary bodies opened orphanages, day schools and undertook domestic instruction in the families of middle and higher classes. "The Serampur Mission, which has from the first zealously advocated the cause of the female population of India, maintains a school for one hundred Heathen girls. The Rev. W.H. Pearce, of the Baptist Mission, was early occupied with this branch of the work, and missionaries of other denominations have collected children."

Raman discusses that free schools had begun to mushroom around Madras^ by the I9th century; as at Nagercoil, Palayamkottai, Tirunelveli, Tiruchirapalli, Kumbakonam, Madurai, Coimbatore, Salem, Tirupattur and around Madras. Billington' comments on the difficulty of reaching Mohammedan girls and mentions Lady Hobarts' efforts in Madras. She adds: "The Church of England Zenana Mission is well to the fore also in this work, and in the schools under Miss Oxiey's care, the drill and singing are notably good." To a large extent, these missionary schools, as opposed to home education or zenana education provided by missionaries, tended to include children from those social groups so far outside the pale of education. This was partly due to the philosophy of working for the needy and partly to the fact that upper class Hindus and Muslims held the missionary schools in some suspicion and would be unwilling to send their daughters to these institutions. J.E.D. Bethune notes Indian apprehension of Missionary activities. "The failure of every attempt to induce respectable Natives to send their daughters to a Missionary School, and the conviction which 1 have that the system of the Government Schools is best calculated for producing a rapid and salutary effect in the country induced me to establish my school on the same principle of excluding from it all religious teaching, though I was well aware of the additional difficulty which this restriction would cause to me for procuring efficient female teachers." Again we find that missionary efforts were able to survive due to Indian munificence. Rani Lakshmibai donated land in Travancore to the Church Missionar Society (CMS) to maintain teachers, widows and orphans, while Parvathi Bai, her successor, and the Raja of Cochin did the same. In 1827, Tyerman and Bennet, of the London Missionary Society (LMS), mentioned the liberal Ranis thus; "All schools in Nagercoil are making excellent progress... the girls' school and seminary are entirely supported, clothed, fed and educated from the proceeds of land given for this purpose, and the sale of lace made by the girls."

Zenana or Home Education

Even after the introduction of formal schools, indigenous modes of transmitting knowledge such as zenana or home education for girls continued. "While educated men often taught women in their family zenana education or group teaching within a suitable home was soon recognized as a feasible alternative to education in a school.

By the end of the century, the Government of India started funding tutors for these rapidly expanding home-oriented schemes of education. In 1882, the Education Commission stressed the importance of zenana education in a culture where women's seclusion was still prevalent. In the Bengal Presidency, by 1907, the number of girls being instructed through this system rose to 1431 recorded cases as against 1200 at the end of the earlier quinquennium."

Female missionaries were very active in providing zenana education. "1 saw several instances in which the ladies of the Church of England or other Zenana Missions had been asked to instruct in English and other branches of knowledge the girl-wives of young men at the universities" But Indian families feared conversions of the young students. This is clear from Mrs. Wilson's testimony: "Seventeen years ago a native gentleman asked for a 'Lady teacher' for his females; one went regularly for a few months; after which he called again on the gentleman to say he must give it up....."

Gradually, missionary sponsored zenana education for groups of girls became more acceptable to Indians. Under the urging of Mrs. Isobel Brander, Inspectress of Schools, Madras, an earnest attempt at home education was made. Billington mentions one such scheme at Madras. "At the present time about a hundred and twenty women are studying thus, carrying their reading on to English, arithmetic, history and geography, being visited at home weekly by the native governesses and occasionally attending lectures. I was present at one of these series organized by the Hindu Reform Association, given in Tamil, upon the world and its movement,..." Speaking of the colonial rulers supporting the zenana system, Desai and Krishnaraj discuss, while in part, this approach was in keeping with the overall attitude that women, whether Indian or British middle classes, should be trained not for careers, but to be good wives and competent mothers, it also reflected a general indifference to prevailing social relationships and role expectations of the subject people. The education of girls and of women was regarded as the legitimate responsibility of Indians: it neither suited nor interested the rulers to take much initiative in this area. It is also interesting that the colonial male administrator and the Indian male joined hands to maintain the patriarchal system through reinforcing the segregation of women in the zenana system.

19th Century Meagre Official Efforts

The Despatch of 1854 had declared: "The importance of female education in India cannot be over-rated; and we have observed with pleasure the evidence which is now afforded of an increased desire on the part of many of the natives of India to give a good education to their daughters". The Despatch indicated that all grant-in- aid rules should be applied to girls' schools, but it did not recommend that Government should undertake the responsibility of **establishing** girls' schools. Female education was left entirely to private enterprise with assurance of aid from the Government. The grant-in-aid rules meant that the administration would control the curriculum, content of teaching and management of the institution but not assume any responsibility for outcomes or quality of education. The Bethune School, established in 1849, had been perhaps the first instance of Government initiative for female education. Bethune school was started in Calcutta with 21 pupils. In November 1853, the Court of Directors sanctioned "the grant of such monthly allowance to the Bethune Native Female School as shall be necessary to maintain it in efficiency".

Schools continued to be opened by Indians that later received official aid, for example, the various schools opened by Ishwar Chandra Vidyasagar. Manockjee Cursetjee, a Parsi from Bombay requested Bethune to help establish similar female schools in that province. Local inhabitants of Uttarpara and Barasat came forward to establish female schools of their own. Some requests for aid were turned down by the British administration ostensibly due to negative public opinion. One of the Governor-General's Counselors, John H. Littler, opposed the idea of Government support to girls' education by recording: "The scheme of female education is doubtless unpopular and looked upon by the mass with fear and dread, whether Hindoos or Mohammedans. Will it not involve a dereliction of the principle of neutrality to which the Government is pledged in like cases?" Such opinions helped the administration justify its reticence in affording support to girls' education.

Everywhere official efforts relied on Indian support for success. The report of 1861-62 for North-Western Provinces noted that: "The plan adopted by Thakoor Kalyan Singh of the Agra College, of training a class of native ladies, belonging to the families of his kinsmen as school mistresses has resulted in the establishment of really useful schools. They are now 17 in number". The Director of Public Instruction, Madras, in 1859 mentions that in Madras, female education was carried on to a considerable extent by private schools, some of which received aid from the Government. "There are Parsi and Hindoo girls' Schools in Bombay and the European officials with the native bankers superintend others at Ahmedabad. There are also some small schools in the Northern division, mostly owing their origin in private effort."

Monteath summarizes the position in his own note of 1862 which shows that in 3 out of 5 provinces administered by the British, there were more private schools than the government ones, as shown in Table 1.

Table 2 shows that the proportion of private girls' schools to total stopped increasing in the 20"' century showing that the colonial administration began to take the initiative over. However, the aim of education remained the preparation of girls as good wives. Therefore, the end result remained very limited and not emancipatory as education should be.

Table 1 : Position of Girls' Schools, 1862

State	*Govt. Schools*		*Pvt. Schools*		*Total*	
	No. of Schools	*Av. Attend*	*No. of Schools*	*Av.A ttend*	*No. of Schools*	*Av. Attend*
Bengal	—	—	8	199	8	199
NW Province	17	140	19	615	36	755
Punjab	52	1,168	4	484	56	1652
Madras	—	—	124	6,983	124	6,983
Bombay	28	162	20	978	48	1,140

Source: National Archives of India, (1960), op cit, p. 89.

Table 2: Institutions for Girls, India, 1916-17

Year	*Public Schools*	*Private Schools*	*Total*
1916-17	19,365	1,955	21,320
1911-12	14,113	1,960	16,073
1906-07	10,681	1,759	12,440
1901-02	6,176	1,338	7,514
1896-97	6,550	1,459	8,009
1891-92	5,711	1,042	6,753
1886-87	4,906	1.768	6,674
1916-17	*Public*	*Private*	*Total*
Madras	1,815	119	1,934
Bombay	1,216	85	1,301
Bengal	9,566	318	9,884

(Contd...)

UP	1,236	336	1,572
Punjab	1,030	872	1,902
Bihar Orissa	2,561	56	2,617
CP & Berar	365	8	373
Assam	**351**	7	364
NWFP	46	49	95
Other	90	41	131

Source: Bureau of Edu **India.** Ed H Sharp, CSI, CIE (1918). **Progress of Education** *in India* 1912-17: **Seventh Quinquennial Review: Vol II,** Calcutta, S. intendent of Govt. Printing, Ch. II.

Indians continued with more planned efforts for girls' education in Punjab. "Accordingly committees were appointed at each of the two cities, and it was arranged that the family priests of certain of the best families, viz. 30 at Lahore and 40 at Umritsar, should undertake to teach, each of them at least, one female from his own or his client's families.....and as soon as the pupils become proficient enough to impart knowledge themselves, they will be taken into service of the families with which they are connected as Governesses",... ....."I may also mention here that within the last two or three months, Baba Khem Singh, a lineal descendent of the Guru BabaNanak, and greatly revered by all classes of his countrymen, has been preaching at Jullunder and its neighbourhood in favour of Female Education....... The success of his mission has been immense, and Girls' Schools are now starting into existence by scores and even hundreds, 1 believe, in those parts of the Punjab which he has visited."

Around 1860 there were no Government Schools in Oude, Madras or in Mysore but some private girls' schools existed. There were 92 Government Female Schools in the Central Provinces supported from the Education Cess Funds. The Director Public Instruction, Central Provinces, wrote "The largest number (girls' schools) in any district is at Saugar, where there are 26 Schools with 713 pupils; in the districts of Chhindwara and Upper Godavary none have yet been opened . ...they are entirely supported by Local Educational Funds in the same way as the Boys' Schools,...." Private enterprise also existed in Gujerat. "Some of the Private Girls' Schools (under inspection), and especially the Roychund Deepchund School at Surat, are exceptions to my general remark, Capt. Waddington (Appendix A 1, p. 23) reports favourably of the Parsee Girls' Schools attached to Sir Jamsetjee Jeejeebhoy's Benevolent Institution." Thus throughout this period (as in the initiatives of missionaries and foreign private individuals) the efforts of the colonial Government were supported by Indians through donation of land, cash and services.

Where Government girls' schools did exist there was doubt of their quality. The Director Public Instruction, Bombay, wrote in 1865-66, "The first characteristic of our Girls' Schools is extreme irregularity of attendance; the second is that they are in reality Infant Schools, in which it appears to me that the great bulk of the children, being very young, sit looking on, while a few girls at the top of the School receive a little instruction."

Women's Education in 19th Century Contemporary Indian Literature

Indian literature devoted much importance to women's education in the 19th century. Mukherjee brings this out clearly when she examines women protagonists in Bankim Chandra Chatterjee's/«(i/ra **(1873),** O. Chandu Menon's **Indulekha (1888).** Hari Narayan Apte's **LakhshyatKon Gheto (1890),** and Mirza Mohammad Hadi Ruswa's **Umrao Jan (1899).** These novels were all written by men about women protagonists in the]9*" century. Indira in the novel **Indira** was from an affluent landowning family, Indulekha in **Indulekha** was from a prosperous matrilineal Nair family in Kerala, Yamuna in **Pan Lakshyat Kon Gheto** is from a Middle class Maharashtrian family, while Ameeran in **Umrao Jan** is a courtesan in Lucknow. These women are, therefore, from differing social and geographical backgrounds. All these four women were able to read, write and appreciate thoughts and expressions used in the regional literature of the time, analyse their own situations in the light of the times and pass judgement in their minds. These women may not have been part of the formal education system laid out by the British and, therefore, not counted among those who were "enrolled" in school.

Overview and Observations

It is argued that mere "enrolment" ought not be the only indicator of an educated Indian woman; there were many other informal methods and systems by which an Indian woman acquired education, knowledge and information such was required for her to live her life **usefully.** That few were able to record their thoughts or act upon them or share them with a wider public are features surely of the age, which in varying forms would be found in all societies of the time. But to condemn Indian social arrangements completely, and state that very few girls were educated because very few were 'enrolled' at school, fails to capture the true conditions or arrangements made by Indian society, both public and private, for the education of girls and women.

There is thus evidence that the Indian agency made arrangements for girls from certain families to access education and even enroll in school (The Raja of Vizianagaram Caste Girls' School). A concern for quality and attempts to design a suitable curriculum is seen in Indian efforts (as in the Caste Girls' School, Mysore). There are also recorded instances of attempts to bring change in public attitudes to the education of girls (note Baba Khem Singh's efforts in Pubjab). Though these efforts were for a restricted clientele, they indicate the nature of actions by the Indian agency for girls' education. In contrast, as will become clear in the following pages, there is complete resistance by the colonial administration to incurring additional expenditure for girls' education. The main expenditure incurred by the colonial administration was in maintaining the control structures such as inspection and the grant-in-aid systems.

Policy and Efforts for the Education of Girls in India (1900 -1947)

Overview of the Progress

The National Movement was gaining momentum. The Indians demanded that primary education be made free and compulsory and technical and vocational education be introduced. Gopal Krishna Gokhale's resolution for free and compulsory education in 1910 was not passed. But since the colonial Government could not entirely ignore Gokhale's Bill and the growing demand for mass education, the Educational Resolution of 1913 was passed. It was recommended that voluntary effort provide primary education and that the state partially provide secondary education. It also recommended that a special curriculum of practical utility be introduced for women without placing too much emphasis on examination. It recommended strengthening control through increasing the number of female teachers and inspectors. A renewed emphasis on control was in keeping with the British education policy in the twentieth century which was based upon the perception of Curzon that the policy of introducing Western education in India was recoiling upon its rulers.

Despite lack of official support, public agitation at Gokhale's rejected bill resulted in Primary Education Acts being passed in Punjab, United Provinces, Bengal, Bihar and Orissa in 1919; in Bombay, Central Provinces and Madras in 1920; and in Assam in 1926. Except for Orissa and Punjab, the acts were expected to include girls.

Twentieth Century Financial Policy for Girls' Educational Development

In 1886, the colonial Government had suggested "Expenditure from Provincial Revenue on Government Educational Institutions should not ordinarily be increased in proportion to the total expenditure but should ordinarily be constantly decreasing quantity provided that there is assurance that the field abandoned by the Government is occupied by local efforts." The colonial Government continued to refuse to undertake responsibility or financial burden for education of Indians while controlling policy and implementation. The system of grants-in-aid instituted after 1854 was given only to those schools that charged tuition fees — a clear attempt at preventing any initiative towards making education free and universal. In 1920, less than 1/3 of all educational expenditure came from Public Sources and any additional expenditure came largely from Private Sources.

Arguing that the people would not welcome compulsory education, the colonial Government would not make financial provision for it. This was absurd as in Baroda, Compulsory Primary Education was introduced in 1873 and by 1918 that state had achieved a 93 per cent Gross Enrolment Ratio (GER) for the total school going age group including girls. Mysore and Hyderabad too showed high GER and good progress in education.

The inadequacy of British efforts was admitted even by British historians. "The Indian Finance has never provided an amount that was adequate for the support of **this organization (Primary Education .....**The popularity of instruction has depended **more upon the habits of the community than upon the expenditure of the state."** *(emphasis* Author's*). When the Madras Presidency proposed a reorganization of girls' education with the recommendation " In our opinion the scheme is a well considered one, and is likely to benefit the cause of female education...... ", the colonial Government took no immediate action indicating their disinterest in undertaking such expenditure Colonial financial policy for girls' education was influenced even by such extraneous forces as women's groups in England. One suggestion from such a group was...this deputation suggests that, when a woman is recruited in England for an educational appointment under Govt, of India, she should be appointed by the Secretary of State in time for her to arrive in India at least a year before it would be necessary for her to take charge of all the duties of the post." The Board of Education agreed with the suggestions. Thus, where the colonial Government was unwilling to assume the extra expenditure for the benefit of Indian girls it was ready to bear the additional expenditure of European women arriving a year prior to assuming their duties in India. British historians attempting to faithfully exonerate the colonial Government argued that the financial burden of expanding girls' education was too heavy.*

TABLE 3: Increase/Decrease in Expenditure over Educational Institutions Between 1932 -1937

(in Rs.)

Province	*Instit. for Males*	*Instit. for Females*
Madras	-2,40,051	-26,030
Bombay	NA	NA
Bengal	+22,99,252	+4,55,360
UP	+ 10,64,555	+6,70,980
Punjab	+3,60,933	+6,26,103
Bihar	NA	NA
CP/Berar	+6,49,494	+ 1,40,095
Assam	+4,08,193	+99,816
NWFP	+2,86,223	+99,472
Coorg	+21,716	+3,831
Delhi	+ 1,65,447	+ 1,81,387
Ajmer/Merwara	+ 1,12,101	+2,767
Baluchistan	-27,370	-48,102

The colonial administration's fund allocation between boys' and girls' educational institutions was discriminatory as evident from the vast differences in expenditure in 8 out of 13 provinces as per Table 3.

Besides the markedly lower allocations for girls, the colonial Government used the higher cost per scholar for girls as an excuse to project that girls' schooling was iiot cost effective. It is argued that at this point of time, a responsible government should have considered the social benefits of girls' education and undertaken the social marketing of schooling for girls as a parallel to providing school facilities, instead of counting the costs.

Table 4: Cost of Education in British India according to Standard and Sex, 1937

	Expenditure on Institutions (in Rs.)		*Total No. of Scholars*		*Total Cost per Scholar (in Rs.)*	
	Female	*Male*	*Female*	*Male*	*Female*	*Male*
High School	89,50,405	5,31,37,619	1,10,133	10,23,347	79-3-0	49-8-9
Middle School	45,69,658	2,41,5,194	1,64,095	11,99,287	27-13-8	20-2-3
Primary.School	1,39,79,988	6,98,00,051	14,94,783	90,47,007	9-5-8	7-11-5
Special School	26,48,833	1,46,76,118	19,307	2,13,084	137-3-1	56-15-3
Unrecog. Institutions	96,486	6,15,170				

Source: National Planning Commission.(1947), **National Planning Committee Series:** Report of the Sub-Committee: Women's Role in a Planned Economy. **Bombay.** *Vora and Co Publishers Ltd., Ch. IV, p. 132.*

Even the Bombay, Bengal and Assam administrations were emphatic about the requirement of more money as well as the need for faster growth of girls' education encompassing a wider social section of girls. They argued that the education of girls presently required more financial fostering than that of boys; scholarships and studentships must be given more generously. Defending itself, the colonial Government argued that the Census of India, 1911, showed a higher female literacy for British India than for Native States. But, the colonial Government's defense appears fatuous as obviously all Native States were not equally advanced. The level of achievement in British India needed to be viewed against the progress in the advanced Indian States like Mysore and Baroda where more genuine efforts for the education of girls had been made. The colonial Government noted: "In some of the opinions received by the Government of India it is contended that female education is not primarily a matter of money but of social development and it is urged that in many places schools have been opened but have failed to attract scholars." *The colonial Government was unable to appreciate that expansion in infrastructure required to be accompanied by strong efforts at social change and development and that the two were inseparable. Any Government that assumed responsibility for governance could not morally step back from either of these responsibilities.*

Curriculum for Inequality

Educationists and social reformers (both Indian and British) alike had a limited vision of women's emancipation, envisioning women only as housewives and education as the means to further heighten their efficiency in this role. Twentieth century girls' educational content in India was thus not an education for equality but for continuing patriarchal domination over the newly educated women and girls. The Calcutta University Commission Report say "One of the forces already at work and likely to become more potent, in the removal of this disability is growing preference of young men for educated wives whom they will accept with smaller dowry". This argument seems not to take into account the very small numbers of men who were eaucated at the time. Table 5 gives the low literacy rates for nabs and females between 1901 and 1941. Educated males opting for educated wivss would have been few and the number of parents consciously preparing their daughters for such an eventuality would be minimal. Even if the educated boys carried enough status to influence matters of marriage and girls' education, the affected families would be mainly from the upper classes. What then of the lower social and economic classes and castes?

Table 5: Literacy Rates in India (in per cent), 1901-41

Year	*Female*	*Male*	*Total*
1901	0369	9^83	**SJS**
1911	1.05	10.56	5.92
1921	1.81	12.21	7.16
1931	2.93	15.59	9.50
1941	7.30	24.90	16.10

Source: NCERT (1995), **Sixth All India Educational Survey,** New Delhi, NCERT, p. 14.

However, the prevailing notion that educated boys wanted educated wives sealed the fate of girls for many years to come. Thus, "the Sewa Sadan at Poona imparted music lessons, home science, first aid, nursing, mid-wifery etc. apart from teaching of languages to girls. The main idea was that since a girl had to be a wife and a mother, school education should train her to perform that role more effectively."

The question of curriculum was debated again in 1916 and again the colonial administration shirked its responsibility. "There is little doubt that public opinion requires that Indian girls should learn arithmetic and should learn to read and write their own vernacular but the question whether subjects, other than those above, should be taught, might on this principle, be left for the decision of local bodies... It would in this case be inadvisable for the Education Department to insist on any prescribed standard course, so the duty of the Department be confined to indicating groups of subjects for adoption by local bodies, leaving it to these bodies to select form of currency which seems suitable...." There was, in fact, little room for manipulation in choice of optional subjects as the compulsory subjects took ip practically the entire school time.

With regard to a common curriculum in Secondary Schools, the colonial Government deliberated over whether to prepare girls for a University career; or to prepare them primarily for home life. To the credit of the colonial Government, it finally concluded that instruction of girls in Secondary Schools should encourage the development of mental capacity thus rejecting those who sought to relegate Indian girls and women exclusively to the hearth. But it pandered to retrogressive thinking by suggesting that where possible, home instruction would be arranged for those girls leaving school on marriage.

Even where isolated efforts at widening of educational content for girls were attempted these tended to remain within the nurturing roles accepted for women, as teaching, nursing and child-rearing. Loreto House in Calcutta taught English, Mathematics, History, Botany, French and was planning further expansion of courses for its teacher training class. "The new college department is to be considered as a Training College following a 3 year course which combines the 1A Examination after the second year of the course".

Other Policies Negatively Affecting Girls' Education

The policies of the colonial administration usually failed to improve the quality of girls' education. In 1916, the colonial Government declared that co-education was opposed to public opinion and should not be encouraged and recommended that all schools should be under the same management. "Boys' and girls' schools should be placed under the same control though there may be in addition an Advisory Committee for the purpose of girls' education". These Advisory Committees were unable to fulfil their objective and were therefore of little support.

Colonial policies affected Indian women and girls in other ways. That prejudice played a major role in establishing theories of stereotypes and deciding the policy of the colonial Government requires no reiteration and progress of girls' education also had to contend with it. The Indian Women's Education Association made a representation requesting either a grant or scholarships for training Indian women in England. A few years after this, Indian women began to be sponsored for gaining education or training abroad. The letter of the Secretary to the Government of Bombay in*this regard has this interesting passage. "I am to suggest that the scholarship holders should be selected from teachers who have rendered two years approved service in a recognized school in the Presidency, that the selected candidate should be required to pass a rigourous physical examination before proceeding to Europe, and that *scholarships should not as a rule be conferred upon applicants who* *belong to the more orthodox castes of the Hindu community, as their physique, owing to the special diet to which they are bound by caste requirement ordinarily renders them unfit to cope with the climatic conditions of Europe.*" (emphasis Author's).

Similarly, prejudice also played its role in the employment of Indian women. The colonial Government argued that since competent Indian women were lacking, it was advisable to obtain the services of qualified English ladies for the Women's Education Service. As late as 1921, there were a total of 24 posts of Inspectresses of Schools and it appears incredible that this number of competent and suitable women were not available in India. Meanwhile the slow' but relentless Indianization of the bureaucracy built up unavoidable tensions of its own. One Wali Mohammad, Assistant Secretary to the Government of India notes that the Indian bureaucracy suggested that 50% of appointments in Class I of the Women's Education Service be reserved for Indians and that there be no difference in service rules between natives of India and others. These recommendations for moving towards equal opportunities for Indian women were rejected by the Secretary of State in England.

On the other hand, the colonial Government continued to support Europeans or Anglo-Indians by special privileges in service conditions, with scholarships for further study or by reserving job opportunities for them. This continued despite Indian public feeling that the teaching would be more successful and more likely to attract students if it were more largely in the hands of Indians and of non-Christians.

Table 6: Progress of Women's Education, India, 1921-47 (Enrolment)

Institutions	1921-22	1931-32	1941-42	1946-47
Primary School	10,87,131	19,44,070	31,23,643	27,15,230
Secondary School	1,24,954	1,96,170	4,10,333	4,42,403
College	1,207	2,685	11,778	16,284
Prof College	266	521	1725	2468
Prof. School	19,570	17,568	40,869	38,375

Source: Mukherji, S.N. (1969) **Education in India: Today and Tomorrow.** Baroda. Acharya Book Depot, p.255.

Role of Women and Girls in a Planned Economy

Indian women found their champion in Mahatma Gandhi and other social reformers who spoke of the need to educate women. The All India Women's Association demanded equality of educational opportunity for women and girls at its first Education Conference in 1927. Successive Education Reports reiterated the need to improve opportunities for girls. The Hartog Committee

Report, 1929, argued: "priority should be given to the claim of girls' education in every scheme of examination". Despite this, there was uneven improvement in enrolment.

The National Planning Committee was constituted in 1938 under the chairmanship of Jawaharlal Nehru with Sarojini Naidu, Aruna Asaf Ali, Vijaylakshmi Pandit and Mridula Sarabai on the Sub-Committee that considered the role of women in a planned economy. The policy regarding girls' education after Independence was based on the recommendations of the Sub-Committee.

The Sub-Committee made some positive contributions. It noted that despite some increase in girls' enrolment, there existed worrying levels of wastage. Both the Sub-Committee and the Women's Education Committee of the Central Advisory Board of Education (CABE, 1944) considered that local bodies in some provinces had not worked satisfactorily. The Sub-Committee recommended that all local bodies spend an adequate proportion of their educational funds on the primary education of girls.

Table 7: Total Number of Female Pupils in all Educational Institutions (1922-1937)

	1922	*1927*	*1932*	*1937*	*Incr. 1932-37*
Males	6,962,928	9,315,144	10,273,888	11,007,683	7.1
Females	1,424,425	1,842,352	2,492,649	3,138,357	25.9

Source: National Planning Committee (1947). *National Planning Committee Series: Report of the sub-Committee: Women's Role in Planned Economy,* Bombay, Vora and Co. Publishers Ltd., Ch. IV, p. 131.

Table 8: Girls' Wastage in Primary Classes if 100 Admitted in Class 1,1944

Province	*Per cent in Class IV*
Madras	18.4
Bombay/Sind	29.5
Bengal	4.0
UP	12.0
Punjab	19.2
Bihar/Orissa	^1.0
CP/Berar	22.0
Assam	27.3
NWFP	16.4
Coorg	47.0
Delhi	20.8
Ajmer-Merwara	15.0
Baluchistan	2.9
Bangalore	33.2

Source: National Planning Committee, (1947). Op Cit Ch IV, p. 137.

The Sub-Committee found that in some cases "the province cannot afford separate schools for boys and girls in majority of the villages. Hence, in many cases, the alternative is not between co-education and a separate girls' school but between co-education and no education at all for girls." Most states reaffirmed that co-education at the primary stage was the best solution. Punjab adopted the policy of training the wives of existing teachers and engaging married couples in the same school. The Sub-Committee recommended that schools should necessarily have their own playground and physical culture for girls. It recommended that 50 per cent seats be reserved for women in colleges wherever a demand for female teachers existed.

Not all of the Sub-Committee's actions or observations were enlightened or helpful. The Sub-Committee referred to a demand for women's education springing from the growing number of educated men who demanded educated wives, a statement made in earlier official documents. While at this point of time the influence of the rising education level of males upon females of their classes may not be entirely discounted, it needs to be remembered that if this reason was truly so forceful, then the rise in female literacy levels would be more or less in step with that of males. Even today, female literacy levels are way below that of males (Census 1991, All India Male literacy 63.5 per cent, Female literacy 39.29 per cent). The change in attitudes towards girls' education may be due more largely to the entire changing social ethos in which the social and religious reform movements and the freedom struggle of the previous century played a great part.

The Sub-Committee's role with regard to curriculum was ambivalent. First it stated that there was no branch of knowledge that was the special preserve of any one sex and emphasized the use of common institutions and a common course of study for boys and girls. It noted that knowledge of mother-craft may be provided to girls should they evince a need for it; but domestic science on the other hand was as necessary to boys as to girls. In this, the Sub-Committee were far ahead of the thinking of contemporary society. However, having recorded decisions of such egalitarian implications, it is surprising that the Sub-Committee then went on to state that since women have a greater aptitude for music, art, nursery school teaching and nursing, they should be provided special training for these. It also noted that as it had been proved that women make good teachers in the lower classes, they could be placed in charge of the lower classes in all co-educational schools and opportunities provided for their training in these skills. *Perhaps a subsequent rush of women towards these areas and their consequent invisibility in such fields as Science and Mathematics and related professions may have their root in the Sub-Committee's own limited understanding of women's abilities. The above assumptions might have helped the virtual concentration of women teachers in the lower classes and lack of them in the higher. The statement overtly implies that women may not be as well suited to teach higher classes or at*

University level. It is interesting that the highest policy making body of the time should itself have such a limited vision of women's future role in a planned economy. That this should be so is more surprising considering the stature of persons involved in generating this report.

With regard to vocationalization of Secondary Education, the Sub-Committee mentioned music, art, domestic science, etc. as of interest to girls, thus retracting its own earlier statement that neither sex had any special propensity for any particular subject. Since a school level training in any of these subjects is unlikely to be sufficient for the purposes of earning a living, even the objective that Vocational Education should equip the individual to earn a living is not served. Unfortunately, the Central Advisory Board of Education Report, 1944, seemed in agreement with this genderized division of subjects by recommending that suitable courses should be framed for girls attending Senior Basic schools which should include such subjects as cookery, laundry work, needle work, home crafts, care of children and first aid; the remainder of the instruction should be correlated to this course of domestic science.

It would be relevant at this point to quote directly from the note of dissent to the Report of the Sub-Committee by Ms. Kapila Khandvala which supports the comments of this thesis regarding the fundamentally limited conceptual framework within which the Sub-Committee had visualized the women's role in the planned economy.

"I will now take the specific incidents and institutions which, while treated of in the Report, do not, in my opinion express correctly the view of educated and progressive Indian womanhood as regards the role of woman in planned society. Taking first the woman's position as an individual, the Report has as already remarked postulated equality as between man and woman. This equality affects and will condition social status, economic obligations and civic privileges. At the present time all the privileges, obligations or restrictions a woman has to suffer from, are in virtue of her relationship, and not in recognition of her individuality as such. She may have a place in society as a wife or a daughter or a mother, but not as an individual by herself only. This has been conceded in the report, but its obvious corollary is not so clearly brought out, namely, that in planned society woman's individuality must be recognised as such without reference to the relationship she may have contracted of her own will, or which may be forced upon her for any reason. Reading through the Sub-Committee's Report on all points in which woman has to have contracts with society, or to incur any responsibilities vis-a-vis society, I feel that the Sub-Committee has not made it clear that in the future planned society what would count, and count alone, will be the individual personality of each woman or of each man as such, and no relationship that she or he may have to bear with their fellows."

Ms Khandvala's well analysed and insightful criticism brings out the limitations of the report in its very understanding of the essence of womanhood and the limited framework within which her potential role has been placed. It became almost impossible for women/girls to claim educational equality with men under such lame beginnings.

Concluding Observations

It is seen that despite some lip-service to the need to educate girls, the colonial administration refused to invest sufficient funds for girls' education. Secondly, there was little concerted effort for expansion and advocacy for girls' education. Finally, throughout this period administrators, social reformers and educationists continued to regard the girl student only as a potential wife or mother. Therefore, efforts and policy decisions were made within this restricted framework. Even Indian planners fell into this trap and there appears little indication of any policy support for the education of the girl as a citizen and as an equal partner.

Notes

1. Some women scholars have sought to peel away later accretions to the original Indian epics to reveal a less romanticized social vision of women. Sukumari Bhattacharya, researching the Mahabharata and Lima Chakravarty researching the background of the Ramayana, find that the original stories based on material culture and life-as-lived appear to accord women greater freedom and individual dignity. However, the later additions and modifications, making the stories entirely value based, prescriptive and stressing the 'ideal', regard women from a strongly patriarchal view point.
2. The students were taught the rudiments of the three R® on pain of the cane or other punishment, writing and arithmetic being pre-eminent to the exclusion of all else. The formal system of schooling based on evaluation, age-wise distribution into classes, and certification, at a location spatially removed from the homes of pupils, was not the norm.
3. The 1881 census of the Madras Presidency pointed to teaching of girls carried on in the Hindu courtyards and behind the pardah in Muslim homes. "Those returns show a total of 39,104 females under instruction in the Madras Presidency, or 4,062 in excess of the pupils returned by the education department in 1882; and 94,571 not under instruction, but able to read and write." Govt/India, Report of the Education Commission (Hunter Report 1882) 522. Girls were also in Indian schools in addition to home teaching. In 1821 a survey was conducted by district collectors of indigenous and western schools in the Madras Presidency. J. Cotton's results from Thanjavur district revealed that the Mannaargudi royal endowment schools had 10 girls of "Soodra or other castes" mainly temple dancers and 1025 boys.
4. The inability of the official system to capture accurately the extent of education available for Indian girls may have led to obvious errors. Billington quotes India Office figures for girls at school throughout British India in 1877-78 as 66,615

which rose to 162,317 in 1882-83 with 3487 girls' schools. In 1891 -92 the number of girls in public and recognized private institutions was documented as 339,043 with about 8117 girls in private Koran schools. Therefore, she concludes that 99.44 per cent of the entire female population was illiterate. But the accuracy of the India Office figures may have been subject to the same inaccuracies as the Madras Presidency figures quoted above. Billington, Mary F. (1973) *Women in India: A Study of the Medieval Period,* New Delhi, Marko Book Agency, (First Published 1895, London Chapman and Hall) Ch 2

5. Both my grandmothers and their sisters were educated at home and were fully conversant with the regional literature of their time. My grandfather was brought up by his grand mother who was literate and is reputed to have accurately calculated her household expenses for the entire year and put aside that amount of money at the beginning of each year. Similar examples would be found in other Indian homes.
6. In 1882 in the Madras Presidency, there was the Church Mission Boarding School (1837), the Free Church Day School, Madras, (1841), the Free Church Boarding School, Madras, (1842), the SPG Boarding Schools in Tinnevelli, (1842), the Free Church Day Schools in Chingleput and Congiveram (1845), the Native Female Education Society's Central School in Black Town Madras (1845), the Wesleyan Mission Boarding School, Roypettah, Madras (1849). Bureau of Education. (1922). Op. Cit. p.50.
7. The first missionary school for native girls' in the Bombay Presidency was opened by the American Missionaries in 1824. Billington, Mary F (1973) Op. Cit., Ch. 2, p. 26,27.
8. The Society for Propagation of the Bible and the Free General Assembly also ran schools. Billington, Mary F. (1973) Op. Cit. pp. 38-39.
9. Gandhiji's call to women to join the Freedom Movement as equals of men was perhaps of greater importance to the emancipation and educational progress of Indian women than the short-sighted educational policies were.
10. This was in keeping with the colonial government's policy of sponsoring private effort for girls' education rather than expanding its own responsibilities.

References

Aggarwal, J.C. (1993): *Landmarks in the History of Modern Indian Education,* Delhi, Vikas Publishing House, Pvt Ltd., p. 17.

Altekar, A.S. (1938): *The Position of Women in Hindu India.* Benaras. Nand Kishore and Brothers, p.21,187.

Altekar, A.S. (1951): Op. Cit. p.205-225.

Aurangzeb's sister and daughter, Jahanara and Zebunissa. Misra, R(1938), Op.Cit., pp.46- 49.

Babur's daughter, Gul-Badan Begum, wrote the Humayun-Namah, Akbar's wife, Salma Sultan and Aurangzeb's daughter Zebunissa were also poetesses, Misra, R. (1967), Op. Cit., pp.46-49.

Billington, Mary F (1973): Op.Cit., Ch.2, p.41.

Billington, Mary F (1973): Op.Cit., Ch.2, pp.26-29.

Billington, Mary F. (1973): Op.Cit., Ch. 2, p.38.

Billington, Mary F. (1973): Op.Cit., pp.29,30.

Billington, Mary F. (1973): Op.Cit., pp.37-41.

Billington, Mary F. (1973): Op.Cit.,. Ch. 2, p.39, 40,411

Bureau of Education (1922): A letter written by J.E.D. Bethunetothe Marquis of Dalhousie, Governor General, dated Calcutta, the 29th March, 1850.0p.Cit., p.52.

Bureau of Education (1922): Op Cit., p.40.

Bureau of Education (1922): Op Cit., pp.38,39.

Bureau of Education (1922): Op.Cit., p.34.

Bureau of Education (1922): Op.Cit., p.44.

Bureau of Education (1922): Op.Cit., p.47.

Bureau of Education (1922): Op.Cit., p.53.

Bureau of Education (1922): Op.Cit., p.53.

Bureau of Education (1922): Op.Cit., p.95.

Bureau of Education (1922): *Selections from Educational Records, Pt II: 1840-1859.* A Richley, JA, CIE Calcutta, Govt Printing Press, p.32.

Bureau of Education [1886]: Progress of Education in India, Quinquennial Review: 1880- 1885. Vol I, p 6 as referred in Oak, V .V. (1925). *England's Education Policy in India.* Madras. BG Paul and Co. p. 138.

Bureau of Education in India, (1920): *Selections from Educational Records, Pt 1, 1781- 1839. Ed Sharp, H, CSI, CIE.* Calcutta, Govt. Printing Press, p. 18.

Bureau of Education, (1922): *Selections from Educational Records, Pt II: 1840-1859,* Ed Richley, J.A., CIE Calcutta, Govt Printing Press, p. 94.

Bureau of Education, GOI (1913) Resolution of Govt, on Edu Policy, Calcutta Superintendent of Govt. Printing; and Govt, of India/Edu Dept/Edu-A/Simla Records 2, File SI no. 13277, Proc. No. October 1913,81-84, Noting on Proc no 81, p3. Bundle no 287. Re; Distribution of copies of this department's resolution no 301 CD, dated 21 February 1913 on the Education Policy of India.

Bureau of Education, in India. (1919): *Calcutta University Commission Report;* 1917-1919 Calcutta, Superintendent Govt. Printing, p. 24.

Chenanna, Karuna (1996): Op.Cit., p.368.

Chenanna, Karuna (1996): Op.Cit., p.368.

Chenanna, Karuna.(1996): Gender inequality in Primary Schooling in India: The Human *RightsFerspectiwe Journal of Educational Planning and Administration. Vol. X, 104, Oct. 1996,* pp. 361-381, New Delhi, NIEPA p. 369.

Chirol, Sir Valentive (1911): *Indian Unrest.* London Macmillan and Co. p.250.

Chopra, P.N.; B.N. Puri and M.N. Das (1974): *A Social, Cultural and Economic History of India,* Vol. III, Delhi, Macmillan India, p. 224.

Chopra, P.N.; B.N. Puri and M.N. Das (1974): Op Cit., pp. 250-271.

Chopra, PN, BN Puri and MN Das (1974): Op.Cit., p. 258.

Chopra, PN, BN Puri and MN Das (1974): Op.Cit., p. 257, 258.

Chopra, PN, BN Puri and MN Das (1974): Op.Cit., p. 259.

Chopra, PN, BN Puri and MN Das (1974): Op.Cit., p.259; Bureau of Education, (1922), Op. Cit., p.44.

Dept of Edu., Govt of India.(1944): *Post War Educational Development in India.* Calcutta.

Desai, Neera and Maithreyi Krishnaraj (1987): Op.Cit., Ch. 3, pp.148-177.

Desai, Neera and Maithreyi Krishnaraj (1987): *Women and Society in India.* Delhi. Ajanta Books International. Ch. 1, pp.25-49.

Desai, Neera and Maithreyi Krishnaraj (1987): *Women and Society in India.* Delhi. Ajanta Books International, p.34 While discussing these women, Misra gives the Brahma- Upanishad period but no specific dates.Misra, R. (1967), *Women in Mughal India: 1526- 1748,* New Delhi, Munshiram Manoharlal, p. 1,2.

Desai, Neera and Maithreyi Krishnaraj (1987): *Women and Society in India,* Delhi, Ajanta Books International, p. 148.

Fuller, Sir JB. (1913): *The Empress of India.* London. Sir Isaac Pitman and Sons Ltd., p.89.

Govt of India/Edu Dept/ Edu-A/Delhi Records 3. File SI no 13164, Proc. No. June 1913,98- 99, Enclosure p. 13, Bundle no 287. Re:Question of appointment of women to educational posts in time

Govt of India/Edu Dept/ Edu-A/Simla Records 4, File s! no 82/14196, Proc. No Oct 1917, Op Cit, p. 31, 32, 33.

Govt of India/Edu Dept/ Edu-A/Simla Records 4, File si no 82/14196, Proc. No Oct 1917,1- 2, Bundle no 292. Re: Female education in India, p. 13.

Govt of India/Edu Dept/ Edu-A/Simla Records 4, File si no 82/14196, Proc. No Oct 1917,1- 2, Op Cit, Letter of the Secretary to the Govt. of India no 160, dated 22 Feb. 1916 on the subject of female education, p.23.

Govt of India/Edu Dept/ Edu-A/Simla Records 4, File si no 82/14196, Proc. No Oct 1917, Op.Cit., Letter of the Secretary to the Govt of India no 160, dated 22 Feb. 1916 on the subject of female education, p.35.

Govt of India/Home Dept/Edu-A. File SI No 10711, Proc. No. Feb 1905, nos 78-80. Calcutta Records 2, Old bundle No 276, New Bundle No 71. R?: Reorganization of Govt. Girls Schools in Madras Presidency, containing Letter no 59 of 1905, Govt of India, Finance and Commerce Dept, Salaries, Est. etc; Edu. written to the R'ght Hon'ble St. John Brodrick, His Majesty's Secretary of State for India, dated Calcutta 9 Feb. 1905, signed Curzon, Kitchener, ER Ellis, TR Arundale, Denzil Ibbetson, HE Richards, JP Hewett and EN Parker; forwarding for his consideration a letter from the Govt, of Madras, No 643 dated 22 Oct. 1904, "regarding the reorganization of the Govt. Girls' Schools in that Presidency." Para 2 and 3. of letter no 59 of 1905 to the R'ght Hon'ble St. John Broderick.

Govt of India/Edu Dept./Edu-A. File SI no 13077, Proc no Mar. 1913, no 124-125, Delhi Records 3. Bundle no 286. Appendix B, Proc no 124 Re: Affiliation of Loreto House, Calcutta to the Calcutta University in 1] English, Mathematics, History, Botany, French to the lA Standard 2] the Licentiate of Teaching. A report on the proposal of Loreto House Calcutta in Arts to the lA and in Teaching to the Licentiate of Teaching signed by HR James and SC Mahalanabis.

Govt of India/Edu Dept/Edu-A/Delhi records 4. File si no 133/13688, Proc. No Feb 1915,1- 15, Bundle no 289. Re: Request of the Indian Women's Education Association for assistance towards the training of Indian women in England, p. 2-4.

Govt of India/Edu Dept/Edu-A/Simla Records 2. File si no 14619, Proc no Aug 1919, 82- 106, Bundle no 294. Re: Award of State Scholarship tenable abroad for Indian women graduates to Miss Gulzar Mohammad Ali, MBBS, (Allahabad) and Miss Gulbai P Patel, MBBS (Bombay); Govt oflndia/Edu Dept/ Edu-A/ Simla Records 2. File si no 14628, Proc no Sept 1919, 22-32, Bundle no 294, Re: Deputation to England of Miss CK Kaushalya, Headmistress, Govt Secondary School for Girls, Connamore, to undergo a degree in natural science at a British University; and Govt of India/Edu Dept/ Edu-A/ Simla Records 2. File si no 14635, Proc no Sept 1919, 55-58, Bundle no 294,. Re: Proposed Deputation of Miss Nirmala Bala Naik, Asst Headmistress, Ravenshaw Girls' School, Cuttack, to England for a period of a year and a half to study for the Oxford Diploma in Education. Letter from Secretary to Govt of Bombay, Education Dept., to Joint Secretary, Govt. Of India, Dept of Edu, No 2066, dated Bombay, 2 July, 1914.

Govt of India/Edu Dept/Edu-A/Simla Records 4, File si no 82/14196, Proc. No Oct 1917,1-2, Bundle no 292, Re: Female Education in India, p. 31,32, 8.

Govt of India/Edu Dept/Edu-A/Simla records 5. File si no 14762, Proc no July 1920, 8-11, Bundle no 295. Re: Reorganization of the Women's Education Service in India, Proc 8 on 26 April, 1920. Note signed by Wali Mohammad, Assistant Secretary to the Govt. of India.

Govt. of India/Edu Dept/Edu-A/Simla Records 2. File SI no. 13277, Proc. No. October 1913, 81-84, Noting on Proc no 81, p3. Bundle no 287. (Re: Distribution of copies of this department's resolution no 301 CD, dated 21 February 1913 on the Education Policy of India. The resolution called for fostering girls' education).

Govt. of India/Edu Dept/Edu-A/Simla Records 4/file no 14611, Proc. No Aug 1919, 39-55. Re: Selection of Miss Iris KM le Blond for the State Scholarship tenable abroad by domiciled Europeans or Anglo-Indian girls or women; Govt. of India/ Edu Dept/Edu- A/Simla Records 4/file no l4547, Proc no June 1919, 34-55. Re: Proposed creation of a post in the Indian Education Service on Rs 400 per mensem to provide for the Professorship of Physical Science, Queen Mary's College for Women, Madras; Recruitment in England of a lady for the post.

History, the Quran, and *Gulistan and Bostan* by Shiekh Sadi Shirazi, Misra, R. (1967), Op.Cit., pp.87-91.

Kapil, Fatima K. (1990): *Education and Social Change in India,* New Delhi, Radiant Publishers, pp.6,42,

Keay, F.E. (1964): Op.Cit. p. 76, 77, 78.

Keay, F.E. (1964): Op.Cit. p. 76.

Keay, F.E. (1964): Op.Cit. pp. 70-75.

Keay, F.E. (1964): Op.Cit., p. 79, Monserrate, who visited India around 1580 AD mentions Akbar's interest in female education. The curriculum included Persian, Arabic, Theology,

Keay, F.E. (1964): Op.Cit., pp. 70-75.

Keay, F.E. (1964): Op.Cit., pp. 70-75.

Lopemudra, Apala, Visvanara and Saswati wrote Vedic hymns. Gargi Vachaknavi and Maitreyi, the wife of Yagnavalkya, held discussions and debates with scholars (Again no specific dates are given) Keay, F.E. (1964). *A History of Education in India and Pakistan.* Delhi, Oxford University Press, pp. 70-75.

Maham Anga, Akbar's nurse, among others, started a college, Misra, R. (1967), p. 87-91.

Manager of Publication, Government Printing Press, Vol. I, p. 163.

Misra, R. (1967): *Women in Mughal India: 1526-1748,* New Delhi, Munshiram Manoharlal. p. 1, 2.

Mudalier, Lakshmanswami (1960): *Education in India,* Bombay, Asia Publishing House, pp.21-22.

Mukherjee, M. (1984): Reality and Realism: Indian Women as Protagonists in Four 19th Century Novels. *Economic and Political Weekly,* Vol. XIX No. 2, 14 Jan 1984, Bombay, Sameekhsha, Trust Publications, pp.77-80.

National Archives of India (1960): Op.Cit., p.220.

National Archives of India (1960): *Selections from the Educational Records of the Govt of India,* Vol. /: Educational Reports 1859-71 (Being two notes on the state of Education in India compiled by AM Monteath in 1862-1867; and Part II of Education in British India prior to 1854 and in 1870, 1871 by AP Howell) Delhi, Govt, of India, p. 217.

National Archives of India (1960): Selections from the Educational Records of the *Govt. of* India. Vol. 1: Education Reports 1859-7!, *Delhi, Govt. of India Press,* pp. 85-89. National Archives of India (1960): Op.Cit., pp. 85-90.

National Archives of India (I960): Op.Cit. pp.85-89.

National Archives of India (I960): Op.Cit., p.215, 216.

National Archives of India (I960): Op.Cit., p.218.

National Archives of India (I960): Op.Cit., p.220,221.

National Archives of India (I960): Op.Cit., p.220.

National Planning Committee (1947): Op.Cit., Appendix 1, p.232.

National Planning Committee (1947): Op.Cit., Ch.IV, p. 137.

National Planning Committee, (1947), Op.Cit., Ch.IV, p. 134.

National Planning Committee, (1947): Op.Cit., Ch.IV, p. 137.

National Planning Committee, (1947): Op.Cit., Ch.IV, p. 138.

National Planning Committee. (1947); Op.Cit, Ch.IV, p. 130.

Nurullah, S and J.P. Naik. (1962): *A Student's History of Education in India: 1800-1961.* Bombay, Macmillan and Co. Ltd., p. 300.

Oak V.V. (1925): *England's Education Policy in Madras,* BG Paul and Co., p. 86.

Oak, V. V. (1925): Op.Cit., p. 82.

Oak, V.V. (1925): Op.Cit., pp. 27-30, 86.

P.Cherian (1935): The Malabar Christians and the Church Missionary Society: 1816-1840. Kottayam, Church Missionary Society, p. 190.

Paul, Thomas (1964): *Indian Women Through the Ages.* Bombay, Asia Publishing House, pp.280-285.

Presumably this refers to most girls being unable to complete their education even during the Vedic age(no specific dates are given) but also gives evidence of at least the occasional performance of the upanayana ceremony for girls. Altekar, A.S. (1951) *Education in Ancient India,* Benaras, Nand Kishore and Brothers, p.205-225.

R.N. Yesudas (1980): *The History of the London Missionary Society in Travancore: 1806-1908,* Trivandrum, Kerala Historical Society, pp. 45, 46, 53-56.

Raman, S.A. (1996): Getting Girls to School: Social Reform in the Tamil Districts, 1870- 1930, Calcutta, Stree, p. 78, 4.

Raman, S.A. (1996): Op.Cit., p. 3, 4.

Raman, Sita Anantha (1996): Op.Cit., Ch. III, pp. 78,79.

Raman, Sita Anantha (1996): Op.Cit., Introduction, px.

Raman, Sita Anantha (1996): Op.Cit., p. 7.

Raman, Sita Anantha, (1996): Ch. l.

Razia Sultana (1236-40 AD) was known as a scholar of many languages. Misra, R. (1967): *Women in Mughal India: 1526-1748,* New Delhi, Munshiram Manoharlal, p.7,8.

Shastri, K, A.N. (1966): A History of South India: From the Pre-historic Times to the Fall of Vijaynagar, Bombay, Oxford University Press, pp. l 15-145.

Shastri, K.A.N. (1966): Op.Cit., p.315.

Shastri, K.A.N. (1966): Op.Cit., p.320-321.

Shastri, K.A.N. (1966): Op.Cit., pp.303-317.

Sukumari Bhattacharya, "Women in Mahabharata" paper presented in Seminar on Women and Culture, Indraprastha College, N Delhi, 1981; Uma Chakravarty, "The Sita Myth" in Samya Shakti, Vol. 1, No.l, July 1983, p. 70, as quoted in Desai, Neera and Maithreyi K rishnaraj (1987), *Women and Sodet in India,* Delhi, Ajanta Bocks International, p. 26.

Suvira Jaiswal, "Position of Women in Early India" paper presented at the First Conference on Women's Studies, 1981, pp2,3. Also refer R.S. Sharma (1980) Indian Feudalism. Delhi, Macmillan and Co. pp. 112,113,277 as quoted in Desai, Neera and Maithreyi Krishnaraj (1987) *Women and Society in India,* Delhi, Ajanta Books International, p. 33).

The Fourth Annual Report of Her Highness the Maharani of Mysore's Caste Girls School, Mysore, (1885), p. 3, 9.

The Fourth Annual Report of Her Highness the Maharani of Mysore's Caste Girls School, Mysore, (1885), Op.Cit., p. 4, 5.

Westley, F. and A.H. Davis (1831): *Tyerman and Bennet's Travels,* London, London Missionary Society,. p. 460.

3

Elementary Education for Girls in India

Gurminder Singh

Abstract

Educating girls has a catalytic effect on every dimension of economic development including high productivity, faster growth, high economic gains and a step towards empowerment of women. Educated women are also observed to be strong positive role models for female children. Gender discrimination makes girls the first sacrificial victim to be withdrawn from school when times get tough, and it is a more relative disadvantage in SC or ST families. The article examines the causes of gender disparities in access to education and details the initiatives taken at the governmental and societal levels to address this issue.

Introduction

Promotion of female education has been the concern of India since Independence. In this light, the central government and state governments, institutions and other organizations have been doing a lot for the progress of the girl child's education. Yet, the achievements in girl's education are far from the goals set for Universalization of Elementary education. The 86th Constitutional Amendment Act 2002 made education a 'Fundamental Right' for children in the age group of six to fourteen years by providing that 'the State shall provide free and compulsory education to all children of the age of six to fourteen years in such manner as the State may, by law, determine'(Constitution of India, Article 21A) The bill specifies that every parent or guardian of a child has to 'enrol his/her child, or, as the case may be, ward in a recognized school, cause the child to attend such school with at least such minimum regularity as may be prescribed; and provide the child full opportunity to complete elementary education'.

The National Commission set up to Review the Working of the Constitution (22 February, 2000) recommended that children should enjoy the fundamental right to free and compulsory education. In addition, girls and children from scheduled caste (SC) and scheduled tribe (ST) households would have judicially enforceable right to education until they are eighteen years of age. According to the Constitution of India, 'The state shall endeavour to provide, within a period of ten years from the commencement of this constitution, for free and compulsory education for all children until they complete the age of fourteen years (Constitution of India, Article 45, 1951).'

'A far cry from the provisions of the Constitution of India, a land of more than a billion people having slightly less than one-third of the world's non-literate population aged fifteen years and above (UNESCO, 1998).' The goal of Universalization of education as set out in the Constitution seems unrealisable even after six decades. The original period of ten years to achieve this goal was extended to sixteen years after the government failed to meet its target. The Education Commission in its report in 1966 regretted this failure on part of the government and pushed the date further. The new target date was 1985. In 1986, the National Policy on Education extended the date by another ten years. In 1993, the department of education, in its report 'Education For All', set the date at 2001(A Review of The National Policy Of Education 1986). Now, the Indian government has to accomplish hundred per cent enrolments of children by 2008.

Extension of goals, years after years, indicates the lack of sincerity towards the child's betterment. The situation further worsens when the question of the girl child and caste differences arises. Caste plays a very important role in educational attainment in India, alongside affecting other major individual and household level variables. There is no doubt regarding the relative disadvantage faced by children belonging to the scheduled castes and scheduled tribes and other backward classes. The effect is even stronger for girls (Drèze and Kingdon, 2001). Drèze and Kingdon have found strong evidence of sharp gender bias in school participation in rural north Indian states of Uttar Pradesh, Bihar, Madhya Pradesh and Rajasthan. Ramachandran (1996) has shown that rising literacy rates in Kerala were closely linked to falling barriers of caste, class, race, and religion and that, in turn, the reduction of these barriers has been a key factor in furthering the spread of education. The vital importance of education in almost every sphere of women's empowerment has been experienced, making it an issue which must not be ignored. There is little argument that ending illiteracy amongst women raises their capabilities, enhances their agency, and involves them in the development process. The relationship between education and development is also a dialectical one.

In this paper we have tried to point out some of the government's endeavours and societal approaches towards the girl's education in the last century and therefore, especial emphasis has been given on Indian education policies after Independence. However the Government of India has made efforts at some levels but still lot has to be done to bring greater numbers within the ambit of education. Disparity in female education is still widespread in Indian society due to the patriarchal outlook or societal taboos towards sending a girl child to school. Further this paper has tried to show the evidence for this view i.e. elementary education for girl child is based on societal approach as well as government initiatives. It is also an attempt to understand, some of the issues confronting practitioners, policy makers, and researchers in female education in India and what they can do to move toward high-quality and gender-equitable education for all.

Gender Inequality in Access to Education

Greek philosophers thought a 'woman is an unfinished man left standing at a lower step in the scale of development. The male is by nature superior and female inferior. The one is the ruler and the other ruled. Woman is weak of will and, therefore incapable of independence of character and position.' Such prejudices prevail even today. On the threshold of a new millennium the status of woman is still to be elevated to that of man.

Given all these difficulties of conceptualization, measurement, quality and accessibility of data, the scorecard on gender equality and female education in Asia is intended to expand understanding and facilitate comparison with regard to achievements of gender equity in and through schooling.

The ideas that have driven the construction of this scorecard are multi-faceted. Existing measures for access to and efficiency in the school system are very limited as measures of gender equality, even though there have been marked improvements in sex-disaggregated data. These access and retention measures cannot, in their raw form, point to a wider understanding of gender equality neither in schooling nor as a result, in the area of education more generally. Thus, the idea for developing a scorecard that weighs enrolment, participation and survival into adulthood originated from concern over the need to find a publicly accountable measure that could distil some general components of human flourishing linked to education and schooling. There are some interesting issues that arise when the scores of India are high in most of the South-Indian states, while in most northern states, they are low (Drèze and Sen, 2000). The very large numbers of districts where enrolment and achievement are low contributes to India's low score. Firstly, coordinated government policies with strong local champions within government, NGOs or a women's movement can lead to significant increases in the score. Good scores, once attained, yield value over decades. Secondly, little action on gender equity in education, coupled with large internal inequalities, can lead to a fall in score. Thirdly, the effects of war linger for many decades after fighting officially ends. Reconstruction requires much sustained programmes.

Schooling has innumerable benefits, and yet vast majorities of Indian children, especially girls are deprived of these. Despite various measures undertaken by the government and local bodies to reduce the inequality in education between genders, castes, classes and religions, this inequality still persists (Divya Vaid, 2004).

India alone has 26.8 million primary school-age children who are not enrolled in primary school, accounting for 23 per cent of global absentees (Unicef, 2005, P. 14-15). Today, the total number of girl students enrolled in the upper primary education are much better because of many policy interventions on behalf of the girl child, such as the Report of the National Committee on Women's Education (1958-9), the Kothari Commission Report (1964-5) and above all the National Policy (1968) and the National Policy on Education (1986), which stressed the need for empowering women, thereby making them capable of guiding their own destiny and becoming self-reliant through exposure to education and survival skills, including income generation (Ramachandra, 2001).

India, being a predominantly agrarian country (*According to the 1991 Census, about 67.7 per cent of Indian Population were engaged in agriculture*), a substantial number of girls are expected to contribute to the family income by their own labour or to look after their younger siblings (Aggarwal, 1997) The opportunity cost of educating girls is thus especially large in rural and low-income families (Sengupta and Guha, 2002). The National Committee on the Status of Women in India (1975) accepted that poverty plays a major role in the attitude to girl's education especially for people below subsistence level (Aggarwal, 1987). The Public Report on Basic Education in India (PROBE, 1999) finds that in northern states of India, such costs are substantial: 'In fact, "schooling is too expensive" came first (just ahead of the need for child labour) among the reasons cited by Probe respondents to explain why a child had never been to school' (PROBE, 1999). 'The development paradigms have generally failed to address the unequal relationship between men and women, and failed to account the potential of women to contribute in the private and public sectors to a country's development. As a result, issues affecting women and girls are nearly invisible in the theories, policies and practices of the development' (UNICEF, 2004).

Girls and women endure numerous violations of their human rights, from social and economic discrimination to physical, psychological and sexual violence, to exclusion from positions of power within and outside the family. Among all the issues facing girls and women, why has education taken centre stage? Educating girls has a catalytic effect on every dimension on economic development including higher productivity and faster growth (Wolfensohn, 1995).

Equal access to educational opportunity is a basic human right essential to well being. Besides, it is now well established, that in developing countries, the economic gains from educating females, at least up to a minimum level, are much greater than the gains from educating males. Educating girls has a catalytic effect on every dimension on economic development including higher productivity and faster growth (World Bank, Report 1995). In the case of the poor girl who must work, her right to education is being infringed upon because she is unable to attend school. There seems to be very little difference between an infringed right and a violated right in this situation. Existence of gender gap in educational attainment thus becomes an important dimension of entitlement failure that threatens sustainable human development.

The primary role of the rights approach is to change public perceptions of what is due to Indian children. In particular, the rights approach can help to put children's issues on the political agenda, and to forge new social norms on these issues. To illustrate, the recent recognition of elementary education as a fundamental right of every child has helped to dispel the resilient notion that education is 'unnecessary' for some sections of society. A similar consensus needs to be built regarding the rights and entitlements of children. One symptom of the marginalization of children (especially young children) in Indian democracy is the low coverage of children's issues in the mainstream media (FOCUS, 2006).

India is still biased towards female education even after sixty years, a wide pervasiveness of the gender disparity, especially in rural areas where education is most sorely needed, the record in education is dismal, there exists a shamefully low literacy rate and disparities based on caste, religion, gender and region still flourish in the access to education, the quality of that education, and the benefits that arise from it. But positively the issue of female education in particular, has increasingly come into the focus of Indian policy makers in recent years.

As mentioned in Focus on Children Under Six (FOCUS 2006) report there are two types of intervention that are needed. First, a need to address the structural roots of child deprivation, including mass poverty, social discrimination, lack of education, and gender inequality. Second, there is a need for immediate protection of children under six, by integrating them in an effective system of child development services that leaves no child behind. It is with this immediate task that this report is concerned.

There is a need to adopt a rights-based approach in emergencies. The enforcement of girls' rights must be accorded the highest priority since many violations of girls' rights are only possible because of the invisibility of girls and the vulnerabilities they face. Therefore, protection, which embraces both the material conditions of children's lives as well as their psychological and emotional well-being, may be seen as a cross-cutting objective of humanitarian action. Agencies' child protection efforts should be focused on addressing and preventing violence, abuse and neglect, exploitation and discrimination as well as forced recruitment in armed groups. Education should be further recognized as a means for protecting and rehabilitating girls affected by armed conflicts (Mathieu, 2006).

Those who are illiterate are denied basic human rights because illiteracy ultimately 'suffocates the consciousness and the expressiveness of men and women who are forbidden from reading and writing, thus limiting their capacity to write about their reading of the world so that can rethink about their original reading of it.' (Freire, 1998: 4)

It is also significant that these conflicts have affected an Asian region that is 'still one of the most iniquitous regions in India as well as in the world in terms of gender, with discrimination against girls and women widespread (Boyden J., 2002)'. Therefore, the impact of conflict and post-conflict settings on female education in Afghanistan, Bangladesh, Bhutan, India, Nepal, Pakistan and Sri Lanka requires an in-depth research in order to take concrete actions and meet the gaps identified. A Girl said in Darfur, 'Education is light. When you don't know how to read and write – ignorance is like darkness.' And she also said to Rima Salah (UNICEF, 2005), 'Please continue to give us light, because we don't want to stay in darkness.' When we talk about education, it is like light. Education is the means towards empowerment of women, and the empowerment of girls. Studies have also linked education levels to lower rates of malnutrition, higher levels of economic empowerment and productivity, lower wage differentials, higher sex ratios, and lower mortality rates. There are intrinsic and extrinsic benefits to education (Sen, 1997), not the least of which is that educated women are strong positive role models for female children and other mothers.

Whatever be the cause, there is a gap in enrolment. The social barriers standing in the way of girls attending schools — poverty, compulsions of older girls in families having to look after the home and siblings, the misconception that girls do not need education and/or that what is taught in schools is irrelevant to them, parents seeing limited (economic) benefits in educating daughters, lack of women teachers and separate schools for girls, supportive facilities (like adequate and clean toilets in schools) and transport facilities to travel to school and back, all these inhibit parents from getting their girls enrolled.

The gender discrimination in schools is an extension of what we think in the family, in society and in the community in which we live. Unless there is camaraderie, dignity and partnership among the members of and within the family, it is difficult to expect the school to create it artificially in its own environment, and to pursue it without reference to what is happening in society. Gender discrimination remains rife in both the curriculum and organization of the school. The most effective way to ensure quality education for all children is to eliminate the barriers for girls: schools that are at long distances from home, high school fees and other hidden costs, lack of safe water and sanitation, discrimination and the threat of violence.

There has to be a democratic environment in the home for the child to be democratic in her lifestyle. Any programme of gender discrimination, elimination in educational institutions, must take into confidence the parents and guardians and undoubtedly the teachers, for whom there must be continuous programmes, orienting them to equality in thought and deed. This manifests itself in language, gestures, postures and action as seen in the way girls and boys are seated in the classroom. We neither need to exceed the limits of decency nor need we show prudishness — again it is for teachers and the administrators in schools to ensure that girls and boys are comfortable in each other's company. Quite often more chances are given to boys than to girls (by a kind of reflex action) to answer questions or to take on responsibility. Girls keep away from sports and physical activity and nothing is done to see that they are talked out of this preference by providing them with some transport or other facilities for getting home safe and encouraging them to take part in all the games and fitness programmes of the school. In addition, all students should be encouraged to take part in life planning — both girls and boys, planning as individuals and as members of a family.

Rightly does it emphasize the role of the community in helping the school to combat gender stereotyping? It encourages local communities, particularly women to play an active role in every aspect of the programme. This includes intensive capacity building for groups in the community to focus on issues relating to the education of girls. Involvement of the community is also required in monitoring enrolment, retention and levels of achievement and classroom behaviour and transaction, with emphasis on girls. The equal treatment promoted in the schools ought to be able to transform the thinking within families. Within the school itself, there is need to identify the overt and covert discrimination, arising out of ignorance and deeply ingrained ways of thinking, on the part of teachers and educational administrators (Karuna, 1988). Freedom and equality have to be seen in relation to the culture and structure of specific societies, and differences in male and female roles do not *ipso facto* result in inequality between sexes. Mukherjee, P. N. proposed three counter concepts to understand equality; discrimination, exploitation and oppression (Karuna, 1988). It seems that all these intervention are designed to programme a fixed social construction of girls.

Government Initiatives: Apprenticeship of Womanhood

After independence, the Government of India has taken number of steps to strengthen the educational base of the persons belonging to the girls and children of Scheduled Castes and Scheduled Tribes. Pursuant to the National

Policy on Education-1986 and the Programme of Action (POA)-1992, the following special provisions for SC's and ST's have been incorporated in the existing schemes of the Departments of Elementary Education and Literacy.

The right approach would be to replace the current practice of setting timeless global targets for the whole country with disaggregated targets for different states and UTs. This would inject the much needed sense of realism to the whole exercise of assessing the magnitude of the task and setting time frames. Considering that education is on the concurrent list and the centre has rightly provided high priority to elementary education, appropriateness of a proactive approach by the centre in designing development activities cannot be questioned. Going by past experience, there is a danger that after the initial enthusiasm, the implementing agencies may seek financial assistance under *Sarva Shiksha Abhiyan* but lose interest in and ownership of the programme and action soon after. Proactive approach of the centre may be taken as a license by many states to be inactive. The real test of *Sarva Shiksha Abhiyan* would be its adaptability to the changing contexts of different states and its ability to enthuse the state governments to continuously innovate the strategies for demanding central assistance. Therefore norms for support under *Sarva Shiksha Abhiyan* should have flexibility to accommodate new initiatives (Kainth, 2006, p. 3291).

The introduction of water, sanitation and hygiene is one factor in India's overall commitment to school quality and improving girls' enrolment. *Sarva Shiksha Abhiyan* is a Government flagship designed to get all children into school, especially girls disadvantaged by caste, tribe or disability. It relies on community participation and monitoring with an emphasis on the recruitment of women and members of disadvantaged groups. The initiative evaluates every aspect of the learning spaces against gender-friendly standards, including the provision of safe water and sanitation. To ensure the enrolment and retention of girls, schools serve midday meals and offer girls scholarships for uniforms and supplies. Teacher training and recruitment are part of an overall push for quality. Advocacy is a strong component of 'back-to-school' campaigns for children who have dropped out, messages directed to parents about the importance of education, a zero-rejection policy for disabled children and adolescent tutorial camps for girls (Unicef, 2005).

As Jean Drèze (1999) has said 'the schooling revolution has raised the literacy status in general and women in particular in Himachal Pradesh. Fifty years ago, educational level in Himachal Pradesh was no higher than Bihar or Utter Pradesh. Today, Himachal Pradesh is second only to Kerala in terms of school participation and literacy rate in the younger age-groups.' In 1951, the first post-Independence census showed Himachal Pradesh's literacy rate to be 19 per cent. By 2001 it had gone up to 77 per cent, with male literacy at 86 per cent and female at 68 per cent. In the fifteen to nineteen age groups, literacy rates were 95 per cent for females and 97 per cent for males, second only to Kerala, where the corresponding figures are 98 and 99 per cent respectively. Of all the states, school attendance rates in Himachal Pradesh in the six to twelve age group are the highest in the country. The distribution of educational performance in terms of gender and caste is also an impressive aspect of schooling in Himachal. In the seven to fifteen age groups not only are the aggregate levels of literacy very high, the gender gap (female literacy 94 per cent; male literacy 96 per cent) and caste disadvantage (SC female literacy 92 per cent; SC male literacy 95 per cent) have also greatly reduced (FOCUS, 2006).

A great deal of variation exists among states. In Rajasthan, the primary gross enrolment ratios for girls in primary and upper primary are 50 and 23 respectively, while the corresponding figures for Kerala are 98 and 104 respectively. Unexpectedly, primary gross enrolment ratios for Dalit girls are only marginally lower than the overall female average, though for tribal girls the difference is more marked. Low gross enrolment ratios at the secondary level reflect a disturbing trend in female education: a high drop out ratio. Drop out rates are highest amongst girls and Dalit communities, though in the latter boys and girls are equally likely to drop out. According to Mily Roy Anand and Mona Yadav (2006) 'A large number of SC girls do not have access to successive stages of education. The drop-out rates of Scheduled Caste girls are another crucial indicator in the field of educational development.'

One of the three elements of the strategy for Universal Elementary Education (UEE) of the National Education Policy of 1986 in India, was a large and systematic programme of non-formal education for children of habitations without school, working children and girls who cannot attend whole day schools.

- relaxed norms for opening of primary/middle schools; a primary school within one km walking distance from habitations of population up to 200 instead of habitations of up to 300 population.
- Abolition of tuition fee in all States in Government Schools at least up to the upper primary level. In fact, most of the states have abolished tuition fees for SC/ST students up to the senior secondary level.
- Incentives like free textbooks, uniforms, stationery, schools bags, etc., for these students.
- The Constitutional (86th Amendment) Bill, notified on 13 December 2002, provides for free and compulsory elementary education as a Fundamental Right, for all children in the age group of six to fourteen years.
- To achieve the long cherished goal of Universalization of Elementary Education (UEE) through a time bound integrated approach, in partnership with States, *Sarva Shiksha Abhiyan,* which promises to

change the face of elementary education sector of the country, aims to provide useful and quality elementary education to all children in the six to fourteen age groups by 2010.

The main features of the programme are:

- Focus on girls, especially belonging to SC/ST communities and minority groups.
- Back to school campus for out of school girls.
- Free textbooks for girls.
- Special coaching remedial classes for girls and a congenial learning environment.
- Teachers' sensitization programmes to promote equitable learning opportunities.
- Special focus for innovative projects related to girls education.
- Recruitment of 50 per cent female teachers.

Some other programmes which directly or indirectly support to the Girl Child educational development are as follows:

- District Primary Education Programme (DPEP)
- Mahila Samakhya (MS)
- National Programme for Education of Girls at Elementary Level (NPEGEL)
- Shiksha Karmi Project (SKP)
- Kasturba Gandhi Balika Vidyalayas
- Jan Shikshan Sansthan (JSS)
- Mid-Day Meal scheme
- Central Institute of Indian Languages (CIIL)
- Kendriya Vidyalayas (KVs)
- Navodaya Vidyalaya (NVs)
- National Institute of Open Schooling (NIOS)
- Adolescence Education Programme (AEP)

Recent assessments show that girls' participation in schooling has improved significantly during the last ten to fifteen years. In July 2003, the government of India approved a new programme called the National Programme for Education of Girls at Elementary Level (NPEGEL) as an amendment to the existing scheme of *Sarva Shiksha Abhiyan* for providing additional support by way of girl child friendly schools, stationery, uniforms, etc, of underprivileged/disadvantaged girls at the elementary level. The scheme has been implemented in Educationally Backward Blocks where the level of female literacy is below and the gender gap is above the national average, i.e. in blocks not covered under Educationally Backward Blocks but have at least

5 per cent SC/ST population and where SC/ST female literacy is below 10 per cent – and also in selected urban slums. Apart from NPEGEL, a new scheme called the Kasturbha Gandhi Balika Vidayalayas has been approved for launch during 2004-05 for setting up 750 residential schools with boarding facilities at elementary level for girls belonging predominantly to SC/ST, other backward castes and minorities in different areas.

India has recently introduced incentives similar to the Bangladesh secondary stipend programme, in which every family with a single girl child will be eligible for free education from Class 6. The motivation seems to be less of an EFA strategy than an attempt to control population and to redress the alarming population imbalance caused by son-preference.

During the eighth five year plan, the target of 'universalizing' elementary education was divided into three broad parameters: Universal Access, Universal Retention and Universal Achievement i.e., making education accessible to children, making sure that they continue education and finally, achieving goals. As a result of education programs, by the end of 2000, 94 per cent of India's rural population had *primary schools* within one km and 84 per cent had upper primary schools within 3 km. Special efforts were made to enrol Schedule Caste/ Schedule Tribe and girls. The enrolment in primary and upper-primary schools has gone up considerably since the first five year plan. So has the number of primary and upper-primary schools. In 1950-51, only 3.1 million students had enrolled for primary education. In 1997-98, this figure was 39.5 million. The number of primary and upper-primary schools was 0.223 million in 1950-51. This figure was 0.775 million in 1996-97.

In 2002-2003, an estimated 82 per cent of children in the age group of six to fourteen were enrolled in school. The government of India aims to increase this to 100 per cent by the end of the decade. To achieve that goal the Government launched *Sarva Shiksha Abhiyan*.

The strategies adopted by the Government to check drop-out rate are:

- Creating parental awareness;
- Community mobilization;
- Economic incentives ;
- Minimum Levels of Learning (MLL);
- District Primary Education Programme (DPEP);
- National Programme of Nutritional Support to Primary Education (Mid Day Meals Scheme);
- The 86th Constitutional Amendment Act was passed by the parliament to make the Right to Elementary Education a fundamental right and fundamental duty;
- National Elementary Education Mission;

- A National Committee of State Education Ministers has been set up with the Minister of Human Resource Development as the Chairperson of the committee;
- Media publicity and advocacy plans;
- *Sarva Shiksha Abhiyan.*

However, the Global Monitoring Report of UNESCO on progress towards Education For All goals considers the progress to be far from satisfactory and emphasizes the goal of gender parity and equality must be met. Are the strategies pursued for girls' education appropriate? It is important that a gender perspective is incorporated into all aspects of planning. For instance, in order to promote girls participation in schooling the Operation Blackboard scheme required that the second teacher appointed to any primary school with one teacher would be a woman teacher. The early 1990s also saw the emergence of an explicit programme for woman's empowerment such as *Mahila Samakhya* as means of improving participation of girls in schools. Unfortunately, no effort has been made to capitalize on the achievements made through these by incorporating complementary measures to retain girls in schools through the full cycle of elementary education, universalizing primary schooling by 2007 and elementary education by 2010. The model and strategies followed by Tamil Nadu and Kerala could be emulated by the poorer performing states. 'Learn While You Earn' scheme could be an effective measure to retain students in schools. 'To improve the quality of results on the part of students, grants are given to all teachers for developing teaching-learning materials, twenty days training is expected to be given to all teachers and free textbooks distributed to all girls and children of SC/ST origin' (Kainth, 2006). It is required to understand why each government initiative has been co-opted with larger cultural framework.

Conclusion

Decades after the commitments and reaffirmations by the government, to ensure quality education to every child, and reduce illiteracy, a large number of girl children are still denied the fundamental right to education. Despite thousand of 'successful' projects in the country, gender parity in education - in access to school, successful achievement and completion is as elusive as ever and girls continue to systematically lose out on the benefit that an education affords.

Emile Durkheim defines education as 'the methodical socialization of the young generation' (Durkheim, 1956). Education opens the 'doors of understanding the world' to girls and helps them be a responsible, increases their self-confidence, expands their sense of potential, their social and negotiation skills, earning power and ability to protect themselves against violence and ill health. Her absence in primary education leads to deprival to higher education as well.

As the world has experienced, girls had played a vital role at every stage of development, in her family, community, national and the universal development. She is a pathfinder to new generations through socializing and upbringing her children the right way. If she is well-qualified obviously she will better nurture the coming generation. If she has this sense of justice inculcated in her, she will also inculcate it in her children. What's happening in the world, the violence being perpetrated is also because we don't have a sense of justice. Because we keep talking about peace, right, But if you don't have justice with this peace, you cannot have peace. All these are, I (we) think, the values that we can get in school. And, of course, boys are important, but more importantly for girls because of the role she plays in socialization (UNICEF, 2005). She (a girl) will play a very important role in her community, but she will also play a very important role in socializing her children and their upbringing.

The stereotyped, persistent and often subtle gender discrimination that run through most societies, make the girls the first sacrificial victims, since being the last enrolled, they are the first to be withdrawn from schools when times get tough. Regardless of social, economic and physical challenges faced by a girl child, education must be ensured to every girl child and, so the government needs to mobilize the needed resources. It has been observed that parents often do not understand the government has the obligation to make available education to all the children (include girl child). The government is obliged to mobilize and make aware the mass, and attribute their children's failure to attend school as the failure of parent and society, both.

Despite the scientific evidence of women's contribution to the society in development and of the country, this has yet be widely recognized. Educating girls is seldom discussed as a strategy in the policy circles, as a way to ensure social progress. As a result, investment in girls' education is often bypassed when budget decisions are being negotiated. Women's role in Policy making must be ensured or reserved for better understanding of issues included here.

The behaviour and attitudes of policy makers and practitioners at best fail to meet particular needs of girls and boys, and at worst sabotage their right to an education without recognition of such differences in the needs of girls and boys, and the inequities in their roles, responsibilities and identities. Education policies and practices are 'gender blind' and the traditional perspectives often fail to take in to account the gender issues that affect girls' access to school.

Denial in any forms, to basic right to education should be considered a nation's failure to provide compulsory, free, available, accessible, acceptable – and adaptable to girls and boys alike. Jean Drèze and Amartya Sen (1995) assert that persistent gender inequality and deprivation of females are among India's most serious social failures. Though women's groups in India work toward progressive change, more efforts from public and private sectors are needed to bring about fundamental social change to reduce gender inequality

Universalization of education, and all the good that it will bring, is possible. Investing in girls' education today – not just with money but with energy and enthusiasm, commitment and concern, focus and intensity – is a strategy that will protect the right of all children to a quality education, and a strategy that will jump-start all other development goals (UNICEF, 2004).

References

Aggarwal, J C (1989): *Indian Women: Education and Status, Including Major Recommendations of the Report of the National Committee on the Status of Women in India, 1971-74* , New Delhi, Arya Book Depot.

Agrawal, S. P. and J.C. Aggarwal (1987): Third Historical Survey of Educational Development in India: Select Documents, 1990-1992. Delhi, Concept Publishing.

Boyden, Jo; de Berry, Joanna; Feeny T; Hart, J. (2002): Children Affected by Armed Conflict in South Asia – A Review of Trends and Issues Identifies through Secondary Research, Refugee Studies Centre, Oxford University, February 2002

Drèze, Jean and Amartya K. Sen (1995): *India: Economic Development and Social Opportunity*, Oxford, Delhi, Oxford University Press.

Drèze, Jean and Gita Gandhi Kingdon (2001): School Participation in Rural India, Review of Development Economics, 5, No. 1: 1-33, February 2001

Durkheim, E. (1956): *Education and Sociology*, The Free Press, New York.

Focus on Children Under Six (2006): Citizen's Initiative For the Rights of Children Under Six, Right to Food Campaign, New Delhi.

Freire, Paulo (1998): *Teachers as Cultural Workers – Letters to those who teach.* Westview Press, Boulder.

Kainth, Gursharan Singh (2006): 'A Mission Approach to *Sarva Shiksha Abhiyan*,' Economic and Political Weekly, July 29, 2006.

Karuna Chanana Edited (1988): *Socialization Education and Women – Explorations in Gender Identity*, New Delhi, Orient Longman Limited.

Mathieu, Alexandra (2006): Reaching the Girls in South Asia – Differentiated Needs and Responses in Emergencies, United Nations Children's Fund, Regional Office for South Asia.

Mily Roy Anand and Mona Yadav (2006): *The Inclusion of SC Girls in Education – A Long Path Ahead, Social Change*, December 2006 Vol. 36 No. 4 114-130, Delhi, Sage India.

Padma Ramachandran (2001): 'Gender Discrimination in School System', *The Hindu*, Tuesday, Dec 18, 2001, Delhi.

PROBE (1999): Public Report on Basic Education in India, New Delhi, Oxford University Press.

Sengupta, P and J Guha (2002): 'Enrolment, Dropout and Grade Completion of Girl Children in West Bengal', *Economic and Political Weekly*, 37(17), Pp1621-37.

UNESCO (1998): World Education Report 1998. Teachers and Teaching in a Changing World (1998, 178 pages), UNESCO's Press Service

UNICEF (2004): The State of the World's Children, Girls, Education and Development, Division of Communication, 3 United Nations Plaza, H9F, New York, USA,

______ (2005): Gender Achievements and Prospects in Education – The GAP Report (Part One), November 2005, New York, USA.

______ (2005): Progress for Children: A Report Card on Gender Parity and Primary Education, No. 2, April 2005, New York.

Vaid, Divya (2004): 'Gendered Inequality in Educational Transitions'. *Economic and Political Weekly* 39:3927-3938. August, 28, 2004

Wolfensohn James (1995): World Bank Report, Washington, DC.

PART – II

FRAMING GENDER IN EDUCATION: EQUITY CONCERNS

4

Education, Caste, Gender Dalit Girls' Access to Schooling in Maharashtra*

— *Padma Velaskar*

The problem of women's educational access and opportunity are receiving renewed and urgent attention today in the context of the national developmental failure to universalise elementary education even at the turn of the twentieth century. At a more fundamental level, the persistence of gender disparities in schooling has cast a long shadow on the feminist project of using education as an instrument of overcoming women's oppression. Simultaneously, however, a proper understanding of changing situations of educational access is hampered by monolithic theoretical approaches that fail to take adequate account of intersections between multiple forms of social inequality and of the significance of socio-historical contexts and dynamics of development. In India, for example, educational issues as related to caste, class, gender, ethnicity and region, and are by and large separately examined. Educational analysis does not take into account the interactive influences of these structural variables and tends therefore to homogenise, simplify or distort a complex and highly differentiated educational reality. Justice is not done to variations and differences between and within larger social categories.

This paper is concerned with examining the implications of the interaction between caste, class and patriarchy for educational access of women belonging to dalit communities, who were subsumed hitherto under two homogenising

* Revised version of paper presented at 'Seminar on Women's Education and Development' held at Malsisar, Rajasthan, (July 31 – August 2, 2004).

categories of 'woman' and 'dalit'. Identified as a key strategy of liberation, education has been increasingly availed by both women and dalits. Yet the question remains as to whether the problem of universalisation continues to basically derive out of the historical legacy of their educational and social exclusion. Do women and dalits continue to remain excluded, and for that matter to what extent and for what reasons? Moreover, due to the tendency to homogenise, when we speak of dalit advance we don't know the gender picture and when we talk of women's advance we don't usually have a caste differential analysis. Following an interactive approach, we explore the specific educational situation of dalit women who have historically occupied a distinctive subordination as a result of their location in untouchable castes and their multiple oppression under traditional caste-patriarchy.

The paper examines the extent to which dalit (viz. ex-untouchable) women have been able to cut across barriers of caste, class and gender to gain access to schooling. To what extent and to what educational level have they achieved parity with dalit boys and "general category", assumedly, non-dalit girls? We focus on dalit girls' access to schooling in Maharashtra, the state where both women and dalits have achieved greater levels of educational parity and educational linked social mobility as compared to their counterparts in some other large states. A comparative historical methodological approach permits exploration of the changing relationship between caste, gender and educational expansion, the focus of which is dalit girl's educational participation at primary and secondary levels of schooling. Issues of women's educational access we believe must also be underlined by a concern with women's freedom from oppression and improvements for them in social opportunities and life chances through education. It is, however, not within the scope of this paper to explore the social impact of education on dalit women's lives.

The paper begins with a brief history of dalit women's education in the colonial context, and of modern educational development among Maharashtra's dalits and women, only in broad strokes, since much historical educational research needs to be done to unravel processes and forces of educational advance among these sections.

The second section of the paper is an attempt to understand the main trends in dalit women's educational trajectory and chronicle patterns of caste/gender inequality in the post-colonial period. It conducts a comparative analysis of the educational progress of dalit girls with that of dalit boys and non-dalit girls, ascertaining patterns of enrolment, dropout and attendance at school. It also attempts to examine temporal change in levels of disparity. Given the historical legacy of regional imbalance in the state, we further examine inter-district variations in dalit girls' access to schooling. Intra-caste (i.e. within the dalit category) disparities are also an historical legacy. However, we are unable to anlayse these due to absence of caste-wise educational data. The data base for the second part of the paper is census data and enrolment statistics published by the Government of Maharashtra. We must, however, state at the outset that, determining these patterns is a difficult task due to limitations of available educational data. Separate time-series data on dalit enrolment are not available up to late seventies in the publications of the Directorate of Education, Government of Maharashtra. A major shortcoming is that the vital rural/urban breakdown of enrolment/institutional data is unavailable. As is well-known to educational researchers, enrolment ratios are imperfect indicators of progress since they do not exclude under-age and over-age children. Ideally they should measure the number of pupils enrolled at a particular level of education who fall within the prescribed age limit for that stage as a per cent of the total number of the eligible within that age group in the concerned population. In the absence of both age and class specific enrolment, our estimates of enrolment ratios tend to be inflated. Further, we do not have reliable estimates of the non-enrolled. In view of all these inadequacies and limitations we can at best, in this paper, indicate broad trends and make broad generalisations. Nevertheless, important trends have been revealed which indicate progress, constraints and contradictions.

The third and final part of the paper reflects on the character of educational advance that is revealed in the earlier section. We attempt, on the basis of existing research and writings and field observations gathered by the author, to hypothesise on the reasons for the patterns found in terms of ideology, structure (caste, class, gender) and state policy on equalising opportunity in education.

Historical Context

Historically, dalit women were placed in most subservient positions in the caste/gender based division of productive and reproductive labour. Despite commonalities on grounds of gender and caste, respectively, with all women and with dalit men, they bore a social oppression that was different in form and experience (Velaskar, 1998b). Under a formal education system that was founded on brahmanical principles of social closure wherein gender, "purity" and caste ranking were primary determinants of access to learning, dalit women shared educational exclusion with both dalit men and upper caste women.

Socio-historic circumstances saw the educational entry of dalit and upper caste women almost coinciding in Maharashtra. Casual factors, however, were different and subsequent developments of course followed completely different trajectories. The social reform movement created the space for upper caste women's educational access whereas dalit women's access was enabled by the anti-caste movement. The emergence of dalit women is intimately linked to the ideology and social impact of anti-caste and dalit movements and we attempt here to capture ideas and actions that stimulated and shaped this emergence. Dalit women's initial inclusion in formal education was closely tied to the pattern of educational inclusion of their caste communities. Colonial education – initially through missionary activity and later through state and indigenous activity – created the first rupture in the caste-education-link. Though it was introduced as part of western imperialist domination and served, for the greater part to consolidate high caste intellectual and social dominance, it had far reaching implications for the lower castes including the most downtrodden castes. Missionary educational efforts targetted both untouchable boys and girls and laid the foundation of low caste educational access.

Education's foregrounding as a potent instrument of liberation of both untouchables and women took place under the combined impact of social reformist actions and powerful anti-caste revolt. Emanating from the nationalist critique of society, nineteenth century Maharashtra, witnessed the emergence of several movements for social, religious and political reform that were to eventually bring about far reaching change in the secular and religious domains of the social order, including a formal acceptance of new ideals and values. The region experienced long and extensive activity and public interest in reform (Heimsath, 1964). The social ferment that was generated at the time reflected the crisscrossing of complex and contradictory economic, social and cultural processes that laid the foundation for a restructuring of caste and gender relations. This volatile situation triggered low caste and untouchable protest, forging change for these communities.

It has become customary and rightly so to locate the beginning of significant change for untouchable communities in the anti-caste movement led by Jotiba Phule (1827-1890). The movement was buttressed by a powerful counter-ideology that represented a fundamental and devastating moral and intellectual critique of Hindu society and religion. In Phule's reading of their historical subordination, it was the debarment of untouchables and women from knowledge and learning primarily responsible for their lowered positions and powerlessness. Modern education, attributed with a secular rationalist purpose would replace and nullify brahmanical education. According to Phule, women's education was the key not only to their awakening and freedom from patriarchal servitude, but to other fundamental changes in patriarchal structure. It would be vital to the development of women as persons and as citizens (Omvedt, 1990). The dogged efforts of Phule and the Satyashodhak movement enabled an educational breakthrough for low castes. Education permeated as a value and fact of life among the "lower" order people. Actual progress of dalit education however, was slow, halting and heavily constrained by shrewd colonial policies of downward filtration and religious neutrality and caste-Hindu orthodoxy. Phule himself faced virulent opposition from the Brahmin community to his educational activities on behalf of women and untouchables. After Phule, indigenous schools for the Shudra and untouchable castes continued to be set up by a number of committed Satyashodhak activists from the higher and lower castes (Velaskar, 1998; Zelliot, 2002). However, the schools were largely meant for boys. As the nineteenth century drew to a close, Phule's agenda for the spread of education among low caste women remained largely unfulfilled.

The larger state level scenario of nineteenth century social reform directed at women was characterised by a strong upper caste/middle class bias. Moderates in general, held an "upliftment" perspective towards both depressed castes and women. Their ideology was oriented towards partial religious reformation without a fundamental attack on Hindu religious philosophy. Clear caste/class and patriarchal interests determined that the primary focus of high caste reformers was upper caste women. The sole exception was that of Vithal Ramji Shinde (1873-1944). A missionary of the Prathana Samaj, Shinde ran a long rural campaign for extending compulsory primary education to girls, including those of low castes. Education was perceived as an instrument of their release and elevation to `the higher culture' (Gore, 1987). Pandita Ramabai, the solitary radical woman leader of the times, too focussed, given one supposes the compulsion of her own location and experiences, on issues and conditions of Brahmin women (Kosambi, 1993).

In the 20th century 'Brahmanetar' (viz. non-Brahman) phase of the anti-caste movement, the battle for socio-political supremacy between the economically dominant Marathas and culturally powerful Brahmans led to rapid politicisation of education. Acquisition of knowledge was a key issue of caste conflict. Educational expansion became part of an action programme of the non-Brahmans to dislodge Brahmans from their traditional positions. Caste organisations gained ascendance and caste-based access to education and its utility for caste-based mobility, status and power became dominant concerns (Omvedt, 1976; Gore, 1989). The result was a considerable extension of schooling and hostel facilities for children of intermediate and lower castes. Simultaneously, the provision of educational facilities and scholarships to needy and deserving students gave a helping hand in accessing education to dalit children also (Gore, 1989). Again, however, educational efforts were characterised by a strong gender bias evident in the categorical focus on boys' education (Khane, 1994). Moreover, along with progressive, equalising elements there existed narrow sectarian tendencies which eventually became dominant.

A woman's movement had by now emerged, wherein women's education constituted a prime focus in the quest for raising women's familial and political status. The National Council of Women's Education was founded in 1925 to further women's education in a context where women's literacy rate was a miniscule 1.8 per cent. As is widely recognised, the substantive impact of the movement was restricted to higher castes and class urban women, as it failed to address the conditions and issues of the masses of women (Mazumdar, 1976).

An autonomous dalit movement which first took root among the Mahars revived concern about the social condition of untouchable women. Its early ideology was rooted in the tradition of social reform. Close connections with Shinde and the Depressed Classes Mission led to the pioneering of autonomous dalit educational effort. Despite the frenzy of caste hatred and violence, there were continued attempts at founding schools and hostels, and vigorous campaigning for spreading educational awareness. They signified a new mood of confrontation and challenge (Moon, 1987; Kolte, 1975). Phule's ideological influence was evident in starting of special girls schools and in efforts of male reformers to educate their wives (Kolte, 1975, Pawar and Moon, 1989).

The Ambedkarian phase of the dalit liberationary struggle drew the dramatic entry of dalit women. The movement saw a new radicalised mobilisation which was galvanised by a new radical Ambedkar ideology of liberation. Though anti-caste and anti-untouchability in its primary thrust, the movement incorporated a separate gender agenda that sought to redefine dalit women's economic, political and cultural position. Following Phule, Ambedkar defined education as a key instrument of dalit men's and women's liberation, emphasising a secular-educational axis of mobility and the carving of a new secular social identity based on principles of equality, freedom and fraternity. He challenged archaic notions of women's intellectual inferiority and emphasised the essentiality of knowledge and learning equally for women and for men. He guided dalit women's political education through their induction into the public arena. Education became a crucial dimension of dalit women's political involvement. Women political activists emphasised the importance of female education for changing the social conditions of their caste communities as well as women's position in families and society. Ordinary women as mothers and learners waged struggles to educate their daughters and themselves (Velaskar, 2001). However, the processes of accessing education were slow.

Overall, the pre-independence history of women's education suggests that educational participation was restricted to urban high caste women. Though enabling conditions for educational access of dalit men as well as women were created by anti-caste social movement, women's actual progress was almost negligible. It is not difficult to imagine the root cause – a simultaneous operation of caste and caste-patriarchal ideology and relations at the societal and caste/community levels. Further more mass education received attention of the colonial state only with the devolution of powers in 1937. The colonial state, societal structures and hierarchal ideologies were far too powerful to be shaken by the efforts of the few dalit and non-dalit reformers. The Ambedkarian movement, however, laid the ground for far reaching change in social conditions and educational status of the dalits. What shape did post-colonial struggles and politics take and with what consequence for dalit women's educational status? The next section examines the issue.

Expansion of Schooling, Trend in Caste/Gender Equity and Dalit Girls Schooling in Post Independence Maharashtra

After independence, the democratisation of education, wherein expansion of educational facilities was coupled with compensatory discrimination, constituted the two-pronged strategy of the Indian effort at equalisation. As we have seen, in Maharashtra, the dynamic history of social reform and social movements fuelled the processes of democratisation of education. Conducive educational climate for expansion of education was created which was manifest in the public demand for education as well state response to the provision of education. A rapid spread of schooling occurred, but from the outset it was imbalanced and uneven, reflecting the pattern of a politically motivated, regionally imbalanced and generally iniquitous economic growth (Government of Maharashtra, 1984).

Within a post-independence socio-political context of elite Maratha dominance and large-scale containment of dalit politics, education gained primacy over political struggle as an instrument of freedom and dignity for ordinary dalits. Equally, education held a special symbolic material and political significance in the context of a widespread dissemination of Ambedkar ideology. The educational struggle however, was long and hard as first generation dalit learners attempted to overcome old and new structural forces (of semi-feudal service, poverty, social stigma, and caste discrimination) and gain education (Velaskar, 1998a). How did dalit women progress vis-à-vis dalit men and non-dalit women? What are the regional and caste-wise patterns of advance and caste/gender equity? We examine this situation in the following section.

The Educational Progress of Dalit Girls

Earlier analyses show that progress of girls' education in the first three decades after independence was commendable only at the primary stage. Girls' enrolment, however, increased at a faster rate than boys. Gender inequality existed at all levels but was most pronounced at higher levels (Kamat, 1985).

Separate educational data for dalits were not made available for this period. Thus, literacy figures of 1971 will have to serve as an index of (past) educational opportunity. In 1971, the literacy rate for dalit women was only 13 per cent as compared to 37 per cent for dalit men, a gap of 24 per cent that indicated women's great educational backwardness. In the same year, the general women's literacy rate stood at 26 per cent and that of males at 51 per cent. The gender gap within the general category was as large as that among the dalits, viz 25 per cent. The caste gap in literacy within genders was much lower at 14 per cent among men and 13 per cent among women. It is also significant to note that by 1971, dalit men had achieved a much higher literacy level than general category women. This fact together with the fact of the smaller gap between dalit and general category women, indicate the significance of patriarchal factors and women's general backwardness. That the caste gap in literacy was lower than the gender gap indicate a slow implementation of the gender agenda even after its accommodation in the Constitution and in the state policy. The women's movement lost its radical edge and was institutionalised and the dalit movement became male-centric.

Separate educational data for dalits are available from the mid seventies. Four sets of schooling statistics will be employed in our analysis to provide some understanding of dalits girls' access to and representation in schooling and of the nature of gender disparity that prevails. In the four sub-sections that follow, we provide an analysis of educational growth for a twenty-year period from 1979-80 to 1998-99. The sections relate to: (1) growth in enrolment (including enrolment ratios); (2) dalit girls' and boys' enrolment as per centage of relevant enrolment totals; (3) gender equity at various levels of schooling within dalit and non-dalit categories; and (4) age-specific attendance rates. With respect to the second and third issues, we examine regional (district-wise) variations in dalit progress. Finally, we make use of NSSO data for 1999-2000 to get an indication of where dalits and dalit girls currently stand in education.

Enrolment Expansion and Growth

Table 1 shows the remarkable expansion and growth in total and dalit girl's enrolment in both absolute as well as relative terms as compared to the educational advance of boys, from 1979-80 to 1998-99. Girls enrolment increased dramatically from 1981-82 to 1993-94 and growth rates for girls are higher than those for boys among both general category and dalit students.

Table 1: Enrolment Growth for General and Dalit Boys and Girls at All Levels of School Education (1979-80 – 1998-99)

Year	*Standard I-IV*			
	Total		*Dalit*	
	Boys	*Girls*	*Boys*	*Girls*
1979-80	4038635	3100255	587331	405971
1981-82	4172781	3264738	602844	433176
1993-94	4847193	4331840	745456	665527
Growth Rate in (81-82 to 93- 94)	674412	1067102	142612	232351
Growth Rate (81-82 to 93-94)	16.1	32.6	23.6	53.6
1998-99	5679213	4685079	773884	717522
Growth Rate (93-94 to 98-99)	17.1	8.15	3.8	7.8
Overall Growth Rate (1979-80 to 98-99)	40	51	31.7	76.7

(Contd...)

	Standard V-VII			
	Total		*Dalit*	
	Boys	*Girls*	*Boys*	*Girls*
1979-80	1616337	981158	197262	94898
1981-82	1805105	1113597	234721	116550
1993-94	2741627	2154683	386940	283174
Growth Rate in (81-82 to 93-94)	936522	1041086	152219	166624
Growth Rate (81-82 to 93-94)	51.8	93.4	64.8	142.9
1998-99	3095311	2699418	468915	402725
Growth Rate (93-94 to 98-99)	12.9	25.28	21.18	42.2
Overall Growth Rate (1979-80 to 98-99)	91	175.1	137.7	324.3
	Standard VIII-X			
	Total		*Dalit*	
	Boys	*Girls*	*Boys*	*Girls*
1979-80	972587	461103	112224	38968
1981-82	1105066	532526	133743	51134
1993-94	1960335	1281684	275238	163071
Growth Rate in (81-82 to 93-94)	855269	749158	141495	111937
Growth Rate (81-82 to 93-94)	77.3	140.6	105.7	218.9
1998-99	2304814	1758211	332191	241099
Growth Rate (93-94 to 98-99)	17.57	37.17	20.6	47.84
Overall Growth Rate (1979-80 to 98-99)	136.9	281.3	196.0	518.7

Source: Education at a Glance (1979-80 – 1998-99), Directorate of Education, Government of Maharashtra.

At the elementary stage (I-VII) the growth rate for dalit girls outstrips that of general category girls. Girls' enrolment at lower and upper primary enrolment levels has increased by over 10 lakhs within the general category. The corresponding figures for dalit girls are 2 lakhs and 1.6 lakhs. The growth rates registered are 32.6 and 93.4 per cent for general category girls and 53.6 and 142.9 per cent for dalit girls at lower primary and upper primary levels respectively.

At the secondary level, enrolment growth rates for girls of general and dalit categories are 140.6 per cent and 218.9 per cent respectively. Dalit girls' enrolment doubled from 51,134 to over 1.1 lakh. Between levels, the greatest growth has occurred at the secondary level. Quantitative progress over the two decade period (1979-80 – 1998-99) reconfirms the trend of highest growth rates for dalit girls.

Trends in enrolment ratios provide an added indication of educational growth. The main historical trend that is apparent from a consideration of the figures in the Table 2, in conjunction with Table 1 is that the educational system has accommodated an increasing proportion of girls and dalits. A dramatic swelling of dalit enrolment ratios is witnessed at the primary level. Middle level enrolment has advanced in the decade of the eighties and more particularly from eighties to the nineties for dalit boys and girls. At the secondary level, it is striking to note that the enrolment ratios of dalit boys and girls surpass those of general category children. Even as we keep in mind the problem of inflated enrolment ratios, and do not count them as valid indicators of "real" progress, the ratios do indicate a great post 80s spurt in educational enrolment at all levels.

Table 2: Stage-Wise Enrolment Ratios at Different Levels for Total and Dalit Population (1978-79 to 1998-99)

Level	*Primary (I-V)*				*Middle (VI-VII)*				*Secondary (VIII_X)*			
Year	*General*		*Dalit*		*General*		*Dalit*		*General*		*Dalit*	
	Boys	*Girls*	*Boys*	*Girls*	*Boys*	*Girls*	*Boys*	*Girls*	*Boys*	*Girls*	*Boys*	*Girls*
1978-79	124.2	96.9	142.4	99.1	61.7	35.9	58.6	26.4	41.6	20.0	37.7	13.1
1981-82	122.8	98.5	140.5	102.5	64.9	39.3	66.2	31.7	41.7	20.6	40.1	15.5
1993-94	104.5	94.7	142.6	128.4	64.4	51.1	82.4	59.4	68.6	47.7	86.7	54.7
1998-99	103.9	99.7	142.2	137.4	96.4	85.8	127.0	111.0	71.6	63.3	84.6	79.7

Source: Education at a Glance (1978-79 – 1989-99). Directorate of Education, Government of Maharashtra.

Per Cent Dalit Girls and Boys Enrolment to Their Population Per Cent

To ascertain dalit educational advance in another way, we may compare figures of dalit enrolment as per centage of total enrolment with their per centage in the total population. However, we need to point out a difficulty that such a comparison holds due to inter-censual discrepancies in population data. As per the census of 1981, dalits constituted 8 per cent of the total population in Maharashtra. The census of India 1991 shows a jump in this per centage to 11.09 due to the enumeration of Buddhists as dalits after the Constitutional Amendment Act of 1990. Dalit males constitute 11.04 per cent of the total male population and dalit females constitute 11.16 per cent of the total female population of Maharashtra in 1991. The Ministry of Education of the Government of Maharashtra, however, has always recognised and included neo-Buddhists as Scheduled Castes in compiling educational data. We thus proceed with the analysis using 1991 census figures for all years, keeping in view underestimation in earlier censuses. The 1991 figures are likely to be closer to actual for preceding years.

Table 3 below depicts the aforesaid per centages from 1979-80 to 1998-99. It reveals that standing at 14.54 per cent and 13.09 per cent respectively, the per centage of both dalit boys and girls' enrolment outstripped their population per centage at the lower primary level in 1979-80 itself. However, the per cent enrolment of dalit girls was much lower than population per centage at successively higher levels of schooling i.e. at the upper primary and at the secondary levels in the same year. For dalit boys, it was higher at the upper primary stage also. In 1981-82, dalit girls' enrolment again fell short of the population proportion at the upper primary and secondary levels. The corresponding figures for dalit boys showed higher enrolment at all the three levels of schooling. The situation improved for dalit girls' enrolment at all levels between 1981-82 and 1993-94. In the latter year, their representation in enrolment was higher than in the population. By the year 1998-99, both dalit girls and boys consolidated their advance and both registered higher enrolments at all levels of schooling.

Table 3: Dalit Boys and Girls Enrolment as Percentage of Total Boys and Total Girls Enrolment in Maharashtra (1979-80 and 1998-99)

	Lower Primary		*Upper Primary*		*Secondary*	
Year	*I-IV*		*V-VII*		*VIII-X*	
	Boys	*Girls*	*Boys*	*Girls*	*Boys*	*Girls*
1979-80	14.54	13.09	12.20	9.67	11.54	8.45
1981-82	14.4	13.32	12.99	10.46	12.10	9.6
1993-94	15.38	15.36	14.11	13.14	14.04	12.72
1998-99	15.24	15.32	15.12	14.92	14.41	13.71

Source: Education at a Glance (1979-80 – 1998-99), Directorate of Education, Government of Maharashtra.

The data lend substantiation to trends of rising enrolment noted in the earlier section. Dalit girls, particularly since the eighties, became part of general dalit educational advance and seem to have gained from the impact of ongoing social and economic changes in the state.

Inter District Variations in Enrolment Per Cent

Regional imbalance in all developmental aspects, including the historical diffusion of schooling, has been a persistent characteristic of development in Maharashtra. It should thus be important to examine unevenness of spread in dalit education also. Table 4 below gives a district-wise distribution of the data presented in the earlier section. It shows Maharashtra's erstwhile thirty districts (today, they number 35) in terms of whether they achieved higher, lower or equal dalit enrolment per centage as compared to dalit population per centge in the year 1998-99.

The Table shows that per cent enrolment of dalit girls and dalit boys surpasses population per cent at the lower primary stage in twenty-eight of the thirty districts in the year 1998-99. This suggests that erstwhile educationally backward districts from Marathwada and other pockets have in general registered quantitative progress towards the goal of universalisation of elementary education. Gadchiroli and Solapur are a cause for concern. It would also be important to highlight the districts where dalit girls have recorded notable advance. We define as "advanced" an enrolment per centage which is higher by 5 or more per cent points than population per cent. So defined, the advanced districts at the lower primary level are Mumbai, Pune, all districts of Konkan, Aurangabad, Jalna, Parbhani and Nanded of the Marathwada region, and Buldhana, Akola and Wardha and Nagpur of Vidarbha. Of these, Parbhani, Nanded, Buldhana, Akola, Nagpur and Wardha are in an advanced position at the upper primary level also.

Table 4: Dalit Girls and Dalit Boys Enrolment (in per cent) as Compared to Their Percentage in Population at Various Levels of Schooling (1998-99) [30 Districts]

Schooling Level	*Gender*	*No. of Districts by Whether Percentage Enrolment to Percent Population is*		
		Equal	*Lower*	*Higher*
Lower Primary (I – IV)	Girls	-	2	28
Boys	2	2	26	
Upper Primary (V – VII)	Girls	2	2	26
Boys	4	1	25	
Secondary (VIII – X)	Girls	2	8	20
Boys	2	4	24	

Source: Computed from data available in Education at a Glance (1998-99), Directorate of Education, Government of Maharashtra.

The picture changes for the worse at the upper primary level and even more markedly at the secondary level. At the latter level, a smaller number of districts viz. twenty districts record higher enrolment than population per centage with respect to dalit girls. Eight districts which register lower enrolment per centage are Pune, Ahmednagar, Solapur, Kolhapur, Sangli of Western Maharashtra, and Beed, Osmanabad and Latur of Marathwada. The situation in the latter three is much worse than the former three. Dalit boys are behind in only four districts.

Remarkably, in Konkan and Vidarbha regions, dalit girls show advance at the secondary level also. Buldhana, Akola, Nagpur perform exceptional progress. In Marathwada, only Nanded maintains its advanced position. On probing the situation in Vidarbha even further, we find that the ratio of dalit to non-backward category girls is markedly in favour of dalit girls at all three levels. In Amravati, Akola, Yavatmal, Nagpur, Wardha and Chandrapur, dalit girls have surpassed non-dalit girls.

Gender Equity in Dalit Education

To examine the issue of gender equity/disparity within and across social groups, we examine per cent female enrolment to total enrolment in both dalit and general categories.

Table 5 indicates gender distribution within total enrolment and dalit enrolment at different levels. Schooling, it is revealed, was certainly male dominated in 1979-80. Girls of both categories were placed in a situation of great inequality, especially at the upper primary and secondary levels with dalit girls being worse off. The Table further attests to a rise in girls' representation in general and in dalit categories and at all levels of education over the twenty-year period. By 1998-99, gender inequality is reduced at all levels and girls' enrolment is more than 45 per cent of the total in both social groups. There continues, however, to be greater disparity at the secondary level where the female enrolment per centages are 43 and 42 respectively for general category and dalit girls. If one separately examines ratios for the NBC category (arrived at after subtracting all BC category pupils from the total number of pupils), the ratio improves sharply for these girls revealing greater gender disparity among dalits.

TABLE 5: Per cent Girls Enrolment to Total Enrolment and Dalit Girls Enrolment to Total Dalit Enrolment at Different Levels (1979-80 – 1998-99)

Year	*Lower Primary (I - IV)*		*Upper Primary (V – VII)*		*Secondary (VIII-X)*	
	Per cent Girls	*Per cent Dalit Girls*	*Per cent Girls*	*Per cent Dalit Girls*	*Per cent Girls*	*Per cent Dalit Girls*
1979-80	43	40	37	32	32	25
1981-82	43	41	38	33	32	27
1993-94	47	47	44	42	39	37
1998-99	47 (48)	48	46 (47)	46	43 (44)	42

Figures in parentheses represent per cent NBC girls to total NBC enrolment.
Source: Education at a Glance (1979-80 – 1998-99), Directorate of Education, Government of Maharashtra.

The district wise scenario of gender equity at the lower primary level shows that dalit girls' enrolment is near about or above the state average of 48 per cent in most districts. At the upper primary level also, only three districts fall markedly below the state average of 46 (viz. Nasik, Solapur and Jalna). At the secondary level however, as many as fifteen districts register a lower dalit female enrolment than the state average of 42 per cent. They include districts from Khandesh, Western Maharashtra and all the districts of Marathawada. The districts of Nasik, Solapur and Jalna continue to figure as poorest performers and show largest gender inequity. In commensuration with the advance indicated in the earlier section, in most Vidarbha districts dalit girls perform exceptionally well at the secondary level. The pattern is more or less repeated in the general population, at the primary level in terms of number of districts. However, the districts vary. At the upper primary level five districts are below average, three of them from Marathawada. At the secondary level, all the districts of Marathawada and two each from Nasik and Pune divisions are below the state average.

Drop Out

Retention at a particular stage of education and progression between education stages are both important aspects of educational opportunity. It is difficult to compute either kind of dropout rate with any reasonable degree of accuracy for Maharashtra. Phenomena that are external and internal to schooling viz. inter-district migration, the numbers of repeaters in every class, an admission policy that admits new entrants at any level deemed "appropriate" for the pupil by local authorities, are all factors that preclude an accurate calculation. The data provided in Table 6 below is thus a very rough approximation of drop out levels. It is concerned with "continuation drop out" rates of dalit and non-backward category students. By continuation drop out rates we mean the extent to which cohorts entering levels I, V, and VIII in 1993-94 and slated to reach standards IV, VII and X respectively in 1996-97, 1995-96 and 1995-96 actually do so.

The Table reveals that dalit girls and boys have a higher level of dropout at the primary stage as compared to the NBC children. The dropout of dalit girls is lower than that of dalit boys. At the upper primary level, dropout of dalit girls is higher than dalit boys and higher than NBC girls. But strikingly at the secondary stage dalit girls' dropout is lower than that of NBC girls. The gender difference in dropout within dalits is smaller. This suggests that those dalit girls who do survive elementary school and enter the secondary, stay on till the end. For NBC girls, the secondary level appears to be the critical stage of dropout. They probably belong to the dominant yet orthodox segments of the Maratha caste-cluster, which constitutes a significant proportion of this category.

TABLE 6: Drop-out Among Dalits and NBC Population at Different Levels (1993-94 – 1995-96)

Social Group	*Lower Primary (I – IV)*		*Upper Primary (V-VII)*		*Secondary (VIII – X)*	
	Girls	*Boys*	*Girls*	*Boys*	*Girls*	*Boys*
Dalit	15.87	18.30	17.38	14.14	25.88	26.40
NBC	15.41	14.60	16.31	16.95	30.45	27.29

Source: Computed from enrolment data for year 1993-94 and 1996-97. Education at a Glance, Directorate of Education, Government of Maharashtra.

District-wise variations in dropout reveal that Osmanabad, Raigad and Jalna, show the highest rates of dalit girl dropout at lower and upper primary levels. At the secondary level, diverse array of districts in terms of developmental levels show very high rates of dalit boys and girls dropout. They include the educationally advanced districts of Mumbai, Pune, Jalna, Thane, Sangli, Osmanabad, Ahmednagar, Satara, Ratnagiri, Beed and Latur

Wardha; Bhandara, Nagpur, Aurangabad, Akola and Kolhapur are districts with lowest dropout.

Age-Specific Attendance Rates

The census provides data on school attendance by age groups. The major limitation of this data is that information does not include the stage at which children are attending school. Nevertheless, the data cover the entire span of school going ages and also give a useful rural/urban breakdown. On the whole, age-specific attendance rates are better indicative than enrolment ratios of educational situations. Though figures for 2001 are not available, we analyse census 1991 figures to provide further insight into the schooling situation.

Table 7 provides rural and urban wise breakdown of school attendance rates for dalit and non-dalit girls and boys. The Table shows that girls' attendance rates are lower than those of boys in all age-groups in both social groups and in both urban and rural areas. For dalit girls, they range from a high of 78.2 per cent in the 10-12 years age group in urban areas to a low of 32.51 per cent in 16-17 years age-group in rural areas.

Table 7: Age Specific School Attendance Rates in General and Dalit Populations and Caste/Gender Disparities in Rural and Urban Maharashtra (1991)

Age Group	*Rural Attendance Rates*				*Percentage Difference in Rural Attendance Between*			
	Dalit		*General*		*Dalit Boys and Girls*	*General Boys and Girls*	*General and Dalit*	
	Boys	*Girls*	*Boys*	*Girls*	*Boys*	*Girls*	*Boys*	*Girls*
6-9	61.46	50.19	66.30	57.04	11.27	9.26	4.84	6.85
10-12	80.62	60.65	80.64	64.94	19.97	15.70	0.02	4.29
13-15	73.53	51.16	72.24	49.90	22.37	22.34	-1.29	-1.26
16-17	59.34	32.51	56.20	27.97	26.83	28.23	-3.14	-4.54
Urban Attendance Rates								
6-9	67.19	64.16	75.84	73.16	3.03	2.68	8.65	9.00
10-12	85.13	78.2	88.26	84.37	6.93	2.89	3.13	6.17
13-15	80.64	69.99	81.67	75.81	10.65	5.86	1.03	5.82
16-17	67.41	52.31	68.98	58.43	15.10	10.55	1.57	6.12
Total Attendance Rates								
6-9	63.59	55.39	69.77	62.83	8.21	6.94	6.17	7.44
10-12	82.27	67.45	83.48	72.00	14.83	11.48	1.20	4.55
13-15	76.06	58.52	75.75	59.51	17.53	15.84	-0.30	1.38
16-17	62.42	40.84	61.46	40.97	21.58	20.49	-0.96	0.13

Note:-Sign denotes higher dalit attendance as compared to general attendance.

Source: Census of India, 1991 Series – 14, Maharashtra, Part VIII (II) Vol. I/Part VIII (I).

Attendance rates are highest for girls of both categories in the 10-12 years age group, indicating better retention at the two elementary (lower and upper primary) stages. For rural girls, they fall significantly in the higher age groups of 13-15 years and 16-17 years, indicating withdrawal. However, it is significant to note that in rural Maharashtra, general category girls lag behind dalit girls in school attendance in the higher age-groups. Some further support is thus lent to the earlier finding of a lower secondary stage dropout for dalit girls. Against the rural situation, urban dalit girls lag substantially behind their general category counterparts in all age groups.

The Table further shows the impressive advance of dalit boys' education not only vis-à-vis dalit girls but also boys. Rural dalit boys closely follow rural general category boys in school attendance in the 6-9 and 10-12 years age groups. They surpass the latter in the 13-15 and 16-17 years age groups. Like the girls, however urban dalit boys' attendance is lower than that of general category boys in all age groups. However, the difference is much smaller than that with respect to the girls in all categories except in the 6-9 years category.

Gender disparity, both within rural dalits and non-dalits, is very high in all age groups, especially the higher age groups indicating post-elementary withdrawal of girls. Urban gender disparity within dalits is smaller than rural, but exists at all levels. It is sizeable in the 13-15 and 16-17 years age groups. For the general category, it is sizeable in the 16-17 years age group. Thus gender constraints continue to affect participation of girls belonging to both categories especially at the higher levels of schooling.

Current Educational Levels of Dalits as Compared to OBC and Other (Non-BC) Category Women and Men

To conclude the inquiry into dalit women's educational progress, we look at educational levels achieved by dalit, OBC and 'others' (presumably non-BC population). In the context of the current non-availability of caste-wise literacy figures of census 2001, we have analysed NSSO data for the year 1999-2000 and attempted to gauge the impact of the processes of educational development in terms of final educational attainment.

Table 8 reveals that the per centage of illiterates is the highest among female dalits (viz. 49.87 per cent) as compared to any other sub-group. Illiteracy is also fairly substantial among OBC and "other" category women. The gap between dalit and other women seems to be narrowing at lower primary and middle levels of education. However, a much higher per centage of women from the 'other' category have attained secondary education as compared to dalit women. The 'other' category women are consistently better placed than the dalit or OBC women with respect to each level of education.

Though overall expanding school enrolments have meant increasing educational attainments for dalit women and narrowing gender disparity in terms of literacy and education, the disparity continues to be largest for dalits as compared to other categories. Dalit men are educationally way ahead of women. The gender gap in literacy is 20 per cent for dalits as compared to 18 per cent for OBC and 14 per cent for "others" in 1999-2000. It appears to have narrowed over time if one uses 1991 census figures as a comparative point of focus. It then stood at 29 per cent for dalits as compared to 24 per cent within the general population. When available, Census of India 2001 figures for SC/ST will confirm the trend of declining gender disparity within dalits and non-dalits.

Table 8: Dalits, OBCs and Others by Educational Levels and Gender Disparity in Educational Levels in Maharashtra (1999-2000)

Educational Level	*Dalits*		*m-f disparity*	*Other Backward Classes*		*m-f disparity*	*Others*		*m-f disparity*
	Male	*Female*		*Male*	*Female*		*Male*	*Female*	
Not Literate	29.80	49.97	-20.17	24.98	43.36	-18.38	19.95	33.97	-14.01
Literate	17.01	15.17	1.84	18.11	16.25	1.86	16.83	16.11	0.72
Primary	17.90	15.42	0.01	17.21	14.79	2.42	15.57	15.91	-0.34
Middle	19.68	11.82	8.06	19.36	15.64	3.72	18.37	15.43	2.94
Secondary	8.86	4.19	4.67	11.49	6.48	5.01	14.78	9.38	5.4
Hr. Secondary	3.34	2.02	1.32	5.01	2.07	2.94	6.45	3.98	2.47
Graduate	3.14	1.08	2.06	3.77	1.38	2.39	7.95	5.08	2.87
NR	0.27	0.33	-p	0.07	0.05	-	0.11	0.15	-
Total	**100.00**	**100.00**	-	**100.00**	**100.00**	-	**100.00**	**100.00**	-

Source: NSSO 55th Round (July 1999-June 2000). NSSO, Ministry of Statistics and Programme Implementation, Government of India, 2001.

Note:- sign denotes higher female than male illiteracy/education level.

Summing Up and Explaining the Patterns of Dalit Girls' Educational Access

To sum up, we highlight patterns of school access and caste/gender disparities. The picture is one of quantitative advance, but also of constraint and contradiction. Advance is reflected in the high growth rates in dalit girls' enrolment and growing gender and dalit non-dalit parity. Obstacles are reflected in persistent gender disparity and in uneven and unequal diffusion of education based on caste, gender and region.

It is obvious that there has been an unprecedented expansion of dalit girls' access to schooling from 1979-80 to 1998-99 in Maharashtra, the hallmark of which is a quantitative spurt in enrolment post-80s. During this period, dalit girls' access to elementary levels of schooling widened dramatically. The expansion is indicated by the highest growth rates, high enrolment ratios and the rising proportion of dalit girls' representation in total girls' enrolment.

Gender disparity within the dalits has substantially reduced but not eliminated and opportunities seem to be increasingly availed by dalit girls at the lower primary level. Opportunities for secondary education are also availed and steady increases noticed in the proportion of dalit girls entering and staying on in secondary school. The proportionate representation, however, is much less at the secondary level than at the primary level. There seems to be a considerable dropout of girls and dalit girls between elementary and secondary stages and also within the secondary stage leading to lower gender equity. We need better quality data to make to a firm conclusion about rates of dropout. However, attendance rates force us to exert an overall note of caution. They suggest that gender equalisation even at the elementary level is still very elusive. A large gender gap persists in rural and urban areas among dalit and non-dalits. Lower attendance rates in higher age-groups suggest that despite increasing access, opportunities at the secondary school level are very unequal. Urban dalit girls are doing better than rural, though they are behind non-dalit urban girls. However, rural dalit girls' attendance is very significantly higher than that of rural non-dalit girls in the two higher age groups, suggesting greater progress of the former.

Following the historical pattern, there exist regional variations in dalit girls' educational progress as well as in caste/gender disparities. However, changes have also occurred in these patterns which do not suggest a neat correspondence anymore between economic development and educational development. Despite the socio-economic lag, districts of Vidarbha and Konkan and also Marathwada, have experienced impressive dalit educational development. In most districts from Vidarbha, girls have advanced and there exits gender disparity at all levels. Indeed these districts account substantially for the state's progress and have contributed to the changed picture of caste/gender educational inequality. There are districts however, including those from Vidarbha that lag behind in dalit girls' education and also display huge gender disparity. Some Marathwada districts continue to be the most backward. Thus, high rates of enrolment growth registered by dalit girls have been insufficient to wipe out historical disadvantage in some parts of Maharashtra.

As we mentioned at the outset, intra-dalit educational disparities too are a characteristic feature of Maharashtra's educational scenario. Macro-level analysis of literacy data has established that Mahars/Neo-Buddhists and Chambhars are more educationally advanced and the Mangs and many other smaller dalit castes are educationally backward (Wankhede, 2002). The Mahar (an overwhelming majority of whom are now Buddhists), Mang and Chambhar castes constitute an overwhelming proportion (80 per cent +) of the dalits in the state. Five castes viz. Bhangi, Lingader, Khatik, Holar and Dhor, together constitute 8.42 per cent. The remaining 51 castes constitute the rest (Wankhede, 2002). The neo-Buddhists and Chambhars have achieved far superior education levels than the rest. In recent times, some others, such as Dhor, Khatik and

Lingader have achieved better progress. But the overall picture is of low access and schooling attainment of these most backward caste groups (Velaskar, 2005; Wankhede, 1998 and 2002; Velaskar & Wankhede, 1998). We not only need data to know the extent of exclusion and deprivation of very backward communities, we also need data to establish class-based differences in educational access within dalits. Micro studies indicate that there is ground for such variations (Wankhede, 1998).

Contemporary situation of dalit girls' schooling in the State can be summed up in terms of three trends: (1) increased access and opportunities to enrol at all levels; (2) persistence of gender disparities in retention at all levels, and sharply so at the secondary level; and (3) the continuing though changed levels of regionally unequal educational development. The cumulative impact has been the enhanced but as yet the lowest levels of literacy and education among dalit women as compared to dalit males and non-dalit females. Thus, though neither caste nor gender have remained definitive predictors of educational access today, they certainly are not irrelevant.

We now attempt an explanation of the changing patterns of caste/gender disparities in education terms, of the larger ideological, material and political factors at play, as well as the dynamics of state educational policy and action. Given the paucity of correlational explanatory or qualitative research that examines such linkages, only a broad speculative analysis is possible of facilitative and constraining factors – social, economic, ideological and cultural – that have resulted in the patterns. What factors account for the dramatic improvement in dalit girls' access to education as well as for the persistent gender disadvantage? How do we explain the changing patterns of regional imbalance in dalit girls' educational attainment?

The brief survey of educational developments in the colonial period revealed a history marked by social cleavages of caste, class, gender and tribe. In such a context, educational entry of dalit girls was directly tied to socio-political and ideological change in their caste communities. In post independence Maharashtra too, the expansion of schooling facilities did not have an immediate impact on dalit girls. Dalit boys availed these to a much greater extent. Thus, the educational benefit of great ideological impact of the dalit movement and Phule Ambedkarian ideology was largely restricted to boys. Post-Ambedkar transformatory action on dalit women's behalf had almost come to a standstill. Women and women's issues became peripheral to dalit politics. Their unchanging, inferior position as "women – dalits" was reflected in poor prospects for dalit girls' education, despite available opportunities. Caste gender barriers persisted in the form of traditional ideologies of untouchability, of early marriage and of an enforced participation in both domestic and productive caste-sexual division of labour in a context of poverty. Greater opportunity costs were involved of educating girls as compared to boys. Caste discrimination and sharply negative attitudes to girls' education from within the caste communities pervaded several regions, particularly those historically more feudal.

It is well known that the rapid socio-economic development of Maharashtra has tread a highly skewed and distorted pattern. The state's position as economically advanced hides tremendous disparities between and within its regions/districts, between its urban and rural areas, and between castes, tribal/ non-tribal populations. The situation has been aggravated by the emergence of class inequalities and the persistence of poverty. Imbalanced development was also reflected in unequal geographical diffusion of educational facilities at all levels of education (Govt. of Maharashtra 1984). In the immediate post independence period, politico-economic rural interests emphasized mass education and accelerated the spread of rural education (Rosenthal, 1977). School and teacher provision and investments in education aimed to set right the imbalances and bring about a more equitable diffusion of educational facilities. Compensatory discrimination in schooling was provided albeit unsatisfactorily to the economically disadvantaged and to dalits in the form of freeships, scholarships, special classes and provision of books. Later periods witnessed a slowing down of the state impetus to the equitable distribution of primary education and an overall shift towards greater support of secondary education. In terms of special promotion of girls' education, the overall record of Maharashtra government's educational policy and action has been mixed. Schooling has been primarily coeducational and factors known to have a direct impact on girls' education, such as accessible schools, girls' schools, women teachers and scholarships, have not received sufficient attention.

Iniquitous economic and educational development has had a multi-faceted and contradictory impact on dalits and on dalit girls' education. On the one hand, it created the context for socio-economic advance of the dalits reflected in impressive levels of urbanisation, educational development, occupational change and social mobility which was aided primarily by the policy of reservations. Akin to the experience of the higher castes, middle class formation had a favourable impact on girls' educational participation. Higher income levels, better educational climates, greater exposures and ability to pay were the material factors that have enabled girls' education. On the other hand, dalits, including those from Buddhist and Chambhar castes, have been greater victims of uneven development processes across the state and especially in some regions. The persistence of caste structure and ideology is evident in that there continue to exist marginal and socially excluded castes and sections within the dalit category. They continue to lead a poverty-stricken and oppressed existence outside the pale of village societies. Children of these lower most classes and communities largely stay away from/are excluded from education as they cannot bear the costs of educating any or all children. Dalit women are concentrated in caste/gender segmented rural and urban labour markets and gain work as cheap labour in caste occupations and informal economies. Patriarchal ideology is reinforced. It is strong in custom, law and attitude and gets further compounded by economic deprivation and social oppression. Strong counter-veiling cultural religious norms serve to curtail enrolment and school attendance and legitimise female child labour, early marriage, early withdrawal of girls from school, low aspirations, etc. Micro-studies have attested to this grim reality (Velaskar, 1999; Berntsen, undated; Apte, 2004; Chauhan, 2004).

Against this background still prevailing in certain regions the counter scenario of very impressive figures for dalit girls' enrolment in parts of the same region creates a paradoxical phenomenon. It points to the operation of other factors of significance. It is suggested here that dalit liberation ideologies and dalit politicisation have made an independent educational impact. A key factor that has positively influenced dalit girls' education as it has of boys is the profound impact of Ambedkar ideology (Velaskar, 1998). It is strongly prevalent among dalits and Buddhists in particular, through the dalit movement, especially its cultural politics and through dalit civil society. The Chambhars have been keen competitors and have made rapid strides. In regions where the dalit movement has been strong such as Marathwada and Vidarbha, various social, political and cultural organisations functioning within overarching Ambedkarian, Phule-Ambedkarian, Ambedkarian-Buddhist ideologies, have engaged in spreading the Ambedkar ideology, including his educational thought. They have worked to mould dalit society's attitudes to girls' education and where possible to engage in educational action. With the rise of the militant dalit protest in the form of Dalit Panthers in the seventies, the movement acted as a pressure group on issues of scholarship, reservation policy and caste discrimination in educational institutions, enhancing educational motivation. The protracted agitation over the renaming of Marathwada University after Dr. Ambedkar heightened political and educational consciousness of dalit society. Despite lacking in material conditions, pro-school values have been adopted by dalit girls and their families. Dalit parents displayed considerable willingness to invest in their daughters' education and many dalit families defied costs and poverty for this purpose. In contrast, the rural Marathas continue to display a patriarchal bias and uphold early marriages and lower education levels for girls as compared to boys.

Since the eighties, the direct impact of the women's movement set favourable changes in social values and beliefs about women's "proper" place to a greater pace. This radical second phase made a widespread impact across caste and class on gender consciousness in Maharashtra (Datar, 1992). New cultural norms set by urban educated middle class women began to gain wider societal acceptance. The special significance of the women's movement to dalit women was that it radicalised gender agendas of dalit organisations and revived Phule-Ambedkarian ideology of gender. The dual impact gave rise to the phenomenon of dalit women leaders within malestream dalit politics, dalit educated working women in rural and urban areas, and eventually to the emergence of a separate dalit women's movement. Education of dalit girls is a key agenda item and the escalation of female demand for and participation in education could well be attributed to the joint impact of dalit women's movements and the new "dalit feminist" consciousness. The gender component of Ambedkar ideology which had challenged caste-patriarchal traditionalism and placed equal emphasis on the education of girls and boys is more vigorously advocated today in order to promote greater inclusion of girls at all educational levels. Girls are increasingly utilising dalit pre-matric scholarships which were earlier consumed largely by boys (Wankhede and Velaskar, 1998).

We do not have systematic empirical studies that ascertain the impact of hierarchical ideologies and patriarchal values on schooling system and their adverse effect on dalit educational enrolment, retention and attainment. Micro level studies indicate that hierarchical organisation of schooling systems and internal caste and gender hegemonic curricular and teaching-learning processes compound the educational difficulties of disadvantaged children in general and girl children in particular. Thus, the mass inclusion that has been achieved by the state system of education is an incredibly weak inclusion (Velaskar, 2005; Berntsen, undated). Caste-patriarchal policy of the state has been evident in the poor quality of government primary schools, their inadequate presence at the secondary level, failure to adequately recruit women and dalit teachers etc. Currently, only 3.28 per cent of primary schools and 8.77 per cent of secondary schools are girls schools in Maharashtra. In an overall situation of unequal provision, middle class dalit girls alone can access "better", private schools and single-sex schools. The large majority, however, are confined to poorly equipped and far away local body schools. This is a known factor for dropout and low attendance.

The government woke up to the reality around the eighties. Schemes were launched to foster girls' education through various kinds of economic support, such as provision of free uniform, textbooks, bus fares and midday meals. In 1991, a most important policy change sought to directly redress gender inequality by making education 'free' till Std. XII for girls. It would be reasonable to assume some positive impact of all these measures on girls' education though systematic policy evaluative studies need to be conducted. Dalit girls seem to have benefited both from general expansion and specific policies targeting dalits and girls. But it does appear that variations in schooling attainment are equally or more a consequence of liberative secular trends and Ambedkarian ideological impact on dalit communities.

Conclusion

The paper has attempted to examine the combined impact of caste, class and gender through a focus on patterns of dalit girls' access to schooling. It has been found that dalit girls were late starters but have considerably improved their educational situation. However, there is marked gender disparity within the dalits and also regional variations which results in continuous educational disadvantage for dalit girls in same pockets. The enhanced but as yet unequal educational progress of dalit girls appear to be the result of a combination of significant factors, socio-economic and cultural, related to society and state; macro socio-economic processes, in particular class formation and urbanisation; the decline yet persistence of unequal caste relations; the ideological impact of dalit and women's movements, in terms of changing values pertaining to girls' education; and an open but yet inadequate government policy and unequal state provision. The state through its caste-class-gendered institutions and policies and half-hearted remedial actions continues to function as a central agency of reproduction of inequality. A situation of overall greater gender than caste disparity in school educational attainment suggests that gender continues to be a formidable structural obstacle in accessing education. The influence of caste, however, has certainly not disappeared – it persists in the educational exclusion of several dalit castes and caste discrimination. Further, class has emerged as a fundamental category of exclusion – including a few but excluding the overwhelming majority. We need further disaggregated macro analyses by region, sub-caste, class and gender to reveal the exact patterns and their correlates. We also need micro studies that draw linkages between economic inequality, class stratification, poverty, caste disadvantage, institutional casteism, hierarchical ideology and patriarchal cultures. More conclusive explanations must await further fine-grained research that will systematically and coherently illuminate the numerous and cross cutting factors at play in determining patterns of both educational participation and deprivation of dalit girls.

References

Aggarwal, Yash (2000): An Assessment of Trends in Access and Retention. New Delhi, NIEPA.

Apte, Meenakshi (2004): *Maharashtrateel Mulinche Shaleya Shikshan* in Swadhar (Ed.): Shodh Bai Manasachya Jeenyacha (Marathi). Mumbai: Akshar, pp. 69-81.

Basu, Aparna (1988): *A Century's Journey: Women's Education in Western India* in Channa, K. (Ed.) Socialisation Education and Women. New Delhi: Orient Longman, pp. 65-95.

Bernsten, Maxine (n.d.): *Kunachya Khandyavar, Kunache Oze* (Marathi), Unpublished paper.

Bernsten, Maxine (n.d.): *Shoshitanche Shikshan* (Marathi), Unpublished paper.

Bernsten, Maxine (2002): Collapse at the Foundation – A Study of Literacy Among Third Standard Students in Western Maharashtra, Phaltan. Unpublished Manuscript.

Chakravarti, Uma 1998: Rewriting History: The Life and Times of Pandita Ramabai. New Delhi: Kali for Women.

Chauhan, Vijaya (2004): *Bharatateel Mulinche Shikshan* in Swadhar (Ed.) Shodh Bai Manasachya Jeenyacha (Marathi), Mumbai: Akshar, pp. 62-68.

Chitnis, S. and P. Velaskar (1988): Education in Maharashtra: Strengths and Weaknesses, A Report prepared for the World Bank. Bombay: Tata Institute of Social Sciences (mimeo).

Datar, Chhaya 1992: *The Women's Movement in Maharashtra: An Overview* in C. Datar (Ed.) The Struggle Against Violence. Calcutta: Stree, pp. 1-50.

Dhani, Shantibai (1989): Ratrandin Amha (Marathi as narrated to Bhavana Bhargave) Nasik: Bhavsarita.

Deshpande, Sudha (2003): *A Tale of Distorted Development: Economic and Demographic*, in Mungekar, B. (Ed.) The Economy of Maharashtra: Changing Structure and Emerging Issues. Mumbai: Dr. Ambedkar Institute of Social and Economic Change, pp. 147-177.

Forbes, Geraldine (1980): *The Indian Women's Movement: A Struggle for Women's Rights or National Liberation?* in Minault, Gail (Ed.) The Extended Family: Women and Political Participation in Indian and Pakistan. Delhi: Chanakya Publications, pp. 49-82.

Forbes, Geraldine 1996: Women in Modern India. Cambridge: Cambridge University Press.

Ghugare, S. (1983): Renaissance in Western India. Bombay: Himalaya Publishing House

Gogate, B. (1986): Marathwadyatil Shikshan (Marathi). Pune: Continental.

Gore, M.S. (1987): Vitthal Ramji Shinde, Mumbai. Tata Institute of Social Sciences (mimeo).

——— (1989): Non-Brahman Movement in Maharashtra. New Delhi: Segment Book Distributors.

Government of Maharashtra 1980: Education at a Glance 1979-80. Pune: Directorate of Education.

———1984: Report of the Fact-Finding Committee on Regional Imbalance in Maharashtra. Bombay: Government of Maharashtra.

———1994: Education at a Glance 1993-94. Pune: Directorate of Education.

———1999: Education at a Glance 1998-99. Pune: Directorate of Education.

Kadiyal, R.A. (1987): Karmaveer Bhaurao Patil – Contribution to Education in Maharashtra. Kolhapur: Indumati Publication.

Kadiyal, R.A. (1994): *Contributions of Rajashree Shahu Chhatrapati Maharaj to the Progress of Education*, in Salunkhe, P.B. and Mali M.G. (Ed.) Chhatrapati Shahu – The Pillar of Social Democracy. Mumbai: Education Department, Government of Maharashtra, pp. 427-32.

Kaldate, Sudha (1988): *Striyanche Shikshan* in Kulkarni, B. (Ed.): Marathwada 2001, Aurangabad: Jaihind Pub.

Kamat, A.R. (1985): Education and Social Change in India. Bombay: Somaiya Publications.

Karnik, Ajit (2003): *State Finances: Issues and Concerns,* in Mungekar, B.(Ed.) The Economy of Maharashtra – Changing Structure and Emerging Issues. Mumbai: Dr. Ambedkar Institute of Social and Economic Change, pp. 237-69.

Khane, R.D. (1994): *Shahu's Crusade Against Untouchability* in Salunkhe, P.B. and Mali, M.G. (Ed.) Chhatrapati Shahu: The Pillar of Social Democracy. Kolhapur: Indumati Publication, pp. 143-68.

Kolte, V.B. (1975): Jaibai Chaudhari, in *Asmitadarsh* (Marathi), Vol. No. 3, pp. 31-38.

Kosambi, Meera (1993): At the Intersection of Gender Reform and Religious Belief – Pandita Ramabai's Contribution and the Age of Consent Controversy. Mumbai: Research Centre for Women's Studies, SNDT Women's University.

K. Seetha Prabhu & Sangita Kamdar (2003): *Social Sectors Without Human Development* in Mungekar, B. (Ed.) The Economy of Maharashtra: Changing Structure and Emerging Issues. Mumbai: Dr. Ambedkar Institute of Social and Economic Change, pp. 335-70.

Mazumdar, V. (1976): *The Social Reform Movement in India from Ranade to Nehru* in Nanda, B.R. (ed.): Indian Women – From Purdah to Modernity, New Delhi: Vikas.

Moon, Vasant (1987): Madhyaprant Varhadatil Dr. Ambedkarpurva Dalit Chalval (Marathi). Pune: Sugava.

NCAER (2002): Human Development Report, West and Central India. New Delhi: Oxford University Press.

Omvedt, Gail (1990): Jotiba Phule ani Stree Mukticha Vichar (Marathi). Mumbai: Lokvangmay Gruh.

Omvedt, Gail 1994: Dalits and the Democratic Revolution. New Delhi: Sage.

O'Hanlon, Rosalind (1985): Caste, Conflict and Ideology – Mahatma Jotirao Phule and Low 1985 Caste Protest in Nineteenth-Century Western India. Cambridge University Press, London.

Phule, Jotiba (1991 a): Slavery, Collected Works of Jotirao Phule, Vol. I. (Translated from Marathi by Patil, P.G.). Mumbai: Education Department.

——— (1991 b): Selections. Vol. II. Bombay: Education Department.

Ranade, Pratibha (1989): Stree Prashananchi Charcha (Marathi). Bombay: Popular.

——— (n.d.): Mahatma Jotiba Phule, Social Reformer and Philosopher: A Feminist Point of View. Unpublished manuscript.

Rosenthal, D.(1977): The Expansive Elite. Berkeley: University of California Press.

Sarkar, S. (1997): Writing Social History. New Delhi: Oxford University Press.

Tilak, J.B.G. (1996): How Free is Primary Education in India. *Economic and Political Weekly,* Vol. 31, No. 6, pp. 355-66.

——— (2000): *Education Poverty in India.* Occasional Paper, New Delhi: NIEPA.

Smock, A. (1981): Women's Education in Developing Countries. New York: Praeger.

Wankhede, G.G. (1998): Intra-caste Educational Variations Among the Scheduled Castes of Mumbai Metropolis. Bombay: TISS.

——— (2001): Educational Inequalities Among Maharashtra's Scheduled Castes, *Economic and Political Weekly,* Vol. XXXVI, No. 18, pp. 1553-58

Wankhede, G.G. & Padma Velaskar (1999): The Post-Matric Scholarship Scheme for SC/ST in Maharashtra and Goa – An Evaluation. Mumbai: TISS, (mimeo).

Varde, S. (2003): *Badaltya Maharashtratil Shikshan* (Marathi), in Bhole, B. and K. Bedkikal (Eds.): Badalta Maharashtra. Satara: Dr. Babasaheb Ambedkar Academy, pp. 123-38.

Velaskar, Padma (1998 a): *Ideology, Education and the Political Struggle for Liberation: Change and Challenge Among Maharashtra Dalits,* in Shukla, S. and Kaul, R. (Eds.) Education, Development and Underdevelopment. New Delhi: Sage. pp. 210-40.

——— (1998 b): Caste Patriarchy and the Nature of the Dalit Women's Subordination. *Sugava: Dr. Ambedkar Special Issue,* Vol. 4, pp. 54-67.

——— (1999): *Educational Disparities and Social Process – The Declining Structure of Opportunity for Downtrodden Communities,* in Contemporary India. Paper presented at South Asian Conference on Education, University of Delhi. New Delhi: (Unpublished manuscript).

——— (2001 a): Dalit Women's Struggles and Meanings of Education. Unpublished Manuscript, Mumbai: Unit for Research in Sociology of Education, Tata Institute of Social Sciences.

——— (2004): Caste and Gender in Education – Recent Trends in Access and Equity for Dalits of Maharashtra. (ongoing study). Mumbai: Tata Institute of Social Sciences.

——— (2004): *Asaman Vikas – Samakaleen Maharashtrateel Jat, Varg, Ling ani Dalit Striyanche Shoshan va Pratikar* in Swadhar (Ed.) Shodh Bai Manasachya Jeenyacha (Marathi). Mumbai: Akshar, pp. 195-212.

——— (2005): *Educational Stratification, Dominant Ideology and the Reproduction of Disadvantage in India*, in Dahiwale, S.M., Understanding Indian Society – The Non-Brahmanic Perspective. Delhi: Rawat, pp. 196-220.

Zelliot, Eleanor (1992): From Untouchable to Dalit – Essays on Ambedkar Movement. Delhi: Manohar.

——— (2002): *Experiments in Dalit Education: Maharashtra, 1850-1947*, in Sabyasachi Bhattacharya (Ed.): Education and the Disprivileged – Nineteenth and Twentieth Century India. Hyderabad: Orient Longman Private Ltd.

5

EQUITY AND EDUCATION*

— DHANWANTI NAYAK

Abstract

This paper focuses on the concept of equity and attempts to develop a framework for conceptually engaging with it in the sphere of education. It makes a heuristic distinction between human rights and social justice, and while locating the primary significance of equity squarely within the discourse of ethics, briefly describes some of the implications of taking a human rights perspective in education vis a vis of social justice. It draws out the difference between equity and equality and uses the distinction between means and ends, and between the formal and the substantive, to locate the importance of focusing on a process-based rather than on outcome-based approach to equity. Lastly, it distinguishes between equitable education and educational equity to clarify the ways to understand the role of equity in education, and draws attention to the fact that only by engaging with both of them can we broach the question of an equitable society. In the context of equitable society, it also raises the question of whether reforms in education will impact on society by drawing attention to the way power and hierarchies are deeply embedded in social structures. It thus brings in the issue of the extent to which educational reform is

* This paper was written as a background paper for the 3rd National Learning Conference 2007 on 'Equitable Education for Equitable Society' organized by Azim Premji Foundation, Bangalore. The positions taken in this paper, and the understanding thereof, do not necessarily reflect those of the Foundation and are solely the responsibility of the author. I am grateful to Geetha Nambissan and B K Anitha for detailed feedback on an early draft of the paper; Sharada Jain, Vimala Ramachandran, Giridhar S. Padma Sarangapani for their encouraging comments; Shantha Mohan, Medha Marathe and Vijay Gupta for discussions. Usual disclaimers apply.

possible without addressing the hierarchies of the larger society which may, in fact, go against achieving substantively in education.

Introduction

In a country where poverty and deprivation are still widespread (conservative estimates indicate one out of four people to be still below poverty line) and surviving is a matter of daily struggle, it cannot be assumed that all sections of the population will be able to prioritize education to the same extent, and for several years at a stretch. The opportunity cost of going to school is so high that in many cases it means the child is not just fending for herself, but many times for the survival of the family. Given the critical nature of education in human development, poverty cannot be used as a reason for not providing education to the masses. State and civil society have to engage in meaningful ways to achieve education for all. Though several initiatives have taken place over the last two decades to achieve this, yet, even conservative estimates reveal that more than 15 million children in the age group 6-14 years are still out of school even today ((MHRD 2006), warranting the continued push for universalizing elementary education.[1]

Deprivation has thus combined with stratification making the composition of those who are out of school to include traditionally marginalized groups, such as the Dalits, Adivasis, religious minorities and "challenged" children. Critically, another group common to all of them - girls – still constitutes below 50 per cent of enrolment at all stages (Mehta 2006), and regional disparities are also differently spread inter-state, intra-state, and between urban and rural areas. New "groups" such as children with HIV/AIDS, those who are the victims of civil war, juvenile delinquents and so on, are being formed continuously and, in turn, having difficulties in accessing education, further compounding the situation.

Whatever the multiple and complex causes of educational marginalization, there have been two major challenges which continue to confront education: one is enhancing the quality of education and the second is ensuring equality. Both have also been pitted against the constant need to address 'quantity' by providing access to increasing sections of the growing population (Naik 1975; Rao 2000). Thus the close connection between quality and equality has always been acknowledged. Increasingly, however, the commonly accepted interpretation of this connection is that one should not compromise on quality of education while ensuring equality. The other interpretation, not as well articulated, defines quality of education *in terms of* equality, so that a good quality education/ school is that which *enables equality*. By this interpretation (but not necessarily by the first), the absence of marginalized groups in a "mainstream" school and equally of the "mainstream" children in schools for the marginalized, would itself be an indicator of poor quality. Thus, while there seems to be agreement on the connection and need for quality and equality, the interpretation given to this link is critical because the first interpretation emphasises quality, while the second focuses on equity.

This paper gives us an opportunity to look at the conceptual development of equity. It attempts to clarify the ways in which equity plays out in education and their implications. It also raises the question of the extent to which reforms will create an equitable society when hierarchies and power are as deeply entrenched as they are in our society.

Equality and Equity: Formal and Substantive Equality

There is a conflation of the terms equality and equity and they are often used interchangeably in common parlance as well as in academic literature. In order to bring out the nuances, we start by trying to understand the nature of equality through a simple statement: "All humans are equal". Clearly, this statement does not mean that they are so in *every* respect but that they are equal in *relevant* respects and are to be treated as such in those respects. However, by the very same reason, this does not rule out treating them differently in those respects where they are, in fact, unequal. Such distinctions are important, particularly when equality is considered as a moral and social ideal (Benn 1967, p. 39). The distinctions are critical to the sector of education.

The above statement on equality of all humans can be modified to state: "Everyone is equal in the eyes of the law." Equality can thus also be seen as a legal standard, a formal or *de jure* concept, which may draw upon distinctions of "relevant" aspects. Strictly speaking, it may not be necessary from this perspective to take into cognizance socio-historical and other causes which have led to inequalities, unless a case is made for them as being "relevant". A focus on equality thus implies that different people are to be treated "the same" by some specified "agency" (in the above example, the legal system) and according to some specific, "relevant" aspect or parameter.

However, controversies arise precisely in the perceptions of inequalities that exist among people due to differing ideas on what is considered "relevant". Since entitlements in a society are usually set forth in more general terms, such as "all human beings are born free and equal in dignity and rights" (*Universal Declaration of Rights* adopted by the UN General Assembly in 1948), or "equality before law" or "equality of opportunity", these are also open to contestation about what equality means and what is to be done when there are evident inequalities or when there is a conflict, as for instance, when the "opportunities" available to one person are compromised by the opportunities available to another. Such contestations, while having their genesis in society, tend to end up in the interpretative domain, including in the judicial system, for redressal.

To clarify the concept of equality a little further, the discussion needs to address two questions (Burchardt 2006):

- Firstly, equality between whom?
- Secondly, equality of what?

The answers to these questions will clarify the conceptual shift from equality to equity.

Equality between whom?

The rationale for answering the question, 'equality between whom', has its basis in two relevant features: firstly, the inequality should be beyond individual control and secondly, it should have a historical source (Burchardt 2006). In India, the answer to this question is focused on two encompassing groups: gender and social groups (the latter including Dalits, Adivasis, minorities, the challenged). The law grants them equality. But since these groups have been *historically/traditionally* discriminated against and because membership of these groups is beyond *individual* control and choice, when inequalities are perceived between these groups for which existing law is inadequate, the concept of equity is invoked to ensure the redressal of such inequalities. Thus, although the law guarantees equality, it is also recognized that to make equality a reality, *we need to invoke a concept of fairness which shifts the terminology from equality to equity.*

Equity in law, according to the dictionary, is the resort to general principles of fairness and justice whenever existing law is inadequate.[2] In order for some people to realize equality of status, additional efforts have to be made which will remove existing barriers to equality and enable them to access opportunities so that there is a greater distributive justice. Equity, in this sense, includes all the means or approaches to achieve the goal of equality. It also includes actions, attitudes, and assumptions that provide such opportunities. Regardless of the complex ways in which equity is defined, having understood that inequities arise due to many deep-rooted causes and are shared by groups of people, there is now sufficient consensus that while outcomes are a way of assessing equity, the focus should be on its processual aspect. By this yardstick, equality can be seen as a goal that society aspires for and works toward, with constant negotiation among members in the society on what it means in specific situations.

Implications of focusing on equality rather than equity

Why is it important to make this distinction between equality and equity? Other than the reasons mentioned above which have to do with enabling access by focusing on equity, when we say everyone is "equal" (in common parlance as much as before the eyes of the law), the underlying danger is that they will be treated *according to the standards of one group,* usually the dominant one, which makes other marginalised groups further disadvantaged because of the inherent group differences. If default standards or so called "neutral rules" are always those of the advantaged groups, then achieving equality becomes difficult, if not impossible.[3] Sometimes an excessive focus on universalization may actually have adverse affects because it doesn't really take cognizance of such differences[4] as we shall see in the next section.

Hence, any framework built to eliminate discrimination must take into account that although *de jure* or formal equality is important, one must also ensure *de facto* or substantive equality which would be a more powerful one for realizing the rights of marginalized groups.[5] For example, *de facto* equality of the sexes may be defined as "women hav[ing] equal entitlement to rights, benefits and results as men but that there may have to be differential or preferential treatment for women in order for them to enjoy their entitlement to equality" (CEDAW[6]). Focusing on putting in place mechanisms and processes for improving access to resources, and removing barriers to them, is in the purview of equity. Equity, in this sense, is what enables substantive equality.

In discourses within the social sector, such as in education, an approach focusing on equality would be limited to equality of status while an approach focussing on equity would be more inclusive and bring in the equality of opportunity. It emphasizes that equality is possible in only relevant aspects and when situations arise whereby there is a gap between different groups in those aspects, then this "equity gap" is not justifiable and must be redressed. Such an approach also allows an understanding of equitable education as distinct from educational equity.

Equality of what?

Assuming that this "equity gap" exists in certain specified domains, as for instance in education, then it brings us to the second question 'Equality of what?' This can be addressed along three dimensions, viz., equality of opportunity, equality of process and equality of outcome (Burchardt 2006).

Of these, equality of opportunity is the most complex and open to interpretation. If we assume that it depends upon talent and effort, then equality of opportunity tends more towards the meritocracy position in which case there is a lack of acceptance of the role played by institutions in systematically creating (and depriving) opportunities to select groups. However, efforts can be made to equalise opportunities through addressing institutional barriers as, for instance, by providing resources (and *additional* resources) to some sections of the population. It operates in education at the formal level by including aspects like the provision of schools, uniforms, textbooks and bicycles to girls and other groups.

Equality of process is the most difficult to ensure but it is the one with maximum long-term effect. Rather than focusing on the distribution of particular resources, it is concerned mainly with the relations and interactions people have and generate between and among themselves, and between people and institutions ((Burchardt 2006, p.10). In education, it is concerned very closely with pedagogical practices with a focus on more process-based learning of children.

Equality of outcome is the most popular and convenient but also the crudest form along which to measure equality and is not well-supported philosophically ((Burchardt 2006, p.10).[7] Particularly when outcomes are defined in terms of "results", then outcome evaluation analysis tends to be flat and reveals less in and of themselves.[8] Equity, however, is usually defined in terms of outcome – in the proportional participation of certain groups in various sectors. This, however, is an indicatory function, a measure of participation, and can be seen as comprising the concept of educational equity which is elaborated upon later.

Another reason for de-emphasizing outcomes is because there is an acknowledgement that even with substantive equality of opportunity, there will be a difference in outcomes on account of variety of grounds, not the least being the assertion of individual choice, the pursuit of talents which has nothing to do with capability, and may be even differential capacity to work. Thus, for instance, "whilst the actual activities and states of being of individuals are observable, the activities and so on that the individuals could do, but are choosing *not* to do, are unobservable" ((Burchardt 2006, p. 17, emphasis in original).[9] Since elementary education is considered a "basic" activity, it is presumed that differences in outcomes are caused by differences of substantive access to opportunities rather than differences in choice.

One of the ways of using outcomes in a more profound way is define them in terms of consequences, as Sen (1985) does with "capabilities" in his capability approach. It makes for a richer understanding of what barriers prevent people from achieving certain goals or fulfilling needs.[10]

In the next section, an attempt is made to expand this shift between equality and equity by exploring how it plays out in the concept of "human rights and social justice".

Human Rights and Social Justice: From Equality to Equity in Education

Several specific reasons are invoked to focus on equity, some of which are as follows (World Bank, 2006):

- If we do not focus on equity, the long term development of the country on almost every index will be compromised. Health, education and economic growth will stagnate or even decline in the long run if equity issues are not addressed.
- In a functioning democracy, polity and civil society are constantly under threat when benefits accrue or are perceived to accrue to only

certain groups, and there is a perpetuation of the ideas and world views of a few privileged groups at the expense of other groups.

- The accompanying inequalities get reproduced over several generations leading to a trajectory of hopelessness, underachievement and what has been called "inequality traps". These tend to be quite stable over time as they are successfully perpetuated by the elite and internalized by the marginalized.
- Society consistently skews its resources in such a way as to systematically favour those who are wealthy and/or politically influential and limits the scope of upward mobility for certain groups.
- Several stereotypes and prejudices combine to further prevent genuine engagement with "the other", however broadly conceived.

Additionally, a society which has various kinds of inequities may conceal deeper problems. For instance, "meritocracy" positions in society get strengthened by which people believe that opportunities in a society should be available on the basis of talent and efforts. Such positions "fail to take into account the cumulative effects of advantage on the talents one has been able to develop" (Burchardt 2006, p. 4) and are represented by arguments such as "selecting the best person for the job" and "using resources effectively".

Most importantly, these viewpoints have also allowed the perceived "failure" of other individuals to be divorced from the socio-historical groups they belong to, i.e they fail to take into account the cumulative effects of disadvantage on the talents one has been unable to develop. Such viewpoints thus have ignored the systemic and institutional roots of inequities.

While we can enter into the discourse on equity from several disciplines such as economics or politics, in this section we use ethics. This gives us the entry point into further understanding equity – through the discourse of human rights and social justice. Both are interlinked and often not clearly differentiated, as manifested in the use of the phrase "human rights and social justice". Indeed, they do go together. However, separating them for heuristic purposes shows their different emphases and thus implications in education.

Human rights basically focus on those aspects which are guaranteed to an individual by virtue of being human – thus the emphasis is on the individual and how each one must be allowed to develop their individual potential. Although the interpretation of specific human rights may differ from case to case, or example to example, they are generally understood as "the minimum standards to which every individual is entitled" (Burchardt 2006). Human rights perspectives thus advocate and guarantee the *equality of individuals regardless* of group membership.[11] The imperative to universalize elementary education, for instance, can be seen as arising from this perspective. Within it, there is an emphasis on poverty and deprivation and it thus invokes human rights to make a case for minimum standards of living, education, and so on. In practice, for some political philosophers, this perspective is based on ideas stemming from humanitarian aid which involves a transfer of resources and its equalization (Chandoke 2006).

Human rights are thus unconditional and guarantee the same minimum entitlement. *From this perspective, there is nothing wrong with inequalities which exist between and among people after having taken care of providing a minimum level.* "Everyone has the same minimum entitlement, but there is nothing objectionable, from the point of view of human rights, in inequalities between individuals above that threshold level" (Burchardt 2006, p. 6).[12]

Perspectives rooted in social justice, on the other hand, look more at individuals as members of groups and recognize the fact that individuals belong to different socio-economic groups, with specific historical and other relations between them. According to this perspective, such membership should not be a preventive factor in the development of human potential. Discourses on equity in education for marginalized groups stem from this perspective – equity as distributive justice. There is thus a moral and ethical imperative that is at the basis of social justice. It compels the nation-state as well as civil society to ensure that diverse needs of different groups are met because some characteristics which people possess such as sex, disability, racial and caste membership and the like are beyond individual choice and control and these should not prevent their access to resources of the society. Taking the perspective of social justice therefore acknowledges the inequality of people because of group membership.

For our present purposes (and based on the two factors mentioned above, firstly, the inequality should be beyond individual control and secondly, it should have been so historically), we can thus isolate three basic or main causes[13] for the existence of group inequalities (Chandoke 2006), which are economic, social and socio-economic. The discourse on human rights is focused largely on the first level (economic) where certain rights are guaranteed to those suffering from poverty and extreme deprivation as human beings and therefore as individuals.[14] Social justice is concerned mainly with the other two groups. As Chandoke (2006) points out, this perspective allows for remedial actions such as land reforms, income-generating schemes and the like, which will redress the social inequalities of the second group. Most significantly, according to her, when such social inequalities combine with poverty then this perspective also allows for additional and specific measures such as protective discrimination to redress the socio-economic inequalities. *Such measures are also consistent with the notion of substantive equality, whereby unequal or preferential treatment may be required in order to achieve equality.*

Such a perspective combines ethical individualism (whereby individuals are valued for themselves rather than as members of a group), with methodological pluralism (which recognizes that individuals influence and are influenced by larger social structures) and thus affirms human rights without compromising on social justice.

Typology of Equity: Gender Equity, Social Equity and Educational Equity

From the discussion in the above section, we can make some general observations on equity: that the term equity is used when we want to differentiate between inequalities that exist between groups rather than individuals; when such inequalities are of socio-historical origin or have causes beyond individual control, such as being born with a disability; it focuses on process-oriented approaches rather than terminal assessments for the removal of barriers and creation of opportunities; its discourse includes all mechanisms allowing differential treatment for achieving equality; it aims at achieving distributive justice.

The manner in which disadvantages emerge from gender and social hierarchies and reinforce inequalities in the domain of education, are consistent enough to generate a basic typology of equity for our present purposes along the major parameters - gender and social groups - before seeing how equity is engaged in the domain of education.

Given our understanding of equity, we can now see that gender equity and social equity may be seen as the two main types of equity.[15] Gender equity refers to the degree of participation[16] of both men and women in activities of society. Usually when we ask whether gender equity has been achieved, we mean to focus on those differences that exist between men and women as two groups rather than as individuals; that have their origins outside the context of individual agency; focus on those mechanisms, policies and practices which remove systemic barriers to their access to opportunities within society to develop themselves fully; and those mechanisms which allow for differential treatment for them as a group to create opportunities which they would otherwise not have access to, such as free education for the girl child in government schools.

Similarly, social equity refers to the participation of members of all social groups in society. Thus, when we ask about social equity we mean to ask whether all social groups (including people of different castes, tribes, religions and the disabled) have equal access to opportunities to develop themselves in various spheres along the lines of reasoning used above.[17]

Educational equity then is an outcome based assessment like the above, and indicates the degree of participation of all marginalized groups in the sphere or domain of education i.e. the participation of girls, Dalits, Adivasis, minorities, and the challenged in education. When children from all social groups and both sexes participate in education, this is a measure of educational equity. It is thus gender and social equity operating in the domain of education. In keeping with the description of equity mentioned above, we would look at everything in terms of groups, not individuals. Although educational equity has been sometimes used interchangeably in the literature with equitable education, looking at the proportional participation of children from marginalized groups in schools is in the domain of educational equity according to the framework outlined in this paper.

Education and Equity: Equitable Education, Educational Equity and Education for an Equitable Society

Equity operates in education in at least three ways: (a) by enabling equality of opportunity for *all* children, including those from educationally marginalized groups *within the sphere of education itself.* Initiatives for this fall under 'equitable education', i.e. education for equity with an emphasis on diversity; (b) by enabling participation of children from all marginalized groups (including girls, Adivasis, Dalits, challenged, minorities, rural poor) in that equitable education. This falls under 'educational equity', i.e. equity in education with an emphasis on "relevant" diversity; and (c) by education in turn enabling equal opportunity in other fields such as the job market. This falls under 'education for equitable society'.

The CABE Committee (2005) defines equitable education in terms of quality, thus referring to equitable quality of education as "providing all children access to, participation in and completion of elementary education with the prescribed courses of study..." In this definition, equitable means of equal or comparable quality. Equitable education thus is concerned with *every* child's education, not just those from the marginalized groups. It recognizes that all children may be marginalized for various reasons within the school or classroom situation. It must be stressed that all children in the classroom, regardless of group membership, "may feel alienated due to non-relevant curriculum and teacher-centred pedagogy" (Jha 2002, p.179). *Equitable education thus has the power to (directly) affect the educational experience of all children, not just those of the marginalized groups. In effect, it would look at the quality of the educational experience of children as individuals, not as members of groups.* Thus, even those children who do not come from educationally marginalized communities could feel marginalization due to factors restricted to education itself, such as curriculum and pedagogy. Educational equity, on the other hand, would refer to participation of certain marginalized *groups* in education at levels of access, process and outcome.

For instance, inequitable quality of education may include teaching styles that prevent all children from actively participating in the classroom, leaving some children bored and others inattentive. Curriculum may be in favour of some subjects over others, pedagogical styles may overemphasize a lecture mode at the expense of experience or team learning. Text books may not be appropriate to the child's own intellectual level, emphasizing abstract concepts at an age when they find it easier to deal with the concrete – all these may leave some children groping for meaningfulness. Language used by the teacher may be gendered or even simply different from the language used by the child at home; examination questions may be framed in ways that make no sense to the children's worldviews and so on (Jha 2002). All these result in an inequitable education since *regardless* of group membership, some children even from the "mainstream" communities may be left out due to irrelevant curriculum and curricular inequities, unimaginative teaching and other inadequacies in curriculum transaction etc.

How can we further understand how equity works in equitable education? Nambissan has analysed "equity in education" along three dimensions, viz., access, process and outcome (Nambissan 1996, p. 1016). Using these same dimensions, we can see that in "equitable education", these play out in the following way: the provision of educational infrastructure must be such that it enables children of all backgrounds to access education through a school system that factors in diversity. For some people, equitable education may be a sound basis, for asking for common schools based on the neighbourhood school concept. For others it may be through providing equitable quality education in government schools, and still for others, it may be important that the children from poorer sections of society be allowed access into private schools as has happened with the recent Delhi ruling to private schools to reserve 25 per cent of their seats for such children.

Process in equitable education retains all children through adequate pedagogical practices which factor in diversity in conscious ways – for example, by the use of two or more languages in teaching, individualized curriculum, focus on interests of children which may not coincide with the rest and so on. When these pedagogical practices are conceptualized and constructed such that all children's educational experience is enhanced by them – for instance, by child-friendly, activity-based teaching, appropriate language(s) as medium of instruction, context-specific learning, and the like – then this would go a long way towards ensuring that no child is marginalized. Having now located the larger discourses among which equity is situated, it can be seen that in terms of curriculum transaction and pedagogical practices, equitable education does not mean treating all children the same; it means treating some children *differently* in order to treat them *fairly* (ACSA, 1). This is because there is a recognition that the entry point for children is *not* on a level playing field.

Outcomes in equitable education is simplistically a completion of the course of study. It can be broadened to include the outcome or performance of children. These are a reflection of how testing is conceptualized to make evaluations germane to the child and encourage them to draw upon their own understanding. Learning outcomes need to factor the contexts children live and learn in, rather than focusing on terminal outcomes, such as ability to read and write which may itself not be a skill so easy to attain for first generation learners. Coming to the same place every day, remaining there for several hours at a stretch, exclusively interacting with peers may all be equally important achievements for children to learn.

Similarly, we can map how the three dimensions of access, process and outcome play out in educational equity. For instance, if the educational infrastructure provided is of the quality that attracts children from the marginalized groups, then this can be seen to be access in educational equity.[18] It is quite possible, for instance, that seen from this perspective, ashram schools, bridge schools, EGS schools and even *madarsas* and the like, may be justified as means of reaching educational equity. However, without clear linkages to a shared educational experience, such as common or neighbourhood school, these initiatives will provide equity of a superficial kind since they are more in the form of specialized schools for children with special needs and go against the larger and more fundamental discourses of inclusive education. Unless there are concrete linkages to so-called mainstream schools, these schools will provide education of a dubitable kind to both children going to them as well as children in mainstream schools since they encourage the segregation of experience for children both from the "mainstream" as well as the "marginalized".

Process in educational equity would look at ways in which children from marginalized groups would be retained through special attention in classrooms, such as using the language most familiar to the children's mother tongue as the medium of instruction, using examples which are relevant to their experience and world views. Outcomes would look at the group learning outcomes of children from marginalized sections, keeping in mind that these may not be restricted to literacy and numeracy.

This brings us to the last way in which equity engages with education: education for equitable society. When the quality of education is of a kind that enables genuine (or substantive) access to *other opportunities* in society such as jobs, livelihood, shelter, leisure, arts and culture, etc, then this refers to education for equitable society.

Drawing upon Amartya Sen's distinction between endowments and entitlements, we can say that education is both an *end* in itself - an entitlement - as well as a *means* to achieve equity - an endowment. We can also see how the capability framework he has developed can be used to enhance our understanding of equitable society. Sen's capability framework "advocates that in making evaluations of well-being and policies, we focus *on what people can do and be*, instead of exclusively on their mental states or on the goods they have at their disposal" (Robeyns 2002, emphasis mine). Thus, for Sen 'substantive freedom' and 'capability' are used interchangeably.

The questions that thus must be addressed in this context are: What are the components of this equitable quality of education and how do we promote it? What is the relation between a diverse education system and equity? Are homogenizing or universalizing systems a solution to inequities? How do we address the issue of language and its role in equity? The scope of such questions is too large to be addressed here except to note the following.

It is clear that inequitable systems of education (which in turn were characterized by educational inequities) along the lines which traditionally existed in India cannot lead to the formation of an equitable society. However, providing an equitable education does not, in and of itself, result in social, gender and other kinds of educational equity either. Nor is there any guarantee that having achieved educational equity, an equitable society is inevitable, or even possible, as we briefly describe it in the last section on social change.

But since education itself is one of the means by which equity is possible in other domains (an entitlement which enables access to endowments), we can posit at this point that an equitable education is a necessary condition for both educational equity and equitable society. Further, it is a moot question whether educational equity even at the level of number of children enrolled may be achieved, without revamping of the pedagogical practices to ensure that equitable education. Thus equitable education can be seen as that kind of education which ensures educational equity, making the close and uncompromising linkage between quality and equity that was mentioned in the beginning of this paper. Such a perspective directly links quality with equity by unconditionally including the participation of children from marginalized groups in the educational experience of children from more privileged groups and vice versa. Segregated schools thus compromise on quality when the educational experiences of children are isolated and exclusionist. They encourage the "ghetto-ization" of educational experience which breeds other kinds of problems in society. If universalization of elementary education is achieved at the cost of inclusive education i.e. if 'hierarchies of access' (Ramachandran 2002) are maintained, then this will have serious implications for the larger society.

Conclusion: Equitable Society – The Possibility of Social Change

In the previous section we dealt with factors within the educational system itself in terms of access, process and outcome through types of schools and the larger schooling system, pedagogical practices and issues, and outcomes in terms of the actual participation of marginalized groups. There are some factors, particularly at the policy level, which have enabled educational equity, such as the midday meal plans that have nothing to do with education per se but have impacted on bringing more poor children in to schools. Similarly, with the abolishment of child labour. Thus the linkages of education with the larger society are clear. In this section the question addressed pertains to the relation between education and equitable society. This brings in structural issues directly into the discussion and also raises the question of the limits of educational reform. If for instance, the needs of the working culture shape and influence the quality of education (Apple 1995, Bowles and Gintis 1976), then it appears that educational reform will always be limited by the economic structures which determine relations in the society. Although a case is increasingly made for stronger linkages between the so called "real" world of work and education, there is also a parallel understanding that this is a short term view with accompanying short-term benefits, and that education must instead be viewed as an end in itself.

Another aspect central to the understanding of social actions/movements seeking to change their status relative to the rest of the society is the concept of power. No discussion on equity would be complete without factoring this in, since this is an important ground for preventing or enabling social change. The traditional conceptualization of power as the ability to exert power *over* people, resources and structures has broadened into newer conceptions of power as one which is fluid, relational and connected to discourses and knowledge (Parpart 2004). Both these conceptualizations need to be factored into the discussions on equity in education and the possibility of equitable society, as this would allow us to examine whether, and to what extent, reforms in education actually are effective when seen against the structures of the larger society.

Secondly, while these structures would include institutional structures like caste, class, family, job market, and the like, some of these structures also include the discursive ones. Perhaps part of the limited success of the education "war" with regard to equity has been that the focus has been on the traditional conceptualization of power, while relegating the latter conception of power related to discourses and knowledge to some peripheral space which plays no significant role. In fact, the opposite is true – discourses and knowledge systems occupy and change the deep space of personal and group imagination, since they articulate images of the self and society and thus are equally, if not more, important in effecting change.

Thirdly, it is important to see how power is inextricably woven with hierarchy (in addition to structures and discourses), and thus whether, and to what extent, the larger society will act to enable substantive change for the marginalized. Kumar asks, "Why should the community with its caste-based and gendered power structure act in concert to educate the poor?" (Kumar et al 2001, p. 565). In fact, although it sounds processually sound, we need to deconstruct the nature of power in order to understand how vested interests can and probably will prevent change from occurring when based in community initiatives. "Experiences of rural social mobilization and dalit upsurges in recent years confirm the idea that the community is often an upholder of a casteist and sexist position" (Kumar et al 2001, p. 565).

Lastly, questions have been raised about the extent to which power structures underlying democratic but market-driven societies will permit educational equity through appropriate reforms in education. After all, such a capitalist system *depends* on hierarchies prevalent in the work environment in order to produce and generate profit. Thus, there is a built-in contradiction that although "education is more democratic than most other institutions...[it] helps reproduce unequal relations in society" (Carnoy 1983, p. 400). We need to engage with this question much more deeply than is possible in this paper.

There is a need to understand several things concerning equitable society: firstly, an educational praxis devoted to changing systems by programmatic approaches to reforming education has limitations and may not be sustained without integrating elements of the discursive aspect. Secondly, we need to understand the nature of these limitations in a hierarchical society whose vested interests get severely compromised by the success of educational reform. Thirdly, the relation between the state and the market in the sphere of education must be understood. Fourthly, educational reform must address its limitations when seen in the context of the work environment. Thus, it must engage with the sociology of the work place in order to understand the boundaries of educational praxis. Understanding educational reform at this level automatically and substantively engages with empowerment. Without such an understanding of it, universalisation of education may at best be simply a numbers game, divorced from the larger social realities in which it is embedded. Worse, it may continue to propagate bias, prejudice and social stereotypes which education is in fact meant to eradicate.

References

Apple, Michael (1995): *Education and Power*. 2nd edition. New York: Routledge.

Association of California School Administrators: Position Paper. Accessed at www.acsa.org/ doc_files/ ACSA per cent20Position per cent2020Paper.pdf

Benn, Stanley (1967): Equality – Moral and Social, in *Encyclopedia of Philosophy* (ed. Paul Edwards). Vol 3. New York: The MacMillan Company and the Free Press.

Bowles, Samuel and Herbert Gintis (1976): *Schooling in Capitalist America – Educational Reform and the Contradictions of Economic Life*. New York: Basic Books.

Burchardt, Tania (2006): Foundations for Measuring Equality: A Discussion Paper for the Equalities Review. London: ESRC Research Centre for Analysis of Social Exclusion, London School of Economics. Accessed at http://sticerd.lse.ac.uk/dps/case/cp/CASEpaper111.pdf and www.theequalitiesreview.org.uk/foundations4measuring.pdf

Carnoy, Martin (1983): Education, Democracy and Social Conflict. *Harvard Educational Review;* Vol.53 No.4; November 1983.

Chandoke, Neera (2006): Three Myths about Reservation. *Economic and Political Weekly*. June 10, 2006: 2289-90.

Cunningham, CD, M Galanter and NR Menon (1997): Rethinking Equality in the Global Society Conference Proceedings. *Washington Law Quarterly*; Vol 75; 1561-1676.

Govinda, R. (2002): *India Education Report: A Profile of Basic Education*. New Delhi: OUP & NIEPA.

Jha, Jyotsna and Dhir Jhingran (2005): *Elementary Education for the Poorest and Other Deprived Groups – The Real Challenge of Universalization.* Delhi: Manohar Publishers.

Jha, Madan Mohan (2002): *School Without Walls – Inclusive Education for All.* New Delhi: Madhuban (Original Heinemann Publishers).

Kumar, Krishna; Manisha Priyam and Sadhna Saxena (2001): Looking Beyond the Smokescreen – DPEP and Primary Education in India. *Economic and Political Weekly*; Vol 36(7); February 17-23, 560-68,.

MHRD (2006): *Assessment of Sarva Shiksha Abhiyan 2006.* National Report on Household Survey March 2006. New Delhi: IMRB International, Social and Rural Research Institute.

Mehta, Arun C. (2006): *Elementary Education in India – Progress Towards UEE.* Analytical Report 2004-2005. New Delhi: NIEPA & Dept of Elementary Education and Literacy, MHRD, GOI.

Naik, J P. (1975): *Equality, Quality and Quantity: The Elusive Triangle in Indian Education.* New Delhi: Allied Publishers.

Nambissan, Geetha B. (1996): Equity in Education? Schooling of Dalit Children in India. *Economic and Political Weekly;* Vol 31(16-19); April 20-27, 1011-24.

Parpart, Jane (2004): *Gender, Power and Governance in a Globalizing World.* Development Research Series, Research Centre on Development and International Relations Working Paper No. 120. [www.ihis.aau.dk/development/working_papers/working_papers_pdf]

Ramachandran, Vimala (2002): *Gender and Social Equity in Primary Education: Hierarchies of Access.* New Delhi: European Commission.

Rao, Nitya (2000): Quality with Quantity. *Economic and Political Weekly;* Vol 35(48); November 25, 2000, 4181-85.

Robeyns, Ingrid. (2002): In Defense of Amartya Sen. *Post-Autistic Economics Review,* No. 17, 4 Dec 2002. http://www.paecon.net/PAEReview/Issue17/Robeyns17.htm

Sen, Amartya (1981): *Poverty and Famines: An Essay on Entitlement and Deprivation.* Oxford, UK: OUP.

Sen, Amartya (1985): *Commodities and Capabilities*. Oxford: North-Holland.

Sen, Amartya (1992): *Inequality Re-examined.* New Delhi and Oxford: Oxford University Press.

UNDP (2005): *Human Development Report 2005.* Oxford and New York: Oxford University Press and UNDP.

Webster's New Universal Unabridged Dictionary (1983); Second Edition. New York: Simon and Schuster.

World Bank (2006): *World Development Report 2006 – Equity and Development.* Washington DC: The World Bank and OUP.

Notes

1. These figures vary depending upon factors taken into account, such as enrolment, attendance, drop-outs, etc. For instance, estimates based on population projections and age-specific enrolments, calculated the figures for 6-13 age group to be in the vicinity of 60-70 million children in 2001 (Tapas Majumdar Committee Report 1999, mentioned in Jha and Jhingran 2005, p. 20).
2. For example, when a hen is lost by a peasant in a car accident caused by someone else, a court of law may only ensure payment of the market price of the hen to the farmer. However, a court of equity (or invoking equity principles) can gain the peasant a sum closer to the "real" value of the hen since it would consider that it is a source of income from eggs and this too has been lost to the peasant.
3. For instance, if women are to be the treated equal to men in the workplace, then it is the male standards by which they will be evaluated and these will not take into account the fact that they are still the primary caregivers in the family. Unless the gendered structure of family roles are themselves radically changed, many women think that they must be given additional special rights to enable their equality in the workplace. This position while clearly consistent with fairness, problematizes it *vis-a-vis* impartiality.
4. Millennium Development Goals are in this category since they are "distribution neutral" and therefore do not directly address inequality. "Progress is measured by aggregating and averaging change at a national level and thus even as they are being achieved, many poor people get left behind" (UNDP, 2005, p. 51).
5. The Indian Constitution, according to Justice B P Jeevan Reddy, which guarantees formal equality before law in Article 14, interestingly also envisages substantial equality between individuals in Articles 15(1) and 16 (1) as well as measures to bring about substantial equality between groups in Articles 15 (4) and 16(4). In addition, he says, the Indian Constitution is one of the few which not just provides equality before the law but also equal protection of the laws, unlike the American Constitution, for example, which speaks only of the latter (Cunningham, Galanter and Menon 1997, p. 1595).
6. The Convention for Elimination of All Forms of Discrimination Against Women (CEDAW) is a treaty adopted by the UN General Assembly in 1976 and ratified by India in 1993. It is an international Bill of Rights of Women advocating equality between men and women. It obliges member states who have ratified it to act against inequality with affirmative action.
7. For instance, outcomes are seen to not reveal anything about why or how something has occurred or what is preventing them from being achieved. For this kind of understanding, we need to do further micro-studies to flesh out the reasons for the outcomes, whatever they may be. Further, it risks ignoring differences in need, values, preferences, agency and responsibilities (Burchardt 2006, 10).
8. The other problem with focusing on equality of outcome is its measurement or evaluation. For instance, assuming that sharing of power is taken to be one such outcome, it is ambiguous how this can be evaluated without incorporating process itself, especially as empowerment of girls is defined as a process, not a product.

9. It is difficult, for instance, to evaluate whether the case of one woman being employed while another not, is due to differences in substantive opportunities available to them or due to differences in personal choices they have made.
10. Capability focuses on "the freedom people have to do and be rather than exclusively on their mental states or on the goods they have at their disposal" (Sen 1985; Robeyns 2002). Sen's capability framework is able to keep context in mind. It incorporates process, differences in need, preferences, values, structural constraints and the like.
11. Right to life can be seen as an example of this.
12. Burchardt (2006) gives the following example to illustrate this: Everyone has the right to life as the minimum entitlement guaranteed under the European Convention on Human Rights, and the existence of large inequalities in life expectancy for different social groups are seen as being consistent with the state having met its obligations under the ECHR.
13. The selection of economic, social and socio-economic as main causes may seem arbitrary in this case. However, "[T]here are diversities of many kinds. It is not unreasonable to think that if we try to take note of all the diversities, we might end up in a total mess of empirical confusion. The demands of practice indicate discretion and suggest that we disregard some diversities while concentrating on the more important ones" (Sen 1992, p. 117).
14. For instance, specific needs of all individuals who live below the poverty line have to be met regardless of which marginalized social group they may belong to.
15. Strictly speaking, a sociologically more nuanced understanding of equity would give us gender equity as well as social equity (referring to caste groups), religious equity (referring to all religions), and cultural equity (referring to "ethnic" categories such as Adivasis). Additionally we would need to add a category of equity for differentially challenged groups.
16. We have deliberately not problematized the concept of participation in this section, preferring to take a simple view of it, without getting drawn into other discussions not directly related to this one.
17. The focus on equity in the manner described above again has the benefit of de-emphasizing outcome-based evaluations, especially in societies which suffer from deeper inequities which need to be redressed.
18. Nambissan (1996, p. 1016) quotes an example from Mencher's study of Pariyan children who were inhibited from accessing education since they had to walk through the upper caste sections of the village in order to reach the school. This would be seen as a socially inaccessible school.

6

Gender, Educational Deprivation and Exclusion A Case Study of Madhya Pradesh and Chhattisgarh

— *Madhumita Bandyopadhyay*

I. Introduction

The Indian Constitution guarantees equality and social justice in all walks of life including education. The policy pronouncements have viewed provision for free and compulsory elementary education for all as a critical prerequisite for achieving the goal of education for all. Promotion of gender and social equity has also been guiding principle for policy planning and implementation. Further commitments to the Universalization of Elementary Education as well as the legal, administrative and financial frameworks for the government-funded education system are found in two main sources. These are the on-going series of Five Year Plans for National Development and the National Policy on Education (NPE, 1986), with its Programme of Action (1992). As a result of these five year Plans as well as NPE, changes are being made on the ground. Various Centrally Sponsored Schemes including Operation Black Board, District Primary Education Programme etc. were initiated as per suggestions given by NPE, 1986 and POA, 1992. Government of India has been implementing a countrywide programme- *Sarva Siksha Abhiyan* since the year of 2000-01. The Right to Education Act, 2009 has made education up to the grade VIII as fundamental right of children of 6-14 years age-group from the year of 2010 by enforcing 86th Amendment. As a result of many such initiatives, it is heartening to see that, during last decade India has already witnessed unprecedented expansion of schooling facilities along with increase in enrolment of children both boys and girls from different socio-economic, ethnic and linguistic groups. In India, the number of schools has grown rapidly from 767,000 in 2005 to 858,916 at the primary level and at upper primary from 275,000 to 589,796. This improvement in access definitely indicates a rapid increase in enrolment and number of teaching staff in primary and upper primary level during recent years. In 2013-14, as many as 198.8 million children are enrolled in more than 14 lakh schools which are served by 7.7 million teachers (NUEPA, 2014). In view of this, one has to admit that developments in recent years have made significant impact on the situation, raising the hope that universal basic education would be a reality within a reasonable period of time. However, despite such improvements, many challenges still remain unresolved.

While many government documents and recent researches indicate the impressive growth of schooling provisions, more in-depth analysis is required to assess what is the nature and extent of impact of these developments on improving access to and participation of children in elementary education across the country? Are more children irrespective of their caste, class and gender accessing and completing the elementary education cycle and moving to secondary schools? What factors seem to facilitate or hinder the smooth flow of children within the school system? To what extent are school factors responsible for ensuring that all children are attending schools regularly and they are being able to achieve the expected levels of learning? What is the actual nature and magnitude of exclusion of children from schooling? Who are the children that remain excluded and where do they live? Why they are excluded and how their fundamental rights can be addressed? These are some critical questions that might possibly determine whether India achieves the targets and goals set at the national level.

Using the secondary as well as empirical data of a recent study conducted under CREATE, this paper attempts to answer some of these critical questions from gender perspectives as in India more girls than boys face the threat and challenges of exclusion. The paper will also make an attempt to explore the strategies and actions required to promote gender equity in education. The data used for this paper have been collected through community and school survey (CoMSS) covering 88 schools and 6431 households from 36 villages selected from four blocks of three different districts namely Rajnandgaon district of Chattishgarh, Rewa and Dindori districts of Madhya Pradesh. These villages were covered in another study conducted earlier eighteen years ago in 1990 (Govinda and Varghese, IIEP-NUEPA, 1993) and have been revisited while conducting the present study under CREATE-NUEPA project. In addition to 35 primary schools studied earlier, schools with middle and lower secondary grades located in same villages also have been included making the total number of schools 88. It is primarily because this present study intends to examine inclusion and exclusion of children of 3-15 age groups who are eligible for different levels of schooling ranging from pre-primary to secondary level. In earlier study, house hold survey was not conducted but in the present study, data have been collected from households from these 36 villages. These three areas still represent developed rural area (Rajnandgaon), underdeveloped rural area (Rewa) and a tribal area (Dindori) respectively as it was found 18 years ago while conducting earlier study (Govinda and Varghese, IIEP-NUEPA, 1993).

II. Exclusion and Education: Conceptual Framework

Educational exclusion has close association with social exclusion which has been explored by many other researchers (Sen, 1995; Subrahmanian, 2004; Sayad, 2004). According to Oxford Dictionary, the social exclusion occurs due to lack of participation of any individual in society. It is multidimensional in nature as it is an outcome of factors. For example, exclusion of any individual or group may be outcome of poverty as well as other kinds of disadvantages such as social norms, cultural biases, social relation etc which also cause exclusion under different circumstances Functioning of social institutions like schools and existing social relations among different groups within schools and outside determine the process of exclusion. In the context of educational exclusion it needs to be understood as a 'process', not just an 'event' and a mere statistic or figure. Many events preceding schooling shape the life of the individual child who gets excluded later on from educational system. Some of these events are located in the family, some in the community and the peer group, and many are located in the school where the child is supposed to be studying. So it is required to capture the events that surround their life (Govinda and Bandyopadhyay, 2008). As it has been mentioned in another earlier paper (Govinda and Bandyopadhyay, 2010), most notably, social exclusion is linked with the denial of equal opportunities among different groups with different social backgrounds (De Hann, 1997; Thorat, 2003). Social exclusion is seen as "lack of access to resources and consequent inability to utilize them. It is further accentuated by denial of opportunities which enhance access to resources and their utilization" (Ziauddin and Kasi, 2009). Since education is considered as essential means to access resources and its effective utilization, denial of educational opportunities definitely causes social exclusion. As mentioned by Popey and others (2006) that "exclusionary processes impact in different ways to differing degrees on different groups and/or societies at particular times." This holds true in case of educational exclusion too as it is the deprived groups who remained excluded for ages and many of them are still found not availing schooling facilities. Girls constitute a significant proportion among these out of school children due to various reasons ranging from cultural norms, socio-economic background, household responsibilities, gender roles in society to different policy related issues (Bandyopadhyay M. & Subrahamanian, R. 2011). It is because of this, a large section of population is still found illiterate. The NSS data show that literacy rate (Table 1) increases according to the social classes, with lowest literacy rates for SC females in rural areas followed by ST females. While the proportion of total literates has been recorded as 72.8 per cent with considerable difference in literacy rates of rural and urban population of age five years and above, around 36 per cent of females in rural area are still not literate and majority of them are from socially disadvantaged and economically weaker sections.

Table 1: Literacy rate among persons of age five years and above for different social groups

Social Group	*Rural*			*Urban*			*Rural + Urban*		
	Male	*Female*	*Person*	*Male*	*Female*	*Person*	*Male*	*Female*	*Person*
ST	701	526	615	880	720	804	717	544	631
SC	721	523	623	831	691	764	743	555	654
OBC	780	575	679	886	753	822	808	621	716
Others	842	685	767	935	860	900	879	757	821
All	773	585	682	900	789	848	811	640	728

Source: NSS 66th Round Report (543), Employment and Unemployment Situation among Social Groups in India, 2009–2010, p. 29.

Similar social and gender gaps are visible in case of school enrolment across the states. Educational access along with their participation behaviour considerably varies among different social groups.

It has been realized over time that the children who fail to access or complete a basic education cycle do not constitute a homogenous group. For some children, physical access to school is difficult while others fail to access school due to socio-economic reasons. Some join school, but are silently excluded because they rarely participate in the educational process. According to Govinda (2009), "Many children simply leave school without mastering basic skills of literacy and numeracy. Such excluded children grow up as non-literate or semi-literate youth and adults, subsequently lowering the national literacy rates". So the question arises that "what about the right of those children who suffer silent exclusion (i.e. low achievers), even while sitting in the classroom as schools fail to impart any learning?" (Govinda, 2009). As mentioned earlier, an attempt has been made to identify those children who are in the Zone of silent exclusion in all four countries (South Africa, Ghana, India and Bangladesh) under the CREATE study and the proportion of such at risk children is quite prominent in all these countries including India (CREATE, 2011).

Section III: Zones of Exclusion in Indian Context: Drawing the Contours

The analysis presented in this section is two-fold. It gives a quantitative picture of the children in various Zones of exclusion on the one hand, and on the other, field based research findings on the processes involved and the reasons for children continuing to face the risk of exclusion. It should be mentioned at the outset that databases in India do not fully follow the categories identified under the different Zones. Consequently, discussions of the different Zones to some extent over-lap. The data collected from field are also presented as evidence in support of incidence of exclusion and inclusion at the grass root level. It has already been mentioned in the Country Analytical Review (CAR) prepared under CREATE (Govinda and Bandyopadhyay, 2011) that the Children who fail to access or complete a basic education cycle do not constitute a homogenous group. So, it is important not to categorize all these children together, as they have different access needs and contexts. It is also required to look at these children differently as they are living in different circumstances. In the CAR, using secondary data, an attempt has already been made to configure the different Zones of educational exclusion in India and assess the magnitude and nature of exclusion in each Zone. Since the understanding the dynamics between schools and children requires an analysis of access from a range of viewpoints, looking at children in different circumstances, this paper again configures these distinct Zones of exclusion and educational access at the elementary level is described in terms of six Zones of exclusion: The Zones of Exclusion model has been developed by the Consortium for Research on Educational Access, Transitions and Equity (Lewin, 2007). These Zones have been adapted to suit the structure of the Indian education system (Govinda and Bandyopadhyay, 2008) and to assess the magnitude and nature of exclusion in each Zone.

As mentioned earlier this paper uses the existing database developed under CREATE. These data have been collected through Community and School Survey conducted in 2008 in 36 villages located in three areas namely Rajnandgaon of Chhattisgarh, Rewa and Dindori of Madhya Pradesh. It will attempt to capture the intricacies of journeys that different sections of children in India pass through. The distribution of children according to their schooling status in the selected clusters is given in Table 1 that highlights that majority of the children of 6-15 years age group are enrolled in school. The proportion of drop out and never enrolled is not too high but their number is a matter of concern. The highest proportion of never enrolled and drop out children both could be found in Dindori. Rajnandgaon has larger number of dropouts whereas Rewa has more number of never enrolled. This section provides an in-depth analysis of data to identify the children falling in different Zones of exclusion.

The data reveals that although access of both boys and girls to education has improved, patterns of access are gendered. More than half of the parents of girls who never attended school were of the opinion that they do not need to send their girl children to school. The reality of girls' exclusion is further complicated by caste, religion, ethnicity and age. The per centages of girls amongst those never enrolled in the three clusters are 57 per cent in

Rajnandgaon, 47 per cent in Rewa and 54 per cent in Dindori (Bandyopadhyay, 2012). This indicates that some girls face difficulties in initial physical access to education and their proportion is higher in rural areas inhabited by disadvantaged groups like SC, ST and OBCs. The proportion of never-enrolled was higher among tribal girls (13 per cent) than boys (10 per cent) but there has been no difference between boys and girls in case of dropouts as 9 per cent of boys and same proportion of girls belonging to ST category dropped out from schools In case of Scheduled Castes too there is hardly any difference between the proportion of boys and girls in case of never enrolment and dropout in these three clusters. On an average around 8 per cent of boys and 7 per cent of girls among SC children remained never- enrolled, around 5 per cent boys and 4 per cent girls dropped out from school.

The following sub-sections provides details about the children falling into different Zones of exclusion

3.1 Zone 1: Children Not Entering Primary School

The National Sample Survey Organization (NSS) in its survey conducted in 2009 (GOI, 2010) has provided the data on never- enrolled children and reasons for their non-enrolment. Around nine per cent children of 6-10 years' category and six per cent children in the 10-13 years' group were recorded as never-enrolled in school at the time of the 64th NSS survey. As per the NSS data, 'lack of interest of parents in studies' has been attributed by the highest proportion of respondents (34.7 per cent for 6-10 years and 31 per cent for 10-13 years old) as the reason for non-enrolment of children in school, followed by the reasons like financial constraints (23 per cent for 6-10 and 29 per cent for 10-13 years old) and 'education not considered as necessary' (17 per cent for 6-10 and 20 per cent for 10-13 years old). Gender difference is visible while mentioning the reason. For example while 28 per cent boys remained never enrolled because of lack of parental interest in studies, it is increases to 33 per cent for girls. Very few children were found non-enrolled because of their engagement in paid and unpaid work, sibling care or other household chores. However, higher proportion of girls cited these reasons as well as the reason like 'no tradition in community'. Contrary to this, more boys than girls remained never enrolled because of financial constraints and other economic reasons.

An attempt has been made to examine the extent to which this problem of never-enrolment is persisting in the villages under study. The total number of never enrolled children in 6-15 years age group is 265 and out of them more than half (147, 54.5 per cent) are from Dindori cluster while in Rewa and Rajnandgaon 76 (16 per cent) and 42 (18 per cent) such children have been recorded during the survey. More girls than boys are found never enrolled particularly in Dindori (Table 2).

Table 2: Age-wise Never Enrolled Children in Three Areas

Clusters	*Age -wise Never Enrolled*														
	3-5 Age group (Zone 0)			*6-10 Age group (Zone 1)*			*11-14 years old (Zone 1)*			*15 years old (Zone 1)*			*Total (Zone 0+1)*		
	B	***G***	***T***	***B***	***G***	***T***	***B***	***G***	***T***	***B***	***G***	***T***	***B***	***G***	***T***
Rajnandagaon	5	7	12	15	18	33	1	4	5	2	1	3	23	30	53
Per cent	*22*	*23*	*23*	*65*	*60*	*62*	*4*	*13*	*9*	*9*	*3*	*12*			
Rewa	1	1	2	29	28	57	10	8	18	1	0	1	41	37	78
Per cent	*2*	*2*	*3*	*70*	*73*	*73*	*24*	*22*	*23*	*2*	*0*	*1*			
Dindori	4	9	13	38	49	87	22	29	51	2	4	6	66	91	157
Per cent	*6*	*10*	*8*	*58*	*59*	*55*	*33*	*32*	*32*	*3*	*4*	*4*			

Source: HH Survey, 2008.

A considerable proportion of respondents in the study area has cited poor quality of school as a reason of never enrolment which indicates that without even availing schooling facilities parents felt the ineffectiveness of schools and expressed their dissatisfaction about the functioning of school. While 34% children were never enrolled because of household related reasons, particularly their family's economic condition and their engagement in household chores, rest of the children remained never-enrolled because of school related reasons. It is noteworthy that, in Rajnandgaon cluster majority of never enrolled children could not go to school as they are engaged in household work. Contribution to household income and lack of interest of parents and children in education are other major reasons as it is also the case in NSSO. Around one third of children remained deprived of education due to the single reason like lack of interest of children in studies. Though distance of school from residence is not found an important reason in Rewa and Rajnandgaon but in Dindori 15 children remained never enrolled due to this reason and majority of them are in lower age group. In general, more numbers of younger age group children were found never enrolled indicating practice of late entry despite having a primary school within the village itself.

3.2 Zone 2 and Zone V: Children Dropping Out from Primary and Upper Primary (Middle) School

Although most states in India have done well in enrolling more and more children in recent years, the inability of schools to retain those children has continued to be a serious problem. Although country level data indicate the progress made in reducing drop out rates over the last decade and a half, still around 25 per cent children dropped out during 2006-07, even though there was an unprecedented level of developmental action in primary education. The 61st NSS (2004-2005) (GoI, 2006b) also shows the problem of drop-outs prevails at large scale. It shows physical access to school is now only a minor reason for dropping out. A substantial number of children were found to be dropping out because education was not considered necessary, they had to support household income (especially urban boys) or they had to attend to domestic chores (girls in particular). The situation with respect to drop out at the primary and upper primary level in the study area is analysed below (Table 3).

Table 3: Age and Level Wise Distribution of Drop out Girls and Boys in Study Area

Last Class Attended before dropping out		*6 to below 11 years*			*11 to below 15 years*			*15 to below 19*			*Total*		
		M	*F*	*T*	*M*	*F*	*T*	*M*	*F*	*T*	*M*	*F*	*T*
Primary level (Grades 1-5)	Number	22	20	42	58	56	114	21	24	45	101	100	201
	Per cent	100	95	98	72	74	73	40	53	46	65	70	67
Middle level (Grades 6-8)	Number	0	1	1	21	20	41	25	20	45	46	41	87
	Per cent	0	5	2	26	26	26	47	44	46	29	29	29
Secondary (Grade 9)	Number	0	0	0	2	0	2	7	1	8	9	1	10
	Per cent	0	0	0	2	0	1	13	2	8	6	1	3
Total (N=100)		22	21	43	81	76	157	53	45	98	156	142	298

Source: Household Survey, 2008.

The Table 3 highlights that, total 298 children from 6-19 years old were found drop out during the household survey of CREATE. Majority (67 per cent) of them had to drop out even at the primary level and 29 per cent dropped out at the upper primary level. While more boys than girls of 6-19 years old had to drop out from school, the proportion of girls (70 per cent) who dropped out at the primary level was much higher than that of boys (65 per cent). In case of upper primary level, their proportion has been almost same.

Table 4: Drop out of 6-10 and 11-15 Age group Before Completion of Primary Schooling (I-IV)

Clusters	*6-10 years old*			*11-15 years old*			*Total Drop out before class V (I-IV)*	*Total*
	Dropout at the Primary Stage (I-V)	*Per cent*	*Total Drop out of 6-10 years age group*	*Dropout at the Primary Stage (I-V) (N=100)*	*Per cent*	*Total Drop out of 11-15 years age group*		
Rajnandgaon	8	88	9	28	29	95	36	105
Rewa	6	67	9	11	17	66	17	75
Dindori	23	95	24	34	46	74	57	98
Total	**38**	**88**	**42**	**73**	**31**	**235**	**110**	**278**

Source: HH Survey, 2008.

According to the household survey data of 2008, very few children of 6-10 agegroup are found dropout and therefore falling under the category of Zone 2 in all the three clusters (Table 4). While altogether 272 children were recorded as dropout, 110 children had to dropout at the primary stage and only 42 children were of 6-10 years age group. Similarly, although total 235 children of 11-15 age group were recorded as dropout, 31 per cent of these children had to drop out at the primary stage itself.

Almost all data sources indicate that dropout rate among older children (11-14 years) is much higher than among lower age groups. The situation at the upper primary level (grades 6-8) is quite alarming as around half of the children who enroll in upper primary schools do not complete the upper primary cycle (GoI, 2007a). Table 5 indicates the number and proportion of such children of 11-15 years of age is quite significant in the study area. While more boys than girls in the age group of 11-14 are found dropout in Dindori, girls are found more disadvantaged in Rewa and Rajnandgaon. The trend is just reverse in case of 15 years old. At this stage girls as well as boys in some households are required to get engaged in paid or unpaid work to contribute to household income.

Table 5: Children in Zone 5 (Drop out of 11-14 and 15 Years Old)

Clusters	*11-14 Age group*			*15 years old*			*Total Drop Outs (6-15)*		
	B	*G*	*T*	*B*	*G*	*T*	*B*	*G*	*T*
Rajnandagaon	28	33	61	16	12	28	49	49	98
Per cent	57	67	62	33	24	29			
Rewa	23	18	41	21	11	32	49	33	82
Per cent	45	54	50	42	33	39			
Dindori	30	25	55	8	13	21	48	52	100
Per cent	62	48	55	17	25	21			

Source: Household Survey, 2008.

Like Zone 2 Zone 5 also includes over aged children but their proportion is not too high as indicated by data given in above able. It is interesting to see in Table 6 that a considerable proportion (42 per cent) of 6-11 years old children dropped out at the Grade I and this proportion is higher among girls. It is disheartening to see that these children could not even complete early grades of their basic education. It is noteworthy that majority of children had to leave their education at Grade V as this is the grade in which the highest proportion of children of 11-15 years and 15-19 years old dropped out. It is disheartening to see that 87 children (44 girls and 40 boys) left their education at the Grade V alone and 117 (56 girls and 61 boys) more children left their education even before Grade V. Substantial number of children, boys as well as girls also dropped out after entering upper primary school. Altogether maximum exodus took place at the Grade VII in the area under study where 30 children reported that they have dropped out at this grade.

Table 6: Age, Gender and Grade Wise Percentage distribution of children attended last class before dropping out

Last Class Attended before dropping out	*Grade 1*	*Grade 2*	*Grade 3*	*Grade 4*	*Grade 5*	*Grade 6*	*Grade 7*	*Grade 8*	*Grade 9*	*Total (n=100)*
6 to below 11 years										
Male	7	3	8	2	2	0	0	0	0	22
Per cent	32	14	36	9	9	0	0	0	0	100
Female	11	3	3	1	2	1	0	0	0	21
Per cent	52	14	14	5	10	5	0	0	0	100
Total	18	6	11	3	4	1	0	0	0	43
Per cent	42	14	26	7	9	2	0	0	0	100
11 to below 15years										
Male	6	7	9	11	25	7	12	2	2	81
Per cent	7	9	11	14	31	9	15	2	2	100
Female	4	13	5	9	25	11	4	5	0	76
Per cent	5	17	7	12	33	14	5	7	0	100
Total	10	20	14	20	50	18	16	7	2	157
Per cent	6	13	9	13	32	11	10	4	1	100
15 to below 19 years										
Male	1	0	1	6	13	8	7	10	7	53
Per cent	2	0	2	11	25	15	13	19	13	100
Female	0	4	3	0	17	2	7	11	1	45
Per cent	0	9	7	0	38	4	16	24	2	100
Total	1	4	4	6	30	10	14	21	8	98
Per cent	1	4	4	6	31	10	14	21	8	100

Source: Household Survey Data, 2008.

Based on above analysis, it is discernible that, boys and girls both had to leave schools early in all the study areas though reasons of their dropout are different.

It has been found that school related reasons determine children's access and participation in schools more critically than household related reasons in the villages under study (Govinda and Bandyopadhyay, 2011c). These include lack of sensitivity of school system towards the need of poor children and parents, lack of inclusivity in schools and its poor functioning. It is the school which could not encourage children and parents to grow their interest in school (Govinda and Bandyopadhyay, 2011b) and it is the school which could not provide any support to poor children who are engaged in paid or unpaid work to provide financial support to their family and consequently they had to leave their study. The children's lack of interest in study which has been mentioned as a major reason for non-enrolment indirectly points to poor quality of education (Tilak, 2000).

Substantial gender gap is found in proportion of children who have become unschooled due to household related reasons. While 34 per cent boys dropped out and 29 per cent remained never enrolled due to these reasons, proportion of girls who left school (40 per cent) and remained never-enrolled

(33 per cent) (due to these same reasons) is much higher indicating discriminating attitude of parents and families towards girls' education and continuation of gender stereotyping. It is also mention worthy that despite having schooling facilities within reach, dropout of children continued in the subsequent years. According to the data collected from schools located in the sample villages, the incidence of drop out increased in 2009 when altogether 446 children dropped out. The number of total drop out children further increased to 602 (Figure 1) in 2010. The highest proportion of drop out was in Dindori during both years, followed by Rajnandgaon, which has better schooling facilities than Dindori and Rewa. More girls than boys dropped out in Rajnandgaon but the case was reverse in Dindori. In Rewa while girls' retention was better than the boys in 2009 but this trend got reversed in 2010.

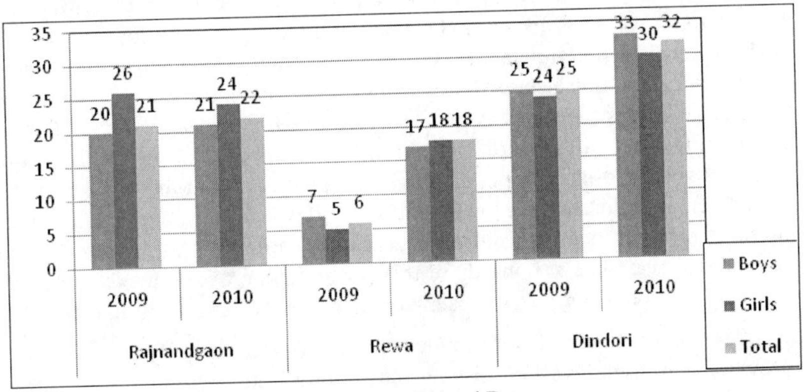

Source: Household Survey and School Roster Merged Data.

Figure 1: Percentage of Drop out Children in 2009 & 2010

3.3 Zone 3: Children at Risk of Silent Exclusion

In addition to children who never-enroll or drop out at the primary stage, there are also children who continue to be enrolled at school, but who are at risk of dropping out. These children are often silently excluded from schools; they are physically present but gaining little cognitive benefit from the learning experience.

The active presence of children and their imbibing of knowledge and skills in the classroom become important issues once they get enrolled in a school. The central characteristic of meaningful access (Lewin, 2007; Govinda and Bandyopadhyay, 2009; Little, 2008) to school education is the sustained and active participation of children in teaching learning processes and classroom activities. Irregular attendance, low levels of learning, previous temporary withdrawals, overage learners and grade repetition tend to make children at risk of the permanent exclusion i.e. dropout. On the other hand, it has been found that students who attend school regularly score higher in their achievement tests than their peers, who remain frequently absent. Although the low attendance and low learning level of children is rampant across the country, many studies found these problems are more prominent in case of disadvantaged groups (Govinda and Bandyopadhyay, 2008; Pratham, 2012; Dreze and Kingdon, 1999). Many of these children are characterized as 'not interested in studies' by different reports like NSS (GOI, 2001), NFHS (IIPS and ORC Macro, 2000), and PROBE (1999) and eventually drop out from school. This particular reason, however, may be related more to school-related factors which act as barriers for children to learn effectively and to move further. In addition to these surveys, several other studies like The Annual Status of Education Report (ASER; Pratham, 2014) PROBE (2011) have demonstrated poor quality of teaching-learning processes in many schools, which results in low levels of basic skill attainment, i.e. reading, writing and arithmetic. The ASER argues that even after attending school for five or even eight years, many children face severe learning deficit. Along with poor learning level, grade repetition also seems to be high despite having a policy of automatic promotion across the states as per RTE Act, 2009. The data collected for the all-India District Information System in Education (NUEPA, 2014b: 37) in 2013-14 showed that 1.24 per cent had to repeat grades at the primary level. Moreover, as children move to higher classes, low level of attainment becomes more significant making children at risk of dropping out at the middle and secondary level. The magnitude of this phenomenon of silent exclusion can be analysed with reference to absenteeism, repetition and performance.

The data collected from sample schools (located in study area) indicate prevalence of high levels of absenteeism among students in all the localities. As mentioned by Govinda and Bandyopadhyay, (2011c), "the rates are in particular staggering in Rewa and Dindori. What is most intriguing is the unduly high proportion of children remained absent in EGS schools which are supposed to be established and managed by local communities. It is interesting to note that the proportion of girls who missed their schools for 'three days and less' is much higher than boys. This indicates, that once girls manage to access to school, they tend to attend it regularly, contrary to general perception. The proportion of long duration absentees is higher in case of boys in all three areas (Table 7)

Table 7: Absenteeism of girls and boys in previous month of Data Collection in the Study areas (in per centage) in 2008

Period of absenteeism	*Rajnandgaon*			*Rewa*			*Dindori*			*Total Area*		
	B	*G*	*T*	*B*	*G*	*T*	*B*	*G*	*T*	*B*	*G*	*T*
0 - 3 days	54	63	59	48	52	50	50	61	55	51	59	54
4 - 6 days	25	22	23	22	20	21	20	15	18	23	20	22
7-15 days	17	13	15	24	24	24	20	16	18	19	17	18
.>15 days	4	3	4	6	4	6	11	8	9	7	4	6

Source: School Roster data, 2008.

An important feature of good schooling is the smooth progression of children from one grade to another. The policy of automatic promotion which has been adopted by both states much before the enforcement of RTE Act, 2009 is expected to ensure that the children do not repeat same grade and lose their motivation to learning. However, the data collected from schools suggest that the incidence of repetition is rampant in all EGS and government formal schools though very few repeaters could be found in private schools. Although higher proportion of repeaters is found among younger age group, still the repetition rate is quite high among older age group who are still continuing at the primary stage despite being already over aged. Obviously these children would need different interventions to improve their learning level.

Despite states having no detention policy, altogether, 1408 (15 per cent) out of the total of 9286 children enrolled in 88 schools under study were found repeaters. While repetition rate was little higher for girls in Rewa, boys showed higher repetition in the other two clusters (Figure 2).

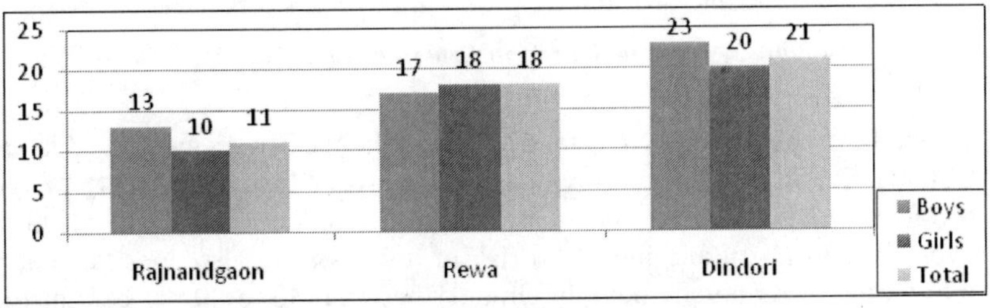

Source: Roster data, 2008.

Figure 2: Gender difference in rate of repetition in all three clusters

The overall repetition rate (Figure 3) shows a declining trend over the last five years but around 10 per cent of the boys and 8 per cent of the girls repeated their grades in Rajnandgaon in the year of 2007-08. It is found that there had been a gradual increase in repetition of both boys and girls in Rewa cluster till 2006-07. In 2007-08 although the number of repeaters declined, still more number of girls (294) than boys (275) had to repeat their grades. Maximum number of repeaters was recorded in the year 2006-07 when the proportion of repeaters was 34 per cent among boys and 33 per cent among girls.

In Dindori, the repetition rate has also shown an increasing trend and around one fifth of the girls and around one fourth of the boys were found repeating their grades in 2007-08. In view of this, one can say that, a large section of children could not learn adequately and schools could not make adequate efforts to reduce the incidence of repetition.

The repetition has been a perpetual problem, as discussed above and as many studies have mentioned, the children experiencing repetition become

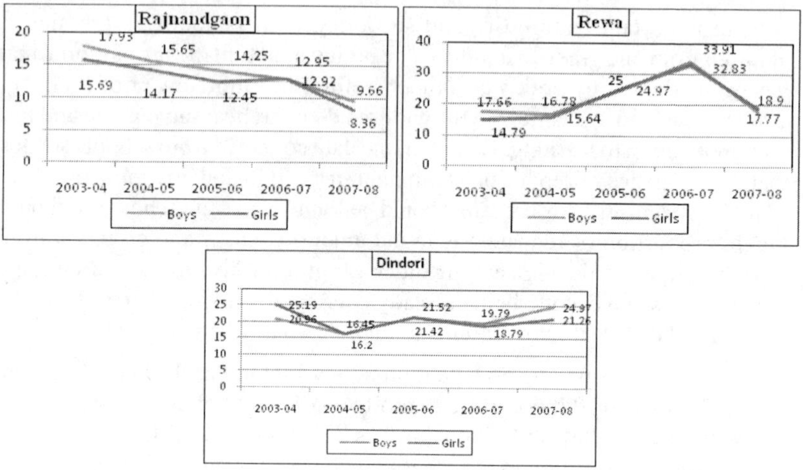

Source: School baseline data, 2008.

Figure 3: Trend in Repetition Rate from 2003-04 to 2007-08

vulnerable to exclusion as they tend to leave school early. As mentioned in the Country Summary Report (Govinda and Bandyopadhyay, 2011, 14), "High levels of repetition should be a serious cause of concern since they lead to over age enrolment and increased risk of drop out. So also does late entry into Grade 1. As noted above in Grade 1 between 30 to 40 per cent of the children are 7 years old or more. By Grade 5 in Rewa and Dindori more than 60 per cent are one or more years over age and by Grade 8 over 70 per cent. In Rewa over 25 per cent of those in Grade 8 of primary school are 16 years or

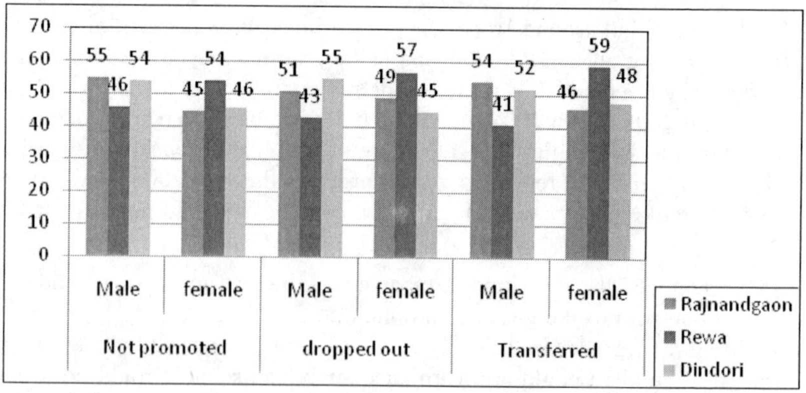

Source: School Roster Data.

Figure 4: Status of Repetition, Dropout and Transfer of Students in 2009.

older and in Dindori their proportion is over 33 per cent. Older children are more likely to drop out, especially if they are girls". The following Figure indicates the process of exclusion and silent exclusion at the schools (primary to secondary level) under study and to what extent girls and boys are vulnerable to exclusion in these three clusters.

As data show that some children also have taken Transfer Certificates mainly for continuing study in some other institution. While in 2009, proportion of boys was much higher than girls among those who took TC in Rajnandgaon and Dindori, it is just opposite in Rewa. However, there is no guarantee that all children who have taken TC will be able to get transferred to higher level or not.

From the above discussion, it emerges that, despite enhanced inputs and special efforts some children are still unable to attend schools regularly and facing the threat of exclusion due to poor learning level. Following section will throw some light on status of learning outcome of sample children who appeared for a competency test in Hindi and Mathematics conducted for this study.

3.4 Learning Outcome

The learning disparity is closely linked with the disparity in schooling facilities and quality of school functioning as it has been observed in the CREATE study (Govinda and Bandyopadhyay, 2011c). It has been found that most of children who were enrolled in private schools in Rajnandgaon and Rewa could perform much better than those enrolled in the government schools located in the same areas (Govinda and Bandyopadhyay, 2011c). Learning outcomes also differs because of poverty, caste and gender as girls from poorer and disadvantaged households attend mostly government schools with poorer facilities. As per the competency test scores, higher proportion of girls than boys performed very poorly as they secured below 30 per cent marks in both Hindi and Mathematics. Gender disparity in learning outcome both in Hindi and Mathematics was higher in Rewa as the proportion of poor performers (below 30 per cent) was much higher in the case of girls (41 per cent) as compared to boys (26 per cent) in this cluster.

In addition, it also depends on the nature of area where the schools are located. The schools located in advanced areas with better facilities and teachers seem to be able to address learning needs of children in better way. It is noteworthy that in the tribal cluster of Dindori, around half of the children who appeared for the test obtained below 30 per cent both in Hindi and Mathematics. It is mainly because like many other tribal dominated blocks and districts, Dindori has been neglected for ages and has remained underdeveloped with a serious consequence on education of children. During the school survey, most schools in Dindori were found devoid of adequate physical facilities and qualified teachers. It is heartening to see that on an average, more girls than boys could perform better in Hindi in Dindori. Another important point is that, despite the poor learning environment as mentioned above, around one fourth of the girls and boys could secure above 70 per cent in Mathematics in this cluster. Higher proportion of girls (19 per cent) than boys (9 per cent) could secure more than 40 per cent marks in Mathematics.

Table 8 shows the mean and standard deviation of marks obtained by children in the competency test of Mathematics as well as Hindi. Broadly speaking, considerable gender gap in the mean scores of Mathematics is persisting in all three areas and it is in alarming situation particularly in Dindori. It is noticeable that the standard deviation has crossed 20 in all the three clusters and in Dindori it has reached 28 for girls and 30 for boys. This indicates that a large section of children, both boys and girls could not learn adequately and face the threat of silent exclusion as mentioned earlier. The mean scores in Hindi are abysmally low in all the three clusters and it was much lower than the Mathematics mean scores. The mean score in Hindi was much lower in the case of girls than boys in Rewa as well as in Rajnandgaon putting girls in a more disadvantaged situation. The mean scores in Dindori, both for boys and girls are abysmally low indicating that absolutely no learning was taking place in the schools of Dindori so children are not getting any benefit of attending school. Thus, broadly speaking, the analysis of competency test marks showed that learning levels of both, boys as well as girls was far from satisfactory in all the three clusters especially in Dindori. It may be because Majority of the children in all these clusters speak the local dialects at home and their mother

Table 8: Mean and standard deviation in Mathematics and Hindi competency test

	Mathematics			*Hindi*		
	Total children who appeared in the test (N)	*Mean*	*S.D.*	*Total children who appeared in the test (N)*	*Mean*	*S.D.*
Rajnandgaon						
Boys	181	51.29	23.374	208	41.86	18.357
Girls	195	44.37	22.894	228	35.13	18.069
Total	376	47.70	23.354	436	38.34	18.494
Rewa						
Boys	159	55.83	23.163	183	45.92	19.881
Girls	166	41.80	24.165	186	38.69	21.232
Total	325	48.67	24.666	369	42.27	20.861
Dindori						
Boys	54	33.74	30.633	54	29.66	20.456
Girls	63	35.79	28.388	64	30.49	20.016
Total	117	34.84	29.335	118	30.11	20.136

Source: Competency test results, 2008.

tongue was not Hindi. This might have caused a great disadvantage in learning Hindi. This aspect needs immediate attention of teachers and other service providers. More detailed analysis shows that children of Grade V could perform much better than the children of Grade IV.

3.5 Zone 4: Children Who Complete Primary School But Do Not Enter Upper Primary School

In addition to children who leave school early, it is quite common phenomenon that some children do not transit to upper primary level though they complete primary education on account of various reasons. One of these is the non-availability of upper primary schools in the vicinity. In India, according to DISE data, the trend for transition rates from primary to upper primary level, has found 89.58 per cent in 2012-13. This indicates that 10 per cent of children attending lower primary schools do not transit to next level. This suggests that, simply passing the grade V examination, however, does not ensure transition to upper primary school as it depends on availability of schools with upper primary section within reach of children. It is also related to low learning level of basic competencies, which leads to failure and exclusion from the schooling system beyond grade V. DISE data from 2008-09 also shows more than 50 per cent of children performed at an average or below average level in class V[1].

The data collected from the villages under study indicate that due to poor learning level at the primary stage many children experience failure at the primary level and those who somehow can manage to complete primary grades, they fail to enter upper primary stage and falls under the Zone 4. However, their proportion is not too high in these three clusters. This indicates barring a few, most children who get chance to complete primary education, take admission in upper primary section and try to continue. It is evident from the household data shows that altogether 79 such children could not transit to upper primary education in these three clusters and majority of these children (48) are in the older age group (14-15 years). Their proportion is the highest in Rewa cluster although many villages in Rewa have been provided with upper primary schooling facilities within reachable distance.

3.6 Zone 6: Children Who do not transit to secondary Level after Upper Primary Education

This Zone includes the children who are repeating grades at the upper primary stage along with those who are irregular in schools and also not performing as expected. A substantial proportion of children particularly in Rewa could be found repeating different grades at this stage. While their proportion among 11-15 age group is around 6 per cent in Rajnandgaon and Dindori, in Rewa it is 18 per cent and therefore falling under Zone 6.

The above analysis suggests that merely increasing enrolment in lower levels of schooling is no guarantee that children's participation in higher levels will improve. The non-availability of facilities for accessing secondary education could have a significant backwash effect on the participation of children in the elementary stage, and particularly in upper primary schools. Thus, poor learning achievement at the elementary stage on one hand and lack of schooling facilities at the secondary stage on the other compels many children to leave schools at this stage. It is evident from the data gathered from the three clusters, very few children (27) could be found who left their study after completion of upper primary school and hence can represent this Zone. Number of such children is higher in Rajnandgaon where 21 from 11-15 age group and 66 from 16 and higher age group were found already left their education after completion of elementary schooling. This Zone also includes those who are vulnerable to drop out at the secondary stage. In Dindori altogether 19 repeaters were found in the age group of 11-15 years in 2008 while 14 were from the age group of 16 and above. Age wise dropout has already been discussed in previous section but level wise repetition and dropout are highlighted in following Table that explains the situation with respect to exclusion and silent exclusion in case of Zone 5 and Zone 6.

Section IV: Possible Reasons for Silent Exclusion

While discussing about never enrolment (Zone 1) and Dropout (Zone 2 and Zone 5) It has already been mentioned that, lack of interest of children and their parents, putting less value to education, engagement in paid and unpaid work and financial constraints have been the main reasons for non enrolment and dropout. As mentioned in a CREATE policy brief (Bandypadhyay, Das and Zeitlyn, 2011), "absenteeism is multi- causal phenomenon" involving home -related and school- related factors. While children's engagement in paid or unpaid work, sibling care etc. reduces their chance of attending school fully and perform better in classroom, the quality of services provided in the schools, the infrastructure and the level of teacher's qualification and training may also act as determining factors for these. Many researches have also indicated that effective systemic management as well as internal management of schools can improve the quality of educational services that, in turn, influences the access and participation of children particularly girls (Govinda and Bandyopadhyay, 2011c, Bandyopadhyay and Dey, 2011 Dayaram, 2011, Dayaram, 2013).

One of the major reasons for unequal access, participation and uneven learning outcome is the diversification of Service Delivery of Education. One can see that Disadvantageness of an area and poor provision is linked with each other. This linkage is found putting children at further risk of exclusion in varied manner. Poor condition of schools with untrained and low qualified teachers makes quality education out of reach for many children. During the study, in addition to the variation between government and private school, considerable variation is also found even among different government schools. Apart from alternative schools, Education Guarantee Schools, NFE centres (which are not allowed now after RTE Act, 2009), many government schools located in the study area were found in dilapidated condition and being run by single or two teachers without any school Head. Following Table shows the skewed distribution of qualified teachers which determines the teaching learning process in school to a great extent.

Table 9: Availability of Qualified Male and Female Teachers

Types of School	*Qualification of Male Teachers*						*Qualification of Female Teachers*				
	X	*XII*	*Graduation*	*PG*	*Others*	*Total (n=100)*	*XII*	*Graduation*	*PG*	*Others*	*Total (n=100)*
Govt & EGS	7	2	14	26	1	61	44	36	66	0	153
Per cent	11	3	23	43	2	100	29	24	43	0	100
Private	0	1	10	4	0	26	10	9	16	1	36
Per cent	0	4	38	15	0	100	28	25	44	3	100
Total	7	3	24	30	1	87	54	45	82	1	189
Per cent	4	3	28	34	1	100	29	24	43	1	100

Source: Teachers' Profile, 2008.

The majority of schools (90 per cent) in Rajnandgaon have some trained teachers whereas in Dindori only 41 per cent of schools have some trained teachers. However, even in Rajnandgaon there are a few schools where there is no trained teacher. According to the data, there are 21 schools (70 per cent) of Rajnandgaon, 28 schools (80 per cent) in Rewa and only 3 schools (13 per cent) in Dindori where all teachers could be trained. Apart from training, "poor subject mastery of teachers is a major concern, with large proportions of even very well qualified teachers reporting difficulty teaching any subject. The frequency with which difficulties were reported was twice as high amongst Grade 10 qualified teachers (40 per cent) as amongst those with under graduate and postgraduate qualifications (20 per cent). Some teachers reported that they didn't feel competent to teach the subject that they were assigned to teach, although this proportion decreased with higher levels of qualification" (Bandyopadhyay, Umabati and Zeitlyn, 2011, 3). Many had problems with multi-grade teaching, although this is a common phenomenon in most of the schools. Very few teachers meet parents to inform them about their child's poor performance. It has also been found that, the higher the level of the teacher's qualification, the less likely that they are to meet the parents but more likely they provide extra time to weaker students.

This type of skewed distribution of schooling facilities particularly teachers seem to perpetuate disadvantage and inequality as it works against the participation and progression of girls, children from SCs, STs and other minorities, first generation learners and the poor. One has to understand that school is the only source of their education and they have no other resource and home support in case school fails to provide quality education to them. Since majority of poor girls attend government schools, more efforts are to be made to make these schools well functional and equipped with physical and academic resources including qualified and trained female teachers. It is required to look into these aspects with reference to RTE Act, 2009.

It has been discussed earlier that, the incidence of student absenteeism was rampant in the sample 36 villages covered under CREATE study. In addition to long absenteeism and sporadic attendance, around 22 per cent children in Rajnandgaon cluster, 35 per cent students in Rewa cluster and 47 per cent in Dindori cluster were found absent on the day of visiting 88 sample schools located in these 36 villages. The household data reveals that, most commonly cited reason for absenteeism was ill- health and sickness of children. Higher household income and higher parental education are positively related with children's attendance in school. The study further discusses the vicious cycle of absenteeism and repetition. Often, despite attending regularly, children do not learn at the optimum level due to loss of effective teaching time. Persistence of gender and caste- based discrimination inside and outside the classrooms has been manifested in teachers' attitude with regard to classroom management, seating arrangement and mid-day meal distribution. Gender and caste - based stereotyping was also visible in the allocation of different tasks to children in schools. It is known to all that, eventually these children who face discrimination are pushed out of the school system because of such discriminating attitude of teachers and unequal treatment they get in school because of their gender and social background. It is required to define good schools not only based on good facilities and learning outcomes but also how children are being treated to promote effective

Table 10: Performance of Students As Rated by Teachers

Performance of child		*Rajnandgaon*			*Rewa*			*Dindori*		
		Male	*Female*	*Total*	*Male*	*Female*	*Total*	*Male*	*Female*	*Total*
Very good	Number	290	252	542	242	159	401	18	26	44
	Per cent	13	11	12	16	10	13	2	3	3
Good	Number	776	762	1538	540	510	1050	170	142	312
	Per cent	34	34	34	35	33	34	19	18	18
Average	Number	926	921	1847	526	602	1128	369	327	696
	Per cent	40	41	41	34	40	37	41	41	41
Below average	Number	261	268	529	156	179	335	256	216	472
	Per cent	11	12	12	10	12	11	29	27	28
Very poor	Number	57	28	85	63	74	137	81	86	167
	Per cent	2	1	2	4	5	4	9	11	10
Total (N=100)	**Number**	**2310**	**2231**	**4541**	**1527**	**1524**	**3051**	**894**	**797**	**1691**

Source: HH Survey, 2008.

participation of children in school. Another major in-school factors that determine silent as well as primary exclusion is teachers' perception about the performance of their students which has been highlighted in the following Table.

A clear gender difference in investment on education is also visible through CREATE study which seem to be determining factor for their learning outcome and continuation of study. For example, more boys than girls are found availing private tuition particularly in Rewa. Typically, a higher proportion of boys than girls are availing private tuition and paying higher tuition fees, indicating parental preference for education of sons. In Rewa and Rajnandgaon both clusters some parents have also spent money for purchasing books but proportion of boys is higher than girls with this respect. The difference is quiet visible in case of Rewa cluster and higher amount is spent for purchasing books for boys than girls.

All these above mentioned reasons possibly exclude girls more than boys. Discriminating nature of parents, teachers and community, poor quality of schools and teachers, insensitivity of peer group, low investment on education all are responsible for educational deprivation and exclusion of some children particularly girls which has been revealed by many studies including CREATE.

Section V: Profile of Excluded Children: Who Goes to School and Who Does Not?

A study of meaningful access to and participation of children in elementary education has to include an understanding of the various contextual and background factors that interact to influence the participation of the children in school. The previous section has already presented the picture of exclusion from education in the different Zones which characterize the nature and magnitude of exclusion from primary and upper primary classes in the study area. These excluded children include those who are deprived of schooling in some or other ways due to different factors like ill-health, poor nutritional status; poverty, child labour; children of illiterate parents: first generation learners; children from SC and ST communities; disadvantaged girls; children in difficult circumstances; and children with disabilities.

An analysis of the social composition of household members indicates that, Dindori cluster is predominantly tribal area with 87 per cent of total population is of tribal origin. Other two clusters are dominated by OBC population though the proportion of OBC in Rajnandgaon exceeds 80 per cent while in Rewa it is only around 44 per cent. Rewa is also having higher proportion of general category and scheduled caste both as compared to other two clusters. Half of the households in all the three clusters mainly depend on manual labour as main source of income. A large proportion is also engaged in farm activities and belongs to lower income group. Further, it is also evident that the number of people below BPL is more in Dindori whereas it is comparatively less in Rewa and Rajnandgaon. Dindori has 66 per cent Household belonging to BPL card holders followed by Rajnandgaon (47 per cent) and Rewa (24 per cent). Parental occupation and education in general have an immense impact on children's education. Majority of parents in these clusters are typically engaged in agriculture or wage labour. It is also heartening to note that there has been increasing willingness among all parents including illiterates to educate their children and that has resulted in increase in number of first generation learners in schools particularly those are run by the government.

The data reveals that, during last few decades there has been a steady increase in male and female literacy rates in these three clusters. However, there has considerable variation in literacy rates among these three clusters under study. While Rajnadgaon cluster which is a developed agricultural area has 71 per cent literates followed by Rewa, less developed locality where the literacy rate is slightly less i.e. 66 per cent. The literacy rate is much lower in Dindori cluster as compared to other two clusters which is around 37.02 per cent. Further, the status of literacy of women is much lower as compared to their male counterparts across the three clusters. It has not even reached 30 per cent in Dindori. The situation is not encouraging in Rajnandgaon also where more than half of the women were found illiterate in 2008. There is around 16 per cent gender gap in the literacy rate in all three clusters (Figure 4).

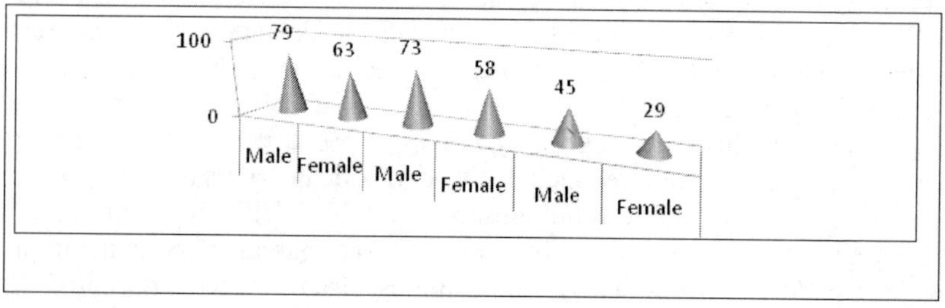

Source: HH Survey, 2008.

Figure 5: Status of Literacy

In light of the above analysis, one can assume that, majority of children are first generation learners and belong to low income group. Although most of the eligible age group children have already entered schools, a small section is still left behind. Perhaps they are the hardest to reach group in these localities. It has been found (Bandyopadhyay, 2012 a) that, out of 148 drop out boys, 48 per cent have illiterate fathers and 69 per cent have illiterate mothers. These per centages have shown considerable increase in case of drop out girls. More than half (51 per cent) of the drop out girls have illiterate father but around

80 per cent dropout girls have illiterate mothers. Similarly proportion of never-enrolled children with illiterate mothers is also very high and it is 72 per cent in case of never-enrolled girls. Barring a few, most children with educated parents were attending schools. Again children of illiterate parents remained frequently absent from schools and also repeated their grades (Bandyopadhyay, Das and Zeitlyn, 2011). Access of children to schools and their participation have its close association with occupation of parents, main source and amount of household income as well as expenditure.

The aspiration level of parents also differs for girls and boys and it varies also from one cluster to another (Bandyopadhyay, 2012a, 2013). It was found that girls mostly are not expected to be highly educated whereas parents aspire for higher education beyond school for their sons particularly in Rajnandgaon. The data show that, parents of 63 per cent boys in the advanced cluster of Rajnandgaon wanted their children to continue education beyond school level, the proportion of such parents is only 40 per cent in case of girls. It may be because of limited opportunities available for education after primary education in this cluster. The situation is more prominent in case of Rewa with considerable number of people from general caste and OBC. The proportion of SC is relatively higher than other clusters under study. In Dindori, parental aspiration has been low both for boys and girls but most parents wanted their sons and daughters both should complete at least primary education. This skewed pattern of expectation of parents might have an impact on the schooling status of the children which needs further investigation. The parental aspiration and education may also impact on their decision regarding household investment on children's education which is discussed subsequently. In addition to education and high aspiration level, parental economic status and occupation also have an impact on their decision regarding access of children to education as well as investment for this purpose. In an earlier paper (Bandyopadhyay, 2012b), an attempt has also been made to see the extent to which the social background contributes to the process of children's access to schooling opportunities. For example, children from SC /ST categories mostly attend government schools while children from general category constitute majority in private schools particularly in Rewa cluster. Being OBC dominated region Rajnandgaon and Rewa both have significant proportion of OBC children attending private schools (Bandyopadhyay, 2012b). There has been considerable gender gap in access to private schools particularly in the cluster of Rewa district. Thus, majority of girls are attending government schools available near to their residence irrespective of the quality of schools. This has considerable impact on their level of school participation and learning as discussed above.

Section VI: Conclusion

The preceding analysis establishes the fact that despite enormous expansion of the system at the national level in recent years and enrolling majority of children of 6-14 years age group, a large proportion drop out without completing the compulsory education period of 8 years. The deeper insight into the present situation through the field study reveals that even while there has been a perceptible improvement in access, infrastructure and enrolment, still a large section of children are already excluded or at the risk of silent exclusion posing severe challenge before initiatives taken for UEE.

The above analysis indicates that the gender and social background of learners play an important role in this process of exclusion as well as silent exclusion. It has been found although girls are increasingly gaining physical access to schools particularly those run by Government, they become educationally disadvantaged in case these schools are not gender friendly and devoid of basic facilities compromising with quality of services. It is because of this, many children particularly girls are found lagging behind boys with serious learning deficit as it is found in the backward and remote cluster of tribal dominated Dindori district. The socially disadvantaged children particularly girls remain educationally disadvantaged as compared to other children in advanced areas as well. For achieving Universalisation of Elementary Education and also for overcoming all kinds of exclusion in school education, these children need immediate attention of policy makers and service providers at the local as well as higher levels.

It has been observed that, differentiation in educational facilities has perpetuated inequality to such extent that instead of bridging gender and social gaps it is widening these gaps rapidly. Thus one can see that, despite policies aim at bridging disparities and achieving greater social equity, schooling facilities seem to be reproducing the hierarchies and inequalities that exist in the society, if not aggravating. This is indeed accelerating the process of exclusion putting children one or another Zone of exclusion as described above, though demand for education has increased tremendously even among poor, illiterate and disadvantaged groups. The need of the hour is to respond to this demand through effective strategies at the school level and by moving the focus from input provisions to learner entitlements to deal with the situation of silent exclusion. One has to understand that eventually the silent exclusion of any child leads to his or her permanent exclusion which is evident by increasing dropout of children even at the early grade of schooling. Under these circumstances, overcoming exclusion is indeed a serious challenge before a country like India with a large proportion of young people and provisioning of quality education is most essential to meet this challenge. It has already been discussed earlier that how quality and equity are intrinsically related to each other. In view of this it is understandable that, more serious efforts are to be made to promote gender and social equity both preventing the children from falling into different Zones of exclusion as mentioned by CREATE study (Lewin, 2007; 2011).

References

Bandyopadhyay, M. (2013). Gender equity in educational access in India. *Southern African Review of Education (SARE)*, Volume 18, Number 2: 9-24.

Bandyopadhyay, M. (2012a). Gender and School Participation Evidences from Empirical Research in Madhya Pradesh and Chhattisgarh. Occasional Paper, NUEPA and also published at CREATE website http://www.create-pc.org/pdf_documents/Gender%20and%20school%20participation.pdf

Bandyopadhyay, M. (2012b). Social disparity in elementary education. *Seminar*, October, pp. 21–25.

Bandyopadhyay, M. and Subrahmanian, R., (2011) Gender Equity in Education: A Review of Trends and Factors. *Who Goes to School? Exploring Exclusion in Indian Education*. New Delhi: Oxford University Press, p 123-165.

Bandyopadhyay, M. & Dey, M. (2011). *Effective School Management Committees*, CREATE India Policy Brief No. 4, NUEPA, New Delhi.

Bandyopadhyay, M., Das, D. & Zeitlyn, B. (2011). *Absenteeism, Repetition and Silent Exclusion in India,* CREATE India Policy Brief No. 3, NUEPA, New Delhi.

Bandyopadhyay, M., Umabati, S., and Zeitlyn, B., (2011) Teachers and Teaching in India, CREATE India Policy Brief No. 5, Delhi, NUEPA

Bandyopadhyay, M. & Dey, M. (2010). *Hierarchy in Access to Elementary School in Rajasthan and Haryana: A Report*, NUEPA, New Delhi (Mimeo).

Dayaram (2011). School Management Commitee and the Right to Education Act 2009 Resource Material for SMC Training. *America India Foundation*, New Delhi.

Dayaram (2013). School Development Plan Under RTE Act 2009: School Mapping and Micro-planning - Participatory Tool for School Development Plan. *America India Foundation*, New Delhi.

De Haan, Arjan. (1997). Poverty and Social Exclusion: A Comparison of Debates on Deprivation. Working Paper No. 2, Poverty Research Unit at Sussex. Brighton: University of Sussex

GOI (1986). *National Policy on Education: 1986*, Ministry of Human Resource Development, Department of Education, New Delhi.

GOI (1992). *Programme of Action: 1992*, Ministry of Human Resource Development, Department of Education, New Delhi.

GOI (2006). Report No. 516(61/10/2) *Employment and Unemployment Situation Among Social Groups in India,* NSS 61st Round (July 2004 – June 2005).

GOI (2010). *NSS Report 64th Round—Education in India, Participation and Expenditure*, Ministry of Statistics & Programme Implementation, New Delhi

GOI (2013). *NSS 66*th *Round Report (543), Employment and Unemployment Situation among Social Groups in India, 2009–2010.*

Govinda, R. (2008). Literacy and Elementary Education in India: Regional Imbalances and Social Inequities. In: Prakash, V. & Biswal, K. (ed) Perspectives on Education and Development. Revisiting Education Commission and After. pp.157-201. New Delhi:Shipra/NUEPA.

Govinda, R. & Bandyopadhyay, M. (2008). Access to Elementary Education in India, Country Analytical Review, CREATE, Delhi / Brighton: NUEPA / University of Sussex, UK.

Govinda, R. & Bandyopadhyay, M. (2010). Educational Access in Madhya Pradesh and Chhattisgarh, Country Research Summary. CREATE, Delhi / Brighton: NUEPA / University of Sussex, UK

Govinda, R., & Bandyopadhyay, M., (2010). Social exclusion and school participation in India: Expanding access with equity, *Prospects*, Vol. 40, No. 3, *Universal primary education in South Asia: A right that remains elusive* edited by R. Govinda and Manzoor Ahmed.

Govinda, R. & Bandyopadhyay, M. (2011a). Access to Elementary Education: Analytical Overview. In Govinda, R (ed.). *Who Goes to School? Exploring Exclusion in Indian Education*. New Delhi: Oxford University Press, 1–86.

Govinda, R. & Bandyopadhyay, M. (2011b). *Overcoming Exclusion Through Quality Schooling*. CREATE, University of Sussex, U.K. Available at www.create-rpc.org [accessed 6 June 2013].

Govinda, R. & Bandyopadhyay, M. (2011c). Changing Framework of Local governance and Community Participation in Elementary Education in India in Govinda, R (ed.). *Who Goes to School? Exploring Exclusion in Indian Education*. New Delhi: Oxford University Press, P: 248-285

Jennie. Popay, Etheline Enoch, Heidi Johnston & Laetitia Rispel (2006). *Social Exclusion Knowledge Network (SEKN) Scoping of SEKN and proposed approach* http://www.who.int/social_determinants/resources/sekn_scoping. pdf)

Lewin, K. M., (2007a) Improving Access, Equity and Transitions in Education: Creating a Research Agenda. CREATE Pathways to Access Research Monograph No. 1. Brighton: University of Sussex

Little, A. (2008): EFA Politics, policies and Progress, CREATE, Research Monograph, 13, Path ways to Access, www.create-rpc.org

NUEPA (2014). *Elementary Education in India: Progress Towards UEE*, Flash Statistics, DISE, 2013-14, Provisional; NUEPA, New Delhi.

Thorat S. K. (2003), *Caste, Ethnicity, and Religion: An Overview Paper on Exclusion/ Discrimination and Deprivation*" Concept Paper for DFID, Delhi. May, 2003.

Tilak, J. B. G. (2000). Why Do Some Children Never Go to School in Rural India? *Kurukshetra*. October. Annual Issue, 49(1): pp. 55-59.

Sayad, A. (2004). *The Suffering of the Immigrant*, Cambridge, UK: Polity Press

Sen, A. (1999). *Development as freedom.* New Delhi: Oxford University Press.

SRI-IMRB (2014). *National Sample Survey of Estimation of Out of School Children of Age 6-13 in India*, GOI, New Delhi, September 11, 2014. http:// www.educationforallindia.com/ssa

Subrahmanian, R. (2004). Introduction: Exploring processes of marginalisation and inclusion in education. IDS Bulletin, 34(1), 81-89.

Ziyauddin, K.M. and Kasi, E. (2009) *Dimensions of Social Exclusion: Ethnographic Explorations,* Cambridge Scholars Publishing, UK

7

HETEROGENEOUS GENDERED REALITIES AND MULTIPLE DISADVANTAGES ISSUES THAT FRAME WOMEN AND GIRLS EDUCATION IN INDIA

— *VIMALA RAMACHANDRAN*[1]

Introduction

Progress on the gender equality and education front has been carried out periodically in the last two decades, especially since the run up to the Jomtien meeting in 1990 and subsequent national and international events that compel attention on the march towards gender equality. This assessment once again provides an opportunity to introspect and focus on the good news and the not so good news emanating from the ground.

Education for All (EFA) assessment done in the years 2000[2] and 2003[3] started with appreciating the enormous progress made in access. While this was important and is indeed a heartening trend, the big question that is worrying administrators and the larger education community is the persistence of high drop out rates, low transition from primary to upper primary and high school.

1. This phrase "heterogeneous gendered realities and multiple disadvantages" has been taken from the NCERT report 3.2 – National Curriculum Framework 2005, Position Paper on Gender Issues in Education, New Delhi 2005. This paper is a combination of the EFA Mid-decade assessment commissioned by NUEPA in 2007 and Gendered Inequality in Education published in Devaki Jain and C P Sujaya (Ed), Indian Women Revisited. Publications Division, Ministry of Information and broadcasting, Government of India, New Delhi 2014.

Poor learning outcomes have now been brought on the front burner and have been acknowledged as the biggest challenge facing Indian school education.

It is now well established that gender equality in education and enhancing the access of girls to basic education is influenced by three inter-locking sets of issues – systemic; content and process of education and economy, society and culture (as captured in the following grid). This issue need not be reiterated now as this approach has now become an integral part of mainstream analysis.

There is almost unanimous acceptance of the fact that gender – as a category – needs to be seen within the larger social, regional and location context. India is a land of rich diversity and it is also a country of sharp disparities. The interplay of socio-economic inequalities and gender relations creates a complex web that either promotes or impedes girls' ability to go through schooling[4]. While economic disparities and social inequalities are certainly important, a number of researchers argue that cultural beliefs and practices and regional characteristics play an important role (Colclough et al, 2000[5]). As Shireen Jeejibhoy and Zeba Sathar point out "the cultures of South Asia are largely gender stratified, characterised by patrilineal descent, patrilocal residence, inheritance and succession practices that exclude women, and hierarchical relations in which the patriarch or his relatives have authority over family members. Levels and patterns of female autonomy vary considerably within the region… region plays the major conditioning role…"[6] The social and educational status of Muslim girls in Kerala and Tamil Nadu is appreciably better than that of the majority community in Rajasthan or Eastern Uttar Pradesh. Similarly, the social relationships and status of Dalit students vary with region / state and even within districts. The position of women in different communities and their access to education also differs as we move from region to region, social group to social group and between urban and rural areas.

In India it is therefore important to understand the intermeshing of poverty, social inequalities and gender relations. The three intersect in different ways in different regions of the country – with one reinforcing the other in some and offsetting one in others. Understanding and unravelling this is the biggest challenge today[7]. In this context there is a need to acknowledge the following:

- Rural-urban differences in enrolment, attendance and completion are greater than male-female differences;
- Backward–forward areas/regional differences are greater than gender and social group differences;
- Disparities between very poor households (below poverty line) and the top quartile is much higher than gender, social and regional differences;
- Differences between social groups – especially between tribal communities, Muslims and specific sub-groups among the SC on the

one hand and the forward castes / Christians and other religions is high.

- Inter-community differences are often as severe as intra-community differences. For example the literacy status of some tribes is better than others and some Dalit groups better than others.

In the early years after Jomtien (1990) most of the analysis on gender gap in education started with mapping the provision of schooling (access / supply) and the "demand" – meaning readiness of families to send their children, especially girls to school. However, with the march of years there was a realisation that one cannot separate supply and demand for education – where ever there are schools within access and where ever these schools were regular and functioning well – demand increased (Rekha Wazir, 2000)[8]. Conversely, where schools were dysfunctional / indifferent, where not much teaching was happening and where communities did not have confidence in the school as a safe place for their daughters, demand fell sharply. There was recognition that the availability of well functioning schools is indeed an important variable that influences household decisions (Ramachandran et al, (Snakes and Ladders) 2004, Subramanian, 2002, PROBE 1999[9]). Research on what happens inside the school and the push out factors highlighted by the attitudes and practices of teachers and of children from relatively forward social groups affects the readiness of children from socially disadvantaged social groups remaining in school (Robert Jenkins, 2005, Geetha Nambissan 1996, 2000 and 2001, Vimala Ramachandran and Taramoni Naorem 2013[10]) Experience of NGOs like MV Foundation highlighted the push out factors and over the years there is a recognition of the need to interrogate classroom practices, teacher / administrator attitudes and prejudices and the curriculum that may reinforce social biases / discriminatory practices and gender stereotypes. (NCF Position Paper 3.2, NCERT 2005, Vimala Ramachandran, 2004)

Twenty-four years after Jomtien it is now recognised that the prevailing gender gap in educational achievement remains quite significant – as evident from the tables below.

Table 1: Graded Inequities in Literacy rates

	Census 2001	*Census 2011*
Rural Female ST	32.4	46.9
Rural Female SC	37.6	52.6
All Rural Female	46.13	57.9
Rural Female Non SC/ST	50.2	61.1
Rural Male ST	57.4	66.8
Urban Female SC	57.5	68.6
Urban Female ST	59.9	70.3
Rural Male SC	53.7	72.6

(Contd...)

All Rural Male	70.7	77.1
All Urban Female	72.86	79.1
Rural Male Non SC/ST	74.3	79.9
Urban Female Non SC/ST	75.5	81.0
Urban Male ST	77.8	83.2
Urban Male SC	77.9	83.3
All Urban Male	86.27	88.8
Urban Male Non SC/ST	87.6	89.7

Source: Adapted by Vimala Ramachandran from Marie Lall and S Srinivasa Rao 2011[11]

Table 2: Graded inequality in drop out rates, 2010-11

Primary classes 1 to 5		***Elementary classes 1 to 8***		***Secondary classes 1 to 10***	
ST Boys	37.2	ST Girls	55.4	ST Girls	71.3
ST Girls	33.9	ST Boys	54.7	ST Boys	70.6
SC Boys	29.8	SC Boys	46.7	SC Boys	57.4
All boys	28.7	All Girls	41	SC Girls	54.1
All Girls	25.1	All Boys	40.3	All boys	50.4
SC Girls	23.1	SC Girls	39	All Girls	47.9

Source: SES, GOI 2012.

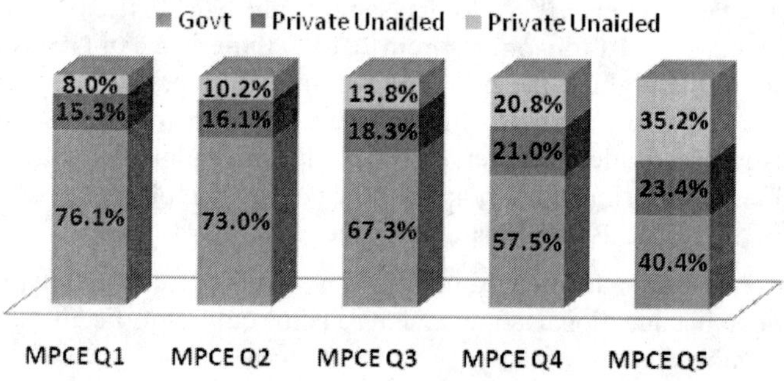

Source: NSS 64th round, 2008-09

Fig. 1: Types of schools attended by secondary stage students as per MPCE quintiles

NSSO data throws some light on who studies up to what level and who goes to what kind of school. If we are to take the poorest quintile of the population, 76.1 per cent of children go to government schools and only 9 per cent go to private unaided schools. However, as we go to the richest quintile, only 40.4 per cent go to government schools and 35.2 per cent to private unaided schools. The distribution of boys and girls within each quintile would be different. Therefore, analysing educational access on the basis of data that is only disaggregated by gender does not make much sense in India because girls and women all over the country do not face same challenges or same barriers.

Till early 1990s most of the analysis on gender gap in education started with mapping the provision of schooling (access / supply) and the "demand" – meaning readiness of families to send their children, especially girls to school. However, over the years there was a realisation that one cannot separate supply and demand for education, where ever there are schools within access and where ever these schools were regular and functioning well, their demand increased (Wazir, 2000). Conversely, where schools were dysfunctional / indifferent, where not much teaching was happening and where communities did not have confidence in the school as a safe place for their daughters, demand fell sharply. There was recognition that the availability of well functioning schools is indeed an important variable that influences household decisions (PROBE 1999; PROBE Revisited 2011, Subramanian, 2002; Ramachandran et al, 200412). Research on what happens inside a school and push out factors highlighted by the attitudes and practices of teachers and of children from relatively forward social groups affects the readiness of children from socially disadvantaged social groups remaining in school (Nambissan 1996, 2000 and 2001; Ramachandran and Naorem 201213) There is a recognition of the need to interrogate classroom practices, teacher/administrator attitudes and prejudices and curriculum that may reinforce social biases/discriminatory practices and gender stereotypes. (NCF Position Paper 3.2, NCERT 2005; Ramachandran, 2004, 2012) It is now recognised that the prevailing gender gap in educational achievement is more than just a combined effect of both supply and demand factors and one cannot ignore children's experience of schooling, the role of the teacher and the overall school environment.

So where do we stand today?

Technically, almost 98 per cent of children up to 11 years of age have access to schools near their home, within 1 km walking distance. But the grand access story ends there. When it comes to upper primary school, high school and later on post-secondary education and training in colleges, technical institutions, vocational institutions and the more we move away from main roads and rural hubs, access goes down significantly. Even if all children who enter primary school were to demand to enrol in high school, there are just not enough schools to accommodate them. The hard reality in India is that close to 50 per cent of children who enrol in class 1 drop out before they reach class 10 and the worst statistics is of ST girls with 71 per cent of them dropping out before they reach class 10. The gender gap widens as we move from primary to secondary and higher (as evident in the graph given below). Therefore, enrolment statistics of India needs to be tempered with data on attendance, drop out rates, learning outcomes and transition from one level to the next.

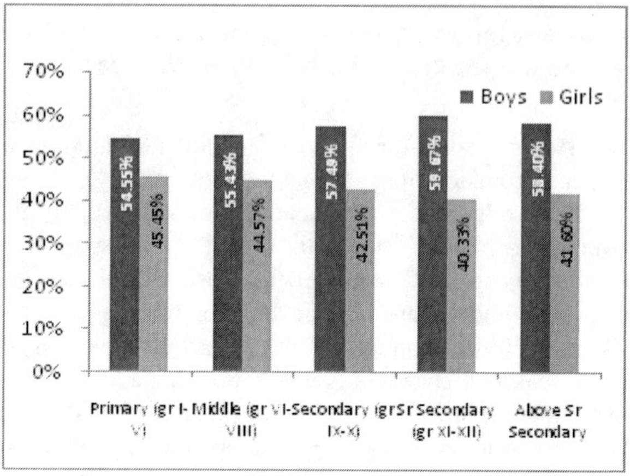

Source: Deepa Sankar, 2011.

Fig. 2: Shares of boys and girls in total students attending: NSS 64th round (2007-08)

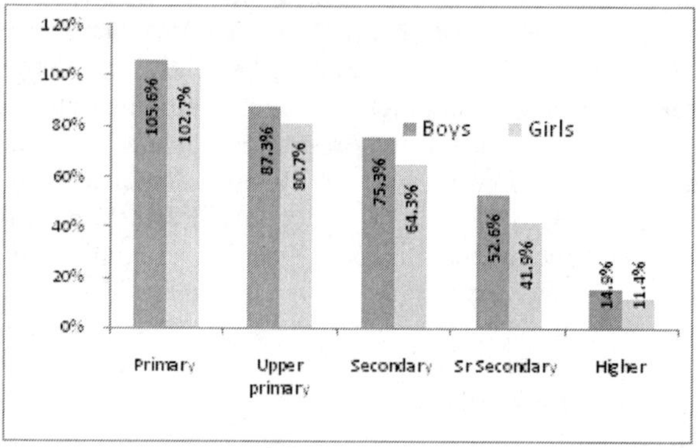

Source: Deepa Sankar, 2011.

Fig. 3: GAR among boys and girls estimated using NSS 64th round 2007-08: All India

Equally, data on enrolment gives us a limited understanding of children's participation in schooling. One reason is that enrolment figures are collected by the school system and many researchers argue that the data collected does not always reflects a true picture. Sample survey data, especially the National Sample Survey has recorded some progress, as evident in the tables below. However, male female gap in current attendance in all communities is significant. Equally, the gap between "others" (meaning forward communities) and that of SC, SC and OBC is quite significant and this gap is far more pronounced in rural areas.

Table 2: Current attendance rates in educational institutions per 1000 persons on different age groups and social groups NSS 55th (1999-2000) and 61st (2004-05) rounds

Social Group	*55th Round 1999-2000*						*61st Round 2004-05*					
	5 to 14 years						*5 to 14 years*					
	R (M)	*R (F)*	*U (M)*	*U (F)*	*R All*	*U All*	*R (M)*	*R (F)*	*U (M)*	*U (F)*	*R All*	*U All*
ST	632	527	809	740	582	776	767	678	871	850	726	865
SC	701	586	792	739	647	766	809	737	850	793	775	822
OBC	743	621	824	786	687	806	843	763	881	878	805	880
Others	802	738	880	854	771	868	876	842	915	914	860	914
All	739	638	845	808	692	827	835	767	890	879	491	885

Note: R: Rural, U: Urban.

Source: NSSO 55th Round and 61st Round.

The Age Specific Attendance Ratios (ASAR) given in the 64th Round (NSSO, 2008) for different age groups and in rural and urban areas tell a slightly nuanced story. According to this report, in 6-10 years group only 88 per cent children are reported attending school (rural 82 per cent and urban 90 per cent) and this comes down marginally to 86 per cent (85 per cent rural and 89 per cent urban) for children of 11-13 years. It is interesting to note that the "overall age-specific attendance ratio drops steadily from 88 per cent in age-group 6-10 to 86 per cent at age 11-13, to 64 per cent for age 14-17, 18 per cent for the age-group 18-24, and finally to only 1 per cent for age 25-29 (Statement 4.4). Rural-urban differences are more pronounced than male-female differences, especially in the higher age group" (NSSO 64th Round, Report No 532, p. 44).

Table 3: Net Attendance Ratio, comparing NSSO 52 and 64 Rounds

Class Group	*Rural*			*Urban*			*Rural + Urban*		
	Female	*Male*	*Total*	*Female*	*Male*	*Total*	*Female*	*Male*	*Total*
NSSO 52nd Round 1995-96									
Class I to V	56	68	63	77	80	78	61	71	66
Class VI to VIII	32	44	39	57	60	58	38	48	43
Class IX and X	17	26	22	40	41	40	23	30	26
Class XI and XII	8	13	11	28	25	26	14	16	15
NSSO 64th Round, 2007-08									
Class I to V	83	86	84	84	86	85	83	96	84
Class VI to VIII	54	59	57	64	67	65	56	61	59
Class IX and X	35	40	38	51	52	51	39	43	41
Class XI and XII	19	25	23	39	40	40	25	29	27

Source: Report 532, Page 45, NSSO 64th Round.

Furthermore, when we look at Net Attendance Ratio (ratio of the number of persons in the official age group attending a particular class-group to the total number of persons in the age group) the enrolment story is punctured again. While there has been significant improvement in the last decade or so, there is still a significant gap between enrolment and attendance figures.

The story gets more complex when we move beyond male-female and rural-urban categories. India is a country with huge diversity and massive inequalities. All-India (National) data makes little sense and so does overall age-group information. The schooling experience is determined by a number of inter-related factors, namely:

- Location – rural/urban, remote/desert/mountainous, international borders, inter-state borders, conflict areas;
- Identity – caste, religion, specific occupational group within the caste / community (Maha Dalit, Musahar, Valmiki etc.), language spoken at home;
- Economic status – those who live below poverty line or the lowest economic quartile, permanent or seasonal migrants;
- School type - what type or kind of school they are enrolled in such as government (including municipal/local body schools), private aided, private unaided, private unaided and unrecognised;
- Ability / disability – within all of the above, children living with disabilities face huge challenges that may vary across different locations, different castes/communities and between boys and girls.
- Gender – within all of the above gender relations exert a strong influence. It is important to acknowledge that they may be different and affect boys and girls differently.

For many decades, India has been arguing that access to schooling has improved steadily and that the country has turned the corner in basic education. Equally significant is that from 1980 to the end of the eleventh plan (March 2012), government's approach was to focus on access issues and address quality issues later. However, this approach was not only badly thought out but has also proved to a very costly. The effect of separating access from quality can be seen across the country. While enrolment rates have increased and there are many more school today, the harsh reality is that learning levels continue to be a matter of grave concern in India. Education involves developing the ability to read and write with comprehension and understand and apply mathematical concepts appropriate to the grade in which the child is studying. Education also involves developing a positive self-image, display active learning and self-learning ability and be self-confident. However, most assessments of "quality" done by NCERT and non-governmental agencies are limited to assessing grade-appropriate skills in language, mathematics and environmental science at the primary level with science and social science replacing environmental science at the upper primary level.

Furthermore, one important element of schooling is to contribute to the overall development of a child, building her self-esteem and confidence, enabling her to stand with her head held high in the family and in the society. Given the nature of our schools and the attitudes of administrators and teachers, practices of exclusion and humiliation, especially of girls and boys from socially disadvantaged groups and children of extremely poor people, does not always lead to a healthy overall development of a child. A recent study across six states of India, a qualitative study that explore inclusion / exclusion of children in schools, in classrooms and among peers (Ramachandran and Naorem, 2012) threw up disturbing findings. Blatant and subtle forms of discrimination were found in almost all dimensions of the school: (i) how children are seated in class, (ii) whom the teacher focuses her attention on, (iii) whom does she ignore, (iv) who gets to clean the toilets and do menial tasks, (v) who gets to drink water first and who has to wait in line, (vi) who is asked to lead the assembly, (vii) who can perform special duties during school function, (viii) who eats the mid-day-meals etc. This list is endless. Issues such as gender, caste, poverty, appearance, skin colour, overt symptoms of illness or disease, cleanliness, language spoken at home emerged as important markers of equality. A girl child from a poor Dalit or ST family, who is not "properly" dressed, is at the bottom of the pecking order in schools. Attitudes and practices of teachers in the classroom and in the school reflect prevalent social practices. Adolescent boys and girls that we interviewed and worked with said that the situation is much worse today than it was during the time when their parents went to school.

Another deeply disturbing trend is the incidence of sexual harassment and sexual abuse in our schools. Even though newspapers have reported many cases where schoolteachers were accused of raping or sexually molesting their students, there is a lot of resistance from the government to do any systematic research on the prevalence of sexual abuse in schools. During the course of the inclusion / exclusion study we asked girls and boys (separately) in FGD about sexual abuse and violence, both verbal and physical. After a hushed silence, some of them talked about what they had heard or seen. Women teachers also talked about their own experiences. Dalit and Adivasi women teachers had to face the dual burden of caste and gender, which makes them far more vulnerable. These issues are rarely talked about and there is little research-based evidence that we can go by. Similarly, a recent study revealed, "children were physically punished, often quite brutally, mentally tortured, humiliated and even sexually abused in schools. Corporal Punishment is rampant in both low cost private, private elite and government schools, both English and vernacular medium. The difference being that the number of private schools where such cases are reported far outnumber the government schools and the similarity being that majority of these schools, irrespective of type appear to cater to disadvantaged sections of the society" (Nawani, 2013[14]).

Gender and education is not easy to unravel. Given the layers of inequalities and the growing prevalence of caste and community based mobilisation there is a need to go beyond standard indicators of enrolment and transition and go deeper into the schooling experience of children. May be one way to go about it is to develop a framework that could help us locate and position how each dimension of our identity, our schooling experience and social organisation could be juxtaposed to help us gain a deeper understanding of the situation. Women and girls education needs to be situated within this context, as attempted in the grid below.

Tools that are used to measure gender gap / progress towards gender equality in education reveals little about the texture of inequalities inherent in the society and reinforced by the prevailing education system. Coming to grips with gender and social equity issues in education requires a framework that can capture heterogeneous gendered realities and multiple disadvantages. Gender is embedded within a complex social and institutional structure in India. Therefore, it is necessary to look at gender inequalities in education within the broader framework of social, economic and location specific inequalities on the one hand and the prevailing school system on the other. A global study on girls education has summarised these issues: "Already excluded because of their gender, many girls face multiple barriers, making it more difficult for them to enrol in and complete primary school and continue on to secondary school... reaching excluded girls generally means higher costs and alternative policies and strategies because their needs differ from those of majority population…" (Lewis and Lockheed, 2007, p. 19-20)

Feminist scholars and those working on social exclusion have tried to tease out the texture of exclusion by identifying the levels, sources and also the forms of exclusion. While the government has provided schools in most areas, discrimination or non-inclusion takes different forms for people from different social groups / locations.

The grid / table below attempts to capture this complex scenario:

Table: Heterogeneous gendered realities and multiple disadvantages that frame girls and women's ability to access meaningful education

Prevailing school system > ***Socio-economic Factors ∨***		***Physical access***	***Teachers and teaching***	***Learning***	***Monitoring and supervision***	***Accountability***	***Transition to next level***
Poverty	In abject poverty Above poverty line	No access to schools or school not within reach (walking or bus)	Teacher attitude/ prejudice	No support at home, no money for tuition	Does not capture work load of girls / child labour / trafficking	No voice in community / in the school	Poor learning, cannot afford tuition
Location	Rural Urban Tribal	Teacher absent, irregular, take turns. Parents fearful of sending girls to school.	High teacher-pupil ratio leading to low teaching time	School not supervised, Little teaching-learning	No oversight, and school level committees ineffective	Schools not visited by officials, no oversight	Access to next level difficult
Community	Tribal SC Muslim Others	Formal access yes, social distance may prevent children from enrolling	Teacher unfamiliar with tribal language Culture/caste/community/class biases	Social/cultural language barriers	Not a priority	No voice in village or in school	No girls-only high schools
Occupation	Home based Outside, wage labour	Work burden on children	Attitude/ prejudice of teachers	Poor learning, irregular in school Seasonal work, absenteeism	Not factored in as an area to track, monitoring system insensitive	Parents cannot participate in meetings	Children drop out and join parents in work
Migration	Seasonal	Long absence	Teacher indifferent, not equipped to handle children joining mid stream	Irregular in school	Not factored in as an area to track	No voice in community	No hostel facilities/ other alternatives
Displacement	Permanent Periodic	Move to new location	Teacher indifferent	Irregular in school and language can also be a barrier	Not factored in as an area to track	No voice	No hostel facilities/ other alternatives
Conflict	Communal Insurgency Insurgency	Poor access due to insecurity, fear	Teacher attitudes/ prejudice; teacher absent	Low learning due to Fear, insecurity and frequent absence / schools shut	No monitoring	No voice in the administration	Fear of movement

(Contd...)

Violence & abuse	Home School Society	Poor access due to fear, low self image	Corporal punishment, verbal abuse	Low learning due to fear, insecurity	Not part of monitoring protocol	Not accountable to children or parents	Lead to dropping out
Gender relations / attitude	Eldest/ older children	Burden of work, eldest at risk	Teacher attitudes, sexual abuse, harassment. Gender and social stereotypes in textbook and in the classroom	No time to study at home, work burden	No specific monitoring done through data / information disaggregated by gender as well as social group	Gender issues not taken on board	Leading to dropping out
	Girl child	Reaching of menarche					
Disability	Mental	Identification and assessment of requirement	Ignored, not equipped to handle special requirements	No support	No specific monitoring	IED programme not gender sensitive	Drop out
	Physical	Identification and assessment of requirement. No physical access					
Health	HIV, Scabies, visible symptoms	Prejudice in school/ community	Teacher attitudes	No support	Not specifically monitored	Not part of monitoring protocol	Drop out

Given the situation described above, what is the way ahead?

Meaningful access[15]

The number of schools being built has gone up, infrastructure in terms of boundary walls, drinking water facility and number of schools with girls' toilet has improved and to top it all the Right To Education act has made elementary education a fundamental right of every child. The sad reality is that while the RTE act has made education a fundamental right, administrators and teachers have a rather warped understanding of the right – they believe that the act asks them not fail a child, not to hit a child and not let children drop out of school. As a result the spirit behind the RTE is lost in the race to count children in school.

The question is what happens to a child once we surrender her to the formal education system in India. What happens to the child once he or she enters school but no stimulus to learn? What about the increasing number of teachers in the system who are recruited but feel no accountability to student learning? What about those working children – girls and boys – who enrol by rarely attend? The new Child Labour law proposed by the government could exacerbate this phenomenon. What happens to first generation learners from disadvantaged groups who choose to not attend school because they do not have the ability to cope with the system – especially those who cannot afford private tuitions or do not have any support at home? What about those children with special needs who are formally included in school but do not have teachers who are willing to accept them or have the skills to work with them? Are we then truly looking at education for ALL?

While everyone is in agreement that there is a need for more number of schools, improved infrastructure, universal enrolment and better PTR, what we miss is the granularity of the issue of actual teaching and learning happening in the classroom. Meaningful access is providing not just the physical access to participate in the formal education system but more importantly an equitable opportunity for all children to engage with a quality education system. Meaningful access needs to happen at every single step of the education delivery system, right from bringing the child to the school or for that matter taking the school to a child. Right from ensuring that schools are available for all children from any social group to ensuring that once the child reaches the school, it is a safe haven of learning and growth to achieve his or her potential. Meaningful access includes access to teachers, who will provide differentiated support catering to varied learning styles and who will pay special attention to those that need extra nudge to keep pace. And most importantly, meaning full access is to provide a safe, gendered space with room to find and express one's own identity shaped by membership in any social group without the fear of mockery or discrimination.

Meaningful access can reduce dropout rates, ensure transitions to higher levels of education, higher learning levels and most importantly an equal platform for all children to achieve their potential.

Safe and non-discriminatory environment for teachers and students

It is said that a school is a microcosm of the society in which we live. More often than not inter-personal and inter-group dynamics prevalent in the community is also reflected in the school. Teachers, if they are not adequately sensitised and trained, may just transfer behaviour pattern and prejudices to the school. Educational administrators and politicians give this as an excuse for persisting discrimination in schools. This is where we have a lot to learn from countries that have successfully combated this tendency and have insisted that schools and other publicly funded institutions adhere to constitutionally mandated rights and obligations. Taking the right to equality and the right against discrimination enshrined in the Constitution of India, teachers and all educational administrators are duty bound to ensure a non-discriminatory environment in school. Teachers and headmasters do not have the freedom to discriminate on the basis of case, religion, gender, ability or economic status.

Taking the Constitution of India as the guiding spirit, teachers, administrators and community leaders need to be told that any violation of the right to equality and the right against discrimination will invite strict penal action. A non-negotiable code of behaviour needs to be communicated to all those who are involved in school education. This needs to be done in writing and prominently displayed in all schools and educational institutions. Simultaneously, children, especially boys, need to be involved in activities that enable them to understand and appreciate diversity, respect differences and formulate school level norms of behaviour towards other children, and towards girls. Involving children in creating an egalitarian atmosphere could bring moral pressure on teachers, administrators and local leaders not to differentiate or discriminate. (Ramachandran and Naorem, 2013)

As it stands today teacher orientation and training is often limited to administrative requirements and subject knowledge.There is also growing evidence of training fatigue among teachers. Equally, short duration training programmes are not able to do justice to supporting basic subject knowledge and pedagogy issues. Creating alternative forums/platforms where teachers and community leaders can come together to communicate the need to ensure that schools are free of discrimination may well be a worthwhile exercise. Essentially, what is required is that we start looking seriously at discrimination in schools and work at all levels to bring about lasting change on the ground. There are no short cuts and the government and civil society organizations need to take this issue seriously and address it in every context. (Ramachandran and Naorem, 2013 forthcoming)

Curriculum "free" of biases and one that actively encourages critical thinking.

"In my textbooks I learned that only men
are kings and soldiers.
Till I read a book in which famous
queens ruled and fought against enemies.
In my textbooks I learned that only men
Are doctors.
When I went to a doctor I saw that she was a woman.
In my textbook I learned that only men
do farming in my country,
until, on a train journey I saw women
working in the fields.
I have learned that I have a lit to learn by seeing"

(Pooja, Ramya, Anuj, Utkarsh students of class VII, Baroda, quoted in NCF 2005 Focus group on Gender Issues in Education. NCERT, 2005)

Despite over two decades of noise about purging our textbooks of blatant and subtle forms of prejudice and stereotypes, the fact is that textbooks reinforce gendered inequalities and social hierarchies. Traditional notions of what is masculine and feminine and caste specific occupations persist and peep out from illustrations, phrases and examples in out textbooks. Rural urban stereotypes are not only promoted, but urban is given precedence over rural, and non-tribal over the tribal. Most of the examples across subjects are mostly urban centric. Heroes and leaders are invariably men, and caregivers and homemakers are always women. Given this reality NCF 2005 focus group argued that, "education is an integral part of these arrangements that govern children's lives. Thus in orderto achieve substantive and equal citizenship, special curricular and pedagogic strategies have to bedeveloped to empower children, specially girls, to overcome disadvantages *and develop theircapabilities to exercise their rights and choices*. The aim is to achieve a *substantive equality of outcome*, notmerely a formal equality of treatment. In fact, we may even require inequality of treatment, i.e.special treatment for the socially disadvantaged learners, to enable them to achieve equality ofoutcome..." (NCF 2005, Focus on Gender issues in Education)

In order to achieve this goal educators and those who frame the curriculum, write textbooks, train teachers and monitor schools have to adopt a substantive and corrective approach to equality. There is a need to be concerned with not only equality of treatment and equality of outcome. Curriculum and textbooks could be the only vehicle to transmit egalitarian values and respect for diversity and difference and guard against discrimination. Boys need to be taught to respect others, and respect when someone says no.This is essential to combat the culture of sexual harassment (inappropriately called eve-teasing). Equally, the sharp divide between what is masculine and what is feminine needs to be questioned. Such an approach would help educators recognize that gendered differences between girls and boys is not a given and instead it enables them to "examine the assumptions behind it, tries to assess the disadvantageresulting form it, and develops a "different"treatment that **dismantles** *that disadvantage...* Girls are also circumscribed by a genderedsocialisation that differs across caste, tribe andcommunity, and the rural-urban divide; thisresults in the creation of differentiatedaspirations, capacities, and levels of confidence.This approach to equality *addresses such differencesin ways that help learners to overcome disadvantages,value their differentiated capabilities, and develop themto the fullest..."* (NCF 2005, Focus on Gender issues in Education)

Conclusion

May be a lot more can be said and a longer list of issues that frame women and girls participation in education can be presented. In the last fifty years, several commissions and committees have brought out long laundry list of issues and concerns and many strategies have also been listed. Reflecting on why these recommendations and strategies have remained unimplemented, I realized that, we need to first and foremost agree on a few non-negotiable maxims or principles. If they are adhered to, then the chances of other inputs falling into place is far higher. It is with this in mind that I have highlighted only three: meaningful access to education, non-discrimination and fore-grounding gender in the construction of knowledge. If we are able to push for these three, then may be we can start moving towards greater gender equality and social justice.

References

Bhattacharjea, S., Wadhwa, W., & Banerji, R. (2011). Inside Primary Schools: Teaching and Learning in Rural India. New Delhi: Annual Status of Education Report Centre.

De, A., Khera R., Samson, M., and Kumar, A.K.S. (2006). *PROBE Revisited: A Report on Elementary Education in India.* New Delhi: Oxford University Press.

Government of India (2008). *NSSO 64*th *Round*, Report No. 532. New Delhi.

Haan, A. D. (2004). Disparities within India's Poorest regions: Why do the same institutions work differently in different places?, in Equity and Development: *World Development Report 2006 Background Papers*, World Bank, Washington DC, 2004.

Jeejibhoy, S. and Sathar, Z. A. (2001). Women's Autonomy in India and Pakistan: The influence of Religion and Region. *Population and Development Review*, 27(4), 687-712.

Kabeer, N and Subramanian, R (1999) Institutions, Relations and Outcome, Kali for Women, India

Lall, M. and Rao, S. S. (2011). Revisiting the equity debate in India and the UK: Caste, Race and Class Intersections in Education. In Marie Lall and Geetha B

Nambissan: *Education and Social Justice in the era of globalisation: Perspectives from India and the UK* (p. 34). New Delhi: Routledge.

Lewis, M. and Lockheed, M. (2007). *Inexcusable Absence: Why 60 Million Girls Still Aren't in School and What to do about it?* Washington DC: Centre for Global Development.

Nambissan, G. (2009). Children, Social Exclusion and Development. *Working Paper Series, Vol 1, No. 1.* New Delhi: Indian Institute of Dalit Studies.

Nambissan, G. B. (1996 April). Equity in Education? Schooling of Dalit Children in India. *Economic and Political Weekly,* 31(16-19), 1011-1024.

Nambissan, G. B. (2001): 'Social Diversity and Regional Disparities in Schooling: A Study of Rural Rajasthan' in Vaidyanathan, A. and P.R. Gopinathan Nair (ed.) *Elementary Education in Rural India: A Grassroots View.* New Delhi: Sage Publications.

Nawani, Disha. (2013 June). Corporal Punishment in Schools. *Economic and Political Weekly*, Vol. XLVIII, No. 24, 23-26.

NCERT. (2005). *National Curriculum Framework.* Position Paper Number 3.2 on Gender issues in education. New Delhi

Pratham. (2012). *Annual Status of Education Report.* New Delhi

PROBE Team. (1999). *Public Report on Basic Education in India.* New Delhi: Oxford University Press.

Ramachandran, V. (2004). *Gender and Social Equity in Primary Education: Hierarchies of Access* (Ed.). New Delhi: SAGE.

Ramachandran, V. and Naroem, T. (2013). *Inclusion and exclusion of students in schools and classrooms in primary and upper primary schools of India – a synthesis of a six state study* (Forthcoming). Government of India, Technical Support Group of Sarva Shiksha Abhiyan (Education for All).

Ramachandran, Vimala and Taramani Naorem. November 2013. What it means to be a Dalit or Tribal child in our schools: A synthesis of Six-State Qualitative Study. Economic and Political Weekly. Vol XLVIII No 44, November 2, 2013

Ramachandran, V., and ERU team (2004). Snakes and Ladders: Factors Influencing Successful Primary School Completion for Children in Poverty Contexts. *South Asian Human Development Sector Report No. 6*, World Bank, New Delhi.

Sankar, D. (2008). What is the progress in elementary education participation in India during the last two decades? An analysis using NSS education rounds. *South Asia Sector for Human Development*, World Bank.

Sankar, D. (2011). Participation in India: An analysis of NSS 64th round data. *South Asia: Human Development Unit*, Report No. 33.

Sankar, D. (n.d.). *Education system performance among Indian states: A public expenditure efficiency analysis using Linear Programming Methods.* SASHD.

Subramaniam, R. (2002). *Gender and Education: A Review of Issues for Social Policy.* UNRISD, Geneva.

Wazir, R. (2002). *Gender Gap inBasic Education* (Ed). New Delhi: Sage Publication.

Notes

1. Vimala Ramachandran: Education and the Status of Women – Year 2000, in Dr R Govinda, India Education Report, Oxford University Press, New Delhi 2002
2. Vimala Ramachandran: Gender equality and education in India, Progress in the last decade, EFA Global Monitoring Report, UNESCO Paris, 2004 (2004/ED/EFA/MRT/PI/59)
3. "There are well-known substantial differences in well-being across social groups in India… Average per capita income of SC/ST at all-India level is about one-third lower than among other groups. Headcount poverty among other (non-deprived groups in 1999/2000) was 16%, 30% for minorities (Muslims), 36% for SC and 44% for ST… Deprived groups also have lower literacy than other groups… Ranking on neonatal, post-natal, infant, child and under-5 mortality indicators for socially-excluded groups are similar to those of other indicators (e.g. IMR for SC and ST are about 84 and 62 for non-deprived groups). Arjan D Haan: Disparities within India's Poorest regions: Why do the same institutions work differently in different places?, in Equity and Development: World Development Report 2006 Background Papers, World Bank, Washington DC, 2004.
4. C Colclough, P Rose and M Tembon: Gender inequalities in primary schooling: The roles of poverty and adverse cultural practices: International Journal of Educational Development, Vol. 20, 2000, pp5-27
5. Jeejibhoy, Shireen and Zeba A Sathar: Women's Autonomy in India and Pakistan: The influence of Religion and Region; Population and Development Review, 27(4): 687-712, 2001
6. Naila Kabeer and Ramya Subramaniam highlighted the "gender intensified disadvantage" wherein "the specific forms of disadvantage faced by girls and not boys that it is also important to acknowledge and that related to roles for girls deriving from gender division of labour, their reproductive cycles and perceptions of risk and vulnerability to sexual violence. These gender-specific forms of disadvantages (Kabeer and Subramaniam, 1999) need to be identified and distinguished from those that are gender intensified in order to facilitate the identification of suitable social policies…" Ramya Subramaniam, UNRISD, 2002
7. Rekha Wazir, 2000
8. Ramya Subramaniam: Gender and Education: A Review of Issues for Social Policy, UNRISD, Geneva, 2002; PROBE, 1999)
9. Nambissan, Geetha B. 1996. Equity in Education? Schooling of Dalit Children in India. *Economic and Political Weekly* volume 31(16-19): 1011-1024, April 20-27, 1996. Nambissan, Geetha B. (2000): 'Dealing with deprivation', Seminar, September, No. 493, pgs. 9. Nambissan, Geetha B. (2001): 'Social Diversity and Regional Disparities in Schooling: A Study of Rural Rajasthan' in Vaidyanathan, A. and P.R. Gopinathan Nair (ed.) Elementary Education in Rural India: A Grassroots View, Sage Publications, New Delhi and Ramachandran, Vimala and Taramani Naorem. November 2013. What it means to be a Dalit or Tribal child in our schools: A synthesis of Six-State Qualitative Study. Economic and Political Weekly. Vol XLVIII No 44, November 2, 2013.

10. *Marie Lall and S Srinivasa Rao 2011: Revisiting the equity debate in India and the UK: Caste, Race and Class Intersections in Education - in Marie Lall and Geetha B Nambissan: Education and Social Justice in the era of globalisation: Perspectives from India and the UK, Routledge, New Delhi 2011. Page34.*
11. Ramya Subramaniam: Gender and Education: A Review of Issues for Social Policy, UNRISD, Geneva, 2002; PROBE, 1999)
12. Nambissan, Geetha B. 1996. Equity in Education? Schooling of Dalit Children in India. *Economic and Political Weekly* volume 31(16-19): 1011-1024, April 20-27, 1996. Nambissan, Geetha B. (2000): 'Dealing with deprivation', Seminar, September, No. 493, pgs. 9. and Nambissan, Geetha B. (2001): 'Social Diversity and Regional Disparities in Schooling: A Study of Rural Rajasthan' in Vaidyanathan, A. and P.R. Gopinathan Nair (ed.) Elementary Education in Rural India: A Grassroots View, Sage Publications, New Delhi
13. Disha Nawani. 2013. Corporal Punishment in Schools, Economic and Political Weekly, Vol. XLVIII, No. 24, June 15. P23-26
14. I would like to acknowledge the contribution of Ms. Archan Iyer to this idea when she worked with me in 2012.

Part – III

Culture vs economic opportunity

8

Women in Higher Education Today— Structure and Agency from a Gender Perspective

—*Nelly P. Stromquist*

Abstract

The growing inclusion of women as students in institutions of higher education in many parts of the world stands in stark contrast to their weak and disadvantaged position as academics. Why does this occur? In an effort to understand more fully the process of change and resistance in relations of gender, this article explores the dynamic interrelation between structure and agency, two core sociological concepts. Structure functions through predetermined and macro-level constraints to the adoption of new ideas and practices; these constraints are examined through two key arenas: the household and the university as an institution. Agency at the individual level is expressed when women seek access to higher education, though dominant gender norms frequently prevail in their choice of study and career fields. However, neither structure nor agency is static. Universities do change over time, through the adoption of anti-discriminatory policies, measures to include more gender-sensitive tenure procedures, and the creation of women's commissions to review the condition of women students and academics. Exogenous forces such as developments in information and technology affecting reproduction and domestic tasks shape women's individual and collective agency. The confluence of these factors opens the possibility for the creation of alternative ways to respond to one's social system, thereby affecting structure itself. The process of change is not linear but is kept alive through multiple parallel developments. The paper ends with a call for more collective action by women academics.

Introduction

Many individuals, institutions, and national governments readily subscribe today to the notion that women are fundamental social actors and that they should be integrated fairly into all aspects of society. Efforts to achieve gender equality in multiple arenas represent some of the most progressive steps in contemporary society, yet these efforts are still few and many of them are weak. Despite the paucity of public policies promoting participation of women in higher education, women have been gaining a presence in such institutions across the world. While this has been occurring largely as a byproduct of the mass expansion of universities—which has been greatly aided by a growing private sector—the enrollment of women in post-secondary education has grown almost twice as fast as that of men (UIS, 2010).Today, women represent the majority of university enrollments in four of eight world regions and their presence is particularly noticeable in Europe and the Americas. In European countries, 60 per cent of higher education degrees are earned by women, including 50 per cent of the Ph.D. degrees (OECD, 2010). A similar pattern occurs in the U.S., where women have earned the majority of the associate's degrees since 1977, the majority of bachelor's since 1981, the majority of master's since 1980, and the majority of doctoral degrees since 2006 (NCES, 2011). As faculty members and high-level administrators, however, the representation of women is still deficient.[1]

Across the world, the greatly increased number of women graduates has not resulted in similar gains in their academic positions. In the U.S., more men than women enjoy tenured and tenure-track positions while women are over-represented in non-tenure positions (AAUP, 2011). Women represent about one-fourth of the full professors (Curtis, 2011)—a figure that has been slowly improving over time—and the majority of instructors and lecturers, positions that offer very limited prospects for promotion and, for those in part-time employment, high job instability with no health or pension benefits.

Institutions of higher education have been changing enormously in recent decades, moving into more part-time positions and fewer permanent appointments (Black, 2005); indeed, some consider that the professoriate has been the occupation experiencing the most drastic change in contemporary society. In the U.S., between 1976 and 1995, a time span of only 20 years, part-time positions increased by 91 per cent while full time increased by only 27 per cent (Dugger, 2001). By 2011, 51 per cent of the faculty worked part-time (AAUP, 2013). Tenure, long a distinctive feature of academic work, has become scarce, representing at present only 30 per cent of the faculty positions; further, 19 per cent of the full-time positions are now non-tenure track (AAUP, 2013). According to the American Association of University Professors (2011), women comprise 63 per cent of the non-tenure track faculty—positions are generally part-time and subject to short-term contracts. Unsurprisingly, US women academics earn less than men at each of the professorial ranks and at any type of higher education institutions. Part-time and low-paid positions among women have also been detected in countries such as the UK, Canada, Australia, and New Zealand. Among women faculty who work full time, it is not uncommon to be assigned heavy teaching, mentoring, and service loads, a practice that faculty of color (i.e., primarily African American and Hispanic) experience in particularly increasing ways. The latter phenomenon has been attributed to racist practices in the U.S. academy (Fries-Britt, Rowan-Kenyon, Perna, Milem & Howard, 2011).

Another important change affecting higher education institutions has been the increase of annual mechanisms to monitor the work of faculty members and to appraise programs and institutions (Black, 2005)—processes that consume considerable time and that reframe intellectual activities along the line of research production, revenue-generating projects, and individual promotion rather than issues related to social justice, an area that would open discussion on the conditions of disadvantaged groups in society. Because of these new practices, reaction to changes in the nature of the professoriate has been timid and sporadic.

In this paper, I seek to explore the tension between permanence and change in gender at the university level by invoking the interaction between structure and agency—two core concepts in sociology. My aim is to contrast spaces and possibilities for reproduction and transformation of gender relations. The paper is organized in two broad sections. The first puts emphasis on current situations characterizing the presence of women as faculty members at their place of work as well as their private domain (the household). The second part explores the various societal and institutional forces that enable structural change and individual action to emerge. I use a gender lens to bring attention to both material factors (salary, ranking of academic women) and symbolic factors (access and choice of fields of study). In attempting to account for both permanence and change in gender relations, this paper takes a holistic approach, incorporating elements such as public policies, institutional procedures, household relations, individual responses, and collective efforts to advance women's conditions. Most of my evidence focuses on the U.S. experience, exploring its institutions and policies toward gender and education as well as faculty responses to changing social contexts. At times, I draw on research findings from other countries to establish noteworthy parallels. I do not seek to generalize but rather to provide a concrete application of the concepts of structure and agency, using a country about which relatively abundant data exist.

Accounting for persistent gender differences

Structure

Structure can be defined as the set of principles that shape social practices as well as the set of the institutions that officially sanction and enforce those practices. Structures create rules, with different levels of adherence and penalty for failure to follow them, and these rules operate configuratively rather than separately (Ostrom, 1986). As historical, embedded, and embodied beings, people constantly experience social and institutional practices that influence their identity and sense of autonomy. Social institutions acquire and deploy power through both the rules they create and the resources they command. Structures function at macro, meso, and micro levels, thus ranging from social institutions and social networks to internalized social norms at individual levels (Sewell, 1992).The concept of structure at first sight implies determinism in social life because it assumes that institutions are powerful forces in society, shaping communal life in stable and predictable ways.

From a sociological perspective, structures and ideologies are connected (as remarked by Gramsci, writing in the 1920s and 1930s [Gramsci, 1971] and by Marcuse, 1964); ideologies justify existing social conditions and relations, and normalize them. In the case of gender rules and norms, these are influenced by both patriarchal structures and ideologies. Patriarchy is an ideology deeply embedded in social institutions (family, religion, law, the economy, education, among others) and many such institutions, despite the fact that they are not static, are implicated in the continuing disempowerment of women (England, 2000; Morley, 2003).

Through such multiple venues, patriarchal ideologies link women to motherhood, caring, and personal service, while men are cast in the position of being assertive, aggressive, and protective of their families and, thus, responsible for their economic well-being (Ridgeway, 2011). Patriarchal ideology is stronger in some countries than in others and is significantly mediated by additional social markers such as ethnicity, "race," socio-economic class, age, and religion. At the same time, gender is a construct that presents variation according to location and context. For instance, gender boundaries have become more flexible in industrialized Western countries, while they have become increasingly constricted in several Arab countries and in Iran in recent years (Connell, 2008; Read & Oselin, 2008; Findlow, 2013).

As Sewell (1992) observes, structures are constituted by mutually sustaining cultural schemas, i.e., rules and sets of resources that both empower and constrain social action, which, in turn, tend to reinforce those structures. Regarding gender, this process of mutual reinforcement, with its penetration of social institutions and concomitant beliefs, naturalizes gender ideology and creates considerable constraints to change. Two institutions fundamental to the conforming of gender ideologies are the home and the educational system.

The Home. Whether closely-knit or loosely organized, households are not merely physical settings where individuals reside but also the center for our cultural understandings of gender (Ridgeway, 2011). Within the household, three key processes take place: a domestic division of labor drawn along gender lines that maintains persistent notions of femininity/masculinity; control over rules and resources vis-à-vis minors in the household; and constant socialization practices in which the questioning of everyday activities is weak and temporal (often reduced to a few adolescent and early adult years).

While women have increased their participation in the labor force, men have not undergone comparable increases in domestic responsibilities; as Connell notes, the gender division of labor in the household "remains intransigent" (2006, p. 448).Home environments generally do not challenge the prevailing stereotypes of gendered family responsibilities or the assumption that men should be more active in the public sphere and women more committed to the private realm of home, family, and relatives. Persistent gender inequalities in home responsibilities foster gender inequalities in access to money and power outside the home (Ridgeway, 2011). Because women are usually responsible for home management and childcare, they are less mobile than men and, thus, accept positions men would not (Dugger, 2001, citing Benjamin). And because all these processes are perceived as "normal," the home is one of the social institutions most resistant to change.

Recent studies of the amount of housework done by U.S. university professors indicate that women spend much more time in domestic work than men. Women professors with children have been found to devote 31.6 hours per week to childcare while men professors with children devote 17.4 hours (MLA, 2009). A survey of professors in the natural sciences in heterosexual relationships found that women performed an average of 19.3 hours per week of domestic work compared to an average of 4.7 hours per week for their male partners (Schiebinger & Gilmartin, 2010). An earlier nationwide survey of faculty with doctorate degrees reported that women faculty with children provided more than 30 hours per week in the provision of care for others, and they provided this support up to age 50, so it was a practice throughout most of their peak academic years. Not surprisingly, for faculty women with Ph.D.s, the combination of marriage and childrearing also decreases the likelihood of entering a tenure-track position (Goulden, Mason, & Wolfinger, 2005).

For a married student or married faculty member, a part-time position is certainly more compatible for women with young families than a full-time position. However, part-time work entails dedication mostly to teaching and generally to large classes. Research requires large blocks of uninterrupted time and cannot be conducted when one's time is fragmented into multiple tasks, including those pertaining to household management. It should be noted that the domestic division of labor is stubborn to change. In Canada, for instance, despite improvement to parental leave policies during the 1970s, women and men asserted about a decade later that parenthood greatly affected women's careers (Baker, 2012).

Barriers to women's full careers vary in intensity across countries but they are similar nonetheless. The combination of forces linked to marriage, housework, and childcare brings to the fore deep ideologies regarding femininity and masculinity that demand women's and men's time and energy in drastically differentiated ways. Leonard and Malina capture it well when they remark: "Being a mother in academic life is a predominantly silent experience. The facts of this motherhood—the personal individual struggles, compromises and solutions to daily problem of attempting to combine being a good mother and a competent, productive academic [are] largely unvoiced at work" (cited in Marchbank, 2005, p. 145).

The University. Centers of learning are first and foremost social institutions and thus not exempt from being gendered institutions; in fact, one of the main functions of formal education is to ensure the integration of young generations into prevailing social norms and expectations. The context of schooling—its cognitive focus, the top-down nature of most of its institutional relations, the enormous mutual influence of peer groups—does little to challenge the stereotypes of wider society (Connell, 1996; Mohammed, 2009). At the university level, the dynamics are very similar.

Although operating at a higher level of intellectual engagement and reasoning than many other organizations, universities are clearly gendered (Brooks, 1997; Blackmore, 2000; Brooks & Mackinnon, 2001; Acker & Armente, 2004; Allen, 2011), as manifested in the dominance of males in authority positions, the strong ethos of competition to the detriment of solidarity, the segregation by fields of study, the growing distinction between research and teaching (with the accompanying belief that teaching is more feminine and research more masculine), and the unquestioned influence of peers in the formation of gender identities. A large number of institutional case studies conducted in the U.S. provides evidence that women-unfriendly academic climates continue to exist, particularly in the fields of science and technology (e.g., Johnsrud & Des Jarlais, 1994; Cronin & Roger, 1999; CWSEM, 2006; Mason, Goulden, & Frasch,, 2009; Moss-Racusin, Dovidio, Brescoll, Graham, & Handelsman, 2012; Duch, Zeng, Sales-Pardo, Radicchi, Otis, Woodruff, & Lunes, 2012). This is aggravated by the fact that women (again due primarily to multiple demands on their time) participate less than men in professional networks, accumulate less publications, and tend to receive less mentoring than men(Chesterman, Ross-Smith, Peters, 2005). While both women and men academics have considerable control over their schedules, women face inflexible service conditions since they are expected to meet similar levels of research productivity and, increasingly, similar levels of grant procurement and entrepreneurship.

In the U.S., there has been a positive response toward women in education by the state through the use of anti-discrimination legislation such as Title IX, which eliminated admission quotas against women that existed for certain fields such as medicine and law, encouraged affirmative action measures, and punished sexual harassment (Stromquist, 2013a). While anti-discrimination policies continue in place, affirmative action has been successfully challenged in the courts, even though such measures were taken much more often regarding Afro-American and Latino minorities than regarding women. Significant gender disparities in rank, salaries, and promotion are visible. In addition, it is more difficult for women to achieve tenure and promotion, equal pay opportunities, research funding, and infrastructural support (Morrison, Bourke, & Kelley, 2005). There also exist an unwelcoming climate, exclusionary practices, and sexual harassment toward women in institutions of higher education (Dugger, 2001; Cotterill & Letherby, 2005; Bozal, 2010; Allan, 2011). The chilly climate, first detected in the early 1980s, refers to small but frequent inequalities, either not noticed or not contested, that cumulatively lower women's self-esteem, confidence, aspirations, and participation (Hall & Sandler, 1982).

Agency

This concept refers to action taken by individuals in response to their environment. Agency is often conceptualized as part of social action theory and defined as the value-motivated action of individuals; this definition recognizes the importance of subjective meaning attached to a situation by an individual actor (Theodorson & Theodorson, 1969). Individual agency can involve *accommodation* to existing rules and norms but it is especially promising when it involve forms of *resistance* to established structures. Agency can also refer to collective action, in which case it often takes place outside traditional institutions and generally in opposition to them.

Gender is activated by deeply ingrained understandings of what masculinity and femininity are supposed to be. In the case of higher education, women exercise individual agency by seeking admission to university, selecting given fields of study, and completing their studies. Whether women are conscious of this or not, many seek to position themselves better in the labor market (Yates, 1997). This instance of agency is clearly affected by other social markers, notably ethnicity, race, and socio-economic status. The career choices women and men make are influenced by gender ideology, which affects their assessment of self-efficacy as well as their career aspirations (Burstyn, 1993; Bradley, 2000; Ridgeway, 2011). Since career "choices" are further shaped by social expectations of appropriate gender roles and functions, in many ways these *individual choices* are in fact *social products*. Because many social factors affect men and women differentially, in the end, women pay an education premium to compete equally with men in terms of salaries. Sociologist Connell (1996) refers to men's advantage over women as the "patriarchal dividend." The fact that women need more years of education to compete for salaries similar to those of men could conversely be called the "patriarchal penalty." The lower salaries earned by women, in turn, are taken as indicators of the low contribution of women's careers to society—a perception that creates a vicious circle for women.

Higher education certainly helps women to compete in the labor market and to make better life choices through increased understanding of their surrounding world. Nonetheless, in the U.S., there are significant differences in financial returns to education between women and men with similar levels of education. As Table 1 shows, women with some college education earn less than a man with a high school diploma, women with a bachelor's degree earn almost as much as a man with an associate degree, and women with a master's or more earn the same as men with a bachelor's degree (NCES, 2010); on average, women need at least two more years of education to achieve salary parity with men. In part, this is due to women's predominance in low-wage fields, as they comprise 87 per cent of those in the childcare industry and 86 per cent of those in the health aide industries (Perry & David, 2011). But gender pay inequalities can be found within the same occupations and positions between men and women with higher education (Alkadry & Tower, 2006).

Table 1: Median Earnings of Full time, Full-Year Wage and Salary Workers, Age 25-34 by Educational Attainment and Sex, US Dollars, 2010

Level of Education	*Men*	*Women*	*GPI**
Less than high school completion	24,000	17,800	.74
High school diploma or equivalent	32,800	25,000	.76
Some college	37,900	29,500	.78
Associate degree	39,900	34,700	.87
Bachelor's degree	49,800	40,000	.80
Master's or above	64,200	49,800	.77

Source: National Center for Education Statistics, 2010. Adapted from Figure 49-2.

* Gender Parity Index. This index is computed by calculating the proportion of women's salary in a given category compared to the salary of men in the same category.

Overtime, the wage gender gap has been decreasing. In 1979, the average woman earned $0.62 cents for every dollar the average man earned; by 2010, she earned $0.80 cents compared to her male counterpart (U.S. Department of Labor and U.S. Labor Statistics, 2011). Still, women in the U.S. earn approximately 30 per cent less than men at similar education levels (Black, 2005). Some occupations have become more female-dominated than in the past. In 1980, women represented 75 per cent of primary school teachers and 68 per cent of social workers; by 2012, they were 80 per cent of primary school teachers as well as 80 per cent of social workers (Coontz, 2012).

The college major has a significant role in the gender wage gap, for example, when comparing engineering vs. education. But it is also the case that within similar professions, women earn less than men. For instance, women today comprise 40 per cent of all full-time managers, but their median salary is 73 per cent of male managers (Coontz, 2012). Moreover, women tend not to be present in two fields central to their empowerment: economics and political science. In the U.S., men are three times more likely than women to major in economics (Dynan & Rouse, 1995); slightly more men than women get degrees in political science but only one-fourth of the full-time faculty in this discipline are women (APSA, 2004).It has also been observed that in society at large, American women continue having lower aspirations for political office.

As academics, women tend to concentrate on a few fields, notably the humanities, the social sciences, and education, which has resulted in salaries lower than those of men. Women earn less than men at each of the professorial ranks and at each institutional category (providing doctoral, master's, baccalaureate, or associate degrees). Table 2 shows the salary differential between women and men professors. While multiple factors operate to create the gap, the key point here is that gaps exist even at high levels of education and within similar professorial ranks. Combining all rankings and types of institutions, the gender gap is 19.6 per centage points, although the gap among tenured or tenure-track professors is less and oscillates between 7.1 and 12.7 per centage points (AAUP, 2014). The situation seems to be improving slowly as a 9 per cent gender gap in salaries was detected several years ago among recently hired faculty members at research-intensive universities (Porter, Toutkoushian, & Moore, 2008).

Table 2: Average Salary in Dollars for Women and Men Faculty. US, 2011-12 All Categories of Institutions

	Men	*Women*	*GPI*
Professor	120,797	105,402	87.3
Associate Professor	82,628	76,797	92.9
Assistant Professor	70,781	65,321	92.3
Instructor	49,802	48,024	96.4
Lecturer	57,563	52,045	90.4
No Rank	68,880	60,141	87.3
All Combined	91,994	73,932	80.4

Source: AAUP, 2014, Table 5, based on 1,142 reporting institutions.

Accounting for social change

For those committed to social change, it is important to perceive structure not as opposed to agency but rather as requiring it. As Giddens (1976) argues, structures are not only those forces that place constraints on human agency but also those that enable it. He, as well as Bourdieu before him (1977, English translation), see structure as a process, not a static state; the processes set in motion by existing structures can themselves change. Further, though resources are unevenly distributed, some measure of human and non-human resources are controlled by all members of society. This opens the possibility for the empowerment of agents (Sewell, 1992).

Challenges to and modifications in structure

Attention to access as the key objective for women's education has distracted us from paying attention to the obstacles to women's inclusion and the use of potential mechanisms to change universities (Morley, 2005). While pervasive gender ideologies may be difficult to combat, several social institutions—including educational institutions—are overcoming the resistance of ingrained social constructs to change by moving beyond parity and increasingly committing themselves to the enactment of social justice. New norms and values emerging from various social arenas, such as the women's movements, government policies on equity such as Title IX in the U.S., and judicial decisions on equity and against discrimination and sexual harassment have compelled universities to allow access to a diverse set of people, which includes individuals from low-income families, ethnic minorities, and women. This has created a space for the incorporation of social actors whose stakes in a new social order are high, and has encouraged them to present demands for institutional change, from increased diversity in the composition of student and faculty members to specialized programs that recognize marginalized identities such as gender and ethnic studies. There have also been initiatives by the federal government to fund projects in several universities to engage in workshops to develop supportive networks among faculty of all ranks to increase their awareness of gender issues in their place of work and move with greater ease through processes of promotion and tenure. Such initiatives have generally been successful.[2]A development that has also been beneficial to women concerns the creation of women's commissions in universities. While some feminist academics have decried their existence as a way to defuse conflict, these commissions have given women a collective voice on campus and have brought to the fore key women's concerns (Allan, 2008). In the absence of systematic research, these commissions have illuminated the condition of women in their respective institutions. Women's commissions and legislation focusing on women are usually perceived as changes made at the structural level, yet many of these outcomes were really the result of active collective agency on the part of women, with the institution (or state) responding to their pressure.

In other spheres of society, crucial positive developments are challenging patriarchy. According to Castells (2004, p. 193), "informational, global economy, technological changes in the reproduction of human species, and the powerful surge of women's struggles" are influencing societies toward the end of patriarchal norms. He takes as indicators of progress the reductions in fertility rates and increases in the marriage age and in divorce rates, as well as increases in women's participation in the labor force. While it seems an exaggeration to declare patriarchy a dying order, important demographic and technological changes are occurring in many parts of the world.

As the number of female faculty increases, educational institutions have developed internal policies to promote equal employment opportunity and equal treatment. For women who seek academic careers, universities increasingly provide support through maternal and parental leave and "stopping the tenure clock"—a mechanism in U.S. universities that allows pregnant professors at assistant and associate levels to take time off for a period following birth without compromising the time allotted to secure promotion.[3] Nonetheless, only 32 per cent of U.S. research universities offer a paid modified duty option as one component of their family-friendly measures (Smith & Waltman, 2006).

A few policies have been in place to create a more gender-friendly space for women's work, including in post-secondary institutions. European countries lead the way in this respect by offering reasonable paid parental leaves, childcare facilities, and gender training of faculty members and administrative personnel (e.g., Husu, 2007, describing Finland; Sporn, 2007, describing Austria). Another positive example comes from Germany, which has institutionalized equity plans, introduced gender studies in all its universities, and created the position of gender equity coordinator. In practice, however, this position tends to be occupied by a graduate student who then has little weight in decision-making. On the other hand, the financing of public universities in Germany depends not only on advancement in research and teaching but also in implementing measures to ensure gender equity (Zapata, 2010). In contrast, in the U.S., such measures are very modest. Parental paid leaves are given in only one-third of universities, and mostly only to mothers. In a study of a major U.S. research-intensive university, while 72 per cent of the mothers took parental leave, 82 per cent of the fathers did not, mostly for fear of social stigma and negative repercussions such as delayed promotion (Lundquist & Misra, 2012). Some fields, particularly those in science, technology, engineering, and math (the so-called STEM fields) are described as having "child-free" department cultures. Childcare remains a major obstacle to women in the academy (as well as in other occupations); some estimates hold that childcare costs at present exceed the annual median cost of housing rent in 24 U.S. states (Durno, 2013). Kanter (1977a), who first detected the need for a work-family balance in our lives, warns us about thinking that institutional change can resolve this great problem that women in particular must endure. She says: "Important questions can be raised about the limits of change in any institution alone. Some people are members simultaneously of an occupational and a family system. Furthermore, some people carry over orientations and pressures from one into the other, in part because norms of the two may converge" (p. 78).

While the gender problem in education is by no means simply one of access to all levels or one of assuring the existence of a substantial "pipeline,"[4] governments and universities continue to reduce it to issues of parity, i.e., the need to achieve equal enrollment of men and women. And since women continue to be the minority in STEM fields, most efforts go into increasing the participation of women in those fields. Given the prevailing practices among universities of competing for high rankings, which are associated more with the natural sciences than the social sciences or the humanities, very limited institutional reflection takes place on the gendered nature of universities, which thus make practically no effort to dismantle the patriarchal ideology and practices that continue to mold institutional life. Not surprisingly, little is done to counter the effects of practices linked to the domestic division of labor; issues of childcare are still seen as strictly private concerns that need not require organizational consideration. Social definitions of academic disciplines and their fit into masculine and feminine conceptions of careers in those disciplines are not problematized and women's selection of fields of study are considered matters of personal choice for which the university assumes no responsibility other than to offer scholarships to reduce expenses for women in S&T careers or to offer limited mentoring.

Some regressive steps are also evident. One example is provided by UNESCO's actions in higher education. In preparation for the 1998 World Conference on Higher Education, UNESCO requested a paper on Higher Education and Women, in which 10 women professional organizations participated (UNESCO, 1998).This document identified several goals to be accomplished by 2010. These were: equal participation of women and men as chairs, professors and heads of department posts, an increase in the number of women rectors and vice-chancellors, and an equal participation of women and men in university senates. When the subsequent World Conference on Higher Education took place in 2009, the priorities for action of the meeting made no mention of the previous objectives in the Higher Education and Women document. The priorities were merely to encourage "women's access, participation and success in higher education" without further development of what this might entail (UNESCO, 2009). In a similar vein, a special study requested by UNESCO in preparation for the 2009 conference, entitled *Trends in Global Higher Education: Tracking an Academic Revolution* (Altbach, Reisberg, Rumbley, 2009), referred to women in passing, only to indicate that their numbers as students in higher education would probably continue to increase. The absence of a deeper treatment of gender by UNESCO, particularly regarding the crucial role of ideological factors in the construction of gender and gendered education institutions, reflects a weak understanding of key issues affecting women in the academy as well as limited interest to learn about them.

A crucial transformative action by the state should be the provision of subsidized childcare and the provision of incentives for a much greater sharing of rearing children and household work with men (England, 2000). This might be possible, but at this time, women are not demanding such cultural shifts or mobilizing for them.

Recognizing agency

Although in many instances universities foster working environments that create negative gender experiences, women are attending institutions of higher education in increasing numbers and seeking positions as academics. Their agency in seeking higher education can be attributed to several factors. Demographic reasons, such as delaying the age for marrying and having fewer children thanks to a greater use of birth-control devices among women, have been invoked. Relying less on marriage, women increasingly realize they need to position themselves as independent workers and to fare well in their search for future jobs. In the U.S., it is not only white women who are increasingly seeking university degrees, but also African American and Hispanic women. In both minority groups, women now have a 9 per cent advantage over men in undergraduate completion rates (Mather & Adams, 2007); within those cultures, therefore, there have been gradual inroads toward making breadwinning a part of motherhood (Connell, 2008). Sociological forces, such as declining discrimination in the labor market, greater possibilities for balancing family and professional life, reduction of discrimination within families in providing access to education to sons and daughters, are also at work. Economic explanations are valid as well: post-secondary education has become the main threshold for access to positive social mobility in the U.S. And even at that level, the competition is high as 30 per cent of the adult population over 25 years now has a bachelor's degree or above (U.S. Census Bureau, 2011).

Today, women recognize that they need more education to compete with men for similar salaries or, as seems to be the case in Europe, they benefit from increasing rates of return to higher education (Vincent-Lancrin, 2008). Academic performance is also at work: girls have been attaining higher reading scores, comparable scores in math, and slightly lower scores than boys in science in all PISA test administrations thus far—a phenomenon observed throughout the world. Naturally, girls' high academic achievement nurtures aspirations for higher education, and higher levels of education dispel social notions of lower competence among women (Ridgeway, 2011), which, in turn, facilitates the incorporation of women into the labor force. Finally, changes in gender ideology are also at work. Changing attitudes and values regarding the roles and aspirations of women, in part due to feminist movements in the 1960s and 1970s, have been considerable. The wide dissemination of democratic norms—a social revolution facilitated by information and communication technologies as well as travel—is conveying the notion that women should strive for autonomous and egalitarian lives.

The subsequent pursuit of academic professions among women seems to be related to, among other factors, the excitement of intellectual life, the relative autonomy of the professoriate, and its high social status. Teaching in universities does have a component that is harmonious with conventional family schedules. But the research and service components of academic jobs are quite demanding and, if family responsibilities by gender continued unchanged, the research activities by women might not be performed at full capacity or may take longer to complete. Thus, women's participation in the academic world is growing but often in part-time positions, distant from high-level decision-making, and in institutions with lower prestige. In the U.S., academic women earn less than men in any field, even in those in which they are the majority, such as the education and health professions. This occurs in part because institutional and social discrimination is at work, as women encounter entrenched masculinist values and practices in the bureaucratic and disciplinary cultures of the university, as described above. But also accounting for salary differences between men and women is the much higher participation of men in better remunerated fields in the natural and physical sciences, math, and engineering, as well as differences in research productivity.

The creation of women's studies and gender studies programs can be taken as a powerful instance of collective agency by women in university institutions. Even though such programs are poorly funded, attract small numbers of students, and have been criticized for being Eurocentric and depoliticizing the understanding of gender (Shanani, 2003; Lind, 2003; Howie, 2007), they represent a new claim on intellectual life. In the U.S., however, these spaces have not been free from conflict. Multiple perspectives have recast women's issues away from material problems and framed them primarily along cultural, ethnic, and LGBTQ lines so that women scholars no longer speak with a unified voice (Glazer-Reymo, 2007).

Women academics exercise agency also in the production of their own research. Given the demands on their time, which are significantly different from those faced by their male counterparts, they engage in more modest levels of productivity. Consequently, women's research projects (as documented in the UK, Canada, and New Zealand) tend to be small in scale, applied or based on local research, and use qualitative research methods; also, few of the women academic projects build on international collaboration, as such requires participation in wide academic networks (Baker, 2012; Sugimoto, 2013). The remarkable point here is that women's agency, in trying to accommodate to mothering and caring duties, results in women occupying positions that reduce their competitiveness for future academic promotions.

Although in universities there is a lack of spaces where experiences may be shared, observers such as Brooks and MacKinnon, 2001, based on the experience of women academics in the UK and New Zealand, argue that women academics are gradually recognizing the gendered dimensions of practices such as leadership, productivity, promotion, workload, discrimination, sexual harassment, mentoring, among others (see also Brooks, 1997). This is facilitating women academics' participation in certain programs that open to them through institutional initiatives, as seen above in the case of the U.S. Women's groups through conferences, their own research, meeting with other like-minded organizations, frequent workshops transmit ideas about change, despite their lack of funding and even facilities (Alexander & Mohanty, 1997). Some of this, unquestionably, influences gender developments in higher education institutions.

On the other hand, women in the U.S. have not organized themselves as faculty of color have done. A number of minority professors have been working together in recent years to investigate processes of discrimination and everyday experiences in the research-intensive universities in which they work (Fries-Britt et al., 2011). Through their published findings, which reveal multiple practices of open and disguised discrimination, these faculty of color are leading some university administrators to correct prejudicial practices and develop specific policies to counter abuse or ill-treatment of minority professors. In contrast, academic women are divided by different perspectives in the conceptualization and theorizing of gender and the distance most of them keep from activists in the world outside universities (Cole &Luna, 2010). Consequently, women's agency is mostly expressed through individual than collective agency.

Structure validates ideology and creates constraints to change, as we stated before. But it is still possible to engage in strategic choices within established constraints. Higher education gives women an identity outside the family and this fuels the desire for control over their own lives and for greater career aspirations. Yet many decisions—i.e., agency by women—still take place under traditional, pre-established parameters. Consequently, women engage in numerous preemptive behaviors that will not create family-work conflicts. They prefer jobs with flexibility regarding family routines, bypassing those with demanding schedules; they prefer jobs that do not require performance in distant settings. So women continue to enter careers in education, nursing, the humanities, and the social sciences. But women have also been entering in substantial numbers some professional fields such as law, medicine, and business—fields that bring prestige and high income, even though they are not at the cutting edge of discovery, as fields in science and technology would be.

Obviously, education alone, even at the highest levels, does not create feelings of feminist resistance or even gender awareness. The evidence shows that highly educated women, as women academics are, can engage in influential activities such as knowledge production and teaching and yet not be able to mobilize themselves as a collective force. A strong force that is discouraging agency—against either sexism or racism—within universities today is the increasing consolidation of an institutional culture that constantly deploys audits, quality assessments, and accountability procedures. Does this detract from questioning the institution and shaping professional identities in conformist ways? Morley (2003) would argue that these procedures have a profound impact on academics. Such being the case, the space left for oppositional behavior, including calls for changing gender relations within universities, seem to be very constrained.

Moreover, under the competitive climate that characterizes academic environments today, there is little time for exploration of shared career concerns with colleagues and the cultivation of collective responses. Seldom do women professors meet to address gender issues; prevailing social norms have succeeded in rendering such a concern subjective and thus a non-academic pursuit. More seriously, research indicates that academic women themselves "tend not to view problems in direct gender terms but as their individual choice, although most explanations given are indirectly gender-related" (Donovan, Hodgson, Scanion, & Whitelegg, 2005, p. 252).

Conclusions

Understanding the interrelations between structure and agency helps to see ways in which women have both advanced to higher levels of education and found limits to their success through education. One thing is clear: cultural norms are not totally shared by all and are, therefore, not impervious to change. DiMaggio (1997, p. 265) remarks that "cultures in which people are socialized leave much opportunity for choice and variation." Some areas remain protected and are deeply defended; others seem more flexible and distant from the watchful eye. DiMaggio is also very accurate when he observes that changes do not happen simultaneously and that structure comprises institutions that follow different logics: capitalism, state, democracy, family, religion, science.

Agency is made possible by self-reflexivity, which is an exercise no one can totally suppress. Acts of self-reflexivity lead to change, first by regarding more critically one's own experience and, later, by resisting the status quo. DiMaggio (1997, p. 282) believes that fostering reflexive efforts are events with an "emotional resonance" to people in their surrounding environment. This line of argument would suggest that social change is inexorable as there will always be events that invite introspection. While there is a constant interaction between structure and agency, it would appear that individual changes precede cultural changes. For example, many more women than in the past are working outside the home and still the model of the full-time housewife dominates, as women continue to conduct most of the domestic and caring responsibilities.

As we reviewed the various policies and practices affecting higher education, in several instances we could observe a clear interaction between structure and agency. Structure and agency affect each other constantly, as structures set boundaries to our perceptions and behaviors and, in turn, through our actions we influence and reshape, albeit gradually, the structures within which we live. In other words, we participate in both recreating and contesting the conditions of our oppression. This creates the ebbs and flows of social change. Much of what we call structural/institutional change has come into being as a result of individual or group agency in which women (in the present case) have challenged oppressive conditions or acted proactively.

Education has given women greater potential and their drive for university access is a strong and widespread manifestation of individual agency. Education has not often fostered substantial gender awareness, however, nor has it enhanced women's desire for a faster and more comprehensive set of changes in the social relations of gender. At the structural level, given the state's safe preference for recognizing gender issues almost exclusively in terms of numerical parity, the increasing presence of women in universities is taken as a sign that previous policies in their favor have been entirely successful. And since there is a widespread belief that knowledge is neutral and that universities impart objective and scientific knowledge, the gendered nature of these institutions remains untouched. The notion that institutions of higher education are harmonic and driven solely by merit is one of the strongest social beliefs, and this deters researchers from examining unequal distributions of rewards and recognition and from questioning gender-socializing practices.

Within universities, education quality is currently being defined as that which leads to saleable products, which gives much more importance to the fields of science and technology. With globalization, universities are becoming lopsided institutions, with a few fields—those in science and technology, all dominated by men—occupying preeminent positions (Blackmore, 2000; Stromquist, 2012, 2013b). Under these conditions, it is difficult to foreground gender as an urgent matter as well as to engage in challenging acts of self-reflexivity. As Morley (2005, p. 215) remarks, based on her profound knowledge of higher education dynamics in the UK, "gender sensitization programs might not be enough to dismantle and challenge deeply entrenched patriarchal practice. We need a theory of male privilege rather than female disadvantage."

Women's agency in the university today is alive and visible but operating mostly at individual levels and within traditional parameters. Thus, the clustering of fields of study, according to gender, persists and the subsequent segregation in careers is reproduced. Agency is deployed for individual advancement—a legitimate concern. Yet, instances of collective agency—the source of substantial social change—are very few and mostly outside the academy.

To break down the gendered nature of higher education institutions, it is clear that structures must be the target of *collective* action, and that both institutional and *cultural* change must be promoted. The household must be brought into continuous examination and contestation for its central role in the reproduction of inequitable social relations. This will require examination and contestation of dominant notions of masculinity and femininity. The influence of the mass media, which thrives on a strongly dichotomous representation of feminine and masculine norms, needs to be met with a countervailing force. In addition, expanded provision of childcare services and medical and family leave is essential to produce a better balance of work and family. The curriculum, at all levels of schooling, should incorporate discussion of the domestic division of labor; waiting until women begin to choose non-traditional fields of study—e.g., STEM—is too little and rather late. Educational work should begin early in people's lives and should present more inclusive family models and egalitarian relations.

The provision of greater social services, a more even distribution of domestic and care work, and recognition of such work in social protection systems remain to be accomplished (UNRISD, 2010) in most countries. However, even in the few countries where substantial childcare facilities and parental leave are provided, women continue to evince limited academic representation as full professors. In part, this might be due to the weak participation of women in political action. Not only are women consumed by domestic duties but they are also more reluctant than men to engage in politics; even in academic settings, they tend to be wary of positions of leadership and seldom engage in collective action to promote the examination of gender issues.

A purposeful process of change is possible but degree of transformation requires understanding of dynamic forces as well as individual and collective agency not only to accommodate pressing gendered demands but also to contest them. A fact that cries for attention is why academic women are not using their numerical advantage to penetrate interstices of power within the university and bring about new institutional cultures. What are women academics doing to advance their still marginal position? Obviously, education alone, even at the highest levels, does not create feelings of feminist resistance or even gender awareness. The evidence shows that highly educated women, as women academics are, can engage in influential activities such as knowledge production and teaching and yet not be able to mobilize themselves as a collective force. Now that more women are becoming professors, classrooms should be more utilized to explore gender issues and sensitize women and men about the functioning and consequences of gender regimes. Further, while it is usually deplored that so very few women are university presidents, women today comprise 50 per cent of senior academic affairs in the central administration and 36 per cent of the academic deans in U.S. universities (Curtis, 2011). Since women have a numerical majority in some influential fields such as education, there exist opportunities for them to develop their collective agency to bring career choices and aspirations under gender analysis.

The power of numbers has brought about gender changes, albeit mild, in private corporations (Kanter, 1977b). Such a collective agency is needed to disrupt traditional ideas about men and women, masculinity and femininity, and ultimately to produce an altered social environment in institutions of higher learning. The numbers of women as academics is substantial. Why not use this resource to increase gender awareness and question gender relations among men and women students and among men and women academics?

References

AAUP (2011): *It's Not Over Yet. 2009-2010 Report on the Economic Status of the Profession.* Washington, D.C: American Association of University Professors.

AAUP (2013): *Trends in Faculty Employment Status, 1975-2011.* Washington, D.C.: American Association of University Professors.

AAUP (2014): *2013-14 Annual Report on the Economic Status of the Profession.* Washington, D.C.: American Association of University Professors.

Acker, S. & C. Armente (2004): Sleepless in Academia. *Gender and Education*, 16(1): 3-24.

Alexander, M. J. & C.T. Mohanty (eds.) (1997): *Feminist Genealogies, Colonial Legacies, Democratic Futures*. New York: Routledge.

Alkadry, M. & L. Tower (2006): Unequal Pay: The Role of Gender. *Public Administration Review*, 66(6): 888-898.

Allan, E. (2008): *Policy Discourses, Gender, and Education: Constructing Women's Status.* New York: Routledge.

Allan, E. (ed.) (2011): Special Issue: Women's Status in Higher Education—Equity Matters. *ASHE Higher Education Report*, 37(1): 1-163.

Allen, M. & T. Castleman (2001): "Fighting the Pipeline Fallacy", in A. Brooks & A. Mackinnon (eds.), *Gender and the Restructured University: Changing Management and Culture in Higher Education.* Buckingham, UK: Open University Press, pp. 151-165.

Altbach, P., L. Reisberg, L. Rumbley (2009): *Trends in Global Higher Education: Tracking an Academic Revolution.* A report Prepared for the UNESCO 2009 World Conference in Higher Education. Paris: UNESCO.

APSA (2004): Women's Advancement in Political Science: A Report of the APSA Workshop on the Advancement of Women in Academic Political Science in the US (11-15 March).Washington: American Political Science Association.

Baker, M. (2012): *Academic Careers and the Gender Gap*. Vancouver: University of British Columbia Press.

Black, P. (2005): Class matters in UK higher education. *Women's Studies International Forum*, 28(2-3): 127-138.

Blackmore, J. (2000): "Hanging onto the Edge": An Australian Case Study of Women, Universities and Globalization. In N. P. Stromquist and K. Monkman (eds.), *Globalization and Education. Integration and Contestation across Cultures.* Laham, MD: Rowan & Littlefield, pp. 333-352.

Bourdieu, P. (1977): *Outline of a Theory of Practice.* Translated by Richard Nice. Cambridge: Cambridge University Press.

Bozal, G. (2010): "Techos de cristal en la universidad", in A. González y Asociados (eds.), *La Construcción de la Sexualidad y los Géneros en Tiempos de Cambio*. Valencia: Ediciones Aurelia, pp. 86-99.

Bradley, K. (2000): The Incorporation of Women into Higher Education. Paradoxical Outcomes? *Sociology of Education*, 73(1): 1-18.

Brooks, A. & A. Mackinnon (2001): *Gender and the Restructured University. Changing Management and Culture in Higher Education.* Buckingham. UK: Open University.

Brooks, A. (1997): *Academic Women*. Bristol, Pennsylvania: The Society for Research into Higher Education and Open University Press.

Burstyn, J. (1993): "Who Benefits and Who Suffers: Gender and Education at the Dawn of the Information Technology", in S. K. Biklen & D. Pollard (eds.), *Gender and Education. Ninety-second Yearbook for the National Society for the Study of Education*. Part I. Chicago: University of Chicago Press, pp. 107-124.

Castells, M. (2004): *The Power of Identity.* 2nd ed. Malden, MA: Blackwell Publishing.

Chesterman, C., A. Ross-Smith, M. Peters (2005): 'Not doable jobs!' Exploring senior women's attitudes to academic leadership roles. *Women's Studies International Forum*, 28(2-3): 163-180.

Cole, F. & Z. Luna (2010): Making Coalitions Work: Solidarity across Difference within US Feminism. *Feminist Studies*, 36(1): 71-98.

Connell, R. (1996): Teaching the Boys: New Research on Masculinity, and Gender Strategies for Schools. *Teachers College Record*, 98(2): 206-235.

Connell, R. (2006): The Experience of Gender Change in Public Sector Organizations. *Gender, Work and Organization*, 13(5): 435-452.

Connell, R. (2008): Process of change: instability, contradiction, colonialism. Draft notes.

Coontz, S. (2012, September 29): The Myth of Male Decline. *The New York Times Sunday Review.*

Cotterill, P. & G. Letherby (2005): Women in higher education: Issues and challenges. *Women's Studies International Forum*, 28 (2-3): 109-113.

Cronin, C. & A. Roger (1999): Theorizing Progress: Women in Science, Engineering, and Technology in Higher Education. *Journal of Research in Science Teaching*, 36: 637-661.

Curtis, J. (2011, April 11): Persistent Inequity: Gender and Academic Employment. Washington, D.C.: American Association of University Professors. Paper presented at "New Voices in Pay Equity" event.

CWSEM (Committee on Women in Science, Engineering, and Medicine, National Research Council) (2006): *To Recruit and Advance: Women Students and Faculty in Science, Engineering, and Medicine.* Washington, D.C.: The National Academies Press.

DiMaggio, P. (1997): Culture and Cognition. *Annual Review of Sociology*, 23: 263-287.

Donovan, C., B. Hodgson, E. Scanion & E. Whitelegg (2005): Women in higher education: Issues and challenges for part-time scientists.*Women's Studies International Forum*, 28(2-3): 247-258.

Duch, J., XTI Zeng, M. Sales-Pardo, F. Radicchi, S. Otis, T. Woodruff, & L .Lunes (2012): The Possible Role of Resource Requirements and Academic Career-Choice Risk on Gender Differences in Publication. *Plos ONE,* 7(12): e51332.doi:10.1371/journal.pone.0051332.

Dugger, K. (2001): Women in Higher Education in the United States: I. Has There Been Progress? *International Journal of Sociology and Social Policy*, 21(1/2): 118-130.

Durno, C. (2013): "I can't afford to be a working mom." *Parenting*, 271, p. 82.

Dynan, K. & C. Rouse (1995): The Underrepresentation of Women in Economics: A Study of the Undergraduate Economics Students. Working Paper 5299 (October). Washington, D.C.: National Bureau of Economic Research.

England, P. (2000): "Conceptualizing Women's Empowerment", in H. Presser and G. Sen (eds.), *Women's Empowerment and Demographic Processes. Moving Beyond Cairo*. Oxford: Oxford University Press, pp. 37-65.

Findlow, S. (2013): Higher education and feminism in the Arab States. *British Journal of Sociology of Education*, 34(1): 112-131.

Fries-Britt, S., H. Rowan-Kenyon, L. Perna, J. Milem, & D. Howard (2011): Underrepresentation in the Academy and the Institutional Climate for Faculty Diversity. *Journal of the Professoriate*, 35(1): 1-34.

Giddens, A. (1976): *New Rules of Sociological Method: A Positive Critique of Interpretive Sociologies.* London: Hutchinson.

Glazer-Reymo, J. (2007): "Equality in the American Research University: Researching the Agency for Women's Rights" in M. A. Sagaria (ed.), *Women, Universities, and Change: Gender Equality in the European Union and Beyond.* New York: Palgrave Macmillan/International Association of Universities, pp. 161-178.

Goulden, M., M.A. Mason, & N. Wolfinger (2005): "Do babies matter? Refining gender equity in the academy", in *Mentoring for Academic Careers in Engineering: Proceedings of the PAESMEM/Stanford School of Engineering Workshop*. Santa Barbara, CA: Grayphics Publishing, pp. 89-105.

Gramsci, A. (1971): *Selections from Prison Notebook.* New York: International Publishers.

Hall, R. & B. Sandler (1982): *The Classroom Climate: A Chilly One for Women?* Washington, D.C.: Association of American Colleges.

Howie, G. (2007): After Postmodernism: Feminisms and Marxism Revisited. *Critical Matrix,* no. 16, pp. 40-57.

http://www.aaup.org/article/housework-academic-issue

Husu, L. (2007): "Women in Universities in Finland: Relative Advances and Continuing Contradictions", in M. A. Sagaria (ed.), *Women, Universities, and Change: Gender Equality in the European Union and Beyond.* New York: Palgrave Macmillan/International Association of Universities, pp. 89-111.

Jaschik, S. (2012, June 14): A "Stop the Clock" Penalty. *Inside Higher Ed.*

Johnsrud, L. K. & C.D. Des Jarlais (1994): Barriers to tenure for women and minorities. *The Review of Higher Education*, 17: 335-353.

Kanter, R. (1977a): *Work and Family in the United States: A Critical Review and Agenda for Research and Policy.* New York: Russell Sage Foundation.

Kanter, R. (1977b): *Men and Women of the Corporation*. New York: Basic Books.

Lind, A. (2003): Feminist Post-Development Thought: "Women in Development" and the Gendered Paradoxes of Survival in Bolivia. *Women's Studies Quarterly*, 31(3/4): 227-246. Lundquist, J. & J. Misra, along with KerryAnn O'Meara(2012): Parental Leave Usage by Fathers and Mothers at an American University. *Fathering*, 10(3): 37.

Marchbank, J. (2005): Still inside, still 'out'—A decade of reflection on exposure, risk and survival. *Women's Studies International Forum*, 28(2-3): 139-149.

Marcuse, H. (1964):*One-Dimensional Man: Studies in the Ideology of Advanced Industrial Society.* Boston: Beacon Press.

Mason, M. A., M. Goulden, & I. Frasch (2009): Why graduate students reject the fast track. *Academe*, 95(1): 1-18.

Mather, M. & D. Adams (2007):*The Crossover in Female-Male College Enrollment Rates* (February). Washington, D.C.: Population Reference Bureau.

MLA (2009): *Standing Still: The Associate Professors Survey.* Report of the Committee on the Status of Women in the Profession. New York: Modern Language Association.

Mohammed, J. (2009): "Sex or Gender Equity: the Organisation of Schooling in Trinidad and Tobago", in E. Page & J. Jha (eds.), *Exploring the bias: Gender and stereotyping in secondary schools*. London: Commonwealth Secretariat, pp. 73-104.

Morley, L. (2003): *Quality and power in higher education.* London: Society for Research in Higher Education and Open University Press.

Morley, L. (2005): Gender equity in Commonwealth Higher Education. *Women's Studies International Forum*, 28(2-3): 195-208.

Morrison, Z., M. Bourke, & C. Kelley (2005):"Stop making it such a big issue": Perceptions and experience of gender inequality by undergraduates at a British University. *Women's Studies International Forum*, 28(2-3): 109-113.

Moss-Racusin, C. A., J.F. Dovidio, V.L. Brescoll, M.J. Graham, J. Handelsman (2012): Science faculty's subtle bias favor male students. *Proceedings of the National Academy of Sciences*, 109: 16474-16479. doi: 10.1073/pnas.1211286109.

NCES (2010): The Condition of Education. Washington, D.C.: Institute of Education Sciences, National Center for Education Statistics. nces.ed.gov/programs/coe/figures/figure-er2-2/asp.

NCES (2011): *Digest of Education Statistics*. Washington, D.C.: National Center for Education Statistics, Institute of Education Sciences.

OECD (2010): Education at a Glance. Paris: OECD.

Ostrom, E. (1986): An Agenda for the Study of Institutions. *Public Choice*, 48(1): 3-25.

Perry, J. & E.G. David (2011): American women and gender pay gap: A changing demographic or the same old song. *Advancing Women in Leadership*, 31: 153-159.

Porter, S.R., R.K. Toutkoushian & J.V. Moore (2008): Pay inequities for recently hired faculty, 1988-2004. *Review of Higher Education*, 31(4): 465-487.

Read, J. & S. Oselin (2008): Gender and the Education-Employment Paradox in Ethnic and Religious Contexts: The Case of Arab Americans. *American Sociological Review*, 73: 296-313.

Ridgeway, C. (2011): *Framed by Gender. How Gender Inequality Persists in the Modern World*. Oxford: Oxford University Press.

Robelen, E. 2012 (11 July): Evidence Persists of STEM Achievement Gaps for Girls. *Education Week.*

Schiebinger, L. & S. Gilmartin (2010): Housework Is an Academic Issue. *Academe Online* (January-February)

Sewell, W.H. (1992): A Theory of Structure: Duality, Agency, and Transformation. *American Journal of Sociology*, 98(1): 1-29.

Shanani, N. (2003): "Resisting Mundane Violence"—Feminism and Queer Identity in Post-colonial India. *Michigan Feminist Studies*, Vol. 17, pp. 27-46.

Smith, G. C. & J.A. Waltman (2006): *Designing and implementing family-friendly policies in higher education.* Ann Arbor: Center for the Education of Women, University of Michigan.

Sporn, B. (2007): "University Adaptation and Gender Equality: A Case Study of the Vienna University of Economics and Business Administration", in M. A. Sagaria (ed.) *Women, Universities, and Change: Gender Equality in the European Union and Beyond.* New York: Palgrave Macmillan/ International Association of Universities, pp. 73-88.

Stromquist, N. P. (2012): "Excellence in Higher Education" in Bob Adamson, J. Nixon, and F. Su (eds.) *The Reorientation of Higher Education: Challenging the East-West Dichotomy*. New York: Springer and Comparative Education Research Centre of the University of Hong Kong, pp. 25-45.

Stromquist, N. P. (2013a): Education Policies for Gender Equity: Probing into State Responses. *Education Policy Analysis Archives*, Vol. 21, no. 65, 2013.

http://epaa.asu.edu/ojs/article/view/1338

Stromquist, N. P. (2013b): "Globalization and "Policyscapes: Ruptures and Continuities in Higher Education", in P. Axelrod, R. Trilokekar, T. Shanahan, R. Weller (eds.), *Making Policy in Turbulent Times: Challenges and Prospects for Higher Education.* Montreal: McGill-Queen's University Press, pp. 222-248.

Sugimoto, C. (2013): Global gender disparities in science. *Nature*, Vol. 504, pp. 211-213.

Theodorson, G. & A. Theodorson (1969): *A Modern Dictionary of Sociology*. New York: Thomas Crowell Co.

U.S. Census Bureau (2011): Educational Attainment in the United States. Washington, D.C.: U.S. Census Bureau.

U.S. Department of Labor and U.S. Labor Statistics (2011): *Women in the Labor Force: A Data book.* Washington, D.C.: US Department of Labor and US Labor Statistics.

UIS (2010): *Global Education Digest 2010. Comparing Education Statistics Across the World.* Montreal: UNESCO Institute for Statistics.

UNESCO (1998): Higher Education and Women: Issues and Perspectives. Paper prepared for the World Conference of Higher Education. Paris: Secretariat, UNESCO.

UNESCO (2009): *Communiqué. World Conference on Higher Education: The New Dynamics of Education and Research for Societal Change and Development.* Paris: UNESCO.

UNRISD (2010): *Combating Poverty and Inequality. Structural Change, Social Policy and Politics.* Geneva: United Nations Research Institute for Social Development.

Vincent-Lancrin, S. (2008): The reversal of gender inequalities in higher education: an on-going trend. Paris: OECD, draft document.

Yates, L. (1997): Gender Equity and the Boys Debate: what sort of challenge is it? *British Journal of Sociology of Education*, 18(3): 337-347.

Zapata, M. (2010): "La equidad de género en las universidades alemanas", in A. Mingo (ed.), *Desasosiegos. Relaciones de género en la educación.* Mexico: Universidad Nacional Autónoma de México, pp. 109-150.

Notes

1. I am fully aware that "women" is not a universal category as it intersects with socio-economic status, race, ethnicity, and age, among others. This intersectionality is not the focus of this paper. However, it should be stated that women from upper social classes are benefiting more than those from low-income families. For instance, in the U.S., more women than men graduate from college among families in the top 25% of the earning distribution; in contrast, there is almost no women's advantage among the poorest families (Coontz, 2012).
2. This federal initiative, known as ADVANCE, provides "institutional transformation" grants that offer on average $4 million over a five-year period. To date, some 35 such grants have been distributed through competitive procedures. Considering that at least 200 research universities exist in the U.S., the possibility of institutional change even among those elite institutions is circumscribed to a few.
3. On the other hand, a study of longitudinal effects of the decision to stop the "tenure clock" (Manchester et al., cited in Jaschik, 2012) found that this decision negatively affects women in terms of salary raises and creates a perception by others of women's "competing commitments" to their profession.
4. A strong critique of the pipeline explanation argues that women's low-level positions in university hierarchies are not merely a consequence of their small numbers as potential candidates to higher office but rather the consequence of current discriminatory and unquestioned gender practices (Allen & Castleman, 2001).

9

GENDER BIAS IN EDUCATION AMONG THE RURAL SIKHS OF PUNJAB

—SATINDERJIT THIND AND
SUSHMA JASWAL

Abstract

Women on the whole are a 'depressed class' in terms of literacy. Regional imbalances in women's education are persisting since independence. Superstitions and false beliefs inhibit literacy and, in a way, superstitious false beliefs are result of illiteracy and backwardness - the vicious circle goes on. The study, designed in this context, was conducted among three cultural zones of rural Punjab to assess variations in attitudes of rural parents with respect to female education. It aimed at ascertaining various reasons for discontinuation of female education. Ethnographic technique was used to collect qualitative data regarding these aspects. The results revealed that learning and performing of household chores were considered important for girls rather than going to school. The most frequent reasons cited by adolescent girls for dropping out of school in childhood were – personal, socio-cultural, economic and situational.

Introduction

In the last few decades, developing countries have attached a lot of significance to the role of education in the development process. Education, both formal and non-formal, plays a crucial role in development programmes, if they are to be meaningful. Women are seen as a definite target group for the simple reason that all over the world, literacy rates among women are lower than men. If women are indispensable to the development process, literacy among women must increase. The seven countries of the South Asian

Association for Regional Cooperation (SAARC) had observed 1990 as the 'year of the girl child'. The decade 1991-2000 was declared as the 'decade of the girl child'. Sundaram (1996) reported that more than 60 million girls in the SAARC countries do not get primary education and the majority does not complete their schooling. Patriarchal norms, early age at marriage and women's work participation have been held responsible for sex discriminatory practices (Gupta, 1995). Sharma (1987) indicated that in rural areas of India about 47 per cent of the agricultural work was done by women. The girls under 15 years of age constitute 20 per cent of the country's population and also share 20 per cent of the family burdens.

Lack of education, exposure and opportunities do not allow women to exercise the right kind of choice. Low level of literacy among women and girls is one of the basic elements of gender backwardness. Even in areas where substantial progress is witnessed with high educational status, female literacy rates especially in rural areas trail behind male literacy rates. In India, female literacy is 39.29 per cent and male literacy is 64.6 per cent and half of the enrolled girls drop out from the schools. In Punjab, male literacy rate is 75.63 per cent and female literacy rate is 63.55 per cent (Census 2001). In Punjab, the district Nawanshahar has the highest female literacy ratio i.e. 75.56 per cent and district Mansa has the lowest literacy rate i.e. 45.07 per cent (Census 2001). The following Table shows the trends in decadal literacy in Punjab state for years 1951-2001:

Table 1: Male and Female Literacy Ratio

	1951	*1961*	*1971*	*1981*	*1991*	*2001*
Male	210	407	404	472	657	756
Female	85	207	259	337	504	636

Evidently, though literacy rate in case of females is less in comparison to males, yet there is continuous increase in the number of females being enrolled for education. This may be attributed to the favourable government policies for the needy and bright students and ever-increasing appreciation for girls' education.

Though the per centage of literacy among women has increased from what it was few years ago, the disparity between girl's education and boy's education is very wide. The question arises; whether the girls have the same educational facilities as are being provided for the boys? So, education and gender equality are at the center-stage of contemporary discourse on development and education but disparities in the education of men and women are continuing.

The government and planners in several developing countries have made efforts to enhance literacy rates and educational levels among women, both as a welfare measure and a developmental necessity. However, spreading literacy among females seems to be complex, difficult and a time consuming task in the tradition-bound society like India. Therefore, the study was conducted to have a broader view regarding education in cultural zones of rural Punjab with the following objectives:

1. To study the attitudes of rural parents with respect to female education, belonging to three cultural zones of rural Punjab.
2. To assess the causes leading to female illiteracy in rural areas of Punjab.
3. To identify parental and adolescent's reasons for discontinuation of studies in different cultural zones of rural Punjab. .

Methodology

Sample Selection: The Punjab state for the purpose of study has been divided into three cultural zones i.e. *Majha, Malwa* and *Doaba*. Each cultural zone is equipped with its own cultural tradition in relation to customs, values and ways of life but, at the same time, there is so much similarity and overlapping of the values that sometimes it becomes difficult to differentiate. Data for the present study was collected from rural areas selected randomly

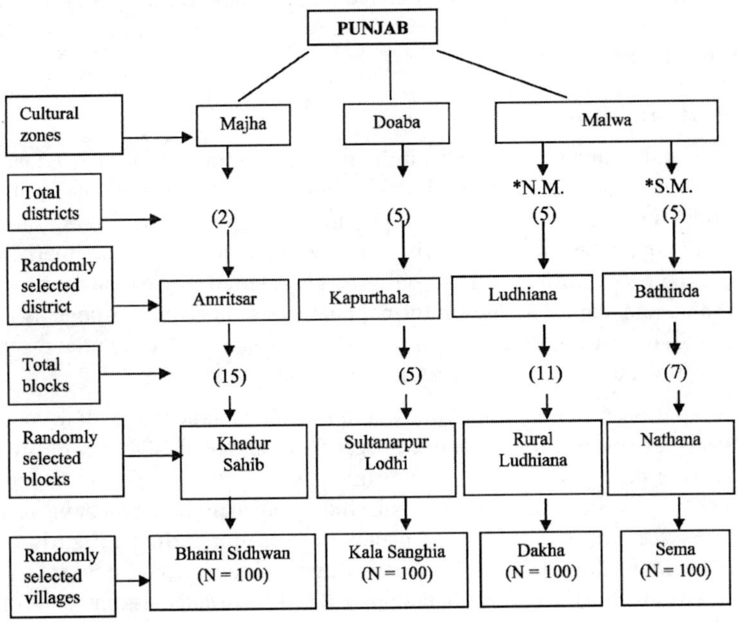

* N.M. = Northern Malwa; S.M. = Southern Malwa

Total sample size: 400 families

Figure 1: Sample Selection

from three cultural zones. The *Malwa* zone, being a big region (having ten districts) and intra-zonal variations in cultural traits being high, two districts were selected from this region. The criteria for inclusion of the sample is that the family must belong to Sikh religion, it should have marginal land or no land and each family should have children of both genders in the adolescent age. Only 100 sikh families who met the inclusion criteria were randomly selected from each of the four randomly selected villages. Thus, the sample comprised of 400 rural sikh families. The plan for sample selection is shown in Figure1.

Technique of Data Collection

For data collection, ethnographic technique was used for a multifaceted interaction between the researcher and the participants, thereby making the data rich and dynamic. This approach helped to understand the culture of the distinct social group through participant (interactive) and non-participant (non-interactive) observations by making extensive field notes and trying to capture the culture's unique values and social processes. Through interactive ethnographic technique, effort was made to talk to all female members in the family for the required information. The observations were also noted on the required issues through non-interactive ethnographic technique by attending social and religious functions. A checklist was also prepared covering all issues intended for discussion.

Results and Discussion

With the impact of western influences, the concept of female education began to change gradually. The introduction and encouragement of missionary schools for both the sexes encouraged girls for going to school on a formal basis. Though, the number of girls was very small, yet it was a landmark in the development of women's education as the girls started leaving the confinement of home and started attending formal classes on the same footings as boys. But, the study in cultural zones of rural Punjab reported wide gender disparity in literacy rate irrespective of socio-economic status.

After partition, Punjab witnessed a radical social change on account of various factors. Several proactive programs were launched for the upliftment of lower cast people. The government's policy of affirmative action strengthened the practices of Sikhism which consider all human beings equal. Then, with the occurance of green revolution, industrialization and urbanization, there is a growing hetrogenity of socio- economic status and life-styles within the caste. The co-existence of caste and class curbs the clear-cut manifestation of caste and class differentiation. People from all castes and classes enjoy friendly social environment.

Among the castes included in the Sikh fold in Punjab, the Jat Sikh is at the top of the hierarchy. The higher land income and greater urban contacts have changed considerably the life-styles, as these are increasingly approximating the urban standards. This section of community enjoys the element of dominance because of being economically well off. They usually send their children to good schools to nearby cities and even at the good residential schools at far away places.

The Government has certain policies for lower caste children such as reservation of seats in technical and professional courses, free education, books and scholarships for them. Parents belonging to lower caste encourage children to ignore their family profession and take up education enthusiastically, along with variety of skilled occupations. They are benefited most from the constitution and have become aware to send their children to schools. Keeping in view the reservation practices and awareness for education, the present study was planned in Punjab state.

The analysis of the data on the attitude of rural parents with regard to education of their daughters, among three cultural zones of Punjab, revealed that families belonging to southern Malwa were least interested in the education of their female children. Parents were of the view that education for girls is wastage of time and money and it is not required for one's life. They were of the opinion that girls should be trained only in household chores/agricultural activities. They reported that instead of wasting money on education of children, the family should accumulate more land/immovable property, as agriculture was the only rewarding occupation for the rural community. It was believed that status of the family was judged by the area of land a family possesses and not by the level of education of members of the family. Children studying at college level were doing so because of their personal efforts and not due to any willingness or motivation on the part of families. Moreover, parents were not happy to send their children in hostels at far away places, particularly the daughters. Sending children to hostels at far away places is inviting problem for children, particularly girls and family members. They felt that education at village school level is sufficient for carrying on day-to-day activities.

It was further observed that among all cultural zones, only a very small proportion of the girls had ventured outside the village for attaining higher education. This is attributed to the fact that females were not permitted to go outside the village and due to the limited facilities in the village school i.e. upto primary/middle/high or 10+2 levels, most of the girls were seen dropping out in between, either to extend a helping hand in the household work, or in the fields. The parents remain apprehensive for finding a suitable marriage partner for their daughters if girls attain higher education. They were also not in favour of granting them freedom to interact with the members of the opposite sex, whereas no such criteria was fixed for boys to go outside the village for higher education. Sex discrimination still prevails in the community for granting permission to daughters to go for higher education. Surprisingly, girls had also internalized this belief so deeply that they never assert for more education.

Punjab ranks 15 as far as the female literacy rate in India is concerned. The gap is wider in rural areas. The rural literacy rate is 65.16 per cent in comparison to 79.13 per cent urban literacy rate (Census, 2001).

An attempt was also made to find out the level of education, parents intend to impart to their daughters and sons. The matriculation or higher secondary levels are generally considered to be high enough for girls and/or whatever is available in the village in the name of education, be it a stitching class. But no such level had been prescribed for boys, they can even go to schools/colleges outside the village. Parents feel the problem of physical security for the girls if they had to travel on their own to places outside the village. They believed that it was not customary to provide higher education to girls in rural areas. Some of the parents preferred to educate daughters upto high school level but learning of household chores such as cooking, stitching and care of animals were considered more important than formal education. The ultimate aim of rural parents was to acquaint the daughters with the household work. Imparting education to daughters was necessary only to make them able to read and write letters, manage their household work/property and become aware of the different happenings in the society. No respondent was seen interested to get their daughters in good jobs in the formal sector but education was most sought for sons so as to help them become economically sound which would in turn enhance the status of family. Similar results have been reported by Joshi (1999) in her study.

It was observed that the primary cause of low priority for female education was the continuation of traditions and out-dated rigid ideas. Women are still treated as unequal to men. They themselves hold traditional notions about their positions. Interestingly, where woman herself was interested to get her daughter educated, resistance came from other members of family, mainly husband and mother-in-law. The resistance was stronger where the husband 'the decision maker' himself was illiterate. This could be an important reason for continued perpetuation of illiteracy among women. The resistance was very much based on the out-dated beliefs that a woman's place was inside the house and education was of no use to her. According to Rana (1995), the low literacy among females is attributed to the prevalence of discrimination against women. This means that status of women cannot be elevated till there is disparity between the two sexes at the educational level.

Household responsibilities were considered another most significant reason which kept the girl child away from school. Young girls were expected to do household chores and were left with no time and energy to do anything else. Again, based on the traditional beliefs/practices, the household work was the sole responsibility of women, hence, mothers trained their daughters on that aspect from early age. The sensitization of girls that they shall be appreciated most by the members of the family and the community for learning household tasks well kills their motivation for studies. Such a situation makes girls to accept psychologically the discrimination favouring boys.

Due to socio-cultural, economic and infrastructural constraints the rural girl child is being neglected and denied opportunities of educational advancement. A rural girl child spent a significant amount of her time in the collection of fuel, in fetching water, in caring for the siblings and in attending to household chores. She was also engaged in family-based economic activity. Girls were, thus, introduced much earlier to the world of work, first, in the household and later, outside, which was one of the most important reasons for her withdrawal from schools. Thus, education, which could have been a major instrument of women's equality, change and empowerment, is unable to play its due role in this regard.

Involvement of women in a variety of on-farm and off-farm activities from early morning till late in the evening hardly leaves any scope for rural women folk to look after the education of their children and for their own leisure time. Their contributions to farm and off-farm activities were not adequately recognised. Women working on their own farm allege that they work without wages and were scolded and beaten by husbands and other family members. Majority of women led miserable life and were victims of prevailing socio-cultural, economic, demographic and political constraints which came in the way of improving their productivity (Malik *et al* 2001)

Farm work, therefore, was identified as a major factor hindering girls to continue education. Girls from low-socio economic status families had to help their mothers in the fields as full-time or part-time workers, along with the household work. Besides cooking and washing, girls also lend their supporting hand to mothers in baby sitting when their mothers were away to the fields.

Further, the parents indicated the following reasons for not educating/ discontinuing education of their daughters.

- No use in investing money on higher education of daughters.
- Household work and care of younger siblings suffer if girls go to school.
- Girls had to work in fields or as maid servants.
- Financial constraints.
- Negative attitude of the family.
- Not appreciated by society.
- Education makes marriage difficult.
- Education makes girls authoritative leading to marital mal-adjustment.
- Lack of interest and motivation among girls for education. .
- No school facilities nearby.
- Absence of female teacher in the school.

Most of the aforementioned reasons are not in favour of girls. They form an integral part of the rural belief system, designed to deny equal rights to both the sexes in matter of education.

Sex discrimination became more obvious when adolescent boys and girls mentioned different reasons for discontinuation/no education to them. The reasons given by them were put into four categories such as personal, socio-cultural, economic and situational. The following were the different reasons stated by adolescent boys and girls.

Reasons	*Girls*		*Boys*	
	Drop-outs	***No-schooling***	***Drop-outs***	***No-schooling***
Personal				
Harsh discipline	√	-	√	-
Fear of examination	√	-	√	-
Dislike of teachers	√	-	√	-
Lack of interest	√	-	√	-
Bad health	√	-	√	-
Stress of domestic work	√	√	-	-
Helping parents in fields	√	√	√	√
Socio-Cultural				
Family not valuing education	√	√	-	-
Negative criticism by neighbourers		√	-	-
Economic				
Poverty	√	√	√	√
Situational				
Lack of school facilities in nearby area	√	√	—	—
Absence of female teacher	√	√	—	—

Socio-cultural and situational reasons were very specific to southern Malwa zone of rural Punjab.

Majority of the adolescent girls and boys mentioned personal reasons. But interestingly, no boy mentioned socio-cultural and situational reasons for discontinuation of studies. As reported in Tribune (2001), girls in Udhampur region of Jammu and Kashmir (India) were determined to study and establish an identity of their own, despite hilly terrains, vast distances, lack of infrastructure and above all, terrorist activities. Because of the constant possibility of coming under attacks on their way to the institution, girls always travelled in groups. Statistics revealed a drastic fall in the number of girl students when they move from lower grades to the higher. It was 28,475 in the middle school and 10,979 in the high school. The reasons stated by government for a swift decrease at high school level was that there are only 12 higher secondary schools, 39 middle schools and 353 primary schools for females. Primary schools can be found in remote villages, while for higher studies the girls have to be sent to far-off places. The area being hilly, parents were reluctant to send their daughters anywhere far away from home. As such, the girls have to abandon their studies after the primary level. This shows that girls, whether residing in plain area or hilly area, share the same kind of social and situational factors.

Conclusion

Though the conditions for the girls' education is not very satisfactory in all cultural zones of rural Punjab, the area of southern Malwa was observed to be behind other zones of rural Punjab. The people belonging to southern Malwa were more interested in display of social ceremonies, irrespective of the occasion. They attach greater importance to dowry in terms of giving expensive cars, heavy jewellery, rich clothes, lavish entertainment programme and free-flowing drinks at the time of marriage of their daughters. They seemed to be firm believers of traditional norms and practices. Their aim of life is to accumulate agricultural land and merry-making – be it a birth of a son or winning panchayat elections, but they are least interested in education of girl child. The remaining other areas such as northern Malwa, Majha and Doaba depicted similar trends as far as education of the girl child is concerned.

Recommendations

Prevalent social constraints, belief system, superstitions and social practices deny equal right to both the sexes. Poverty, unemployment and illiteracy threaten female survival. For removal of inequalities, based on sex discriminating practices against education of girls, attention has to be shifted to the values of society and culture instead of depending entirely on economic growth of the country or academic inputs alone. The eradication of gender discrimination cannot succeed in isolation unless it is accompanied by structural changes such as removal of cultural barriers against women's access to education, employment and equal involvement in family decision-making. Education system needs restructuring so that learning of life skills could take place. For that, shift has to be made from the purely academics to practice. Necessary infrastructure should be developed in rural/remote areas to smoothen the journey to education

References

Anonymous (2001) Girls Defy Hurdles to Pursue Education. *The Tribune*, Dec., p. 9.

Census of India (2001) Series 4 *Punjab Provisional Population Total*, paper - 2

Gupta, V. (1995) Status of Girl Child in Rural Schools of Himachal Pradesh - A Case Study. *Him Shiksha.* Vol. 25, No. 3.

Joshi, S. (1999) *Women and Development - The Changing Scenario*, Mittal Publications, New Delhi.

Malik, P.S. Karwasra, J.L. and Malik, S. (2001) Dilemma of Beast of Burden: Gender Inequality in Employment of Family Farm Labour. *Journal of Agricultural Development Policy* Vol. XIII, No. 1, pp. 27-33.

Rana, S. (1995) Women and Education: New Challenges. *Him Shiksha*, Vol. 25, No. 3.

Sharma, A. (1987) *Resources and Human Well-Being: Inputs from Science and Technology,* 74th Session. Indian Science Congress, Calcutta.

Sundaram, S. (1996) Guarding the Girl Child. Social Welfare 42: 18-20

10

WOMEN'S EDUCATION, DOWRY, BARGAINING AND GAINS TO MARRIAGE*

— *T. LAKSHMANASAMY*

Abstract

Apart from the economic value of women's education, the non-pecuniary returns to investments in women's human capital are substantial. Women's education increases her bargaining power within the household and the human capital investments in children. The models of household behaviour usually use either the non-labour income of the women or the extra environmental opportunities outside the household as bargaining instruments of women in household allocation decisions. However, these models apply the bargaining framework for the post-marital household behaviour only, largely ignoring the premarital bargaining strengths of women. This paper uses investments in women, especially on education and dowry, as bargaining instruments to strengthen the women's gains to marriage in the marriage market. Women's human capital and dowry also act as an instrument for both matching and bargaining. Using primary sample, we find assortative marriage matching, but weak bargaining strengths of women and therefore her insignificant role in household decisions.

Introduction

Apart from its intrinsic value as a crucial development goal, education is also central to one's ability to respond to the opportunities that development presents. The human capital investment not only is a means for enhancing

---

* Revised version of the paper presented in the Seminar on Women's Education and Development held at Malasiss, Rajasthan (July 31-April 2, 2004)

individual labour productivity and earnings, but also is a source of growth, accumulation, and income and earnings redistribution. The investment value of women's education is still higher, both from the individual as well as the society's points of view, as it has not only large monetary but also substantial non-monetary returns for both individual and society. There exists a substantial body of literature dealing with investments in human capital, especially on women's education and health, and the returns, both private and social. There have also been studies that examine the allocation of human capital investments between the sexes, especially among children, in families and in societies. Gender inequalities in education, wages, health and nutrition are widely documented both in developed and developing countries, but they are less often empirically analysed to understand the differential returns and more importantly the gender inequalities within the households. A wide spectrum of results do attempt to quantify the extent of these aspects, but the causes for these unequal outcomes have been less understood.

A basic question that every social science interested in social justice and equality tries to address is: does the increase in the economic status of women translate into progress in their well being as wives and in their overall well-being? In order to understand such deeper questions, one has to go beyond simple individual centered approach to the household level analysis. One has to understand what is the role of women and what happens to them as well as what they can cause within the household. In this respect the social and economic environment in which the families are raised is crucial. In the context of family, the significance of pre-household formation decisions with regard to marriage and marital choices determine women's position within the household and her subsequent roles and outcomes. As we get into the household behaviour, the household decision making process is generally more complex since it reflects the relative preferences and influences of each family member. In this context, the nature of a household is aptly described in the literature as a 'factory'. In the words of Becker, the 'father of economics of family': "A household is truly a 'small factory': it combines capital goods, raw materials, and labor to clean, feed, procreate, and otherwise produce useful commodities" (Becker, 1965). And, as the leading exponents on household models observe: "We too perceive the household as a factory, but like all factories, it consists of individuals who – motivated at times by altruism, at times by self-interest, and often by both – cajole, co-operate, threaten, argue, support, and, occasionally walk out on each other" (Alderman, Chiappori, Haddad, Hoddinott and Kanbur, 1995, p.15). At this juncture, it is highly desirable to understand what goes on within the household, how decisions are taken and resources allocated, what are their implications as to women's position and her role, and why is it so important to understand women's position and power within the household in resource allocation decisions, as well as the importance of her pre-marital investments that are likely to influence her position in the marriage market and in the subsequent family.

In other words, an understanding of the influence of pre-marital investments in women and its impact on the subsequent household decisions is necessary to put in perspective the status of women in contemporary societies. Hence, an attempt is made in this paper to analyse the women's position within the family, using the models of houeshold behaviour. This paper has two main objectives. First, it attempts to provide an overview of theoretical and empirical literature on the economics of family, particularly on the marriage matching and the household resource allocation decisions. Secondly, the paper attempts to empirically test the bargaining theory of household behaviour, and specifically, the productivity hypothesis of marriage market model and the influence of dowry and pre-marital investments in female education as bargaining instruments in the household decisions process in the Indian context, using a primary household survey data from Tamil Nadu.

The rest of the paper is organized as follows: Section 2 presents a brief account of the theories of marriage and intra-household resource allocation decisions. In Section 3, the empirical results are discussed. Finally, Section 4 summarizes the paper.

Economics of Family

In the literature on the economics of family, there exists two major separate strands of analyses on the role of women in the decision making process. There are theories on economics of marriage and household formation. This literature seeks to address the issues of marital choice and gains to marriage. The other literature, generally described as intra-household allocation models, seeks to address the issues of the distribution of power and the consequent outcomes within the household. Two leading economic models of intra-family allocation are: Becker's 'unitary' (altruistic as well as egoistic) or common preference approach, and the 'collective' or Nash-bargaining (divorce threat) models. As an alternative, the non-cooperative or separate spheres bargaining model argues that the threat point is not divorce but a non-cooperative standoff defined in terms of traditional gender roles and greater role of expectations and the non-cooperative standoff. Although such a solution is not optimal, the final equilibrium may be optimal, because of the presence of transaction costs. Carried to extremes, the traditional division of labour and responsibilities suggests a separate sphere equilibrium in the family. Each spouse makes decisions within his or her own sphere, optimizing subject to the constraint of individual resources. Joint consumption economies of scale are an important source of gains and even non-cooperative members enjoy the benefits of household public goods, such as children. This aspect distinguishes a non-cooperative from a pair of independently optimizing individuals.

The unitary model argues that household resources are pooled and shared according to some common household preferences. As long as the household head is sufficiently altruistic, efficient allocation implies that individual member's well-being is taken care of and each member has every incentive to maximize household income or utility. Hence, there is no possibility of conflicts or differential preferences in allocation decisions. Since household decision is common, the unitary model does not visualize any conflict of interests within the household. Even if there exists some sort of free-riding, Becker's Rotten Kid theorem, completely eliminates the scope of rivalry and bargaining. In contrast, Nash-bargained models see the possibility of the existence of conflicting individual preferences among family members, and each member trying to bargain more family resources for own utility maximisation using some threats. The strength of threat or bargain increases with the availability of individual specific resources. The common threat is the divorce threat.

Recent studies provide a more institutional approach to bargaining within the household that moves beyond bargaining models with simplistic fallback or threat points. Bargaining models often define individual's threat points in terms of his or her market earnings or individual assets. But bargaining is affected by legal and institutional aspects that determine how household resources are disposed and that defines enforceable claims on other individual income flows such as child support. Changes in these, described as extra-environmental parameters by McElroy and Horney (1981), such as property rights in land, could easily have a much bigger impact on bargaining power than changes in the relative earnings of men and women. Recent literature in this area has shown that the political and legal institutions as well as the characteristics of the community – the extra-household environmental parameters – that affect the ability of a particular individual to generate income in the event of household dissolution (threat point), or factors that capture sex specific roles of members (to define non-cooperation) can affect allocation within the household could help explain the motive behind collective effects to defend or modify traditional rights. [See Alderman, et. al., (1995); Strauss and Thomas (1995); Haddad, Hoddinott and Alderman (1997); Browning and Lechne (2001); Vermeulen (2002); and Schultz (2002) for an overview of alternative approaches to the bargaining power within the household].

Economics of Marriage

In general, marriage is positively associated with a large number of outcomes, including improved cognitive, emotional and physical well-being for children, better mental and physical health for adults, and greater earnings and consumption for family members. In an economic model, potential spouses compare their expected valuations of economic, social and health outcomes associated with entering into a marriage with those of remaining single. Marriage occurs if the perceived value of marriage exceeds that of the alternative. The early altruistic model by Becker converts a woman's gains into a general increase in her family's income. From there on, how much the wife gains depends on how much her family's altruist (possibly herself) cares for her. Becker (1973) and its sequel (Becker, 1974) were the first to apply rational choice and market model to the analysis of marriage. While previous marriage analysts, mostly sociologists, had focused on the effect of marriage conditions on probabilities and mate characteristics, Becker pointed out that marriage market conditions also affect the individual well-being of each spouse, with possible implications for consumption patterns. Since then numerous studies have convincingly established the positive association between marriage and various measures of well-being. Many studies have also found that marriage is positively associated with market labour supply and earnings of not only females but men's earnings also. Thus, there are productivity gains to marriage through household division of labour and specialization (Becker, 1991). By investing either in home capital or market capital rather than in both, marital partners increase their productivity in their specialized areas, which in turn, increases gains from marriage. There are additional gains in marriage – the gains from association from marriage. Both the gains from specialization and gains from association are likely to increase with education (Tiefenthaler, 1997). Further, Becker's transferable utility model of the marriage market explains how the marriage market also adjusts to changes in the supplies of different types of men and women, different types of living arrangements, and different types of legal environment (Siow, 2003).

Formally, let the welfare W of the married couples depend upon what they bring to marriage:

$$W = f(A_m+A_f, E_m, E_f;Z) \quad (1)$$

where A represents physical wealth, E represents human capital, m and f stand for groom and bride, and Z represents a vector of factors that exogenously affect the gains from marriage. Assume that the utility from marriage increases with wealth and human capital. In case that the human capital is only valued for its income generating potential, the utility from marriage can be written as:

$$W = f(Am+Af+\lambda mEm+\lambda fEf;Z) \quad (2)$$

where λ_m and λ_f (λ_m>0, λ_f>0) are the lifetime return from human capital. Then all brides prefer grooms with high $A_m+\lambda_m E_m$ and all grooms prefer brides with high $A_f+\lambda_f E_f$, thus resulting in an assortative marriage market. However, with positive externalities from one spouse's human capital to the other's, grooms and brides are ranked according to multiple attributes, individual with particular traits may prefer to mate with similar traits, or prefer to mate with traits to compensate for their own.

Since the pre-marital investments, in large part parental considerations, and in third world countries the inheritance takes place at marriage, the choice facing the altruistic parents can be represented as:

$$\max_{A_m, A_f, E_m, E_f} U(S-\Sigma_g A_m-\Sigma_b A_f-\Sigma_g sE_m-\Sigma_b sE_f; Z)+$$

$$\Sigma_g \delta_g f(A_m+\bar{A}_f+\lambda_m E_m+\lambda_f \bar{E}_f;Z)+\Sigma_b \delta_b f(\bar{A}_m+A_f+\lambda_m \bar{E}_m+\lambda_f E_f;Z) \qquad (3)$$

where g and b subscripts denote prospective grooms and brides respectively, U(.) is the utility of parents, S is parental wealth, s is the cost of human capital, and d are the welfare weights for sons and daughters, and the variables $\bar{A}_m$, $\bar{A}_f$, $\bar{E}_m$, $\bar{E}_f$ represent the assets and human capital of the people sons and daughters marry.

The early models on marriage and marital gains did not assimilate the then growing labour market analysis, especially the spousal labour supply. A major obstacle to the integration of labour research with marriage is the lack of integration between Becker's (1965) theory of allocation of time and Becker's (1973; 1974) theory of marriage. Labour research of Becker-Mincer household decision making model ignores that households can be formed or dissolved; marriage model of Becker is not formulated in terms of time use. The concept facilitating the integration of an analysis of labour supply with a marriage analysis is that of spousal labour. The concept of 'wife services' which includes housework activities and child related activities performed by wives for the benefit of husbands was generalized and made gender-neutral by Grossbard-Shechtman (1984), with 'household labour' and later 'spousal labour' by Grossbard-Shechtman (1993) to emphasize the spousal benefit beyond housework, implying spousal workers typically get a material compensation, termed 'quasi-wage' for spousal labour. Many empirical works indicate that most married couples have access to each other's income, more so when the wife is not in the labour-force. The portability/generality of the human capital of spousal workers (and also potential spousal workers) opens the door to an analysis of markets for spousal labour and the analysis of gains to marriage in the labour market.

Empirical studies have shown that male earnings increase with women's education (Benham, 1974) and occupation (Neuman and Ziderman, 1992). However, the empirical relationships are confounded with problems of reverse causality and spurious correlation from omitted variables. Because of these, one is not sure, whether marriage makes people better off, better off people are more likely to marry, or some combinations of the two (Ribar, 2003). While there is a compelling evidence that married men have higher earnings than never-married men, the existence and mechanisms of marriage premium remains elusive. A number of hypotheses has been advanced to explore the nature of marriage premium – why married men earn higher wages. The dominant theory is the Becker's productivity hypothesis where married men have greater opportunity to specialize in the labour market when their wives specialize in home production. An alternative, the selection hypothesis, reverses the direction of causality, proposing that men with higher earnings capacity are valued more in the marriage market and are thus more likely to marry (Nakosteen and Zimmer, 1987; 1997). However, the empirical evidences are mixed. Some studies have shown that, taking selection effects into account, married men still have higher earnings. Thus, there is a potential wage gain from marriage as well as penalty associated with the wives labour market hours, conforming productivity hypothesis (Korenman and Neumark, 1991; Loh, 1996; Chun and Lee, 2001). Whether the same is true in the case of women is unknown as there are virtually no studies on the marriage premium for women. For women, the selection effect may be strong if the marriage market is assortative. As women have to move with their husbands, their labour market attachment may be less and hence their low specialization may not raise their productivity to yield marriage premium. Stutzer and Fry (2003) find some evidence in Germany for selection hypothesis as women gain from actual specialization. It is observed that couples with large relative wage differences and thus a high potential gain from specialization, benefit more from marriage. However, the study is more related with subjective well-being (happiness), than with income gains to marriage.

Another dimension of the marriage market, the quality of match between partners has additional implications for private and social welfare. An individual benefits not only from the increased production possibilities that a more educated spouse brings to a marriage, as assumed in the standard economic models of marriage (Becker, 1991), but also is rewarded by a positive consumption complementarities between the husband's and wife's schooling. Kremer (1997) observes a match correlation between .4 and .6. Further, the correlation between the schooling of husband and wife increases with economic development. Schultz (2001) reports for Taiwan, that there is a decline in gender wage gap in average years of schooling completed from 4.2 years in 1976 to 0.23 years in 1995; consequently, the correlation of schooling of wives and their husbands which was 0.4 in 1976 had increased to nearly 0.6 by 1995. If the private returns to education are of comparable magnitude for men and women, but the social externalities associated with decreased child mortality, increased child health, increased child schooling enrollments and decreased fertility, are all more positively to women's schooling than men's, and these outcomes are valued by the society, it is efficient for society to invest more in the schooling of women than men (Schultz, 2002). But, whether these social externality benefits associated with women's schooling vary by the level of her schooling? Behrman, et. al. (1997), for India, found that mother's literacy and some primary schooling had a larger effect on child's school work and attainment than did her post-primary schooling, suggesting higher social returns for the most basic levels of female schooling. Thus, evidences indicate that assortative marriages have market premium through productivity gains to the spousal education. A deeper understanding of the marriage market may sharpen our insights.

Economics of Intra-Household Allocation

In sharp contrast to the neoclassical economics based theory of marriage, the recent game theory based bargaining models predict that women's gains in economic independence translate directly into increases in their threat points (based on their best possible utility outcomes outside the marriage) and hence into increases in their well-being as family members. Challenging the early unified models of family (Becker, 1991), which could not prescribe how intra-household distribution issues could be resolved, the recent developments in the bargaining models of household behaviour seem to have potentials to fruitfully address the possibility of conflicting interests of family members and the distribution issues within the household. A common approach in the collective models of household behaviour is to allow for the existence of independent preferences among the members of the family and identify the resources under the independent control of family members such as non-labour income, and use it as a bargaining instrument in the allocation decisions. When women control more non-earned income, indicators of child development improves by a greater amount than when men control these resources, holding constant the total budget consumption of the family. The empirical regularity strongly suggests that the pooling of family resources is less than perfect (Fortin and Lacroix, 1997). Further, the existence of legislative support increases a women's utility outside the household and hence it increases her bargaining strengths and threat point utility and thereby her share in the resource allocation. Thus, the existence of women specific resources within the household and options outside the household will have differential impact on household investment decisions, favouring those which will enhance the women's choices (Phipps and Burton, 1995).

The Pareto-only model (Chiappori, 1988; 1992; Browning,et.al., 1994; Browning and Chiappori, 1998; Wooley, 1998; Chen and Woolley, 2001; Lundberg and Pollak, 1993) assume that households will never settle for an allocation that leaves scope for one person to be made better off without detriment to any other family member's welfare. Theoretically, the collective models, both cooperative and non-cooperative approaches, allow for differential treatments and outcomes among household members and resolve conflicts within the household. In general, the existing studies on intra-household allocation of resources use models in which allocation is determined in one of the four ways:

(1) Parents allocate resources based on the differential labour market returns to the members of the family (Rosenzweig and Schultz, 1982).

(2) Parents allocate resources according to their own utility, which depends on the well-being of the members of the family (altruist model) (Behrman, Pollak and Taubman, 1982; Behrman, 1988).

(3) Households allocate resources based on the productivity of individual members of the family (Pitt, Rosenzweig and Hassen, 1990).

(4) Resources are allocated according to the relative bargaining power of the members of the family (Haddad and Hoddinott, 1994; Thomas, 1990).

Formally, consider a household with two individuals, husband (h) and wife (w), both of whom derive utility from a consumption bundle of commodities including a vector of goods and leisure (**x**), conditional on household characteristics (g). The utility of this unitary household can be expressed as:

$$U(\mathbf{x},\gamma) \tag{4}$$

which is maximised subject to a single household income or budget constraint:

$$\mathbf{px} = Y = y_j + y_h + y_w \tag{5}$$

where y_j is household joint income, y_h and y_w are individual incomes. Since preferences are identical, utility maximisation under standard assumptions leads to a set of demand functions for **x** that are functions of a vector of prices **p**, total household income Y, and household characteristics, g:

$$x_i = x_i(\mathbf{p}, Y; \gamma) \tag{6}$$

Thus, under income pooling approach of the unitary model, only total household income Y is relevant for demand and not its components, i.e. specific incomes of husband and wife.

But, in the collective models, the utility function is individual specific in which, under altruistic preferences, both member's consumptions appear:

$$U_j(x_j, x_k; \gamma) \qquad j=h,w \text{ and } k=h,w \tag{7}$$

Then, for all Pareto-efficient outcomes, there exists some weight m for which the household's optimisation problem can be written as:

$$\text{Max } \mu U_h(x_h, x_w; \gamma) + (1\text{-}\mu U_w(x_h, x_w; \gamma) \tag{8}$$

subject to the budget constraint (2). The resulting demand equations are now functions of not only prices, incomes, and household characteristics, but also the weight, m:

$$x_i = x_i(\mathbf{p}, Y, \mu; \gamma) \tag{9}$$

The weight m is the sharing rule, which is related to the relative bargaining strengths of the household members within the household. When m is equal to zero, the model is a unitary and when m equals one, it is a dictatorial model. Let b_h and b_w represent proxy measures (extra-environmental parameters) for bargaining power that influence m, the demand functions can now be expressed as (suppressing the price variation):

$$x_i = /x_i(Y;\mu[b_h,b_w], g) \qquad (10)$$

The unitary model's income pooling hypothesis implies that the identity of the partners is irrelevant, the effect of the proxy measures should be zero:

$$\partial x_i/\partial \beta_j=0 \qquad \text{with j=h,w} \qquad (11)$$

This is a straightforward test of the unitary model. Under Pareto-efficient collective models, the sharing rule is affected by each member's bargaining power:

$$\partial x_i/\partial \beta_j=(\partial x_i/\partial \mu)(\partial \mu/\partial \beta_j=) \qquad \text{with j=h or w} \qquad (12)$$

Under Pareto-efficiency, the ratio of any two such effects is independent of i. That is,

$$\partial x_i/\partial \beta_h]/[\partial x_i/\partial \beta_w] = (\partial \mu/\partial \beta_h)/(\partial \mu/\partial \beta_w)$$

$$= (\partial x_j/\partial \beta_h)/(\partial x_j/\partial \beta_w) \qquad (13)$$

This result that the ratio of husband-to-wife effects is identical across all pairs of goods i and j, provides a simple and powerful test of Pareto-efficiency.

The proxy measures that have been used in the literature, reflecting bargaining power but at the same time not endogenous, include: (1) share of income earned by women (Hoddinott and Haddad, 1995); (2) non-labour income (Schultz, 1990; Thomas, 1990); (3) current assets (Doss, 1999); inherited assets (Quisumbing, 1994); assets at marriage (Thomas, Contreras and Frankenberg, 2002); and the provision of resources to specific household members (Lundberg, Pollak and Wales, 1997; Rubalcava and Thomas, 2002); pre-marital investments (Quisumbing and Maluccio, 2003; Iyigun and Walsh, 2004); and legislative provisions (Chiappori, Fortin and Lacroix, 2002).

The empirical side of relative bargaining strengths of spouses in the household behaviour concentrates on the behavioural impact of the variables that may influence the intra-household distribution of power. There are considerable evidence that resources are not allocated randomly within the households, and that the distribution of resources is unequal within the household in many developing countries (Schultz, 1995; 2002; Strauss and Thomas 1995; Behrman 1997; Haddad, Hoddinott and Alderman 1997; and Schultz 2001 for an overview). Such an unequal distribution of goods usually takes the form of bias against females, that too female children. In India, evidence based on mortality rates and human capital investments (health and education) indicates that there is considerable bias against girls in the intra-household allocation of resources (Bardhan, 1984; Behrman, 1988; Rosenzweig and Schultz, 1982; Sen 1984). Thomas (1990), Schultz (1990), Kooreman and Kapteyn (1990), and Browing, et.al. (1994) have provided evidence that the distribution of total intra-household income has significant impact on outcomes, thus rejecting the standard 'income pooling' prediction. Thomas, et. al., (2002) have shown that the distribution of wealth by gender at marriage has significant impact on child health (an intra-household allocation issue), in those areas in which wealth remains under the contributor's control. Relative incomes are not the only possible variable that may affect the intra-household decision process. It can also depend on a range of variables that change the household environment and, in particular, the members' respective bargaining positions. Factors that may affect the opportunities of spouses outside marriage can influence the intra-household balance of power and ultimately the final allocation of resources, even when the marriage does not actually dissolve (Haddad and Kanbur, 1992).

The variables that proxy situation in the marriage market are natural examples of the factors that change the household environment. Becker (1991, ch.3) emphasized that the marriage market, which depends crucially on sex-ratio, is an important determinant of intra-household utility distributions. Divorce laws and legislations that support females influence the partner's level of income and assigned property rights. The decision process may also be influenced by special features of the marriage contract, like whether agreements are binding or not (Ulph,1988; Lundberg and Pollak, 1993; 1994; Woolley, 1998; Chen and Woolley, 2002). Along these lines, Chiappori, et.al., (2002) provide a structural model of household behaviour and analyze both theoretically and empirically the effects of 'distributional factors', the variables that can affect the intra-household decision process without influencing individual preferences or the joint consumption – sex-ratio and divorce laws, in a collective framework. The results reject the unitary model's prediction that distributional factors are irrelevant to intra-household decisions. They are also at odds with Nash bargaining models that assume that the fallback option is internal to the household. Quite to the contrary, the results support Becker's claim that the state of the marriage market is an important determinant of the intra-household decision process. The internal decision process is a two-step process: first non-labour income is allocated among spouses according to a so-called sharing rule that depends on distributional factors and other variables. Next, spouses choose their labour supply subject to their individual budget constraint.

Thus, the bourgeoning literature on intra-household resource allocation, both theoretical and empirical, ascertains the role and significance of bargaining strengths and strategies of women within the household. However, it frequently turns to the resource allocation patterns within the family, especially on the household labour supply decisions and on the outcomes on child investments, such as health and education. They do not generally address the issues of spousal gains to marriage. Moreover, the intra-household allocation decision literature deals with distributional issues and bargaining strategies once the household is formed and those of decisions prior to marriage, such as pre-marital investments in human capital of potential partners, are not incorporated in the formal analysis. In general, most of the bargaining household models assume marriage decision as exogenous and study the consumption or labour supply behaviour of married women.

There are also some attempts to incorporate the influence of women's education on household resource allocation decisions, as noted by Schultz (2002). "The conclusion of many empirical studies of development is that increased schooling of mothers is associated with larger improvements in child quality outcomes than is the increased schooling of fathers. This has been studied with birth outcomes (e.g. birth weights), child survival, good nutrition, earlier entry into school, increased school enrollment adjusted for age, and more years of schooling completed on reaching adulthood" (Schultz, 2002, p. 212). However, the mechanism of the operation of women's education to influence these remains elusive. The empirical studies differ in how they measure women's control over resources, employing first labour market productivity and then wealth and non-labour income (Haddad and Hoddinot, 1994; Hoddinot and Haddad, 1995; Thomas, 1990; 1994). Empirical evidence from India and Bangladesh suggests that part of the correlation between women's schooling and their children's schooling is due to the marriage matching process, and consequently can be attributed to men's preferences rather than to women's differential productivity in schooling of their children (Behrman, et.al., 1997). Better educated women are able to increase schooling of their children. Men who want better educated children are thus motivated to marry better educated women with increased capacity to produce child human capital. An improved understanding of the joint determination of marriage market and this child/home human capital could affect the magnitude of the estimates of the productivity of female education on child human capital and plausibly reduce them in circumstances where women's schooling is privately valued by men mainly for its productive effects on childrearing. There is an ongoing search to model explicitly family composition, and marriage matching as well as marital status in the household allocation decisions (Behrman, Birdsall and Deolalikar, 1995; Behrman, et.al., 1997; Boulier and Rosenzweig, 1984; Schultz, 1994).

The collective models (as developed by Chiappori, 1988, 1992) suggest – and the empirical evidences support – the notion that relative spousal incomes influence household allocations (Browning, et.al., 1994; Thomas, 1990). In both the collective models of Becker (1991) and Chiappori (1988; 1992) and the exogenous marital bargaining models of Manser and Brown (1980), McElroy and Horney (1981) and Sen (1983) the sharing rule or the bargaining power of the two sexes are determined exogenously and the couples have differential preferences over the choice set. But, while the collective approach to household behaviour takes spousal incomes as given, these incomes are determined at least in part by decisions individuals make prior to marriage. Thus, implicit in the collective framework is the idea that pre-marital investments influence wage earnings, and, hence, intra-marital sharing rules. Nonetheless, existing models neither examine the efficiency of pre-marital investments within the collective framework nor address how such pre-marital choices could influence intra-marital allocations. Just as the early literature on labour supply has not been integrated with the marriage analysis, the intra-household allocation models have lacked a way to be integrated with the marriage market analysis. Again, as the spousal labour did for the integration of the former, the pre-marital investment does for the integration of marriage analysis with intra-household allocation decisions. Earlier, treating spousal incomes as marital public goods, Bergstrom, Blume and Varian (1986) and Macleod and Malcomson (1993) have shown that the equilibrium levels of educational investments are below Pareto-efficient level. Later, Peters and Siow (2002) show how competition in large marriage markets with assortative spousal matching restores Pareto-efficiency. They argue that families make investment in education that is Pareto optimal, once matching is endogenized. In large marriage markets, assortative matching and bilateral efficiency, competitive marriage markets and assortative matching that occur within it guide families to indirectly and reciprocally compensate each other for investments that they have made in their own children. Thus, in Basu (2001) and Iyigun and Walsh (2002), bargaining power of the sexes is determined endogenously according to the actual relative earnings.

However, these papers do not address how pre-marital investments might influence bargaining in a collective household setting. Recently, Becker and Murphy (2000), Browning, Chiappori and Weiss (2003) and Iyigun and Walsh (2004) merge collective household model with marital sorting to explore the implications of spousal matching. In essence, individual's pre-marital investments help determine relative spousal incomes, which in turn influence intra-household allocations. For example, Iyigun and Walsh (2004) incorporate pre-marital investments and spousal matching into a collective household model where marital matching is assortative and an endogenous sharing rule forms the basis for intra-household allocations. The distribution of pre-marital endowments and the sex ratio in the marriage market help determine sharing rule. All sharing rules along the assortative marriage market lead to unconditionally efficient outcomes in which both pre-marital investments and intra-household allocations are efficient. Iyigun and Walsh (2004) show that the bargaining power is again endogenously determined with pre-marital investments and sex-ratio. Thus, incorporating pre-marital investments and marital matching into the collective models is a crucial step in identifying the fundamental determinants of intra-marital sharing rules and their properties.

Moreover, in many developing countries, and in many poor households, women have neither sufficiently large independent sources of income nor adequate legislative or public support to strengthen their bargaining position. Even if such bargaining instruments exist, women in these households do not have any control over them, as they lack education and knowledge to effectively utilize the avenues open to them. In many situations, women are simply not to have any preference of their own and they are not allowed to participate in the household choices. However, there is plenty of anthropological and other evidence from India that parents spend a considerable amount of resources on the marriage of children, especially on female children, both on dowry and marriage related expenses (Bardhan, 1984; Rao, 1993). In fact, lavish expenses on wedding and festivals even under poverty specify a status identity and a strategy to cope with risk and poverty, as well as a mechanism for building networks, representing 'investments in social capital' (Rao, 2004). Browning and Subramaniam (1995) find that the cash dowry, without including in-kind dowry which is also substantial, and expenses, on average, amount to a yearly income for the households. Many argue that, in fact, dowry can be used as a transfer as well as a bargaining instrument in many cases (Zhang and Chan, 1999; Edlund, 2001; Botticini and Siow, 2002). Dowry enhances a women's position in the household and safeguards her interests and welfare. It improves the female's welfare through both income and bargaining effects. Moreover, parents desiring better match for their offspring have to invest considerably on their children both in the human and physical capital from their childhood in order to attract prospective marriage alliances. In this regard, there is a substantial empirical literature suggesting that adding to a mother's schooling will have a larger beneficial effect on a child's health, schooling and adult productivity than would adding to a father's schooling by the same amount. This finding is consistent with recent studies grounded in the bargaining models of family resource allocation which report increments to the non-earned income of the mother, that empowers her, have a larger beneficial effect on the consumption and human capital of children than a similar increase in the non-earned income of the fathers. In order to explore the significance of pre-marital investments as an instrument of bargaining, this paper uses women's education and dowry as indicators of her bargaining strengths. This is accomplished by combining the marriage market analysis with the intra-household allocation methods in a collective framework. It is hypothesized that higher the women's education, higher the probability of assortative mating and thus more the gains to marriage.

The Data and Empirical Analysis

This paper uses a primary data collected for a larger study on marriage and female-age at marriage in Tamil Nadu. The data have been collected though a specially designed questionnaire during September 1996 to March 1997 from both married and unmarried women in both the rural and urban Tamil Nadu. A total of 1014 samples have been collected; compressing 566 (55.8

per cent) married and 448 (44.2 per cent) unmarried women. Due weightage has been given to various socio-economic as well as cultural backgrounds while selecting the sample respondents. The data contain wealth of information about the personal as well as family characteristics of both the married and unmarried females and the personal and family background of the respective partners of married women. Information regarding marriage process, search process, choice of marital partner, marriage expenses including dowry, jewels and wealth transfers, effects of marriage on female employment and post marriage satisfaction and behavior of married women, have been obtained from married females. Beside this information from the unmarried women, the marriage related expectations and the likely choice of marital partners have also been obtained. Though unmarried female sample also furnished some important marriage related expectations, for the purpose of this paper, we have used only the married female sample.

Since the main aim of this study is to examine the influence of women's education on marital bargains and income gains to marriage, first we study the pattern of marriage. The results strongly reveal that the marriage market is characterized by assortative marriage (all tables below consider only valid cases for which the relevant information is available). The results also reveal that females are married either to similarly placed grooms or better than their own background man. Table 1 shows that more than 85 per cent of females married men with similar earnings or higher earnings. This also indicates that there are net gains to positive assortative marriage. Further, Table 2 shows that education is also matched positively in the marriage market. Nearly 88 per cent of females with primary education married either primary (18 per cent) or secondary (75 per cent) educated males; more than 52 per cent secondary educated females married secondary educated males with another 42 per cent marrying college educated males; more than 90 per cent college educated females married degree holder males; nearly 80 per cent of post graduate females married post graduate males, and 50 per cent females with research qualification married research degree holder males.

Table 1 : Marital Matching by Spousal Earnings (Rs Per month)

Female Earnings	*Husband's Earnings*		
	< 6000	*6001 - 12000*	*> 12000*
< 6000	99 (44.6)	110 (49.5)	13 (05.9)
6001 – 12000	10 (07.9)	60 (47.6)	56 (44.4)
> 12000	1 (02.0)	7 (13.7)	43 (84.3)

Note: Percentage figures are in parentheses.

Table 2: Marital Matching by Spousal Education

Education of Female	*Education of Husband*				
	Primary	*Secondary*	*UG*	*PG*	*Research*
Primary	11 (11.5)	47 (74.6)	3 (04.8)	1 (01.6)	-
Secondary	2 (00.7)	144 (52.6)	87 (31.8)	31 (11.3)	1 (00.4)
UG	-	6 (04.4)	45 (33.1)	79 (58.1)	2 (01.5)
PG	-	1 (01.5)	14 (20.6)	44 (64.7)	9 (13.2)
Research	-	-	2 (33.3)	1 (16.7)	3 (50.0)

Note: Percentage figures are in parentheses.

Table 3: Marital Matching by Spousal Occupation

Occupation of Female	*Occupation of Husband*					
	Doctor	*Teacher*	*Engineer*	*Service*	*Business*	*Clerical*
Doctor	8 (88.9)	-	1 (11.1)	-	-	-
Teacher	4 (05.4)	37 (50.0	2 (02.7)	15 (20.3)	3 (04.1)	11 (14.8)
Engineer	3 (30.0)	1 (10.0)	3 (30.0)	1 (10.0)	1 (10.0)	1 (10.0)
Service	2 (02.4)	16 (18.8)	4 (04.7)	43 (50.6)	1 (01.2)	1 (01.2)
Business	-	-	-	1 (12.5)	7 (87.5)	-
Clerical	-	24 (24.2)	3 (3.0)	49 (49.5)	2 (2.0)	18 (18.2)

Note: Percentage figures are in parentheses.

As Table 3 reveals, occupation is also matched positively. Nearly 89 per cent of females with medical education married doctor males; 50 per cent of female teachers married teachers; 60 per cent engineers female married either engineers or doctors; and 88 per cent of females with business background married businessmen. Only females in the service and clerical category married mixed background males. Again 50 per cent of females in service occupations married similar men; among the remaining females, more than 35 per cent married either teachers or clerical males. In the clerical category, 50 per cent of females married men with service oriented jobs, while only 18 per cent females married men with clerical jobs, and 24 per cent married teacher males.

As shown in Table 4 spousal matching by sector of work is strongly assortative. Nearly 83 per cent of females in the government sector jobs married males in government employment; more than 50 per cent of them married central government employed males. Nearly 70 per cent of females working in the private sector married private sector male workers; only 25 per cent of private sector females married government sector workers; 47 per cent of self-employed females married self-employed males; whereas 30 per cent of them married private sector males, with another 24 per cent marrying central government male employees. It is also interesting to note that matching of mates in the marriage market is also positively assortative even with socio–economic background. Table 5 shows matching by parental income. Nearly 80 per cent of females in the low and middle income categories married similar background family males, while in the high income category; more than 75 per cent females married high income family members. Thus, the empirical evidences clearly support the income gain approach to the theory of marriage; there are gains from positive mating and largely likes marry likes.

Table 4 : Marital Matching by Spousal Sector of Work

Sector of Work of Female	*Sector of Work of Husband*			
	Central Government	*State Government*	*Private*	*Self-Employed*
Central Government	8 (28.6)	15 (53.6)	5 (17.9)	-
State Government	13 (15.3)	46 (54.1)	23 (27.1)	3 (3.5)
Private	23 (15.3)	44 (16.4)	186 (68.1)	16 (5.9)
Self-Employed	-	4 (23.5)	5 (29.4)	8 (47.1)

Note: Percentage figures are in parentheses.

Table 5: Marital Matching by Parental Income (Rs per annum)

Parental Income of Female	*Parental income of Husband*			
	< 25,000	*25000-50000*	*50001-75000*	*>75000*
< 25000	79 (38.4)	84 (41.2)	32 (15.7)	9 (04.4)
25001-50000	35 (17.2)	80 (39.4)	54 (26.6)	34 (16.7)
50001-75000	5 (06.2)	30 (37.0)	15 (18.5)	31 (38.8)
> 75000	3 (04.0)	7 (09.3)	18 (24.0)	47 (62.7)

Note: Percentage figures are in parentheses.

The descriptive statistics presented in Table 6 show that the mean age at marriage of females is 21.11 years and the mean age difference between the spouses is 5.68 years, similar to the observations of many cross cultural studies. The mean values of the educational background show that the gap in educational attainment between the marital partners is very minimum. However, husband's earnings are much higher than the wife's earnings. Similarly, the husband's parental annual income is higher than the female's parental annual income.

Table 6: Average Values of Marriage Related Variables

Variable	*Description*	*Mean*	*S.D.*
AGEF	Age of female (yrs)	23.58	1.91
AGMF	Age at marriage of female (yrs)	21.11	1.79
AGEH	Age of husband (yrs)	29.27	2.26
AGMH	Age at marriage of male (yrs)	26.79	2.47
WAGEF	Earnings of females (Rs./month)	6873.08	4679.21
WAGEH	Earnings of husband (Rs./month)	10249.40	6032.39
EDUF	Education of female (yrs)	12.29	3.46
EDUH	Education of husband (yrs)	14.42	3.14

(Contd...)

PINCF	Parental income of females (Rs.x100/p.a)	451.59	395.19
PINCH	Parental income of husband (Rs.x100/p.a)	588.06	480.42
EXPM	Marriage expenses (Rs.×1000)	64.16	70.41
DOW	Dowry for marriage (Rs.×1000)	18.69	27.96
DJV	Jewels for marriage (Rs.×1000)	63.30	53.72
DJQ	Dowry – Jewels (Souvenirs)	15.87	13.56
DMV	Property transferred (Rs x 1000)	40.54	78.59
MGAIN	Income gain to females (Rs./month)	855.86	833.00
N	Sample size	566	

With regard to marital transactions, dowry and jewels are substantial, besides sizable marriage-related expenses. Female's household spent about Rs 64000 on marriage related expenses to marry their daughter. The dowry aspect is really a burden on the female's family: cash dowry has been about Rs 19000 and jewelry amounts to Rs 63000, along with Rs 40000 in the form of property transfers. Thus, a family has to spend nearly Rs 2 lakhs to marry their daughter. These results are in fact a sign of positive assortative mating in the marriage market. Thus, marriage involves high cost and the households are in fact willing to incur this for better marital matching. From the sample, it is observed that even the unmarried females prefer to marry similarly positioned males and nearly 93 per cent of sample respondents expressed that the marriage does not affect either their career or their earnings. Very few felt that the dislocation caused by marriage may affect their employment. The gain in income to marriage for females is also significant. Though only few females reported that they gained, the gain is to the tune of Rs 856 per month after marriage.

Table 7: Correlation Between Spousal Backgrounds

	AGEF	*AGEH*	*EDUF*	*EDUH*	*EARF*	*EARH*	*EDUFF*	*EDUFM*	*DOWRY*
AGEF	1.00	.750*	.527*	.451*	.466*	.206*	.366*	.457*	.140*
AGEH		1.00	.538*	.543*	.461*	.290*	.385*	.406*	.134*
EDUF			1.00	.782*	.682*	.357*	.620*	.645*	.174*
EDUH				1.00	.524*	.419*	.608*	.609*	.180*
EARF					1.00	.312*	.502*	.553*	.247*
EARH						1.00	.526*	.088*	.175*
EDUFF							1.00	.674*	.230*
EDUFM								1.00	.168*
DOW									1.00

	JEWEL	*PROPTY*	*EDUHF*	*EDUHM*	*INCFP*	*INCHP*	*EARHF*	*EARHM*
AGEF	.177*	.119*	.194*	.334*	.292*	.126*	.068*	.096*
AGEH	.280*	.148*	.190*	.346*	.275*	.203*	.066*	.093*
EDUF	.311*	.215*	.402*	.540*	.360*	.238*	.175*	.210*
EDUH	.388*	.205*	.381*	.477*	.343*	.326*	.217*	.128*
EARF	.659*	.240*	.304*	.450*	.374*	.222*	.202*	.266*

(Contd...)

EARH	.321*	.290*	.153*	.239*	.495*	.657*	.327*	.123*
EDUFF	.317*	.224*	.407*	.513*	.384*	.301*	.178*	.152*
EDUFM	.266*	.247*	.400*	.563*	.425*	.270*	.211*	.217*
DOW	.298*	.237*	.149*	.170*	.328*	.327*	.178*	.161*
JEWEL	1.00	.451*	.214*	.306*	.590*	.673*	.423*	.178*
PROPTY		1.00	.005	.075	.332*	.433*	.374*	.158*
EDUHF			1.00	.516*	.196*	.202*	.425*	.170*
EDUHM				1.00	.290*	.233*	.198*	.377*
INCFP					1.00	.573*	.324*	.192*
INCHP						1.00	.398*	.203*
EARHF							1.00	.065
EARHM								1.00

*Correlation co-efficient statistically significant.

Table 7 presents the correlation between some of the important characteristics of marital partners, dowry and their family backgrounds. The correlation between the female education and earnings with male education and earnings are positive and statistically significant. Similarly, the correlation between the female's parental education and earnings with male's education and earnings as well as with his parental education and earnings are also positive and statistically significant. There also exists significant relationship between dowry, jewels, and properties given for marriage with both the families background characteristics.

Table 8: Regression Results of Female and Male Earnings and Gains to Marriage

Variable	*Female Earnings*		*Male Earnings*		*Income Gain*
EDUF	0.164* (10.95)	0.324** (2.00)	0.045* (5.13)	0.222*** (1.74)	-0.255 (1.36)
EDUH	0.018 (1.55)	0.195 (1.23)	0.081* (6.57)	0.163*** (1.70)	0.165 (0.94)
EXPF	0.056** (2.00)	0.085 (0.95)	-	-	-
EXPFSQ	-0.0002 (0.11)	-0.012 (1.33)	-	-	-
EXPH	-	-	0.041 (1.30)	0.389 (1.58)	-
EXPHSQ	-	-	-0.0002 (0.14)	-0.002 (1.53)	-
EDUFEDUH*	-	-0.011 (1.07)	-	-0.008 (1.05)	-
AGEF	-	-	-	-	-0.301 (1.20)
AGEH	-	-	-	-	0.480*** (1.83)
WAGEF	-	-	-	-	0.0006 (0.21)
WAGEH	-	-	-	-	0.0002 (0.77)

(Contd...)

DOW	-	-0.005 (0.88)	-	0.022 ().48)	-0.038*** (1.72)
Constant	2.567* (11.07)	2.700 (1.28)	3.544* (15.26)	2.521 (1.46)	-0.893 (0.20)
R-square	0.54	0.67	0.47	0.73	.031
F	92.30	7.57	68.47	10.25	3.44

Note: Figures in parentheses indicate absolute *t* values.

* Significant at 1 per cent level.

** Significant at 5 per cent level.

*** Significant at 10 per cent level.

In the econometric analysis, first we estimate the wage equations of males and females to identify the effect of own education on earnings, dowry, and spousal education on each other's earnings. Then, we estimate the income gain to women equation to identify the bargaining strengths of females. Table 8 presents the OLS results of the male and female earnings functions as well as the income gain equation. As expected, the effects of own education on earnings are positive and statistically significant in both male and female earnings equations. One year of education generates a return of approximately 16 per cent per year for females and approximately 8 per cent for males. Thus, the rate of return for female education is much higher than that of male education. However, the effects of spousal education are rather weak. While both effects are positive, only female education has some influence on male earnings. The female education coefficient is significant, male education coefficient is insignificant. The effect of female education is approximately 4 per cent per year on male earnings, while the effect of male education on female earnings is only one per cent. Thus, the effects of spousal education are less than the effects of own education on earnings. Further, the effect of the education interaction term is negative and statistically insignificant. This reveals that the productivity gains from spousal education are negative, perhaps due to the reason that females specialize more in the home production than in the market work. As the degree of specialization in the labour market decreases, the gain from spousal education also decreases. Dowry has a negative effect on women's earnings and positive effect on men's earnings, but statistically insignificant in both functions. This shows that dowry may be a bargaining instrument for females; but its effect is only marginal. A 10 per cent increase in dowry reduces female earnings by only 5 per cent.

The results of the productivity effects of spousal education are also reinforced by the results of income gain to marriage estimates. The effect of female education is negative while the effect of male education is positive, but both are statistically insignificant. The dowry variable has a negative effect on gains to marriage and is significant at 10 per cent level. While own education decreases gains to marriage by 2 per cent, dowry decreases the gain by 3 per cent. However, assortative matching increases male earnings by 16 per cent. These results indicate that while males tend to gain from assortative marriage, the gains to females are rather low. The effects of wage rates on income gain are, though positive, low and insignificant. Further, the negative coefficients of dowry and female education in income gain equation are also at odds with the collective approach to household behaviour. They indicate that women have little control over the resources and the allocation decisions within the household. Thus, it seems that in the Indian households women's bargaining strengths are weak and her role in household decisions is rather limited.

Conclusion

This paper has attempted to bring together three strands of research, though not mutually exclusive, on the economics of household behaviour. The marriage market models emphasize productivity gains through assortative matching. The labour market models treat marriage as exogenous and emphasize the returns to human capital investments. The intrafamily decision making models, both unitary and collective models, discuss the patterns of household resource allocation decisions within the household, assuming the existence of a family or household. The missing link for the endogenous model of all three strands is provided by the recognition of spousal labour and pre-marital investments. It has been argued in this paper that parental investments in female education enhances the marriage market prospects of females and hence leads to assortative marriages. With likes married to likes, the division of labour and specialization increases productivity of spouses and hence returns to education. With higher education and better earnings, along with dowry transfers, women have higher resources at their disposal and hence more bargaining power to a greater role in household allocation decisions. In fact, the collective models allow for household member's independent preferences and the household allocation decisions are collective rather than unitary. The collective models have also shown that existence of independent non-labour income or extra environmental factors, such as divorce laws increases women's bargaining strengths and threat point utility. Also the existence of some distributional factors, such as sex-ratio, influences household sharing rules. Empirically, many studies have analyzed all these aspects, and it seems that there appears to be a near consensus that marriage market is assortative, spousal labour and education are important in labour supply decisions, and household decisions are collective. Specifically, the unitary approach has largely been rejected by studies that use independent non-labour income as a bargaining strategy.

In this paper, women's education and dowry have been considered as bargaining instruments to test the productivity hypothesis of marriage and the collective approach to household decision making process. The results of this study show that, like other studies, the market gains of women's education are not limited to the effects of education on own earnings, as the wife's education also increases the husband's earnings. Investments in women's education generate positive labour market returns. Though the same is not the case with husband's education, the effect is still positive. Spousal education and assortative marriage provide for cross-productivity effects. Hence, investment in education of married couples not only increases their own wages, but also increases the wages of spouses. Beyond this productivity effect, women's education does not add to her bargaining strengths over household resources. Neither the presence of large dowry has any significant influence for her independent preferences and household decisions. Thus, pre-marital investments on women, in the form of education and dowry, are not likely to improve women's position within the family, though there are labour and marriage market gains. It seems that in the Indian family structure, women have little bargaining strengths and have limited say in household allocation decisions, even with sizable resources under their control. May be public policies that improve the distributional factors and legislative measures will have important consequences on the bargaining strengths of women and ultimately on the allocation of income and welfare within marriage or households.

References

Alderman, H., P.A. Chiappori, L. Haddad, J. Hoddinott and R. Kanbur (1995): 'Unitary versus collective models of the household – Is it time to shift the burden of proof?'. *World Bank Research Observer*, 10, 1, 1-19.

Bardhan, P.K. (1984): *Land, Labor and Rural Poverty: Essays in Development Economics.* New York: Columbia University Press.

Basu, K. (2001) "Gender and say – a model of household behaviour with endogenously determined balance of power". Cornell University, mimeo.

Becker, G.S. (1965): "A theory of the allocation of time". *Economic Journal*, 75, 2, 493-517.

______ (1973): "A theory of marriage – part I". *Journal of Political Economy*, 81, 4, 813-46.

______ (1974): "A theory of marriage – part II". *Journal of Political Economy*, 82, 2, S11-S26.

______ (1991): *A Treatise on the Family.* New York: Harvard University Press.

Becker,G.S. and K.M. Murphy (2000): *Social Economics.* Mass, CA: Harvard University Press.

Behrman, J.R. (1988): "Intra-household allocation of nutrients in rural India: are boys favoured? Do parents exhibit inequality aversion", *Oxford Economic Papers*, 45, 1, 35-54.

______ (1997): "Intra-household distribution in the family", in M.R. Rosenzweig and O.Stark (eds.): *Handbook of Population and Family Economics*, Amsterdam: Elseiver.

Behrman, J.R., N. Birdsall and A. Deolalikar (1995): "Marriage markets, labor markets and unobserved human capital". *Economic Development and Cultural Change*, 43, 585-601.

Behrman, J.R., A. Foster and M.R. Rosenzweig (1997): "Women's schooling, home teaching and economic growth". *Journal of Political Economy*, 107, 4, 632-714.

Behrman, J.R., R. Pollak and P. Taubman (1982): "Parental preferences and provision of progeny". *Journal of Political Economy*, 90, 1, 52-73.

Benham, L. (1974): "Benefits of women's education within marriage". *Journal of Political Economy*, 82, S57-S71.

Bergstrom, T. C., L.E. Blume and H.R. Varian (1986): "On the private provision of public goods". *Journal of Public Economics*, 29, 1, 25-49.

Boulier, B.L. and M.R. Rosenzweig (1984): "Schooling, search and spouse selection: testing economic theories of marriage and household behaviour". *Journal of Political Economy*, 92, 712-732.

Browning, M. and P.A. Chappori (1998): "Efficient intra-household allocations: a general characterization and empirical tests", *Econometrica*, 66, 6, 1241-78.

Brownning, M. and R. Subramaniam (1995): "Gender-bias in India: parental preferences or marriage costs", Yale University, mimeo.

Brownning, M. and V. Lechene (2001): "Caring and sharing: tests between alternative models of intra-household allocation". University of Copenhagen, mimeo.

Brownning, M., P.A. Chiappori and Y. Weiss (2003): "A simple matching model of the marriage market", mimeo, Unicersity of Chicago.

Brownning, M., F. Bourguignnon, P.A. Chiappori and V. Lechene (1994): "Incomes and outcomes – A structural model of intra-household allocation'. *Journal of Political Economy*, 102, 6, 1067-96.

Botticini, M. and A. Siow (2002): "Why Dowries". Mimeo, University of Toronto.

Chen, Z. and F. Woolley (2001): "A Cournot-Nash model of family decision making". *Economic Journal*, 111, 474, 722-48.

Chiapppori, P.A. (1988): "Rational household labor supply". *Econometrica*, 56, 1, 63-89.

Chiapppori, P.A. (1992): "Collective labor supply and welfare". *Journal of Political Economy*, 100, 2, 437-467.

Chiapppori, P.A., B. Fortin and G. Lacroix (2002): "Marriage market, divorce legislation and household labor supply". *Journal of Political Economy*, 110, 1, 37-72.

Chun, H. and I. Lee (2001): "Why do married men earn more – productivity or selection?" *Economic Inquiry*, 39, 2, 307-19.

Doss, C.R. (1999): "Intra-household resource allocation in Ghana: the impact of the distribution of asset ownership within the household" *in* G.H. Peters and J. von Braun (eds.): *Food Security, Diversification and Resource Management – Refocusing the Role of Agriculture.* Aldershot, UK: Dartmouth Publishing.

Edlund, L. (2001): "Dear son – expensive daughter: why do scare women pay to marry?". mimeo, Columbia University.

Fortin, B. and G. Lacroix (1997): "A test of the unitary and collective models of household labor supply". *Economic Journal*, 107, 443, 933-55.

Grossbard-Shechtman, A.S. (1984): "A theory of allocation of time in markets for labor and marriage". *Economic Journal*, 94, 863-82.

Grossbard-Shechtman, S. (1993): *On the Economics of Marriage: A Theory of Marriage, Labor, and Divorce*. Boulder, Colo, Westview Press.

Haddad, L. and J. Hoddinott (1992): "Household resource allocation in Cote d'Ivoire – Inferences from expenditure data", *in* T.A. Lloyd and W.O. Morrissey (eds.): *Poverty and Rural Development*. London; Macmillan Press.

______ (1994): "Women's income and boy-girl nutrition outcomes in the Cote d'Ivoire", *World Development*, 22, 545-53.

Haddad,L., J. Hoddinott and H. Alderman (1997): *Intra-household Resource Allocation in Developing Countries*, Baltimore. MD.: John Hopkins University Press.

Hoddinott, J. and L.Haddad (1995): "Does female income share influence household expenditure?". *Oxford Bulletin of Economics and Statistics*, 57, 1, 77-96.

Iyigun,M.F. and R.P. Walsh (2002): "Endogenous gender power, household labor supply and the quantity-quality trade-off". mimeo, University of Colorado.

______ (2004): "Building the family nest: a collective household model with competing pre-marital investments and spousal matching". mimeo, University of Colorado.

Kremer, M. (1997): "How much does sorting increase inequality". *Quarterly Journal of Economics*, 112, 1, 115-39.

Kanbur, R. and L. Haddad (1994): "Are better off households more or less unequal?" *Oxford Economic Papers*, 46, 445-58.

Kooreman, P. and A. Kapteyn (1990): "On the empirical implementation of some game theoretic models of household labor supply". *Journal of Human Resources*, 25, 4, 584-98.

Korenman, S. and D. Neumark (1991): "Does marriage really make men more productive?". *Journal of Human Resources*, 26, 2, 282-07.

Loh, E.S. (1996): "Productivity differences and the marriage wage premium for wage males", *Journal of Human Resources*, 31, 3, 566-589.

Lundberg, S. and R. Pollak (1993): "Separate spheres bargaining and the marriage market". *Journal of Political Economy*, 101, 988-1010.

______ (1994): "Bargaining and distribution in marriage". *Journal of Economic Perspectives*. 10, 1, 139-58.

Lundberg, S., R. Pollak and T.J. Wales (1997): "Do husbands and wives pool their resources? Evidence from the United Kingdom child benefit". *Journal of Human Resources*, 32, 3, 463-80.

Macleod, W.B. and J.M. Malcomson (1993): "Investment, holdup and the form of market contracts". *American Economic Review*, 83, 811-37.

Manser, M. and M. Brown (1980): "Marriage and household decision making: A bargaining analysis". *International Economic Review*, 21, 1, 31-44.

McElroy, M.B. and M.J. Horney (1981): "Nash bargained decisions – Towards a generalization of the theory of demand". *International Economic Review*, 22, 333-49.

Nakosteen, R.A. and M.A. Zimmer (1987): "Marital status and earnings of young men – a model of endogenous selection", *Journal of Human Resources*, 22, 2, 248-68.

______Zimmer (1997): "Men, money and marriage – are higher earners more prone than lower earners to marry?" *Social Science Quarterly*, 78, 1, 66-82.

Peters, M. and A. Siow (2002): "Competing pre-marital investments". *Journal of Political Economy*, 110, 3, 592-608.

Phipps, S. and P. Burton (1995): *Collective Models of Family Behaviour – Implications for Economic Policy.* Dalhousie University.

Pitt, M., M.R. Rosenzweig and N. Hassen (1990): "Productivity, health and inequality in the intrafamily distribution of food in low-income countries". *American Economic Review*, 80, 1139-56.

Quisumbing, A.R. (1994): "Intergenerational transfers in Philippine rice villages – gender differences in traditional inheritance customs". *Journal of Development Economics*, 43, 1, 167-95.

Quisumbing, A.R. and J.A. Maluccio (2003): "Resources at marriage and intra-household allocation – evidence from Bangladesh, Ethiopia, Indonesia, and South Africa". *Oxford Bulletin of Economics and Statistics*, 65, 3, 283-327.

Rao, V. (1993): "The rising price of husbands: a hedonic analysis of dowry increases in rural India", *Journal of Political Economy*, 72, 666-677.

Rao, V. (2004): "Poverty and public celebrations in rural India". mimeo, World Bank.

Ribar, D.C. (2003): "What do social scientists know about the benefits of marriage? A review of quantitative methodologies". mimeo, George Washington University.

Rosenzweig, M.R. and T.P. Schultz (1982): "Market opportunities, genetic endowments and intrafamily resource distribution – child survival in rural India", *American Economic Review*, 72, 803-15.

Rubalcava, L. and D. Thomas (2002): "Family bargaining and welfare". mimeo, Santa Monica, Calif.: Rand Corporation.

Sen, A.K.(1983): "Economics and family". *Asian Development Review*, 1, 1, 14-26.

______(1984): "Family and food: sex bias in poverty", *in* A.K. Sen (ed.): *Resources, Values and Development*, Oxford, Basil Blackwell.

Schultz, T.P. (1990): "Testing the neoclassical model of family labor supply and fertility". *Journal of Human Resources*, 25, 4, 599-634.

______(1994): "Marital status and fertility in the United States". *Journal of Human Resources*, 29, 637-69.

Schultz, T.P. (ed.) (1995): *Investment in Women's Human Capital.* Chicago; University of Chicago Press.

Schultz, T.P. (2001): "Women's role in the agricultural household: Bargaining and human capital investments", *in* B. Gardner and G. Rausser (eds.): *Handbook of Agricultural Economics.* Vol.1, Amsterdam: Elseiver, 385-56.

______(2002): "Why government should invest more to educate girls" *World Development*, 30, 2, 207-25.

Siow, A. (2003): "The economics of marriage 30 years after Becker". mimeo, University of Toronto.

Strauss, J. and D. Thomas (1995): 'Human resources – Empirical modeling of household and family decisions", *in* J. Behrman and T.N. Srinivasan (eds.): *Handbook of Development Economics*, Vol. 3A. Amsterdam: Elseiver.

Stutzer, A. and B.S. Fry (2003): "Does marriage make people happy, or do happy people get married?" University of Zurich, mimeo.

Thomas, D. (1990): "Intra-household resource allocation – An inferential approach". *Journal of Human Resources*, 25, 4, 635-64.

______ (1994): "Like father, like son; like mother, like daughter". *Journal of Human Resources*, 29, 950-89.

Thomas, D., D. Contreras and E. Frankenberg (2002): "Distribution of power within the household and child health", mimeo, Santa Monica, Calif, Rand Corporation.

Tiefenthaler, J. (1997): "The productivity gains of marriage – effects of spousal education on own productivity across market sectors in Brazil". *Economic Development and Cultural Change*, 633-50.

Ulph, D. (1988): "A general non-cooperative Nash model of household consumption behavior". mimeo, University of Bristol.

Vermeulen, F. (2002): "Collective household models: principles and main results". *Journal of Economic Surveys*, 16, 4, 533-64.

Woolley, F. (1998): "A noncooperative model of family decision making". TIDI working paper 125, London: London School of Economics.

Zhang, J. and W. Chan (1999): "Dowry and wife's welfare – a theoretical and empirical analysis". *Journal of Political Economy*, 107, 4, 786-808.

11

Enrolment and Dropouts of Muslims in West Bengal

Evidence from NSS 61st Round[#]

Zakir Husain[*]

Abstract

The issue of disparities in educational attainments between different socio-religious communities is a major problem in India. Based on unit level NSS data (61st Round, 2004) this paper undertakes a comparative analysis of the educational status of minorities, particularly Muslim, in the field of primary education in West Bengal. Although the result does not support the popular belief that Muslims do not value education, they are found to lag behind other communities in both rural and urban areas in terms of enrolment and dropouts. Econometric analysis shows that such differences remain even after controlling for household characteristics. We also find that while Muslim girls have marginally lower enrolment rates, the issue of gender discrimination is more complex than commonly believed.

Introduction

The positive effects of education on economic growth have been well documented by the Human Capital School (Schultz, 1961; Weisbrod, 1962). But it is also important to acknowledge the important microeconomic

* The author would like to express his thanks to Prof. Debdas Banerjee for his comments and Saswati Das, Indian Statistical Institute, Kolkata, for assisting in using the NSSO data. Needless to say all deficiencies are the sole responsibility of the authors.

consequences of lower levels of education (what is referred to as "basic education") and its implications for the broader process of development.[1] By improving the functional ability and endowments of individuals, basic education leads to an increase in their entitlements and capabilities, expands their choice set and allows them greater freedom. This has important consequences for social welfare and development (Sen, 1985; Dreze and Sen, 2002).

While schemes like *Mid Day Meal Programme* and *Sarva Shiksha Abhiyan (SSA)* has led to substantial progress in enrolment and retention, the issue of unequal educational attainments across the population remains a major problem. Researchers and policy makers have typically identified girls and children belonging to Scheduled Castes (SCs), Scheduled Tribes (STs) and Other Backward Castes (OBCs) as forming educationally deprived sections of the community, ignoring the poor educational status of Muslims.[2]

A major reason for this neglect is the perceived reason for the poor educational attainment of Muslims. It is commonly argued that Muslims are not interested in education (Hunter, 1869; Sharma, 1978), or if they are at all interested in educating their children, it is boys who are educated (Jehangir, 1991; Ruhela, 1991). Moreover, Muslims are supposed to prefer religious education provided through Madrasahs (Ansari, 1989, Bandopadhyay, 2002; Jehangir, 1991; Ruhela, 1991; Salamatullah, 1994). Since the barriers to educational progress are perceived to be religious and socio-cultural, thereby calling for internal reforms, the nature of vote banks politics in India ruled out the possibility of any targeted intervention by the state towards improving the educational status of Muslims.

This 'social value theory' of educational backwardness has been questioned in recent years (Husain, 2005; Alam & Raju, 2007). Researchers have argued that Muslims do recognize the importance of education, but their 'effective demand' is restricted by their low income levels, while discrimination in the labour market lowers perceived benefits from education. The publication of the "Sachar Committee" Report is an important landmark in this literature (PMHLC, 2006). The Report observed that though enrolment rate of Muslims had increased in recent times, it still remained below that of other communities. Further, dropout rates were high among Muslim students, resulting in low mean years of schooling relative to that of other communities. Rejecting the value theory of educational backwardness, the Report identified economic conditions of Muslims and pessimism about their prospects in the labour market as major demand side constraints. The Report also identified the failure of the state to provide adequate educational infrastructure in Muslim dominated areas as a supply side constraint to improving educational status of Muslims.

In this paper we seek to analyze the educational status of Muslims in the state of West Bengal, India, and identify the socio-economic determinants of their poor educational status. The analysis is based on the following hypotheses:

1. There is a significant disparity in educational attainments between Muslims and other communities.
2. Within the Muslim community, girls constitute a particularly vulnerable section.
3. Educational backwardness is explained not only by household and personal characteristics (like household size, per capita income, gender and education level of head of family, gender of the child, his/her age), but also by the socio-religious identity of the child.

Database and Methodology

This paper is based on unit level data from the National Sample Survey (NSS) 61st Round (2004-05). This database has information on the religion and caste of the respondents. These two variables are combined to create socio-religious communities for analytical purposes. The socio-religious communities are upper caste Hindus, Hindu Scheduled Caste, Scheduled Tribes and Other Backward Castes, Muslims and others (comprising of other minorities and a residual group who did not state their religion). These categories are reclassified into five socio-religious communities, given in Table 1.[3]

Table 1: Socio-Religious Communities in Population in West Bengal – 2004 (per cent)

Analytical Categories used	*Socio-Religious Communities*	*Rural*	*Urban*
Hindu-Upper Caste (H-UC)	Hindu – Upper Caste	27.35	12.64
Hindu-Backward Castes (H-BC)	Hindu – Scheduled Castes	27.17	19.32
	Hindu – Scheduled Tribes	6.37	1.21
	Hindu – Other Backward Castes	6.08	5.95
	Hindu – caste not stated	0.02	0.06
Muslims	Muslims	31.14	14.00
Others	Other Minorities	0.99	1.01
	Religion not stated	0.89	0.30
Total Population		**100 per cent (7.04 crores)**	**100 per cent (2.20 crores)**

The state-level is decomposed by gender and place of residence to get four analytical categories – Urban Males, Urban Females, Rural Males and Rural Females. Our analysis is undertaken for each of these categories as the dynamics of educational decisions may vary between them. For instance, a major reason for not enrolling boys, or withdrawing them from school, is the need to supplement family income. In the case of the girl child, on the other hand, the need to assist in household chores may be an important motivation underlying such decisions.

The focus of this study is on West Bengal since: [a] The size of the minority population in West Bengal is higher than in other states except Madhya Pradesh; [b] The per centage of minorities is higher than in any other major state. Only some small states like Assam, Jammu & Kashmir, North-Eastern states and some Union Territories have a higher proportion of minorities; [c] Ideologically, the Left Front government is committed to secular principles and its electoral manifesto emphasizes upliftment of marginalized sections of the population; [d] Its political stability has given the government the opportunity to implement its objectives of social justice and progress through long-term plans.

We use two sets of methodologies – descriptive analysis and econometric. Firstly, the NSSO data is used to estimate the following:

(a) Children aged 6-15 years who have never attended school, as a proportion of children in the age category; and,

(b) Children aged 6-15 years who had enrolled but have dropped out, as a proportion of all enrolled children in the age category.

We then attempt to identify the reasons for non-enrolment and dropout, based on reasons stated by their family members.

Secondly, we attempt to identify the factors influencing enrolment, completion of primary education and choice of schools based on econometric methods. Now, the dependent variables – whether a child is enrolled or not, whether a child has dropped out or not, and whether the child has completed primary level or not – are binary variables, with values 0 and 1. In this situation, logit or probit models are commonly used, estimated using the Maximum Likelihood Method. These models differ with respect to specification of the error term – if the error term follows a logistic distribution *logit* model is used, while *probit* model is used if the error term follows a normal distribution. Since the cumulative normal and logistic distributions are very close to each other except at the tails, we are not likely to get very different results for the logit and probit models. So we have used probit models to analyse determinants of non-enrolment and dropouts.

Main Findings

Status of Never Enrolled Children

NSSO provides data on children who have never attended (and presumably never enrolled) in any school. It can be seen that more than a tenth of Muslim children aged 6-15 years have never enrolled (Table 2). In urban areas, Muslim children have the highest proportion of never attended children; in rural areas, they do come second after Others, but the sample size of Others is so small (17) that it is not advisable to consider this class.[4] The difference in non-enrolment rates in urban and rural areas is not marked for Muslims and H-UCs; non-enrolment rates among H-BCs is however much higher in rural areas than in urban areas.

Contrary to the common understanding about gender differences within the Muslim community with regard to educational decisions (Jehangir, 1991;

Ruhela, 1998; Hasan & Menon, 2004), Table 2 reveals marginal variations in non-enrolment rates between Muslim boys and girls in both areas.

Table 2: Proportion of Children aged 6-15 Years who have Never Enrolled in Educational Institutions (%)

Socio Religious Communities	*Urban*			*Rural*		
	Total	*Boys*	*Girls*	*Total*	*Boys*	*Girls*
Muslim	11.17	10.52	11.82	12.49	11.87	13.07
H-UC	4.90	6.62	3.37	3.70	4.21	3.16
H-BC	4.76	3.16	6.48	9.90	7.02	13.00
Others	0.00	0.00	0.00	28.26	18.32	39.03
Total	**6.13**	**6.33**	**5.94**	**9.91**	**8.42**	**11.43**

NSSO also provided reasons for non-enrolment. Unfortunately, the categorization is somewhat limited. As a result the residual category of reasons for never-enrolment (Others in the NSSO questionnaire) dominates in many cases (Tables 3-5).

Table 3: Reasons for Non-Enrolment of Children Aged 6-15 Years

Sector	*Socio-Religious Communities*	*School Too Far*	*Supplement HH Income*	*Education not Considered Necessary*	*To Attend Domestic Chores*	*Others*
Urban	Muslim (58)	0	17.48	41.30	1.39	39.83
	H-UC (47)	0	11.16	24.59	2.11	62.13
	H-BC (55)	1.39	3.85	41.21	8.96	44.60
	Others (NA)	0	0	0	0	0
	Total (160)	**0.34**	**12.02**	**34.72**	**3.33**	**49.63**
Rural	Muslim (273)	1.19	9.25	20.05	6.93	62.58
	H-UC (53)	7.54	21.31	5.59	4.68	60.88
	H-BC (171)	1.31	9.00	19.20	8.64	61.85
	Others (17)	12.14	12.53	30.22	12.53	32.57
	Total (514)	**2.27**	**10.26**	**19.08**	**7.69**	**60.71**

Note: Figures in parantheses represent the sample size for respective category. These are estimated without using multipliers.

Among the other reasons, particularly in urban areas, the perception that education is not important is high among Muslims and BCs. Before taking this as supporting the traditional value theory, we should note that education might not be considered important because of many reasons. For instance, pessimism about the prospect of the child in the labour market (Husain, 2005, PMHLC, 2006), the presence of relatively educated but unemployed youths in the neighbourhood (Ramachandra, 2003) and the poor quality of schools (Delap, 1998, PROBE, 1999) may also lead to the belief that the education that the child is getting will be of little use to him/her. Micro studies show that these reasons may significantly contribute to a feeling that education is not important.

Further, we should note that only about 11-12 per cent of Muslim boys and girls in West Bengal are not enrolled. So, even if the traditional value theory is valid – as may be the case for urban girls – it is certainly not a widespread phenomenon within the Muslim community. This supports Hasan & Menon's finding that parental opposition is not an important season in explaining educational backwardness, except in Northern India (Hasan & Menon, 2004).

Table 4: Reasons for Non-Enrolment of Urban Children Aged 6-15 Years

Sector	*Socio-Religious Communities*	*School Too Far*	*Supplement HH Income*	*Education not Considered Necessary*	*To Attend Domestic Chores*	*Others*
Male	Muslim (31)	0	37.41	19.97	0	42.62
	H-UC (24)	0	6.49	32.73	0	60.79
	H-BC (25)	0	11.17	35.15	4.05	49.64
	Others (NA)	0.00	0.00	0.00	0.00	0.00
	Total (80)	**0**	**18.27**	**28.51**	**0.6**	**52.62**
Female	Muslim (27)	0	0	60.00	2.62	37.38
	H-UC (23)	0	19.34	10.35	5.82	64.49
	H-BC (30)	2.13	0	44.39	11.54	41.95
	Others (NA)	0	0	0	0	0
	Total (80)	**0.62**	**5.6**	**41.1**	**6.13**	**46.55**

Note: Figures in parantheses represent the sample size for respective categories. These are estimated without using multipliers.

Disaggregating the rural and urban sample by gender allows us to study variations in motivation for non-enrolment across gender (Table 4). In comparison to 29 per cent for urban boys, only 20 per cent of Muslim boys are not enrolled as parents perceive that education is not important. In contrast, the need to supplement household family income is a more important reason – about a third of non enrolled Muslim boys cite this as the cause for non-enrolment. This would indicate that poverty is a major reason for non-enrolment.[5] Among Muslim girls, however, the perception that education is not important is the major reason for non-enrolment.

Surprisingly, the perception that education is not important does not play a major role in non-enrolment in rural areas (Table 5). This is true for both sexes. On the other hand, opportunity cost of child labour seems to be more important in rural areas, although the dynamics varies across gender. In the case of boys, the need to supplement family income is important, while in the case of girls, the need to attend domestic chores is a major reason for non-enrolment.

Table 5: Reasons for Non-Enrolment of Rural Children Aged 6-15 Years

Sector	*Socio-Religious Communities*	*School Too Far*	*Supplement HH Income*	*Education not Considered Necessary*	*To Attend Domestic Chores*	*Others*
Male	Muslim (130)	0.29	38.9	17.03	9.3	34.48
	H-UC (27)	0.00	43.76	10.59	3.00	42.65
	H-BC (64)	0.00	47.56	14.16	1.51	36.77
	Others (6)	0.00	52.90	0.00	0.00	47.10
	Total (227)	**0.14**	**43.07**	**14.81**	**5.34**	**36.64**
Female	Muslim (143)	0.00	15.31	21.57	24.54	38.58
	H-UC (26)	0.00	10.07	12.81	29.07	48.05
	H-BC (107)	0.00	8.54	16.68	38.48	36.29
	Others (11)	0.00	34.07	31.85	34.07	0.00
	Total (287)	**0.00**	**11.85**	**17.87**	**31.74**	**38.54**

Note: Figures in parantheses represent the sample size for respective categories. These are estimated without using multipliers.

Tables 4-5 provide support to the proposition that opportunity costs of education play an important role in reducing enrolment. This is in line with earlier studies (NSSO, 1997). However, it is necessary to delve deeper into this issue. An important question in this context is what type of work (household chores or productive activities) can be performed by children aged 6-8 years? For instance, in rural areas, children in this age group are more likely to *assist* their parents by carrying food, or foraging for common pool resources, etc. Similarly, children in urban areas either assist in household based productive activities or in household tasks on a part time basis, after school years or on holidays. In neither case the assistance is likely to be of a nature that will *prevent* the child from being enrolled; rather, they may subsequently lead to withdrawal of the child from school.

Table 6: Reasons for Non-Enrolment of Children Aged 6-9 Years

Sectors	*School Too Far*	*Supplement HH Income*	*Education not Considered Necessary*	*To Attend Domestic Chores*	*Others*
Rural Male (84)	-	2.4	-	7.1	90.5
Rural Female (117)	0.9	-	19.7	1.7	77.8
Urban Male (84)	-	3.1	-	-	71.9
Urban Female (27)	-	-	29.6	7.4	62.3

Note: Figures in parantheses represent the sample size for respective categories. These are estimated without using multipliers.

Accordingly, we have re-estimated the reasons for non-enrolment, restricting our sample to children aged below 10 years. In rural areas (Table 6) the main reason for non-enrolment appears to be a lack of belief in the value of education, though the residual category is extremely high. Predictably, the explanation of non-enrolment in terms of opportunity cost loses its explanatory power.

To test this proposition, the age-wise distribution of children who had never been enrolled due to either of these causes was estimated. It was found that only 7.48 per cent (in urban areas) and 3.64 per cent (in rural areas) of such children were aged below 10 years. Since it is unlikely that parents will enroll their children after 10 years, it is likely that such children are merely reporting their current status, rather than stating the actual reason for their non-enrolment.

In urban areas, too, the incidence of children not enrolled in order to assist in household tasks or supplement family income is marginal. Failure to acknowledge the importance of education is important only among H-BCs (both sexes) and among Muslim girls. The sharp variation across gender for the Muslim community may possibly be due to the presence of the fairly substantial proportion of non-Bengali speaking population, with a different attitude towards education shaped by their cultural and religious beliefs.

Before moving on, we should note the high residual proportion in Tables 6 and 7. Coupled with the inability to identify the true reason for non-enrolment of children aged 10 years or more, this makes it difficult to rule out supply side explanations for non-enrolment.

Table 7: Educational Infrastructure in Minority Concentrated and Other Districts of West Bengal - 2001

District	*Per cent Minority Population*	*Schools*		*Population ('000 Covered by Schools*	
		Govt. Schools	*Total Schools*	*Govt. Schools*	*Total Schools*
Puruliya	7.5	2985	3313	0.8	0.85
Bankura	7.7	3914	3914	0.8	0.82
Purba Medinipur	11.6	3490	3878	2.5	2.75
Hugli	15.3	3393	3565	1.4	1.49
Jalpaiguri	16.6	2233	2302	1.5	1.52
Barddhaman	20.4	4138	4800	1.4	1.67
Kolkata	22.1	1532	2007	2.3	2.98
Darjiling	22.7	1371	1388	1.2	1.17
Paschim Medinipur	23.7	4831	5392	0.0	0.03
NON-MINORITY DOMINATED DISTRICTS		27887	30559	1.3	1.5
Koch Bihar	24.4	1872	2070	1.2	1.32
North 24 Parganas	24.7	4049	4644	1.9	2.21
Haora	24.9	2148	2627	1.6	1.99
Dakshin Dinajpur	25.5	1351	1351	1.1	1.11
Nadia	26.1	2787	3063	1.5	1.65
South 24 Parganas	34.1	3604	4396	1.6	1.92
Birbhum	35.4	2371	2774	1.1	1.27
Uttar Dinajpur	48.0	1438	1632	1.5	1.70
Maldah	50.0	1909	2221	1.5	1.72
Murshidabad	64.0	3170	3682	1.6	1.85
MINORITY DOMINATED DISTRICTS		24699	28460	1.5	1.7

Source: Estimated from Census 2001 data: Table C1 (Population by Religious Community - Blockwise) and Table on Educational Amenities in West Bengal (http://www.wbcensus.gov.in/ DataTables/08/ FrameTables-e_1.htm).

As can be seen from Table 7, the population covered by a school is higher in minority-concentrated districts of West Bengal. This holds true for both government schools and all types of schools (that is, government and private). This would imply a deficiency in schooling infrastructure in minority-concentrated areas, which contradicts demand-side explanations of educational backwardness of minorities put forward by government officials. The claim that programmes like SSA have been successful is also important in this context. The SSA is not geared to counteract the negative influence of opportunity costs but is primarily a demand-based programme, involving community participation. Since community participation requires the existence of demand for education, the argument in favour of supply-driven explanations of non-enrolment becomes strong.

Status of Dropouts

While there is still scope to improve the enrolment rates, particularly among minorities and Muslims, schemes like the SSA has led to a sharp increase in enrolment rates in recent years. The next step, therefore, is to ensure that children are retained in schools for a sufficiently long period to ensure that their education has some value in their future life. This calls for an analysis of the incidence of dropouts.[6]

Table 8: Proportion of Enrolled Children Aged 6-15 Years Dropped Out from School

SRC Socio Religious Communities	*Urban*			*Rural*		
	Total	*Boy*	*Girls*	*Total*	*Boy*	*Girls*
Muslim	18.58	21.98	11.12	11.06	14.41	7.80
H-UC	7.28	7.33	6.56	7.84	6.55	9.19
H-BC	11.52	10.24	11.75	10.49	10.36	10.64
Others	12.39	21.94	0.00	16.72	11.06	24.94
Total	**10.85**	**11.59**	**8.83**	**10.19**	**10.97**	**9.37**

About a tenth of enrolled children aged 6-15 years dropout in both rural and urban areas (Table 8). This is not very high; further variations across gender and place of residence are marginal. However, there are substantial differences in dropout rates across SRCs. In urban West Bengal, dropout rate is highest among Muslims. One out of every five Muslim children drops out at some stage of their primary education. Surprisingly, dropout rates are higher among Muslim boys, than Muslim girls. In rural area, too, incidence of dropouts is highest among Muslims (11 per cent). Again, dropout rate is higher among Muslim boys than among Muslim girls.

A substantial gender difference is observed among Muslim in both rural and urban areas (Table 8). However – again contrary to expectations - it is among Muslim boys rather than among Muslim girls in both urban and rural areas, that dropout rates are higher. One reason for this may be that the perceived benefits to education (in terms of increased probability of getting employment) is lower among Muslim boys, discouraging Muslim boys from continuing studies (Ramachandra, 2003; Bhandari & Bordoloi, 2006; PMHLC, 2006). On the other hand, it has been argued that perceived benefits from educating Muslim girls may be high because:

(a) An educated girl has greater prospect of marriage as she is able to teach her children, keep accounts, manage daily expenses, and otherwise run the household more efficiently (Pratichi, 2002; Husain, 2003);

(b) She is better able to fend for herself in the case of desertion by her husband (Hossain & Kabeer, 2004); and

(c) Unlike other communities, the cost of marriage of an educated girl need not increase sharply as it is acceptable for the bride to have a higher educational status than the groom. For instance, it has been found that 26 per cent of educated Muslim women have illiterate husbands (Hasan & Menon, 2004).

As a result, in many cases parents may prefer to continue to educate the girl child till her marriage (Pratichi, 2002).

Table 9: Reasons for Dropping Out of Children Aged 6-15 Years

Sector	*Socio-Religious Communities*	*School Too Far*	*Supplement HH Income*	*Education not Considered Necessary*	*To Attend Domestic Chores*	*Others*
Urban	Muslim (51)	0	70.86	14.87	12.94	1.39
	H-UC (73)	0	18.09	19.93	13.25	48.73
	H-BC (78)	0	26.58	15.47	13.80	44.15
	Others (1)	0	0	0	0	100
	Total (203)	**0**	**38.61**	**16.47**	**13.09**	**31.84**
Rural	Muslim (195)	0.19	30.47	18.65	14.75	35.96
	H-UC (89)	0	24.47	11.86	17.92	45.74
	H-BC (171)	0	29.15	15.35	18.96	36.55
	Others (5)	0	41.45	19.37	20.73	18.45
	Total (460)	**0.08**	**29.15**	**16.17**	**17.11**	**37.49**

Note: Figures in parantheses represent the sample size for respective categories. These are estimated without using multipliers.

Analysis of NSSO data reveals that in urban areas the need to supplement family income is the major reason for dropout among Muslims. The proportion of children dropping out from school to supplement family income is about four times higher for urban Muslims as compared to Hindu - Upper Caste. Seven out of every ten Muslim children dropout to supplement household income in urban West Bengal (Table 9). This is possibly because of lower per capita income levels,[7] coupled with possibility of getting work in the informal sector (Ramachandra, 2006).

Interestingly, a large portion of H-UC dropouts (20 per cent) in urban area consider education not that important. This observation is quite surprising as it is commonly believed that it is the Muslim who value education less due to their conservative attitude (Sengupta & Guha, 2002). However, before emphasizing too much on this, we should note that dropout rate among H-UCs is only 7 per cent.

Disaggregating our analysis for male and female children of both rural and urban areas, we observed causes of dropout to vary sharply between male and female children (Tables 10 and 11).

Table 10: Reasons for Dropping Out of Urban Children Aged 6-15 years

Sector	*Socio-Religious Communities*	*School Too Far*	*Supplement HH Income*	*Education not Considered Necessary*	*To Attend Domestic Chores*	*Others*
Male	Muslim (33)	-	81.58	15.65	0.86	1.91
	H-UC (38)	-	34.48	20.08	-	45.45
	H-BC (42)	-	34.13	25.1	-	40.77
	Others (1)	-	-	-	-	100
	Total (114)	-	**52.6**	**18.98**	**0.35**	**28.07**
Female	Muslim (18)	-	49.98	13.16	36.49	0.38
	H-UC (35)	-	1.78	19.77	26.44	52.01
	H-BC (36)	-	19.48	6.41	26.77	47.34
	Others (NA)	-	-	-	-	-
	Total (89)	-	**20.88**	**13.28**	**29.23**	**36.61**

Note: Figures in parantheses represent the sample size for respective categories. These are estimated without using multipliers.

In urban areas, the need to supplement household income is the main cause of dropout of boys in all SRCs. However, this motivation is particularly strong among Muslim boys – 82 per cent of dropout among Muslim boys is caused by the need to supplement family income. This is not surprising given the fact that per capita income of Muslims is lower than for other communities.

Another interesting observation is that, while the perception that education is not necessary is a major reason for dropouts (about a fifth of dropouts is caused by this belief), this factor is least important within the Muslim community.

Among urban girls, supplementing family income is an important reason for dropout among Muslims (50 per cent) and H-BCs (19 per cent). Not surprisingly, performing domestic chores is another important cause of dropout observed for all SRCs. The perception that education is not important plays an important role only among H-UCs. These results are again linked to relative poverty – forcing the girl child to either undertake productive work generally within the household, or to free older female family members of domestic responsibilities and allow them to work outside the home.

Table 11: Reasons for Dropping Out of Rural Children Aged 6-15 Years

Sector	*Socio-Religious Communities*	*School Too Far*	*Supplement HH Income*	*Education not Considered Necessary*	*To Attend Domestic Chores*	*Others*
Male	Muslim (117)	0.29	38.9	17.03	9.3	34.48
	H-UC (37)	-	43.76	10.59	3	42.65
	H-BC (89)	-	47.56	14.16	1.51	36.77
	Others (2)	-	52.9	-	-	47.1
	Total (78)	**0.14**	**43.07**	**14.81**	**5.34**	**36.64**
Female	Muslim (78)	-	15.31	21.57	24.54	38.58
	H-UC (52)	-	10.07	12.81	29.07	48.05
	H-BC (82)	-	8.54	16.68	38.48	36.29
	Others (3)	-	34.07	31.85	34.07	-
	Total (215)	**-**	**11.85**	**17.87**	**31.74**	**38.54**

Note: Figures in parantheses represent the sample size for respective categories. These are estimated without using multipliers.

It is less easy to identify the reasons for dropout among Muslims in rural areas as the residual category is quite high. Among Muslim boys, economic activity is an important cause of dropout, though its importance is less than among other SRCs. Among Muslim girls, attending domestic chores, followed by a belief that education is unimportant, are the major reasons for dropout. While this is also true for H-UCs and H-BCs, a large proportion of girls from the Other category also dropout to supplement family income.

Econometric Analysis

Variables

Finally, we undertake an econometric analysis to identify the factors determining enrolment and dropout rates. Literature shows that attainments depend upon household characteristics and socio-religious identity of the respondent (Desai & Kulkarni, 2005; Sengupta & Guha, 2002; Husain, 2005; Alam & Raju, 2007). Accordingly we regress our dependent variables on the following independent variables:

1. *Monthly Family Expenditure (MFE):* Higher levels of MFE mean that the household has the resources to invest in education of children. This is important, given the surprisingly high costs of the 'free' primary education (Probe, 1999; NSSO, 1998). Thus, we expect that MFE will have a positive effect on enrolment rate and completion rate of primary education. Correspondingly, dropout should be lower with high levels of MFE. Given the high values of MFE with respect to the values of dependent variables, we have taken the logarithmic transformation of MFE (LMFE).
2. *Household Size (HHSIZE):* The household size is likely to affect educational status adversely, unless the dependency ratio is low.[8]

3. *Gender (FML):* There is a vast body of literature arguing that families tend to invest less in education of the girl child (Probe, 1999). To verify this hypothesis, we have constructed a gender dummy, FML equal to unity if the child is female and otherwise 0.
4. *Age (AGE)*: As a child gets older it becomes more difficult for him/her to join school. This is partly because of incompatibility with other children of the same class, or because of loss of interest in schooling, or because parents tend to engage him in productive or household tasks rather than keep him/her idle (increasing opportunity costs of schooling). After getting enrolled, the probability of dropout increases as the child grows older. This may be because parents have a target level of education that is typically low, or because they want to divert the financial resources for schooling to younger siblings (Husain, 2005). However, the probability of his/her completing primary level will be higher than younger children.
5. *Educational Level of Head of Household (EDU_DM):* Literature shows that if the decision maker is him/herself educated, then he(she) is more likely to educate his(her) children. While studies generally focus on literacy, we have taken different levels of education as defined in NSSO.[9]
6. *Gender of the Head of the Household (SEX_DM):* Gender of the head of the household also affects education related decisions. If a female is the decision maker, it may be expected that she is more responsive to the needs of educating a child, particularly the girl child.[10] On the other hand, if she is also the main income earner then she may have to remove girls from school to undertake household chores, and even boys if gender discrimination in the labour market results in her getting relatively lower wages; then the family income may have to be supplemented.
7. *Socio Religious Community (SRC):* Recent literature shows the presence of inequality in educational attainments at the all-India level between socio-religious communities (GOI, 2006). The analysis in Section 3 also indicates that Muslims, Other Minorities (in rural areas), and Backward Castes lag behind Upper Caste-Hindus in West Bengal in this respect. We have, therefore, constructed dummies to capture differences in educational attainments between SRCs, taking Muslims as the reference category:

   H-UC = 1 if respondent belongs to Hindu Upper Caste, otherwise= 0

   H-BC = 1 if respondent belongs to Hindu Backward Caste, otherwise= 0

Others = 1 if respondent belongs to Non-Muslim Minorities, and Others otherwise = 0

The discussion is summed up in Table 12.

Results

NSSO classifies respondents into three categories – those who have never attended educational institutions, those who had enrolled at some time, but are currently not attending (i.e. dropout), and those who are currently attending. We first consider the probability that a child (in the age group 6-15 years) has ever been enrolled in any educational institution (Model 1). Given the sample of enrolled children, we next identify the probability of the child dropping out (Model 2). The detailed results of the model are presented in Appendix, while Table 12 sums up the main results.

Table 12: Hypothesized and Actual Signs of Regression Coefficients

Variable	*Model 1: Enrolment*			*Model 2: Dropout*		
	Expected	*Actual*		*Expected*	*Actual*	
		Urban	*Rural*		*Urban*	*Rural*
LMFE	+ve	+ve	+ve	-ve	-ve	-ve
EDUDM	+ve	+ve	+ve	-ve	-ve	-ve
SEX_DM	+ve	+ve	+ve	-ve	**+ve**	-ve
HHSIZE	-ve	-ve	-ve	+ve	+ve	+ve
FML	-ve	**+ve**	-ve	+ve	**-ve**	**-ve**
AGE	-ve	-ve	-ve	+ve	+ve	+ve
H-UC	+ve	+ve	+ve	-ve	-ve	-ve
H-BC	+ve	+ve	+ve	-ve	-ve	-ve
Others	+ve	NA	**-ve**	-ve	**+ve**	**+ve**

Notes: 1. Except for H-BC in Model 2 (Rural), all coefficients are statistically significant at 99 per cent level.

2. Coefficients with unanticipated signs are shaded for ready identification.

The regression results show that household and personal characteristics determine educational attainments, with factors like family expenditure, educational level of decision maker, household size and age having expected impacts on probability of enrolment, dropout and primary completion.

Literature has identified girls as a particularly vulnerable section within our society. However, the picture may be more complex than commonly presumed. Probability of enrolment is actually *higher* for girls in urban areas. In rural areas, girls predictably have lower enrolment rates; but, once they are enrolled, girls have greater probability to 'survive' and continue their education. Thus, controlling for other variables, a girl has actually lower probability of dropping out in both rural and urban areas, possibly because of their lower mobility and opportunities outside the household. In the case of probability of completing primary education, however, girls fare worse than boys for the study age group. This is because girls are enrolled at an older age than boys, so that they fail to complete primary level within the age of 15 years. However, the achievements at lower levels of education do not translate into commensurate levels of achievements at higher levels of education, or into greater decision-making power. It is necessary to explore how the linkages between primary education, subsequent levels of education and empowerment can be strengthened for women.

The sign of the coefficient for SEX_DM generally conforms to our expectations. Probability of enrolment and primary completion rates are higher in female-headed households. Rural households headed by female also have lower rates of dropouts. This conforms to intra-household bargaining theory, which argues that a mother may incorporate her child's well-being in her personal utility function (Sen, 1993). In urban areas, however, a child from a female-headed household is more likely to dropout from school.[11]

In urban areas, if women of low income households are the decision makes, then it is likely that she will also be the bread earner. Given the structure of job market in urban areas, her employment may take part of her day. Given the nuclear structure of urban families, this entails shifting part of the responsibility of looking after the younger children and undertaking household tasks to older children, increasing the probability of dropout.

In rural areas, on the other hand, the mother may either have to spend several days outside the home or at least most of the day. In such cases, shifting the responsibility of the entire household tasks to older children may not be practicable. Further, given the presence of older female relatives in the household, household tasks, including supervision of education of children may be undertaken by these relatives. Further, female decision makers may be more interested in educating their children as it will enable them to return to the household sphere and assume traditional functions. The operation of all these forces in the rural areas may lead to empowerment of women having a favorable effect on education.

An important result from the econometric exercise is that, after controlling for household and personal characteristics, the socio-religious identity of the child is important in determining its probability of getting enrolled, continuing education and completing the primary stage. It is expected that Muslims will fare poorly relative to H-UCs. But, contrary to expectations fueled by the myth of minority appeasement, Muslims tend to perform worse than even the backward castes (H-BCs) so far as enrolment and dropouts are concerned. The probability of completing the primary level is higher for H-BC children vis-à-vis Muslims in urban areas. While children from other minority communities, constitutes too small a sample for estimation in urban areas, their status is worse than Muslims with respect to enrolment (rural areas).

However, they have lower dropout rates and higher primary completion rates (rural areas), i.e. Muslim children are less 'robust'.

Conclusion

The analysis undertaken in this paper provides useful insights into the relative status of Muslims and non-Muslim minorities in West Bengal with regard to basic educational attainments. In Section 3 we had seen that levels of non-enrolment and dropout of Muslims are higher than that of H-UC, as also of H-BCs in both rural and urban West Bengal. This may, of course be due to household and personal characteristics, like lower income levels, larger household size, lower educational level of household head, etc. The econometric analysis in Section 4 not only supports our finding that Muslims are relatively deprived, but indicates that even after controlling for such factors, Muslims have higher levels of non-enrolment and dropouts.

This raises the question as to whether Muslims lag behind other SRCs due to cultural and attitudinal traits of the community (Jehangir, 1991), or due to real or perceived discrimination. Policy makers would of course like us to believe the former to be the main reason.[12] While the nature of NSS data prevents us from specifically examining the data to determine valid explanation, the analysis in Section 3 does not provide support for the belief that Muslims are non-appreciative of the value of education. Parents of only 4.6 per cent of Muslim children aged 6-12 years believe that education is not important.[13] It is, therefore, necessary to examine the relative importance of cultural and economic factors in determining the demand for primary education within the minority community, and the nature of this demand.

At the same time, it should be kept in mind that even after controlling for household and personal characteristics, minorities lag behind other SRCs. This calls for affirmative action targeting minorities (like focusing on minority-dominated areas under the SSA, providing scholarships,[14] opening local study centers in minority-dominated areas, slums, distributing free textbooks, and so on) to change their cost-benefit calculations in educational decision making. Despite the fact that only 4 per cent of Muslim children in West Bengal are enrolled in Madrasahs (PMHLC, 2006), the West Bengal government has tended to focus on Madrasahs as the panacea for educational deprivation (GoWB, 2008). Such an attitude and strategy will merely accentuate the gap between minorities and other communities.

References

Alam, M. S. & Raju, S. (2007): Contextualising Inter-, Intra-Religious and Gendered Literacy and Educational Disparities in Rural Bihar. *Economic & Political Weekly*, 42, 18, pp. 1613-22.

Ansari, I.A. (1989): *Muslim Educational Backwardness: New Educational Policy and Programme, The Muslim Situation in India.* New Delhi: Sterling Publishers.

Baig, M. R A (1947): *Muslim Dilemma in India*. Delhi: Vikash Publication.

Bandyopadhyay, D. (2002): Madrasa Education and the Condition of Indian Muslim. *Economic & Political Weekly*, 37, 16, pp. 1481-84.

Bhandari. L. & Bordoloi, M. (2006): Income Differential and Returns to Education. *Economic & Political Weekly*, 41, 36, pp. 3893-900.

Das, S. and Mukherjee, D. (2007): Role of Women in Schooling and Child Labour Decision – The Case of Urban Boys in India. *Social Indicators Research*, 82, 3, pp. 463-86.

Delap, E. (1998): *The Determinants and Effects of Children Income Generating Work in Urban Bangladesh*. Mimeo.

Desai, S. and Kulkarni, V. (2005): *Changing Educational Inequalities in India in the Context of Affirmative Action*. Mimeo: Dept. of Sociology, University of Maryland.

Dreze, J. and Sen, A.K. (2002): *India: Development and Participation*. New Delhi: Oxford University Press.

Govt. of India (2006): *Social, Economic and Educational Backwardness of Muslims in India – A Report*. Unpublished Report, Prime Minister's High Level Committee.

Govt. of West Bengal (2008): *Eleventh Five-Year Plan: Draft*. Development & Planning Department.

Hasan, Z. & Menon, R. (2004): *Unequal Citizens – A Study of Muslim Women in India*. New Delhi. Oxford University Press.

Hossain, N. & Kabeer, N. (2004): "Achieving Universal Primary Education and Elementary Gender Disparity", *Economic & Political Weekly*, 39, 36, pp. 4093-99.

Hunter, W.W. (1869): *Indian Musalmans*. New Delhi, Indological Book.

Husain, Z. (2005): Analysing Demand for Primary Education – Muslims Slum Dwellers of Kolkata. *Economic & Political Weekly*, 40, 2, pp. 137-47.

Husain, Z. (2008): *Employment and Economic Profile of Socio-Religious Communities in West Bengal – Some Evidence from NSS 61*st *Round*. Unpublished. Report, Dept. of Minority Affairs and Madrasah Education, Govt. of West Bengal.

Jehangir, K.N. (1991): *Muslim Women in Bengal – Socio-Economic and Political Status*. Calcutta: Minerva Publishers.

Khalidi, Omar (1995): *Indian Muslims Since Independence*. New Delhi, Vikash Publishing House.

Mondal, S.R. (1997): *Educational Status of Muslims – Problems and Prospects*. New Delhi: Inter India Publications.

National Sample Survey Organisation (1997): *Report No. 412 – Economic Activities and School Attendance by Children in India, 1993-94*. Government of India, New Delhi.

_____ (1998): *Report No. 439 – Attending Educational Institutions in India - Its Level, Nature and Costs; NSS 52*nd *Round (1997-98)*. New Delhi: Dept. of Statistics, Govt. of India.

Pratichi (2002): *The Pratichi Education Report, A Study in West Bengal*. Delhi: TLM Books.

Probe Team and Centre for Development Economics (1999). *Public Report on Basic Education in India*. New Delhi: Oxford University Press.

Ramachandra, V. (2003): Backward & Forward Linkages that Strengthen Primary Education. *Economic & Political Weekly*, 38, 10, pp. 959-68.

_____ (2006): Urban Schooling Mired in Apathy & Prejudice. *Economic & Political Weekly,* 41, 5, pp. 383-4.

Ruhela, S.P. (1998): "Religion, Social Class and Educational Opportunity – Case Studies of Eight Muslim Girls", in S.P. Ruhela (ed.) *Empowerment of the Indian Muslim Women*, New Delhi, MD Publications: pp. 1-21.

Salamatullah (1994): "Education of Muslims in Secular India" Chandigarh: Centre for Research in Rural and Industrial Development.

Sen, A.K. (1985): *Commodities and Capabilities*, Amsterdam, North Holland.

Sen, A. K. (1993): "Economics and the Family", in P. Uberoi (Ed.): *Family, Kinship and Marriage in India*. New Delhi: Oxford University Press, pp 452-463.

Sengupta, P. and Guha, J. (2002): Enrolment, Dropout and Grade Completion of Girl Children in West Bengal. *Economic & Political Weekly*, 37, 17, pp. 1621-37.

Schultz, T. (1961): Investment in Human Capital. *American Economic Review*, 51, March, 1961, pp.1-17.

Shariff. A. and Razzack, A. (2006): "Communal Relations and Social Integration", *in* Council for Social Development. *India: Social Development Report 2006*. New Delhi: Oxford University Press, pp. 96-110.

Sharma, K. D. (1978): *Education of a National Minority – A Reader in Social Class of Indian Muslim*. New Delhi: Kalamkar Prakashan.

Weisbrod, B. A. (1962): Education and Investment in Human Capital. *Journal of Political Economy*, 70, 2, pp. 106-23.

APPENDIX

ECONOMETRIC RESULTS

I. Determinants of Enrolment

Urban

Probit regression, reporting marginal effects

Number of obs =3232758 LR chi2(8) = 1.4e+ve05 Prob > chi2 = 0.0000

Log likelihood = -681403.41 Pseudo R2 = 0.0950

	Never enrolled	*dF/dx*	*Std. Err.*	*z*	*P>|z|*	*x-bar*	*[95% C.I.]*
LMFE	.027577	.0002351	116.39	0.000	8.2253	.027116	.028038
EDUDM	.0056773	.0000408	135.39	0.000	5.8705	.005597	.005757
SEX_DM	-.0610919	.0005896	-134.67	0.000	.086878	-.062247	-.059936
H-UC	.0262025	.0002856	92.73	0.000	.498092	.025643	.026762
H-BC	.0356138	.0002323	135.69	0.000	.285505	.035159	.036069
HHSIZE	-.0051056	.0000558	-90.87	0.000	5.61809	-.005215	-.004996
FML	.0026501	.0002283	11.61	0.000	.509748	.002203	.003098
AGE	-.0026464	.00004	-66.06	0.000	10.8029	-.002725	-.002568
obs. P	.9378265						
pred. P	.9533351 (at x-bar)						

(*) dF/dx is for discrete change of dummy variable from 0 to 1

z and P>|z| correspond to the test of the underlying coefficient being 0

Rural

Probit regression, reporting marginal effects

Number of obs =14348046 LR chi2(9) = 1.3e+ve06 Prob > chi2 = 0.0000

Log likelihood = -3995024.8 Pseudo R2 = 0.1373

	Never enrolled	dF/dx	Std. Err.	z	P>|z|	x-bar	[95% C.I.]
LMFE	.1264464	.0001975	618.10	0.000	7.82165	.126059	.126834
EDUDM	.0135178	.0000259	493.80	0.000	3.80867	.013467	.013569
SEX_DM	-.0021673	.0002715	-8.07	0.000	.05711	-.002699	-.001635
H-UC	.0405894	.0001501	223.88	0.000	.210068	.040295	.040884
H-BC	.0030548	.0001358	22.42	0.000	.389012	.002789	.003321
OTHERS	-.1214299	.000779	-213.89	0.000	.017046	-.122957	-.119903
HHSIZE	-.0189289	.000032	-586.83	0.000	5.97241	-.018992	-.018866
FML	-.0209523	.0001257	-167.46	0.000	.493199	-.021199	-.020706
AGE	-.0024756	.0000215	-115.11	0.000	10.4888	-.002518	-.002433
obs. P	.9010596						
pred. P	.9354884 (at x-bar)						

(*) dF/dx is for discrete change of dummy variable from 0 to 1

z and P>|z| correspond to the test of the underlying coefficient being 0

II. Determinants of Dropout

Urban

Probit regression, reporting marginal effects

Number of obs =3077299 LR chi2(9) = 5.7e+ve05 Prob > chi2 = 0.0000

Log likelihood = -770077.31 Pseudo R2 = 0.2712

	Dropout	*dF/dx*	*Std. Err.*	*z*	*P>|z|*	*x-bar*	*[95% C.I.]*
LMFE	-.0665758	.0002851	-253.81	0.000	8.25118	-.067135	-.066017
EDUDM	-.0040668	.0000412	-98.64	0.000	6.04898	-.004148	-.003986
SEX_DM	.0067101	.0004335	16.20	0.000	.077283	.00586	.00756
H-UC	-.0479891	.0003074	-162.53	0.000	.49761	-.048591	-.047387
H-BC	-.0326051	.0002371	-125.47	0.000	.285661	-.03307	-.03214
OTHERS	.0052411	.0009552	5.71	0.000	.014796	.003369	.007113
HHSIZE	.0076155	.0000582	131.96	0.000	5.6167	.007501	.00773
FML	-.0073666	.0002263	-32.71	0.000	.509763	-.00781	-.006923
AGE	.0253852	.0000531	500.51	0.000	10.7836	.025281	.025489
obs. P	.1084945						
pred. P	.0475428 (at x-bar)						

(*) dF/dx is for discrete change of dummy variable from 0 to 1

z and P>|z| correspond to the test of the underlying coefficient being 0

Rural

Probit regression, reporting marginal effects:

Number of obs =12928445 LR chi2(9) = 2.1e+ve06 Prob > chi2 = 0.0000

Log likelihood = -3195452.5 Pseudo R2 = 0.2496

	dropout	dF/dx	Std. Err.	z	P>|z|	x-bar	[95% C.I.]
LMFE	-.0587599	.0001576	-383.37	0.000	7.84097	-.059069	-.058451
EDUDM	-.0067025	.0000209	-325.72	0.000	3.99073	-.006744	-.006661
SEX_DM *	-.0129492	.0001847	-61.71	0.000	.056374	-.013311	-.012587
H-UC	-.0038833	.0001413	-26.92	0.000	.224501	-.00416	-.003606
H-BC	-.0000981	.0001163	-0.84	0.399	.388961	-.000326	.00013
OTHERS	.0849626	.0008403	143.41	0.000	.013572	.083316	.08661
HHSIZE	.0072451	.0000279	262.28	0.000	5.90964	.00719	.0073
FML	-.0046599	.0001023	-45.57	0.000	.484937	-.00486	-.004459
AGE	.0276411	.0000273	1129.20	0.000	10.4801	.027588	.027695
obs. P	.101974						
pred. P	.0432286 (at x-bar)						

(*) dF/dx is for discrete change of dummy variable from 0 to 1

z and P>|z| correspond to the test of the underlying coefficient being 0

12

HIGHER EDUCATION IN AND FOR A CHANGING WORLD*

KARUNA CHANANA

Abstract

Considerable claims are being made for higher education as an engine of social, economic and political change across the world. There is also counter discourse which questions the optimism of those who support the forces of change as represented by globalization. The first part of the paper focuses on globalization and knowledge society as the two main constructs of the contemporary discourse on change and education and critiques their impact on equity and access in higher education. Scholars are questioning the dependence of globalisation on techno sciences; or the close connection between managerialism and equity; the commodification of knowledge; re-ification of stratification of knowledge generated in the developed and less developed economies while pushing the local knowledge traditions into the margins. All of these have social and equity implications. In the second part, this theme is located within the discourse on higher education in India. Since the 1990s, most of the expansion in higher education has taken place in the 'for-profit' private educational institutions and since profit is the central parametre defining educational priorities and choices, considerations of gender, marginality and caste are pushed to the background. It is argued, on the basis of access and participation of women, minorities and the SCs and STs, that expansion of education has not benefitted the students from these categories. Hence, the role of the State in promoting and pushing for change along with equality and equity through education becomes critical.

---

* Lecture delivered at the Annual Conference of the Comparative Education Society of India, Department of Education, University of Jammu, Jammu, October 11, 2012.

Preamble

Considerable claims are being made for higher education as an engine of social, economic and political change across the world. There is also counter discourse which questions the optimism of those who support the forces of change as represented by globalization. The two main constructs of the contemporary discourse on change and education are globalization and knowledge society focus is on both these. The first part of the paper while locating this theme within the discourse on higher education, especially the Indian higher education system, will provide the context. The basic premise of this paper is that in order to push for change, education itself has to change – a process which is happening at a fast pace across the globe because the educational landscape is expanding. What follows from this is that the relationship between globalization and education is two-way and education cannot push for change without changing itself.

Looking at the history of sociology of education, one cannot think of any time when the social thinkers writing on modern education did not mention change or the contribution of education to change. Change and the functions of education were central to most of their writings. Just to mention a few names, for example, Emile Durkheim, Mannheim, Max Weber, Dewey, etc. They were all concerned about the economic, social and political changes wrought by the industrial revolution and the need for education to respond to them. Education, especially higher education, was seen as the engine of technological growth through skill training and generation of new knowledge, training of manpower as human capital, and to establish and nurture democratic values and promote social mobility. In other words, the functions of education were expected to change in a changing society. Education was to be a 'state capitalist enterprise', i.e., it was to be fully state supported which will enable the universities to retain their professional autonomy considered essential for reflective thinking and for the generation of new knowledge and discovery.

However, education has always been assigned contradictory roles. Its functions tend to be conflictual at times. For example, and as already mentioned, in the wake of industrialization in Western societies, it was expected to push for change and be the main instrument for promoting economic, political and social change. At the same time, it was also expected to instill values and attitudes necessary for maintaining a continuity with the past and the existing social institutions so as to avoid sudden rupture in the social life of the community. For example, at the level of the individual student in the school the values necessary for continuation of social institutions such as the family and society had to be instilled. And at the same time, the younger generation had to be equipped with the new technical skills and be prepared for the job market while getting accustomed to the social changes (Brennan and Naidoo 2006: 225). In other words, socialisation and formal education of the student had to be for change and continuity. Now, some of the traditional functions of education in industrial societies are again being redefined while the new ones are being added in the knowledge society. Education is expected to maintain a balance.

There is no doubt that the changes spearheaded by economic liberalization and globalization are impacting on higher education (HE) worldwide. The relationships between the governments and universities are changing all over the world. Yet the central proposition of the contemporary discourse on higher education, knowledge and globalisation that education can change the future of the world is under a critical gaze.

Additionally, around the time when India began to liberalise its economy in the early 1990s, it was argued by the international agencies and some scholars that higher education is a non-merit or a private good and the developing countries should not focus on its expansion. They should be concerned about primary education which was the public good. This argument reflected a stark reversal of the earlier position that higher education is a public good and should be fully state supported. As a result, more and more governments, including the democratic ones, began to take the stance that the entry or increased participation of the private sector in higher education is not only necessary but healthy for the growth and development of higher education.

So, the question was posed as 'either/or', instead of working in both directions. The Indian government also followed suit and declared higher education as a non-merit good. However, at a later stage there was a remarkable reversal in the global policy promoted by the international agencies such as the World Bank. It began to be argued that higher education is essential for developing countries to become part of the knowledge economy.

Globalisation

"Globalisation has multiple meanings and is manifested differently in different situations.... It takes different forms and looks different in different parts of the world or in different countries. There are also varied perspectives depending on the local and regional contexts" (Macdonell 2008: 145). Globalisation also means many things to many people. According to some, colonialism was globalization while others referred to modernization as globalisation. Here it is referred to as the process of economic liberalization in India since 1991 and its impact on higher education.

What is central to globalization is that the world has become increasingly interdependent and ever-closer a process which started in the last quarter of the 20th century. Communication technology and the global economy have played an important role in this interdependence which is evident all over the globe and in all walks of life (Morris-Suzuki 2008:vii). It has changed the world into a global market and where the jobs are generated is not restricted by geographical boundaries. Macro-developments across the globe affect people at the micro level. Further, the direct nexus between the industry, corporate world and higher education has brought a transformation in the skills needed for jobs. For example, formation of intellectual capital, as a market commodity, is being viewed or projected as an indispensable instrument for a high-skills economy. Therefore, universities become the main sites for the production, dissemination and transfer of knowledge, innovation and technology. Public universities have been forced to downsize; and the language of efficiency and accountability associated with corporate management is being used to run and to evaluate universities. The most salient development is the rise of the for-profit private sector in higher education.

The push for allowing private higher education came from the thinking that the higher education system has become too large and unwieldy and the state could no longer provide funds for it. Second, there was a big question mark about the quality of education in the the state-run system. Further, those who were of the view that private sector can deliver began to push for private universities and colleges. Third, it was argued that competition between the public and private institutions will generally improve quality and efficiency. As a fall-out of this thinking, there has been a fall in state funding of higher education across the world along with tighter control of academic life in order to improve quality for which quality assurance bodies have been set up.

This thinking reinforced changes in the role of education, viz., to harness universities for economic productivity and for knowledge production. Higher education and knowledge produced through it, is also being viewed as a commodity for which a price has to be paid if one wants to buy it. This explains the rise of the private universities and colleges providing self-funded education around the world and in India. The state is no longer viewed as the sole provider of education which has led to a global move away from the traditional forms of funding and regulation according to which it was the sole responsibility of the state to provide funds for higher education. Earlier, there seemed to be a 'social compact' (Brennan and Naidoo: 223) between the state and society to provide for education for all (Slaughter and Leslie 1997). That social compact has broken down. There is also a drastic change in the thinking of the government that higher education should be autonomous and independent from political and corporate influence which was based on the assumption that full state funding will provide professional autonomy to universities. Therefore, new funding and regulatory frameworks are being evolved as a result of the influence of neo-liberal market-oriented mechanisms. At the level of the institutions or at the micro level it means that the higher educational institutions should be financially self-sufficient, thereby forcing the government institutions to cut down on the cost and to think of ways and means to raise funds. One of the easiest ways is to ask the students to finance their own education giving rise to a surfeit of banks providing loans to students. The second is to push the academic community into raising funds for their research and for the university.

Third, the faculty in the state-run universities are either not being recruited or are being recruited on contractual and temporary basis. Fourth, to introduce academic subjects with high market demand.

Slaughter and Leslie call this as 'academic capitalism' which they define as "any institutional and professional market or market-like [sic] efforts to secure external moneys" (1997:8). The emergence of academic capitalism is examined by tracing "the growth of global markets, the development of national policies that target faculty-applied research, the decline of the block grant as a vehicle for state support for higher education, and the accompanying increase in faculty engagement with the market" (1997:11). They refer to "Entrepreneurial Knowledge," and the work of applied scientists as entrepreneurial. Faculties have had to change their conception of knowledge and become academic capitalists. Thus, there has been a change in the perception of the role of the faculty to become instrumental in establishing links with the market and industry and had to acknowledge the economic value of knowledge and its indispensability in raising funds for the universities to pursue research and other activities. Profit and competition became central to this ethos and professors were pushed into this competitive arena. At stake was their survival in the university system. So the nature of academic work and the faculty role changed in response to global markets.

However, the *process of globalisation is complex and generates contradictions and conflicts*. It has become one of the most pressing challenges in the contemporary world. While communication technology in the global world is increasing interdependence ‒ economic, social, intellectual and political — it is also heightening divisions of ethnicity, region, class, caste and religion, and also along national and sub-national lines (Morris-Suzuki 2008: vii; McDonnell 2008:146). Therefore, how should we assess the role of education in change in a world which is still divided along local, regional and national lines especially, in a situation of simultaneous convergence and divergence. While globalisation has increased opportunities and benefits, it also raises serious concerns about cultural identity, social justice and equity. While the higher education system has suffered precipitous decline in state support, the self-funded academic programmes have given rise to debt-ridden graduates and contingent faculty.

Knowledge Society

Along with globalization, scholars have also been re-examining the assumptions underlying the discourse around the knowledge society. Some of the questions raised about knowledge in contemporary society are reminiscent of those raised by the 'new sociologists' in the 1970s. They had asked questions about the universality of knowledge, its control and dissemination in the hands of the few and for a few. Later, feminist scholars raised similar questions. These questions are being raised anew.

According to Weiler "The invocation of the notion of a "knowledge society" has become ubiquitous. Among its many dangers is that it creates the illusion that we know what we are talking about when we talk about "knowledge". He claims that, "when it comes to knowledge, we do *not* know what we are talking about" (2006:61) He asks three questions in the context of the knowledge society: what is knowledge? What are the political consequences of its production and use? Who determines what knowledge is 'valued'? (Neave 2006:18)

Further, scholars (Houtondji: 2006) contend that knowledge society is divided into the developed and developing world, the former creates the knowledge and the latter receives the knowledge created in the developed world. This is reminiscent of Edward Shils' division into the centre and the periphery (Neave 2006:16) in the colonial society which hegemonised knowledge created in the western societies. This framework was an indicator of marginalisation of local intellectual traditions. It focussed exclusively on the western colonial and developed societies as the centre and the knowledge created by them. Universities in the rest of the world were characterised as being on the periphery. Neave goes to the extent of saying that change vis-a-vis the construction of what is knowledge that is being witnessed today is hardly different from what was seen in the colonial and industrial societies. In fact, he argues further that there is no universal knowledge and the so-called universal knowledge marginalises the indigenous or alternative knowledge traditions as was done in the colonial societies and also in the industrial societies. (2006:20). The universal categories denied a place to local social constructs and culture. To quote Neave, "this is no small form of expropriation, and no little exclusion. Assimilating, ostracising or forcing alternative traditions of local knowledge into inner exile effectively evacuates meaning and value from the social structures and communities that produce them" (2006:17). However, now there is evidence of a movement for re-instating the primacy of local identities, knowledge and traditions (Adeoti 2006).

Another argument against globalisation and universality of knowledge in the contemporary context is given by Brennan and Naidoo. They argue that universal knowledge may come in conflict with knowledge which is relevant to the national and local contexts (2006:228). Further, universities are located in national contexts which are experiencing economic, social and political change, each one different from the other. Further, the universities do not merely react to change but also respond and contribute to change. It is because of the interaction of global and local forces which puts pressure on universities to react to change and meet its demands for the benefit of their own society and for the university community. In addition, the global and local forces also create contradictory situations for the university and for knowledge production. But this conflict is being managed by the differentiation of institutional functions. In other words, different sets of institutions are catering to the elite and the masses performing different functions. This reminds us of Trow's division of institutions into elite and mass education which will be taken up later.

Additionally, there is no level playing field in the production of knowledge, what is it used for and by whom? According to Neave, "If there is somewhere a 'level playing field' in which each individual, community or nation may compete on equal terms with its neighbours – ... – It is at present surrounded by high mountains and deep crevasses, both in its formal knowledge infrastructures and in terms of those having access to it" (2006 17). This point is substantiated here by looking at the participation of women vis-à-vis their subject choices, access of minorities and the disadvantaged in India's system of higher education although such disparities are present across nations and within nations.

Equity and Access in the Context of Globalisation

Social transformation or change presumes some fundamental changes in the political, social and economic institutions of society with a positive impact on the relationships between social groups, classes or strata and the distribution of wealth, power and status. However, doubts have been expressed by leading scholars in the field of education. Brown, Lauder and Ashton (2011:3) in their book entitled, *The Global Auction: The Broken Promises of Education, Jobs and Incomes,* say that 'the changing economic world evokes at once a sense of admiration and foreboding'. Clearly, globalisation has not made, and will not make, the world homogeneous' (McDonell 2008: 146). Bowles and Gintis express misgiving and skepticism about the impact of globalization and the equation of knowledge as a commodity when they say, "Today, no less than during the stormy days when Schooling in Capitalist America was written, schools express the conflicts and limitations, as well as the hopes of a heterogeneous and unequal society. Schools continue to be both testing grounds and battlegrounds for building a society that extends its freedoms and material benefits to all." (2002:15)

According to McKinnon and Brooks (2001) the social movements which represent civil society have been questioning the dominance of technology in higher education. They also question the formulation of research agendas around the new technologies and at the marginalisation of social issues and the social policy research areas in which the disadvantaged groups, the marginalised, the minorities and women academic staff and students are generally disproportionately located.

Additionally, globalisation is accompanied by an increased focus on techno sciences which have social and equity implications because the disadvantaged groups, the marginalised, the minorities and women are less likely to be involved in those areas which are frontrunners in the new economy and the market; they are also likely to be at the lower levels; they may also be unable to adjust to the time-space compression that IT demands or fosters (Harvey 1993). Those who are located in the more reflective areas and those who can quickly respond to the call of the market will react differently to these changes.

Moreover, the issue of compatibility between managerialism and equity (Sawer 1989; Yeatman 1990) has also been debated. It is argued that contemporary changes have an impact on pursuing equity issues within the universities because "a commitment to equity and a commitment to cost-cutting" (Bacchi 2001: 120) may not go hand-in-hand. Further, there is tension between promoting a social and democratic ideology, on the one hand and market ideology, on the other. This situation is again a reminder that universities have always contained many contradictions at a single point of time or over several points of time (Brennan and Naidoo 2006:226).

These contradictions can also be viewed as multiple roles which resist as well as draw on global and national forces which simultaneously push for change and also play a reproductive role. An important point is that at the systemic level, differentiation among universities and higher education institutions has become common, for example, there are open or distance education universities, private universities, state universities and other kinds of institutions (such as deemed universities in India), functioning at the same time in many countries. Each of them plays a specific role. Some of them are catering to the elite students while the others are accessed by the masses. Martin Trow's well known distinction between the elite and mass higher education (1974) saw these states as largely sequential or conversion of the former into the latter. Although he saw the possibility of them running in parallel, i.e., elite and mass higher education co-existing in the same society, his framework was based on the former premise. However, it is the latter situation which is characteristic of contemporary society (Brennan and Naidoo 2006:221-33).

This differentiation and variation is also reflected in the academic programmes that are on offer in higher education, for example, there are academic and vocational programmes, applied and market driven professional subjects and those in humanities, social sciences and pure sciences. Internationalization of higher education is also leading to differentiation of higher education. Those parents who can afford expensive education send their children abroad for higher education. Therefore, institutional and subject differentiation is happening along with the diversification of the students in terms of their social composition. These two processes of institutional differentiation among institutions and diversification of students, "allow higher education in the context of change to perform contradictory social functions, namely, help maintain the status and position of social elites while providing some opportunities for social mobility" (Brennan and Naidoo: 229). This is again reminiscent of what has been said long back by Bourdieu when he expostulated the main contribution of education to the systemic reproduction with very limited contribution to change.

Change, Globalization and the Indian Higher Education System

So far as the Indian higher education system is concerned, except for the last few years or in the XIth plan when the government decided to expand the public sector HE, most of the expansion since the early 1990s in the number of institutions and in professional subjects or the male dominated subjects such as engineering, technology, ICT, etc., has been in the private sector.

This development is also linked to the self-financing/self-funded courses which are primarily market driven professional ones and are offered both in the public and private institutions — both are costly but those in the private institutions are much more expensive than those in the public colleges and universities. But both can deny access to the students, especially those from lower and the middle strata due to high cost.[1]

Additionally, the market demand has impacted the stratification of disciplines or subjects leading to the devaluation of arts, humanities, social sciences. Traditionally, underprivileged students and women have entered arts, humanities, social sciences which is a continuing trend. These are also referred to as the feminine subjects. These developments affect students from all the categories under consideration. How are the new developments in the market, its direct impact on the curriculum and higher tuition fees impacting the subject choices of students from these social groups and women students?

Another development is the privatisation of public universities which has two aspects that are likely to affect all the students under consideration. The first relates to the higher tuition fee in the self-financing courses mentioned above and leads to the second aspect, i.e., which parents are able to and are willing to spend higher costs on the education of their children, sons as well as daughters. Those who do, who are they, i.e., which strata of society do they come from?

Access: the Indian Situation

As already mentioned, a very important function of higher education system in social change is to assess the extent of educational opportunities for the disadvantaged groups, the minorities and women. This is a very critical question but is hampered by lack of reliable data. For example, although enrolments in Indian higher education have increased substantially and the student community is diversified, we do not know very much about the social outcomes. Further, we hardly know about the distribution of students from different social groups among the increasingly diversified institutional contexts and new professional and market oriented subjects.

In the last decade, there has been much concern about extending and expanding access to minority groups and Other Backward Castes (OBCs) in addition to the SCs and STs. In view of this, even though India has diversified its higher education system and has, to some extent, implemented widening participation and access initiatives for the disadvantaged and the minorities, its student population has not dramatically changed in composition.

Although there is lack of extensive and reliable database on higher education in India, disaggregated analysis of available enrolment statistics shows continuing inequalities. This is mainly because the number of state universities and colleges is declining since the early 1990s because state support to higher education has been decreasing. Simultaneously, the tuition fees are also increasing in the private sector as well as in the state sector in the name of self-funded academic programmes and subjects. The disadvantaged, the minority and women students have to compete for a few relatively inexpensive seats in state-run system, or they should be ready to shell out the high cost of private higher education. There is no need to emphasize that direct high cost is a barrier to access, not to mention the indirect costs.

Moreover, the new developments have led to the devaluation of disciplines which have been the choice of women, minorities and those from the disadvantaged social groups. It is quite common to hear these days that academic administrators ask the question: why should institutions offer history or sociology or the languages?

Look at the access and participation of women, minorities especially, Muslims and SC/STs[2] in higher education in India. While access is limited to enrolment, participation refers to what happens after the students enter HEIs, i.e., what do they do after admission, namely, do they transit to higher levels; which subjects and specializations do they choose? There can be many other aspects but the nature of the available data puts limits on the analysis.

While choosing to focus on the Muslims, among minorities, in 1993 (Chanana), it was argued that they were an apt example of an educationally backward religious community. This position was taken much before the Sachar Committee report in 2006. The 64th NSSO round conducted from July 2007 to June 2008 has also confirmed that Muslims are educationally backward among other minorities. Additionally, this paper also looks at the intersection of gender with caste/tribe and religion. It may also be added that while these categories are being referred to as if they were uniform; in reality, it is not so. There are sub-groups among them who have done well but a large majority are still excluded from the benefits of higher education.

Women in Higher Education

The two sources on statistics on higher education in India are: the *Annual Reports* of the University Grants Commission and the *Selected Educational*

Statistics (SES) published by the Ministry of Human Resource Development.[3] However, both the reports do not give per centages or proportions of different categories in enrolment. Further, while the subjects have proliferated, in reality, theses two sources divide them into a few outdated categories. These are critical limitations.

In 2009-10[4], there were 436 universities and 25,938 colleges.[5] The gross enrolment ratio was very low at 15.0 per cent for all students: 17.1 for men and 12.7 for women (India 2011: HE2).[6] Indications are that it is higher both for women and men in states with private professional colleges.

At first glance, there is positive change so far as access and participation are concerned since the numbers have increased generally. In this expansion, all the categories under consideration have gained. Women in general and women from specific categories have also gained. But then how do they fare when looked at separately and at disaggregated level?

As per the SES 2009-10, the total enrolment excluding the open universities, is 172,95,086 (India 2011:HE10), of which women form 41.9% (69,69,850).[7] Women comprise 41.6 per cent at undergraduate, 43.9 at graduate and 40.6 per cent at research level (India 2011: HE3-10). In addition, 34,45,654 students were enrolled in distance education of which 38.5 per cent (13,26,290) were women (India 2011: HE16).[8] Thus, the total enrolment including open universities is 207,40,740 (women 40.0).

According to the UGC Annual Report 2009-10, the maximum proportion of women (45.2 per cent) still enroll for arts, humanities and social sciences, followed closely by sciences (43.0) in which it has been increasing due to the devaluation of pure sciences because it is no longer the first choice of men students (Chanana 2006). Again, there has been a gradual increase in women's enrolment in the traditionally male dominated professional subjects such as commerce (37.1 per cent) and engineering (31%), yet they are not more than men in any of these fields, except teacher education (61.5). Their proportions are still low in agriculture (20.4), veterinary science (20.8) and law (24.6). The last three subjects still remain predominantly male domains with women occupying only about 20 per cent seats. Medicine in India has always been preferred by women so that secluded women patients could be treated by women doctors and so this subject stands between the boundaries of feminine and masculine subjects. Therefore, the enrolment of women in medicine, though a professional subject, is 46.5 per cent.

However, gender inequality in participation has declined very little, e.g., in enrolment, men are over-represented in physical, mathematical and computer sciences and women in biological sciences both in the educational and occupational spheres (Chanana 2006). This is also reflected in the choice of sub-fields or specializations. This is confirmed by a report on completed Ph.Ds.

In a latest report on 114,188 Ph.Ds. awarded between 1998-2007, one-third were awarded to women (Kurup & Arora 2010).[9] In all, information was collected from 216 Ph.D. granting institutions which were 42.3 per cent of the existing institutions [511]. The total number of records which were analyzed are 45,561 which cover 39.9 per cent of the Ph.Ds. reported by UGC up to 2005. It provides information by discipline or subject, gender and state.

Out of 45,561 doctorates under discussion, women were 33.6 per cent and men 66.4 per cent. During the period under review, the proportion of women varied from 33.9 per cent in 1998 to 35.1 per cent in 2007. There is subject-wise variation, for example, 42.1 per cent in humanities; 37.1 per cent in the social sciences; 36.1 per cent in medicine; 32.8 per cent in the natural sciences; 24.1 per cent in agriculture and 20.2 per cent in engineering and technology. It records with concern that there has been a major decline in the Ph.Ds. awarded to women in medicine from 40.2 per cent to 31.7 per cent.[10]

It also provides information by sub-disciplines or specializations and gender which demonstrates the horizontal segregation which is replacing the vertical segregation by gender (Chanana 2012). For example, in agriculture, the maximum per centage of women were in agro-chemistry [40.7 per cent], agro-engineering and technology [36 per cent]; and agro-social sciences [32 per cent] while the least proportion of women were in animal studies [18 per cent], plant studies [21.9 per cent] and agriculture [21.5 per cent].

The trends are the same in all other subjects where women are concentrated in a few sub-disciplines or specializations. As for example in the natural sciences 55.9 per cent women are in life sciences followed by zoology [40.1 per cent], botany [39.4 per cent per cent, and biology [38.9 per cent]. They are least in geology with 13 per cent. In engineering and technology, the maximum per centage of 45.6 per cent are in bio-science engineering and the least in mechanical engineering [3.9 per cent], civil engineering [12.6 per cent] and metallurgical and material engineering [13.4 per cent]. The situation is similar in social sciences where women are a large majority in home economics and family living [85.2]; 48.8 in Anthropology, 41.8 in sociology; and least in law (25.5) and management studies (22.4). In humanities, the maximum proportions are in psychology 58.4 and music 57.0 and least in geography 29.1 and religion 26.6 per cent.

Even in medicine, specializations are differentiated in terms of status. In other words, disparities across subjects are being replaced by disparities within specialization through the process of simultaneous inclusion and exclusion. "Inclusion and exclusion both appear to pose dangers and opportunities. Women are simultaneously constructed as winners and losers. Winners because they are gaining access, as students, in significant numbers, but losers because of their lack of entitlement to leadership and prestigious disciplines." (Morley 2009: 384)

Scheduled Castes and Scheduled Tribes

In 2009-10, the proportion of scheduled caste students out of all enrolled students in higher education was 11.8 per cent: 7.3 per cent men; and 4.5 per cent women. The scheduled tribes comprised 5.2 per cent of total enrolment: 3.3 per cent men; 1.9 per cent women. The gross enrolment ratio of scheduled castes was 11.1 per cent and of scheduled tribes 10.3 per cent as compared to 15.0 per cent for all students. The GER of scheduled caste women was 9.0 and for men 13.0; scheduled tribe women 7.5 and scheduled tribe men 13.1 per cent (India 2011: HE17).

For Ph.D., the figures are quite revealing. In 2009-10, a total of 92,211 students were enrolled for it. Out of these, 40.6 per cent (37,436) were women. Again, the number of SC students was 9,119 (9.9), of which 3,666 (4.0) were women and 5,453 (5.9) were men. The ST students were even less with a number of 3,865 (4.2 per cent)—1,594 (1.7 per cent) women and 2,271 (2.5 per cent) men.

These figures substantiate the well known fact that in spite of a very well formulated policy of positive discrimination[11], the representation of the disadvantaged groups of Scheduled Caste (SC) and Scheduled Tribe (ST) students is not adequate and the proportion of women from among them is negligible. Access is very limited to them as a whole but more so to women from these groups. For instance, SC and ST women comprised 11.4 and 4.2 per cent respectively of all women enrolled in 2009-10 (India2011: HE12,14).

Muslims in Higher Education

The report of the Sachar Committee (constituted in March 2005), entitled *Social, Economic and Educational Status of the Muslim Community of India*, looks at the overall situation of the Muslims in India (India 2006).[12] It used the NSSO and Census data. In addition, it collected information on higher education from premier institutes such as IIMs, IITs, universities and colleges.[13] It differentiates between the Muslim Other Backward Castes (OBCs) and the high caste and well-off sections of the community. It provides some analysis by gender and also looks at the intersection of caste, gender, religion. Overall, it observed that this community was generally backward in education and required a special push.

About IIMs, it observed that about one in three Muslim applicants is selected and their success rate was better than others.[14]. Yet, Muslim students comprised only 1.3 per cent of the students in all IIMs [63/4743]. Similarly, the proportion of Muslim students in IITs was low at 3.9 per cent [894/27,161]. The proportion was 1.7 per cent in the undergraduate courses, which are the most important in these institutes. At the postgraduate level, they were around 4 per cent and even better at the Ph.D., level. It is likely that either fewer

Muslim candidates sit for IIT entrance examinations or do not get through the entrance examination.

So far as the select premier colleges of arts, science, and commerce were concerned, the share of Muslims was low in all courses and they were marginal in the science stream. Their proportion was one in 25 enrolled students at the undergraduate level and one in 50 enrolled students at the postgraduate level. However, at the undergraduate level, the ratio of Muslim women is higher than that of men but it falls at the PG level except in the arts programmes.

The per centage of Muslims in management programmes [MBA] other than the IIMs was just 1 per cent both for women and men. Furthermore, the proportion was just about 4 per cent in the top medical colleges at the undergraduate level where they were enrolled in MBBS, dental and nursing programmes. In the medical colleges, except for PG diploma courses, the per centage of Muslim girls is lower than that of boys in all the courses.

In addition, 129 universities and 80 colleges also provided relevant information[15] [out of 300 universities and over 16,000 colleges]. Muslims were 9 per cent at the UG level which is lower than their proportion in the population and significantly lower than the SCs/STs and OBCs. Their participation was particularly low in engineering and medical courses. They were also low in PG courses, e.g., only one out of 20 (5 per cent) is a Muslim, compared to 24 per cent OBCs and 13 per cent SCs/STs.

Wrapping Up

There is no doubt that access has increased for all and it also gets reflected in the higher enrolment, GER, number of HEIs, and preferences for new professional subjects which are applied and market driven. However, the desegregated data presents a different picture. For instance, the gaps by caste, religion and gender continue and in some cases have widened. There is also a close relationship between caste, gender and religious community, on the one hand, and choice of subjects, level of education and the type of institution, on the other. Their proportions decrease as one moves from the undergraduate to the postgraduate and doctoral levels. This indicates lower transition rates and lower participation. Their participation in the most preferred subjects and elite HEIs is very low or marginal. Moreover, specialisations are replacing subjects in terms of concentration of specific students. Therefore, and as mentioned above, while the **vertical dimension of unequal participation** may be declining (e.g. the proportion of women in engineering and science or the fields of study), the **horizontal dimension** relating to specialisation may remain resistant to change. Layers of disadvantage are uncovered when data are disaggregated by ethnicity, gender, caste, etc.

As mentioned earlier, the government revisited its position on supporting higher education in the XIth plan and established new HEIs. However, most of the expansion has taken place in the private sector institution-wise, enrolment-wise and subject-wise. While the private for profit sector has remapped the educational arena and increased the options for the students, it is very expensive and is beyond the reach of the categories under discussion. Again, quality in these HEIs, barring a few, is also suspect.

In this scenario, education has once again been projected as a critical instrument of social change as well as for cultural reproduction. Classic sociological questions about the relationship between education, on the one hand, and economy and society, on the other, are being raised again. One wonders how much of the repositioning of education is change and how much is the reaffirmation of the earlier position.

This brings us to the question: how serious is the state about the role of higher education in promoting change and equality in the age of globalisation and privatisation? This is especially so when global changes are being viewed as gendered, racialized and classed. Again, when profit is the central parametre defining educational priorities and choices, considerations of gender, marginality, race, caste, class, ethnicity are less likely to remain in the foreground but for political compulsions (Brine 1990). Hence, the role of the state in promoting and pushing for change along with equality and equity through education becomes critical. Balancing the two aims becomes the litmus test along with evolving a cogent and comprehensive vision, approach and plan towards the systemic expansion of higher education.

References

Adeoti, Gbemisola Aderemi (2006): Literary Studies in Contemporary Nigerian Universities: The Challenges of Nationalism and Globalisation. In Guy Neave (ed.), pp. 209-20.

Bachhi, Carol (2001): Managing Equity: Mainstreaming and 'Diversity' in Australian Universities, In A. Brooks and A. McInnon (eds.), pp. 119-135.

Bowles, Samual and Herbert Gintis, (2002): Schooling in Capitalist America revisited. In *Sociology of Education,* v.75, no.1, Jan., pp. 1-18.http//www.jstor.org/stable/3090251

Brennan, John and Rajani Naidoo (2006): Managing Contradictory Functions: The Role of Universities in Societies Undergoing Radical Social Transformation. In Guy Neave (ed.), pp. 221-33.

Brine, Jacky (1990): *Under Educating Women: Globalizing Inequality*. Buckingham: Open University Press.

Brown, Phillip, Hugh Lauder and David Ashton (2011): *The Global Auction: The Broken Promises of Education, Jobs and Incomes*. Oxford/New York, Oxford University Press, http://www.amazon.com/The-Global-Auction-Promises-Education/dp/0199731683# reader_0199731683. Accesssed on 22 July, 12 at 1400 hours

Chanana, Karuna (2012): Higher Education and Gender Issues in the Knowledge Economy: Who Studies What, Why and Where? In Deane Neubauer (ed.), *The Emergent Knowledge Society and the Future of Higher Education*, London and New York: Routledge, pp. 177-93.

______ (2006): Gender and Disciplinary Choices: Women in Higher Education in India. In Guy Neave (edited), pp. 267-94.

_____ (1993): 'Accessing Higher Education: The Dilemma of Schooling Women, Minorities and Scheduled Castes and Tribes in Contemporary India' in *Reform and Change in Higher Education in India,* Altbach, P.G. and Chitnis, Suma (eds.), pp 115154. Sage: New Delhi (Also in *Higher Education*, Netherlands, 26, 1993, pp 6992).

Clarke, J.R. (1996): Educational Equity in Higher Education: an International Perspective. In G.D. Postle et.al, *Toward Excellence and Diversity: Educational Equity in the Australian Higher Sector in 1995: Status, Trends and Future Directions*. Queensland: USQ Press.

Government of India (2006): *Social, Economic and Educational Status of the Muslim Community of India: A Report.* Prime Minister's High Level Committee, Cabinet Secretariat, New Delhi. November.

Government of India (2011): *Selected Educational Statistics Abstract – 2009-10*; Ministry of Human Resource Development, New Delhi.

Harvey, D. (1993): *The Condition of Post-modernity: An Enquiry into the Origins of Cultural Change*, Oxford: Blackwell.

Houtondji, Paulin J. (2006): Global Knowledge: Imbalances and Current Tasks. In Guy Neave, pp. 41-60.

Kurup, Anitha and Jagdish Arora (2010): *Trends in Higher Education: Creation and Analysis of a Database of Ph.Ds.,* National Institute of Advanced Studies, Bangalore, India, May.

McDonnell, Mary Byrne (2008): Toward a Globally Connected, Public Social Science. In Morris-Suzuki, ibid, pp. 143-54.

McKinnon A. and Ann Brooks (eds.) (2001): Introduction. In Brooks, Ann and McInnon, A. (eds.) G*ender and the Restructured University*, pp. 1-12, Buckingham: The Society For Research into Higher Education and the Open University Press.

Morley, Louise (2009): Momentum and Melancholia: Women in Higher Education Internationally. In Michael W. Apple, Stephen J. Ball and Luis Armando Gandin (eds.),

Morris-Suzuki, Tessa (ed.) (2008): *Contradictions of Globalisation: Democracy, Culture, and Public Sphere*, Tokyo, International House of Japan.

Neave, Guy (2006): Introduction: Mapping the Knowledge Society Back. In Guy Neave *(ed.) Knowledge, Power and Dissent: Critical Perspectives on Higher Education and Research in Knowledge Society. Paris: UNESCO Publishing, 2006.*

Sawer, M. (1989): Efficiency, effectiveness… and equity? In G.Davis et al (eds.), *Corporate Management in Australian Government: Reconciling Accountability and Efficiency,* Melbourne: McMillan.

Slaughter, Sheila, and Larry L. Leslie (1997): *Academic Capitalism: Politics, Policies, and the Entrepreneurial University.* Baltimore, MD.: The John Hopkins University Press.

The Routledge International Handbook of the Sociology of Education, Routledge International Handbooks of Education. Series, http://media.routledgeweb.com/pdf/ 9780415486637/toc.pdf accessed on 5 Aug, 12 at 1715 hours

University Grants Commission, (2011): *Annual Report-2010-11.*

______ (2010): *Annual Report-2009-10.*

Yeatman, A. (1990): *Bureaucrats, Technocrats, Femocrats*, Sydney: Allen and Unwin.E

Weiler, Hans N. (2006): Challenging the Orthodoxies of Knowledge: Epistemological, Structural, and Political Implications for Higher Education. In Guy Neave, ibid. pp.61-87.

PART IV

WIDER IMPACTS OF FEMALE EDUCATION

13

RETURNS TO EDUCATION BY GENDER AMONG WAGE EMPLOYEES IN URBAN INDIA*

JEEMOL UNNI

Abstract

This study estimates earnings functions for urban wage workers in two states of India, Tamil Nadu and Madhya Pradesh, together with a wage earner choice equation Private rates of return to education ore computed separately for men and women. Returns to education are found to increase with the level of education for both men and women. The relative gap in rates of return to different levels of education is high and so is the relative wage gap between workers at different levels of education. The returns to education are also found higher for women as compared to men with and without the selectivity correction, except for graduates in Madhya Pradesh.

* An earlier version of this paper was prepared while the author was a Post-Doctoral Fellow at the Economic Growth Centre, Yale University, USA. The author is grateful to the Rockefeller Foundation for financial support, to the Economic Growth Centre and the Gujarat Institute of Development Research for the research facilities provided, and the National Sample Survey Organisation for the permission to use individual level data. The support and the encouragement of T. Paul Schultz, Jandhyala B.G. Tilak and an anonymous referee of the JEPA are gratefully acknowledged. The author is also thanks Jignasu Yagnik for computer assistance and Sheela Devadas for word processing support. The usual disclaimers apply.

Introduction

Recent literature on the returns to education has highlighted some distinctive features of private returns to education m low income countries. Some of these are listed below (see Schultz, 1992).

(i) Relatively high private returns to education (in excess of 10-15 per cent) in the early stages of economic development as the expansion of the educational system begins to catch up to the derived demand for educated labour, these returns begin to fall.

(ii) A wide relative wage gap between workers with different levels of education, e.g., primary and secondary educated workers and between secondary and university trained workers.

(iii) Private rates of return differ according to the income levels of the region. As compared to regions with high income, low income regions tend to report higher wage differ-entials by levels of education.

(iv) The evidence on differential private rates of return to education by gender is mixed. In some low income countries, returns to education are found to be higher for women than men. However, the calculation of returns are sensitive to the rate of labor force participation by women (Schultz, 1993).

In this paper the private returns to education in the urban areas of two states of India, Tamil Nadu and Madhya Pradesh, are computed. While Tamil Nadu is an industrially and agriculturally developed state, Madhya Pradesh is a relatively backward state. According to the National Sample Survey (43 rd Round) estimates, the monthly household per capita consumer expenditure in urban Tamil Nadu was Rs 249 in 1987-88, close to the all-India average of Rs 250. Household monthly per capita expenditure was Rs 236 in urban Madhya Pradesh. Among the 17 major states, only in Andhra Pradesh, Bihar, Karnataka, Orissa and Uttar Pradesh, per capita consumer expenditure was below that of Madhya Pradesh. The Central Statistical Organisation estimates of per capita income of states at current prices was Rs 1946 for Tamil Nadu, compared to the all-India average of Rs 2143 in 1984-85. Per capita income was estimated at Rs 1731 for Madhya Pradesh. Only three of the 17 major states recorded per capita state income below this level. Thus, Tamil Nadu may be considered a relatively high income **state and** Madhya **Pradesh a relatively low** income **state in** India

Geographically, Madhya Pradesh is one of the largest states in India, with an area of about 3.5 times that of Tamil Nadu. However, Tamil Nadu is three times as densely populated as Madhya Pradesh. According to the 1991 Population Census of India the population density of the two states was 430 and 149 persons per square kilometre, respectively. This is partly because large tracts of Madhya Pradesh are semi-arid and under forests. Socially backward groups, lower (scheduled) castes and tribes, constitute 38 per cent of its population, while they constitute only 20 per cent of the population in Tamil Nadu. The relative backwardness of Madhya Pradesh is also reflected in its total literacy rate of 44 per cent, compared to 55 per cent in Tamil Nadu in 1991. And finally, Tamil Nadu is a relatively more urbanised state than Madhya Pradesh. In 1991 34 and 26 per cent of the population respectively of the two states reported themselves to be residing in urban areas.

These two states are chosen for their distinctly different economic and social charac-teristics. How do private returns to education differ by gender, age and education levels in these diverse situations?

This paper is divided into five sections. In the next section a description of the data set used and the characteristics of the sample population are discussed. After that, the model and the specification of the variables is presented. The results of the empirical exercise are discussed in the last but one section. The final section summarises and concludes the discussion.

Description of Data and Characteristics of Sample Population

The National Sample Survey Organisation (NSSO) has been collecting data, nation-wide, on employment in its Quinquennial Surveys on Employment and Unemplcyment since 1972-73. The data analysed here were collected by the NSSO in its fourth such Quinquennial Survey (43rd Round) during July 1987 to June 1988. A stratified two-stage sample design was adopted with the first stage units as census villages for rural areas and the NSSO urban frame survey blocks for urban areas. Households formed the second stage units. In all, the survey covered about 130 thousand households spread over about 8400 sample villages and 4600 sample urban blocks.

In the selected districts, the survey covered 2952 households in 297 urban blocks in Madhya Pradesh and 4222 households in 423 urban blocks in Tamil Nadu. The population surveyed in these urban households was 15055 in Madhya Pradesh and 18681 in Tamil Nadu. Information was collected in this survey on the activities, gainful and non-gainful, under-taken by individuals and the wage earnings of the wage employees during the 7 days preceding the date of survey. On a nation-wide basis, very few sources collect information on wages or income accruing to workers. The data on employment and wages of the NSS are considered to be relatively robust since they are collected by well-trained permanent investigators through well developed survey methodology. The survey was spread over the entire year, divided into four sub-round periods of three months duration. The sample was distributed over the four sub-rounds in a manner so as to provide equally valid estimates for the country for each of the four sub-round periods separately and also for the whole year. The reference period was thus a moving week providing an average picture for the entire year. Information collected from all individuals in the sample households forms the data-base in the paper. The analysis is, however, restricted to data on adult males and females between the age of 15 to 64 years.

While estimating the private returns to education among wage earners in India, some distinctive features of the country need to be noted. Firstly, the participation of women in gainful activity is rather low compared to men. It is even lower for women residing in urban areas of the country. The work participation rates for the selected urban samples by age, education and gender are presented in Table 1. The male work participation was 87 and 79 per cent in Tamil Nadu and Madhya Pradesh, while it was 30 and 19 per cent, respectively for women. In the relatively less developed state of Madhya Pradesh, urban women reported very low participation in gainful work. Even in the prime age group of 25-44 years, women's work participation was only 33 and 22 per cent. Among men in this age group, work participation was almost 100 per cent in both states. Participation in gainful employment by education levels show an interesting U-shaped pattern. Work participation is relatively high among the least and most educated populations. This pattern is similar for both sexes in both regions.

A second distinctive feature is that, even in urban areas, the proportion of self-employed persons is relatively large. In urban Tamil Nadu 31.8 per cent of adult male workers and 38.5 per cent of adult female workers were self-employed during the reference week in 1987-88. In urban Madhya Pradesh, it was 42.0 and 46.7 per cent of male and female workers. No distinction is made between unpaid family workers and self-employed workers. Both have been grouped together as self-employed workers. It is difficult to assess the returns to schooling among the self- employed. The probability of being self-employed also increases with age in low income countries. Therefore wage functions estimated across ages for the self-employed cannot be interpreted in the human coital life-cycle framework to determine returns to schooling (Mincer, 1974). The assessment of market returns to schooling may be more accurate if the analysis is restricted to wage earners whose wage rates approximate hourly productivity' (Schultz, 1993).

Thirdly, education is not mandatory and there is no compulsory education even at the primary level. Together with a high level of poverty, this results in a large proportion of the population remaining illiterate even in urban areas. The distribution of the sample population by educational levels across age-groups is presented in Table **2** The per centage of illiterates is relatively low, 13 and 17 per cent among males in urban Tamil Nadu and Madhya Pradesh respectively. However, illiterate women form about 34 and 43 per cent of the urban sample in Tamil Nadu and Madhya Pradesh respectively. The educational attainment of men and women differ considerably. Even in the younger age-group of 15-24 years, female illiteracy is twice as high as male illiteracy in urban Tamil Nadu and nearly three times as high in urban Madhya Pradesh.

Table 1: Workers per 1000 Population by Education, Age and Gender

	15-24	*25-44*	*45-64*	*15-64*
	URBAN TAMIL TADU			
Illiterate	918	963	787	891
Literate	913	983	867	926
Primary School	862	973	902	919
Middle School	674	971	912	841
Secondary School	510	996	873	796
Graduates	801	986	815	931
Total	**728**	**979**	**864**	**871**
	Females			
Illiterate	404	431	yrb	404
Literate	365	421	140	331
Primary School	225	209	184	211
Middle School	160	179	160	168
Secondary School	208	313	243	ISl
Graduates	664	533	513	583
Total	**279**	**331**	**291**	**304**
	URBAN MADHYA PRADESH **Males**			
Illiterate	926	980	833	914
Literate	111	968	869	884
Primary School	654	974	910	826
Middle School	333	980	974	629
Secondary School	375	981	880	721
Graduates	478	952	849	834
Total	**514**	**972**	**875**	**788**
	Female			
Illiterate	170	280	284	256
Literate	186	134	85	133
Primary School	88	112	164	109
Middle School	22	77	0	39
Secondary School	97	206	110	142
Graduates	194	372	467	319
Total	**114**	**225**	**230**	**187**

Note: Computed from estimated workers and population for each group.

Table 2: Distribution of Persons in the Age Group 15-64 Years
by Education, Age and Gender

(per centage)

15-24	25-44	45-64	15-64	
	URBAN TAMIL NADU **Male**			
Illiterate	10.6	11.1	20.0	12.9
Literate	10.6	10.5	17.4	12.1

(Contd...)

Primary School	21.9	20.5	23.6	21.6
Middle School	26.7	21.4	14.0	21.5
Secondary School	26.2	23.9	2G.0	23.8
Graduates	4.2	12.5	5.2	8.1
100.0	100.0	100.0	100.0	
Sample Persons	1925	2730	1363	6018
	Female			
Illiterate	20.7	32.6	56.8	33.7
Literate	12.4	10.7	13.2	11.9
Primary School	21.4	20.5	15.2	19.7
Middle School	20.1	15.3	7.2	15.2
Secondary School	21.6	16.5	6.9	16.2
Graduates	3.8	4.5	0.6	3.4
100.0	100.0	100.0	100.0	
Sample Persons	2042	2550	1356	5948
	URBAN MADHYA PRADESH			
	Males			
Illiterate	10.4	16.7	28.3	17.0
Literate	7.5	10.3	18.6	11.1
Primary School	20.0	15.8	12.5	16.6
Middle School	30.4	15.8	11.2	20.0
Secondary School	23.2	20.7	16.5	20.7
Graduates	8.5	20.6	12.9	14.7
100.0	100.0	100.0	100.0	
Sample Persons	1652	2035	1095	4782
	Female			
Illiterate	28.4	43.2	66.8	42.8
Literate	6.5	9.5	12.2	9.6
Primary School	15.9	12.6	8.7	13.0
Middle School	20.1	8.6	3.7	11.6
Secondary School	22.2	14.0	6.8	15.4
Graduates	6.9	10.6	1.8	7.5
100.0	100.0	100.0	100.0	
Sample Persons	1485	1915	911	4311

Though illiteracy levels are higher in the relatively less developed state of Madhya Pradesh, the per centage of male and female graduates are higher in this state as compared to Tamil Nadu. The higher proportion of graduates in the urban areas in Madhya Pradesh as compared to Tamil Nadu is substantiated by the Population Census of 1981. This anomaly can be explained in terms of the smaller proportion of urban residents in Madhya Pradesh living in larger towns where access to college education is more liberal. There are a larger number of colleges, with lower educational standards for entry and less strict procedures for admissions in this state, as compared to Tamil Nadu. However, the work participation of graduates is lower in Madhya Pradesh than Tamil Nadu, particularly among women (Table 1). This tallies with the general observation of the less developed nature of Madhya Pradesh where employment opportunities for educated persons are perhaps fewer.

The distribution of all wage workers by educational attainment, age and gender are presented in Table 3. The distribution of male wage workers is not very different from that of all males in botih states. However, the distribution of women wage workers by educational levels is different from that of all women. The proportion of illiterate women and graduates are higher among women wage workers than among all women.

The average daily wage earnings obtained during the reference week is computed by dividing total wage earnings during the week by the number of days engaged in wage employment. Average daily wage earnings by educational level, age-group and gender are presented in Table 4. The age-education earnings profiles more or less correspond to the 'well-behaved profiles' (Tilak 1987). That is, earnings are positively correlated with education and age. Since only broad age-groups are reported here, one cannot observe the age at which the profile peaks for each educational level. An inverted U-shaped curve is observed only for women graduates in Tamil Nadu since their earnings appear to peak at a lower age. The earnings profiles for higher educational levels are steeper.

The average wage earning accruing to male wage earners is almost double that accruing to female wage earners in urban Tamil Nadu. The wage differentials by gender are smaller in urban Madhya Pradesh. The average daily wage earnings to both sexes are higher in the less developed state of Madhya Pradesh. This appears to be true at every level of education. The sample of wage workers includes both regular/salaried and casual workers. When tiie daily wage earnings are disaggregated by these two groups it is seen that it is the wages/sala-ries of regular workers that is higher in Madhya Pradesh than Tamil Nadu. Casual daily wage earnings are higher in Tamil Nadu for male workers. (**Sarvekshana,** Vol. 16, No. 3, 1993 and State Series, Special Issues, Tables 80 and 81). Regular wage and salary jobs are mainly in the government sector in Madhya Pradesh, unlike Tamil Nadu where private enterprise is more prevalent. The salary structure in the government sector is relatively higher in Madhya Pradesh than both the government and private sectors in Tamil Nadu. This perhaps explains the anomaly of higher wage earnings in the backward state of Madhya Pradesh.

The differentials by gender and region in the educational and work participation behav-iour are striking. Participation in gainful work and literacy among women in urban areas is much lower than that of men. The proportion of illiterate persons and self-employed workers is relatively higher in the backward state of Madhya Pradesh. Illiterate women and those who have attained graduation participate more frequently in the wa^e workforce. The wage differentials by gender are also quite large.

Table 3: Distribution of Wage Workers in the Age-group 15-64 Years by Education, Age and Gender

(*per centage*)

	15-24	25-44	45-64	15-64
	URBAN TAMIL NADU			
	Male			
Illiterate	14.8	11.1	18.2	13.5
Literate	15.8	9.6	14.0	12.0
Primary School	28.5	18.8	19.5	21.4
Middle School	20.9	20.4	16.1	19.7
Secondary School	15.7	26.5	25.9	23.6
Graduates	4.3	13.6	6.3	9.8
	100.0	100.0	100.0	100.0
Sample Persons	765	1709	687	3161
	Female			
Illiterate	36.3	43.8	72.3	46.6
Literate	18.3	12.6	5.3	13.0
Primary School	19.6	11.0	5.7	12.7
Middle School	5.8	7.6	4.2	6.5
Secondary School	11.7	17.1	10.2	14.2
Graduates	8.3	7.8	2.3	6.9
	100.0	100.0	100.0	100.0
Sample Persons	282	480	174	936
	URBAN MADHYA PRADESH			
	Males			
Illiterate	24.6	15.4	23.3	19.1
Literate	13.7	9.4	12.7	11.1
Primary School	26.3	14.4	11.9	15.8
Middle School	18.7	14.5	14.1	15.1
Secondary School	10.1	23.1	20.7	20.2
Graduates	6.4	23.3	17.2	18.7
	100.0	100.0	100.0	100.0
Sample Persons	346	1110	550	2005
	Female			
Illiterate	58.4	47.5	76.7	56.4
Literate	11.0	3.6	4.5	4.8
Primary School	0.0	3.0	6.2	3.3
Middle School	0.0	1.5	0.0	0.9
Secondary School	13.7	16.8	5.3	13.5
Graduates	16.8	27.6	7.4	21.0
	100.0	100.0	100.0	100.0
Sample Persons	60	224	90	374

Table 4: Daily Wage Earnings by Education, Age and Gender for Wage Earners in Rupees

	15-24	5-44	45-64	15-64
	URBAN TAMIL NADU			
	Male			
Illiterate	11.6	16.1	15.4	14.7
Literate	11.6	19.5	20.7	17.2
Primary School	12.0	18.6	21.8	17.0
Middle School	15.4	22.1	31.3	21.9
Secondary School	15.1	31.7	44.3	31.9
Graduates	24.4	46.4	70.9	47.3
Total	**13.6**	**26.4**	**30.9**	**24.1**
	Female			
Illiterate	7.1	8.0	8.9	8.0
Literate	6.5	8.4	13.8	8.0
Primary School	6.1	10.5	14.7	8.7
Middle School	6.3	14.5	14.9	12.3
Secondary School	8.2	24.8	38.4	22.3
Graduates	21.8	49.1	35.8	38.3
Total	**8.1**	**14.9**	**13.3**	**12.5**
	URBAN MADHYA PRADESH			
	Males			
Illiterate	11.3	18.2	22.4	18.1
Literate	12.2	24.3	24.4	21.7
Primary School	13.2	22.1	29.4	21.0
Middle School	15.4	25.5	40.1	27.0
Secondary School	17.5	34.1	50.4	37.1
Graduates	33.4	46.0	71.6	51.5
Total	**14.8**	**25.4**	**40.3**	**30.4**
	Female			
Illiterate	9.0	10.4	11.4	10.5
Literate	9.3	11.3	16.7	11.9
Primary School	0.0	11.2	14.3	12.7
Middle School	0.0	18.1	0.0	18.1
Secondary School	15.4	29.4	42.1	25.2
Graduates	40.3	42.1	64.6	44.3
Total	**15.2**	**22.0**	**17.4**	**19.9**

The Model and Specification of Variables

The most popular specification of the earnings (y) fimction is semi-logarithmic. The explanatory variables are years of schooling (s), experience (x) and experience squared:

$$\ln y = a + bs + cx + dx^2 + u. \tag{1}$$

This follows from Mincer's pioneering work (Mincer 1974) which showed that this is a good linear approximation of the earnings function derived from a human capital model. The coefficient of s can be interpreted as the private rate of return to education (Dougherty and Jimenez 1991).

A major source of bias in this estimation arises because the earnings are observed only for workers who receive a wage or salary. As noted earlier, the data analysed here consist of a large proportion of self-employed workers. It is much more difficult to measure the productivity of workers who work without a wage in a family enterprise.

The choice of being a wage earner and the earnings received are inter-related, therefore an earnings or wage function for a sample of wage earners alone would be biased. Heckman (1979) developed a statistical procedure for correcting for such a sample selection bias. It requires information on one variable for the entire sample which affects the decision to be a wage earner, but does not affect the market (wage) productivity of the individual. Such a variable influences only the person's non-market reservation wage, but not his market wage offer. It could be the "family's non-earned income, land, or other assets that raise the person's productivity in self-employment and increase the individual's demand for leisure, assuming leisure is a 'normal' economic good" (Schultz 1993).

The returns to education for wage earners is best estimated as a joint analysis of the individual's occupational choice and the determinants of market wage productivity. Such a procedure helps to control for sample selectivity a major bias in estimating returns.[3] The occupational choice of being a wage earner is estimated by a reduced form regression model

$$y * \beta o + \beta_l X + = \qquad \text{Eqn. (1)}$$

where **y*** is an unobservable 'latent' variable. What we observe is a dunmiy variable y which takes the value 1 if the individual^is a wage earner and 0 if he or she is not. X is a vector of individual, family or community characteristics which influence this choice and = is a random error, and = have bivariate normal distributions. The correlation coefficient between u and = is denoted by rho. We have the following probit specification,

$$\text{Prob (y-1)} = \text{Prob } [=> - (\beta o + \beta_l \text{X})] \qquad \text{Eqn. (2)}$$

$$= \text{l-F}[-(\beta o + \beta_l \text{X})]$$

where F is the cumulative distribution of=. The joint maximum likelihood estimate of equations (1) and (2) provides consistent and efficient parameter estimates.

A variation of the Mincerian wage function presented in equation (1) allows the estimated rate of return to education to vary by the level of schooling.

$$\text{In y} = \text{a} + \text{Eb}_k \text{ D}_k + \text{cx} + \text{dx}^2 + \text{u} \qquad \text{Eqn. (3)}$$

D_k are dummy variables where k refers to the level of education. In this specification the rate of return to the k-th level of education can be estimated by comparing the coefficient of D_k with that of D_{k-1} and dividing by the number of years of schooling at the k-th level (Dougherty and Jimenez 1991). The rates of return to education are computed from these estimates corrected for sample selection bias.

The dependent variable used in the wage function is the logarithm of an average daily wage earning. The means and standard deviations of the variables used in the model are presented in Table 5, separately for wage employees and the sample population by gender.[4]

In the NSS data, information on education refers to the levels of education completed by the individual. For our analysis we have converted this information into years of schooling by assigning an average number of years to each level of education as follows. Illiterate persons have zero years of education while literate individuals who did not attend school are assigned one year. Literate persons who attended school below the primary level are assigned 2 years of schooling. It is assumed that persons who completed primary school had 4 years of education. Persons who completed middle school had 8 years of education while persons with secondary schooling did 11 years of schooling. Graduates in agriculture, engineering and medical degrees are assumed to have completed 15 years while graduates with any other subject had on average 14 years of education. Obviously, there is a certain arbitrariness about this procedure.

Table 5: Sample Means and Standard Deviations Separately for All Persons and Wage Workers by Gender and Region

Variables	All Persons			
	Men		Women	
	Mean	SD	Mean	SD
Years of Experience	20.23	13.58	19.80	13.47
Years o f Education	6.64	4.41	4.60	4.47
Literate	0.12	0.33	0.12	0.32
Primary School	0.22	0.41	0.20	0.40
Middle School	0.22	0.41	0.15	0.36
Secondary School	0.23	0.42	0.17	0.37
Graduate	0.09	0.28	0.04	0.19
Land Owned (hectare)	0.26	0.15	0.26	1.36
Homestead Owned	0.46	0.50	0.48	0.50
Daily Wage	25.90	22.77	15.59	16.34
Madhya Pradesh				
Years of Experience	18.81	13.36	18.56	13.23
Years o f Education	6.96	4.95	4.52	5.01
Literate	0.11	0.32	0.10	0.30

(Contd...)

Primary School	0.17	0.37	0.13	0.34
Middle School	0.18	0.38	0.11	0.32
Secondary School	0.22	0.41	0.15	0.36
Graduate	0.16	0.37	0.09	0.28
Land Owned (hectare)	1.24	5.58	1.40	5.94
Homestead Owned	0.56	0.50	0.58	0.49
Daily Wage	35.43	24.56	26.00	22.24
Tamil Nadu				
Years of Experience	21.04	11.73	19.22	11.50
Years o f Education	6.63	4.55	4.00	4.91
Literate	0.13	0.33	0.12	0.33
Primary School	0.22	0.41	0.14	0.34
Middle School	0.20	0.40	0.06	0.24
Secondary School	0.23	0.42	0.15	0.36
Graduate	0.10	0.30	0.08	0.27
Land Owned (hectare)	0.16	0.79	0.11	0.46
Homestead Owned	0.40	0.49	0.44	0.50
Daily Wage	25.92	22.61	15.38	15.61
Madhya Pradesh				
Years of Experience	21.69	11.48	19.79	11.38
Years o f Education	7.17	5.26	5.35	6.24
Literate	0.11	0.31	0.05	0.23
Primary School	0.15	0.35	0.03	0.18
Middle School	0.33	0.34	0.01	0.12
Secondary School	0.21	0.41	0.14	0.35
Graduate	0.21	0.41	0.25	0.43
Land Owned (hectare)	0.64	5.39	0.31	1.64
Homestead Owned	0.41	0.49	0.47	0.50
Daily Wage	**35.36**	**23.89**	**26.00**	**22.24**

Note: The sample means reported here are unweighted estimates. They differ slightly from the relevant estimates in the earlier tables (see Note 4).

Five dummies for the following levels of education are constructed: literate, primary, middle and secondary school and graduates. Illiterate persons are omitted as the reference category.

The experience variable is introduced in quadratic form to capture the non-linearity in the earnings profile. Lack of data on experience usually leads to it being estimated by the expression [age - years of schooling - age of entry into school] (Mincer 1974). However, in developing countries, where much of the labour force is illiterate or did not attend formal schooling, this procedure is inappropriate because it implies that 'work experience' gained during childhood is treated on the same level as adult work experience (Dougherty and Jimenez 1991). To take account of this fact, the experience variable is computed as follows:

For persons with a positive years of schooling,

Experience = [age - years of schooling - 5].

For persons with zero years of schooling,

Experience = [age 14].

Schultz (1993) suggested family's non-earned income, land owned or other assets as the identifying variables which enable individuals to enter self-employment rather than work for wages. Two variables used in this study are land owned and ownership of a homestead. These enter as explanatory variables in the probit wage earner choice equation and not in the wage function.

The joint maximum likelihood estimates of equation (2) and (1) are estimated using years of education and years of experience in quadratic form to check for non-linearity in the relationship to wage earnings.[5] The years of experience displayed a significant non-linear relationship among male in both states and females in Tamil Nadu. The years of schooling, however, did not indicate any such non-linear relationship, except among women in Tamil Nadu. However, in order to assess the differential rate of returns to the level of education the alternative specification with dummy variables for each level of education was used. The experience variable was included in quadratic form.

Empirical Results

The empirical results of the wage earner choice equation (2) and the semi-logarithmic wage equation (1) are presented in Tables 6 and 7, separately for men and women.

Determinants of Wage Earner Choice

The probit equation of the selection into wage employment and the wage function are jointly estimated by the maximum likelihood method. The results for male wage earners (Table 6) indicate that the years of experience have a significant non-linear effect on the selection into wage employment. The probability of being a wage employee increases upto 26 and 28 years of experience, in Tamil Nadu and Madhya Pradesh respectively, and then begins to decline

The education variables are jointly significant at 5 per cent level. The education variable is measured as a set of dummy variables, and the omitted category is the illiterate population. Literacy, primary, middle and secondary school education had significant negative effect on the choice of being a wage earner, with respect to the illiterate category, while being a graduate had a significant positive influence.

Both the identifying - variables land owned and ownership of a homestead - have a significant impact on the choice of being a wage earner. While ownership of land dissuaded participation in wage employment, ownership of a homestead encouraged it. It is likely that persons owning land have enough resources to acquire business assets and undertake self-employment. All these relationships are true for men in both states.

Similar results are observed in the wage earner choice equation for women (Table 7). The probability of being a wage earner increased until 21 and 27 years of experience, in Tamil Nadu and Madhya Pradesh respectively, slightly lower than for men, and then beings to decline. The education variables are jointly significant. As observed for men, all levels of schooling have a negative impact on the selection into wage employment, with respect to the illiterate (excluded) category, except graduation which has a positive impact. Similar negative impact of the level and years of schooling was observed for female wage workers and married women in rural Gujarat (Unni 1992, 1994).

Table 6: Joint Maximum Likelihood Estimates of a Probit Wage Earner and Logarithmic Wage Equation for Men, 1987-88.

Variable	*Probit Wage Earner*		*Logarithmic Daily Wage*	
	Coefficient	*t-ratio*	*Coefficient*	*t-ratio*
Tamil Nadu				
Constant	-0.932	-13.2323	1.610	5.688
Experience	0.101	21.303	0.027	1.827
Experience Squared ('00)	-0.192	-21.271	-0.018	-0.632
Literate	-0.048	-0.739	0.093	0.969
Primary School	-0.181	-3.179	0.204	2.327
Middle School	-0.180	-3.043	0.557	6.217
Secondary School	-0.039	-0.651	1.025	11.410
Graduate	0.168	2.248	1.587	14.803
Land Owned	-0.126	-7.160		
Homestead Owned	0.035	8.391		
Sigma (1)	1.385	23.788		
Rho (1,2)	-0.397	-2.721		
Log Likelihood			-9157.10	3148
Sample Size	6018			
Madhya Pradesh				
Constant	-1.722	-24.061	1.700	7.044
Experience	0.134	23.293	0.022	1.527
Experience Squared ('00)	-0.241	-21.008	-0.005	-0.174
Literate	-0.225	-3.229	0.153	1.479
Primary School	-0.341	-5.358	0.198	2.016
Middle School	-0.334	-4.982	0.578	5.618
Secondary School	-0.125	-1.939	0.897	9.987
Graduate	0.215	3.191	1.381	13.669
Land Owned	-0.024	-8.567		
Homestead Owned	0.083	16.457		
Sigma (1)	1.133	28.718		
Rho (1,2)	-0.232	-2.180		
Log Likelihood			-5759.41	
Sample Size	4782			1999

Note: Due to lack of some observations on wages the sample size of the wage function is smaller than that reported for wage workers in Table 3.

Table 7: Joint Maximum Likelihood Estimates of a Probit Wage Earner and Logarithmic Wage Equation for Women 1987-88.

Variable	*Probit Wage Earner*		*Logarithmic Daily Wage*	
	Coefficient	*t-ratio*	*Coefficient*	*t-ratio*
Tamil Nadu				
Constant	-1.159	-15.790	0.067	0.084
Experience	0.048	7.932	0.064	2.745
Experience Squared ('00)	-0.112	-8.843	-0.123	-2.307
Literate	-0.204	-3.032	-0.117	-0.742
Primary School	-0.517	-8.702	-0148	-0.623
Middle School	-0.763	-10.354	0.245	0.705
Secondary School	-0.286	-4.466	0.975	6.265
Graduate	0.319	3.303	2.197	10.315
Land Owned	-0.180	-3.947		
Homestead Owned	0.013	2.545		
Sigma (1)	1.199	10.046		
Rho (1,2)	0.266	0.689		
Log Likelihood			-3891.43	
Sample Size		5948		931
Madhya Pradesh				
Constant	-2.002	-17.696	1.171	0.671
Experience	0.068	7.261	0.023	0.518
Experience Squared ('00)	*-0.127*	-6.650	-0.049	-0.555
Literate	*-0.477*	-4.172	0.535	1.159
Primary School	-0.854	-6.357	0.436	0.687
Middle School	-1.302	-5.482	-0.250	-0.282
Secondary School	-0.063	-0.699	1.523	5.793
Graduate	0.703	7.574	1.833	3.566
Land Owned	-0.081	-3.695		
Homestead Owned	*0.240*	3.109		
Sigma (1)	1.336	9.463		
Rho (1,2)	-0.157	-0.271		
Log Likelihood			-1751.13	
Sample Size	4311			373

Note: Due to lack of some observations on wages the sample size of the wage function is smaller than that reported for wage workers in Table 3.

Both the identifying variables, ownership of land and homestead, are significant in both ——————The ownership of land in the family reduces the chances of the woman being a wage —————— This perhaps increases the productivity of the woman at home and raises for reservation wage, compared to the market wage, discouraging her participation in wage work. Such a relationship was analysed in detail in an earlier paper (Unni 1994). The other identifying variable, ownership of a homestead, had a significant positive impact on the choice of the woman being a wage earner.

The Wage Equation

The joint maximum likelihood estimates of the semi-logarithmic daily wage equation for men are presented in Table 6. While an earlier specification indicated a non-linear relationship between experience and wage earnings, the years of experience variables introduced in linear and quadratic terms in this equation are not jointly significant. They are, however, retained in the equation. The daily wage earnings increase with experience but do not taper of as expected. The education variables are jointly significant at 5 per cent level. The results show that persons with all higher levels of education earn more than the illiterate persons, which is the reference category. Similar results are observed for men in both states.

The estimated rho, the correlation coefficient between the error terms in the probit wage earner and log wage equations, is significant, in both states. This indicates that the log wage function on a selective sample of wage earners would produce biased estimates. Our correction of this equation for selectivity bias is therefore valid. The OLS estimates of the log wage equation on the sample of wage earners is also presented in Table 8.

Table 8: Ordinary Least Squares Estimates of Logarithmic Daily Earnings Equation for Men Wage Earners, 1987-88

Variable	*Tamil Nadu*		*Madhya Pradesh*	
	Coefficient	*t-ratio*	*Coefficient*	*t-ratio*
Constant	0.904	8.913	1.244	11.889
Experience	0.062	8.111	0.045	5.138
Experience Squared ('00)	-0.86	-5.700		-2.611
Literate	**0.080**	0.856		1.279
Primary School	0.146	1.754	0.156	1.778
Middle School	0.504	5.975	0.542	5.997
Secondary School	1.013	12.290	0.901	11.227
Graduates	1.639	16.561	1.442	17.886
R-Square	0.1511		0.2019	
Adjusted R-Sq.	0.1493		0.1991	
F-Statistic	79.89		71.98	
N	31.48		1999	

The joint maximum likelihood estimates of the logarithmic wage equation for women are presented in Table 7. The results indicate that the wage earnings increase until 26 and 23 years of experience in Tamil Nadu and Madhya Pradesh respectively, and then taper off. The earnings profile for women appears to follow the Mincerian non-linear relationship. The young age at which the women's earnings taper off is probably because a large proportion of these workers are manual workers where physical fitness is a prime criteria for employ-ment. Men are more likely to be salaried workers where experience is more valued.

The education variables are jointly significant at 5 per cent level. The results show that in Tamil Nadu, women who completed middle and secondary school and graduation obtained earnings higher than the illiterate persons, which formed the reference category. In Madhya Pradesh, however, persons with all higher levels of education earn more than the illiterate reference group.6

The estimated rho for women's wage equation is not significant. This implies that estimates based on a log wage equation for a selective sample of wage earners need not be biased. This is a surprising result. The OLS estimates for such an equation are presented in Table 9.

Table 9: Ordinary Least Squares Estimates of Logarithmic Daily Earnings Equation for Women Wage Earners, 1987-88

Variable	*Tamil Nadu*		*Madhya Pradesh*	
	Coefficient	*t-Ratio*	*Coefficient*	*t-Ratio*
Constant	0.579	4.525	0.699	2.686
Experience	0.052	4.303	0.035	1.490
Experience Squared ('00)	-0.094	-3.587	-0.070	-1.428
Literate	-0.062	-0.496	0.458	1.451
Primary School	-0.017	-0.141	0.298	0.741
Middle School	0.444	2.675	-0.431	-0.708
Secondary School	1.044	9.036	1.516	7.085
Graduates	2.124	13.976	1.955	10.793
R-square	0.2321			0.2971
Adjusted R-Sq	0.2263			0.2836
F - Statistic	39.85			22.04
N	**931**			**373**

Returns to Education

The proportionate rates of return to a year of schooling in various levels of education are presented in Table 10 separately for men and women by region. These returns are computed both fi'om the joint maximum likelihood estimates and OLS estimates.

The rates of return to education for both men and women rose with the level of education. They ranged from 8.8 to 21 per cent to a year of schooling at different levels of education for men and 7.7 to 41 per cent per year for women.

Computing private rates of return to education in Andhra Pradesh, another state of India, Tilak (1987) had found that the results for women are sensitive to the treatment of the rate of women's participation in the labour force. While returns of women's education at every level of schooling was higher for women than men, it fell below that of men when non-participation in the labour force is also used in tfie computation.

In our model we have tried to correct for the selection into wage employment using the joint maximum likelihood estimation procedure. The simple OLS estimates are also pre-sented which do not correct for this bias. While the corrected estimates of private rates of return are lower, the gender differentials observed by levels of education are not affected by this correction.

Table 10: Returns to Education by School Level and Gender, 1987-88

Educational Level	*Tamil Nadu*		*Madhya Pradesh*	
	Men	*Women*	*Men*	*Women*
Maximum Likelihood Estimates				
Middle School (4 years)	**8.8**	-	**9.5**	-
Secondary School (3 years)	15.6	24.3	10.6	-
Graduates (3 years)	18.7	40.7	16.1	10.3
(4 years)	14.0	30.5	12.1	7.7
Ordinary Least Squares Estimates				
Middle School (4 years)	9.0	-	9.7	-
Secondary School (3 years)	17.0	20.0	12.0	
Graduates (3 years)	20.9	36.0	18.0	14.7
(4 years)	15.6	27.0	13.5	11.0

Note: Computed from Tables 6-9 by levels of education.

In fact, rates of return by levels of education show an interesting gender differential by region, irrespective of the estimation procedure. While the rates of return to women's education are higher than that of men at all levels of education in Tamil Nadu, they are in fact lower than that of men for graduates in Madhya Pradesh. This latter difference may, however, be interpreted with caution since the size of the sample of women wage in Madhya Pradesh is rather small.

The returns to education computed from selectivity corrected wage equations are lower than those computed from a selective sample of wage earners, except for women in Tamil Nadu. This is particularly true for higher levels of education. This is in contrast to the estimates of the returns to education for male wage earners in Turkey, where the OLS estimates were found to be consistently higher than the selectivity corrected ones (Tansel 1992).

Conclusion

The probability of selection into wage employment increases with age and then declines for both sexes, but at an earlier age for women. All levels of education, except graduation, indicate a negative impact on selection into wage employment for both sexes, with respect to the illiterate category. Ownership of land discoursed participation in wage employment. Similar results were observed by gender and region in the selection into wage employment.

The maximum likelihood method used to jointly estimate the wage earner choice and wage equations indicates that the sample selection bias is important mainly for male workers. The wage function indicates that while daily wage earnings increase with experience for both sexes they t^r off at an early age only for women.

In sum, the returns to education in two urban regions of India rise with the level of education for both men and women. This is in contrast to the estimates of returns observed by Tilak and others (see Tilak 1987) for various regions of India. The relative gap in rates of return to different levels of education is still high ranging from 8 to 20 per cent for men and 7 to 40 per cent for women. Such unconventional returns to reduction have been reported more recently for African countries (Moll 1996; Bennell 1994). A study conducted in Uttar Pradesh has also obtained similar results (Kingdon 1996).

A wide relative wage gap between workers with differential levels of education is also observed. The average daily wage earnings ranged from Rs 14.8 and 8.0 for illiterate men and women, respectively, to Rs 51.5 and 44.3 for graduate men and women in the two states. However, we observed a decline in wage inequality by gender in the two states. While men's wage earnings were almost double that of women among the illiterate and literate groups, wage inequality declined steadily and was the lowest among graduates. Evidently, private investment in education among women also helps to reduce the gender wage gap.

Private rates of return to education and wage differentials are expected to be higher **in** low income as compared to high income regions. If Tamil Nadu may be considered a high income state compared to Madhya Pradesh, the opposite was observed. Returns to men's and women's education were found to be higher in Tamil Nadu. Only at the middle school level returns were observed to be higher for men in Madhya Pradesh.

The returns to education are also found higher for women as compared to men with and without the selectivity correction, except among graduates in Madhya Pradesh. While returns computed from the selectivity corrected equations are lower than that computed from simple OLS regressions, except for women in Tamil Nadu, the correction for selectivity bias did not appear to change gender differentials in returns to education.

The benefits to society that arise from a literate and educated population are many, such as higher age of marriage, lower infant mortality rate, improved child nutrition and family health and a skilled and flexible labour force. Lower private returns to lower levels of education and the low enrolment rates in primary schooling implies that something needs to be done to induce parents to send children to school. The intra-sectoral allocation of resources to elementary education which was quite high in the First Five Year Plan, reduced steeply till the Sixth Plan. However, since the formulation of the National

Policy of Education in 1986, the intra-sectoral allocation to elementary education has increased considerably (Tilak 1995). Unless this trend continues universalisation of education cannot be achieved.

Higher returns to higher levels of education also implies that the demand for such education would be naturally high and rising. A policy response could be a reduction of the subsidy to higher education. However, the debate on privatisation of higher education has pointed out that it might produce uneven and inequitous results (Majumdar and Vaidyanathan 1995).

The economic reforms initiated by the government of India has raised hopes of a high growth of industrial production. But the rapid growth of industry requires an educated and flexible labour force. Various studies have shown that an educated and skilled labour force contributed significantly to the rapid industrialisation of the South East Asian tigers. If India wishes to achieve **rapid** growth which encompasses the large mass of the people, universal education is a basic requirement.

Notes

1. The per centage distributions reported in the Tables 2-4 are computed from a weighted distri-bution of the sample population.
2. In 1992 there were 448 and 233 general educational colleges in Madhya Pradesh and Tamil Nadu respectively {Centre for Monitoring the Indian Economy. Basic Statistics Relating to States of India, September 1994, Table 2.10). There were approximately 26 and 45 thousand persons (rural and urban combined) in the age-group 15-24 per college in Madhya Pradesh and Tamil Nadu, respectively. This was computed using the 1981 Population Census proportion of population in the relevant age-group to the 1991 Census population for the two states.
3. We do not control for a possible omitted variable bias (excluding variables to approximate ability and schooling quality) and simultaneity bias (Behrman and Schneider 1992) due to lack of adequate data.
4. The sample means reported in Table 5 are unweighted estimates. They differ from the weighted distributions and estimates reported in Tables 2-4. This is particularly true for estimates of daily wage earnings since the sample was drawn in favour of higher household monthly per capita expenditure groups. The unweighted daily wage earnings (Table 5) are consequently higher than the weighted estimates (Table 4).
5. These estimates are not presented in the paper.
6. The negative coefficient for middle school category in Madhya Pradesh is perhaps due to its small sample size.

References

Behrman, J.R. and Schneider, R. (1992): Empirical Evidence on the Determinants of and the Impact of Human Capital Investments and Related Policies in Developing Countries: Implications for India, The Indian Economic Review, 27(1): 1-23.

Bennell, Paul (1994): Rates of Return to Education: Does the Conventional Pattern Prevail in Sub-Saharan Africa?, Institute of Development Studies, Working Paper No. 10, University of Sussex, Brighton.

Dougherty, C.R.S. and Jimenez, E. (1991): The Specification of the Earnings Function, Economics of Education Review, 10(2): 85-98.

Heckman, J.J. (1979): Sample Selection Bias as a Specification Error, Econometrica, 47(l):153-161.

Kingdon, Geeta (1995): Education of Females in India; Determinants and Economic Consequences: A Case Study of Urban Uttar Pradesh, Report Submitted under the McNamara Fellowship Programme, World Bank, Washington D.C.

Majumdar, Manabi and Vaidyanathan, A. (1995): The Role of Private Sector in Education in India: Current Trends and New Priorities, Discussion Paper No. 10, Studies on Hunan Development in India, UNDP, Centre for Development Studies, Trivandrum.

Mincer, J. (1974): *Schooling, Experience and Earnings,* National Bureau of Economic Research. New Yorik: Columbia University Press.

Moll, Peter (1996): The Collapse of Primary Schooling Returns in South Africa, 1960-90, *Oxford Bulletin of Economics and Statistics,* 58(1).

Schultz, T. Paul (1992): 'The Role of Education and Human Capital in Economic Development: An Empirical Assessment, Yale University, Economic Growth Centre, Discussion Paper No 670, August.

Schultz, T. Paul (1993): Returns to Women's Education, In E.M. King and M. Anne Hill (ed.): *Women's Education in Developing Countries,* Baltimore: John Hopkins University Press.

Tansel, Aysit (1992): Wage Employment, Earnings and Returns to Schooling in Turkey, Yale University, Economic Growth Centre, Discussion Paper No 661, April.

Tilak, Jandhyala, B.G. (1987): *Economics of Inequality in Education,* New Delhi: Sage Publications.

Tilak, Jandhyala, B.G. (1995): *Costs and Financing of Education in India: A Review of Issues, Problems and Prospects,* Discussion Paper No. 5, Studies on Human Development in India, UNDP, Centre for Development Studies, Trivandrum.

Unni, Jeemol (1992): Occupational Choice and Multiple Job Holding in Rural Gujarat, India, Yale University, Economic Growth Centre, Discussion Paper No 677, December.

Unni, Jeemol (1994): Labour Participation Decisions of Married Women in Rural India, *Indian Economic Review,* 29(2): 177-93.

14

UNDERSTANDING SCHOOL ATTENDANCE AND CHILDREN'S WORK PARTICIPATION IN INDIA*

USHA JAYACHANDRAN

Abstract

A situation analysis of school attendance and workforce participation by children in the 5-14 age-groups at State and district level for seventeen major states is presented from the 1991 Census of India, to identify regions of educational deprivation and high rates of work force participation by these children. Further, possible reasons for low rates of school attendance and high rates of child labour have been investigated and discussed. Disadvantages in terms of rural-urban, male-female and scheduled castes and scheduled tribes are also highlighted.

Introduction

"Education is universally recognised as an important investment in human capital. It contributes to socio-economic development by endowing individuals with the means to improving their health, skills, knowledge and capability for productive work. For society as a whole, education enriches the political and cultural life of the community and strengthens the community's ability to exploit technology for social and economic advancement. Because the benefits are so broad and pervasive, the development of education is a key concern

* This (paper is part of a larger report prepared for the New Delhi Office of the United Nations Development Programme, which funded the data collection and analysis for the same (December 1998).

everywhere." (Tan and Mingat, 1992). Growing global consciousness about the ethical and social implications of child labour and non-participation in schooling by children in their formative years has put the limelight back on the issues concerning children and the various forms of deprivation they face. Many developed countries have made efforts to use trade sanctions as an instrument of coercion to put an end to the use of child labour in various industries. Yet, policy debates at the international level and various international conventions on the rights of the child have not done much to improve the situation in India. Information on the dimension and magnitude of the problem remains quite scarce and in-depth micro-level studies that could contribute towards coherent policy making are notable by their absence.

India offers a rich set-up for studying child labour and non-participation of children in the 5-14 age group in schooling. Various studies at the state and district levels have found the existence of very different educational outcomes in India. Sectoral policies adopted for tackling the interconnected problems of child work force participation and non-participation in schooling are also diverse.

Child population in India, in the 5-14 age-group, increased from 114 million in 1961 to 210 million in 1991, an increase of 1.8 times whereas school attendance saw an increase of three times from 34.6 million in 1961 to 104.3 million in 1991 (Chaudhari, 1996). In India, primary education is not compulsory and neither is child labour illegal. As a result, almost half the child population in the 5-14 age- group — 105 million — is not in school. These children stay at home to tend the cattle, care for younger siblings, collect firewood, work in fields etc. Many find employment in cottage industries, tea stalls, restaurants, household work as domestic help, rag pickers or even bonded labour in the agricultural sector.

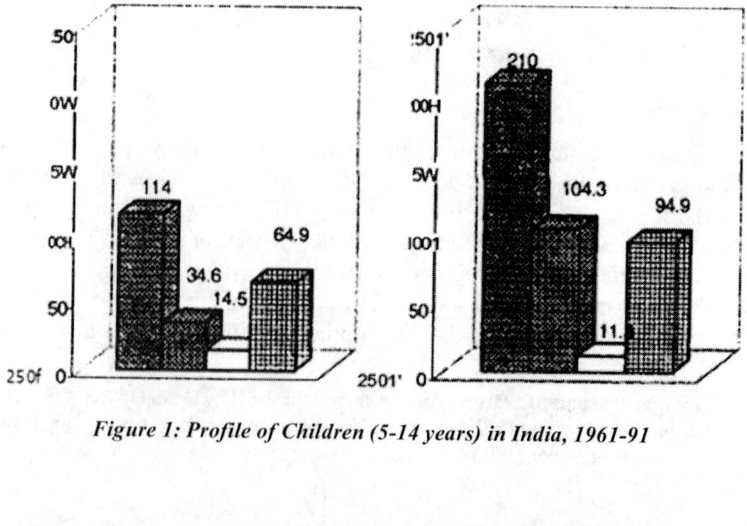

Figure 1: Profile of Children (5-14 years) in India, 1961-91

While looking at children in the workforce and those attending school, it is also essential to consider those children who are neither at work nor at school. Rather than calling them "nowhere children" (ibid), I would prefer to call them "unaccounted children" as they are making significant contributions but are not accounted for because of the Census definition of work (which considers anything done in lieu of wages as work). The Census defines work as participation in any economically productive activity. A person who engages himself/herself in work such as say rice pounding, for sale or wages, or in domestic services for wages for others, or minding cattle for wages or selling firewood or making and selling cowdung cakes or selling grass etc., or any other work like cultivation etc., is treated as working. However, any person engaged only in household duties but doing no other productive work to augment the family's resources is not considered as working (Census of India, 1991).

But in India, there are a large number of children who may actually be working without wages in the fields, in cottage industries (sometimes alongside their parents), on tea plantations, as domestic workers for the middle class, as hawkers, vendors and ragpickers and also load and unload goods. They also work at home fetching water and fire wood, preparing meals etc., but all these activities go unreported by the Census as none of them is done for direct sale or in lieu of wages. Domestic work at home such as minding siblings, cooking, washing, collecting cowdung for consumption at home, grazing cattle for the family, etc. it is done for the household is certainly work for the child though not seen as augmenting the family's resources. It is not reported as work in the Census.

In the rural context specially, these children do make a significant contribution to the households activities, more so the girl child, and their work, although not done in lieu of wages or for sale of any product, should be considered in the formal definition of work. Thus, a large number of children go unaccounted as their contribution is not considered work and they are relegated to the residual category of children neither at school, nor at work. There is also the added problem of children in the 5-7 age-group who are not enrolled in school because of the imprecise nature of their age when it comes to age at admission to school. So many children in this age-group in rural areas and urban slums do not get enrolled into school at the right age and may (or may not) be involved with some household work that is unreported by the Census. These children may also be covered in the set of unaccounted children. In 1961, the proportion of unaccounted children in the 5-14 age group was 57 per cent and this has now fallen to 45.2 per cent in 1991. Although there is a fall in their proportions, their magnitude has risen in absolute numbers. The number of unaccounted children increased from 64.9 million in 1961 to 94.9 million in 1991.

Inequities in terms of educational achievements are seen to be multi-layered in terms of scheduled castes as against non-scheduled castes, women against men, girl child against male child, rural against urban, and backward against the relatively less developed regions. Census data for 1991 clearly brings out these inequities. In 1991, of a total child population of 210 million in the 5-14 age-group, 159.5 million resided in rural areas. A larger proportion of children in the urban areas attend school as compared to those in rural areas. Within rural and urban areas, the proportion of female children attending school is also lower than male children.

Social stratification has played a significant role in the development process in India, leading to inequities between different groups in the context of education as well. Literacy rates show that as against a national level of 52 per cent in 1991, it was 37 per cent for scheduled castes and 30 per cent for the scheduled tribes. Within the scheduled castes, it was 50 per cent for males and 24 per cent for females. The scheduled tribes exhibited even lower literacy rates at 41 per cent for males and 18 per cent for females. Given that these groups together form a fourth of India's population, these literacy rates become important indicators of the levels of deprivation they face in education.

The Study

This study is a situation analysis of school attendance and work-force participation by children in the 5-14 age-group. For this purpose, state and district level data, from the 1991 Census are presented and discussed. Regions of educational deprivation and high levels of work force participation by children in the 5-14 age-group are identified and possible reasons for such patterns highlighted. The disadvantages faced by the female child in terms of participation in the schooling process and work are also studied.

To analyse social disadvantage, the proportions of scheduled castes and scheduled tribes in every district are considered. Literacy rates, adult work force participation rates, with special focus on females are also brought into the study to understand the role they play in determining participation in work and the schooling process at the elementary level.

Analysis

Census data for 1991, when analysed at the All India level brings out the following:

Table 1: School Attendance* (5-14 years), 1991

	Total Population (5-14 yrs) in millions		*Attending School (5-14 yrs) in millions*				
	Male	*Female*	*Male*	*Per cent*	*Female*	*Per cent*	*Per cent*
Total	109.4	100.6	60.8	55.6	43.5	43.2	
Rural	83.2	76.3	42.9	52.0	28.1	37.0	
Urban	*26.2*	*24.3*	*17.9*	*68.3*	*15.4*	*63.3*	

Table 2: Child *Work* Force Participation* (5-14 years) - 1991

	Males		*Females*
	In millions	*Per cent*	*In millions Per cent*
Total	6.2	5.7	5.1 5.1
Rural	5.4	6.5	4.8 6.3
Urban	*0.7*	*2.7*	*0.3 1.2*

Source: Census of India 1991

* Excludes Jammu and Kashmir

Note: The figures in per centage for males and females have beencalculated as a proportion of male and female child population (5-14 years) respectively, for each category.

Table 3: *Unaccounted* Children* (5-14 years) - 1991

	Males		*Females*	
	In millions	*Per cent*	*In millions*	*Per cent*
Total	42.6	39.0	52.3	52.0
Rural	35.0	42.2	43.6	57.1
Urban	*7.6*	*29.0*	*8.7*	*35.7*

Source and Note: As given in Table 2.

- 50 children out of every 100 in the 5-14 age group attend school in India. Out of every 100 boys, 55 attend school and out of every 100 girls, 43 attend school.
- In rural India out of every 100 children 45 attend school. For every 100 boys here, 52 attend school and for every 100 girls, 37 attend school.
- School attendance in urban India is higher with 66 out of every 100 children attending school. 68 out of every 100 boys and 63 out of every 100 girls attend school in urban areas.
- 11.3 million children in the age-group 5-14 participate in the work-force. This is approximately 14 per cent of the global child work-force.
- 95 million children neither attend school nor participate in work in India, of which 78 million are in the rural areas.

State Level Analysis

School Attendance

Country level aggregates often hide state level realities. At the state level, school attendance rates at the elementary level vary from 85 per cent in Kerala to 35 per cent in Bihar. Kerala remains the best performer in rural and urban areas with school attendance rates of 85 per cent and 87 per cent respectively. Bihar shows the worst performance in the rural as well as urban areas with school attendance rates of per cent and 59 per cent respectively. For all the major states, school attendance in urban areas outperforms those in rural areas (Table 4).

Table 4: School Attendance Rates (5-14 years) - Major States, 1991

(per cent)

State/country	*Overall*		*Rural*		*Urban*	
	Male	*Female*	*Male*	*Female*	*Male*	*Female*
India						
Bihar	42.79	25.93	39.82	21.79	63.36	54.07
Uttar Pradesh	44.64	28.00	42.28	23.44	53.37	46.40
Arunachal Pradesh	45.94	36.01	43.37	33.00	63.74	57.92
Assam	49.88	43.46	47.98	41.25	.68.35	65.09
West Bengal	49.88	42.31	45.41	37.26	64.42	59.07
Rajasthan	52.08	25.28	48.20	17.60	66.36	53.19
Madhya Pradesh	53.07	37.82	48.15	30.56	70.08	62.95
Andhra Pradesh	56.00	42.02	51.19	34.29	69.31	63.21
Orissa	56.95	43.13	55.10	40.43	69.08	61.82
Karnataka	61.94	50.99	58.04	‘ 44.22	71.27	67,31
Gujarat	63.11	52.08	60.86	46.81	67.55	62.58
Punjab	65.07	59.17	63.24	55.47	69.50	68.00
Haryana	65.89	52.82	63.60	47.99	73.56	68.80
Maharashtra	68.97	59.92	65.43	53.14	75.05	71.79
Tamil Nadu	73.37	66.14	71.54	62.01	77.13	74.49
Himachal Pradesh	76.60	68.01	75.98	66.89	83.86	82.15
Kerala	*85.50*	*85.54*	*84.97*	*85.04*	*87.09*	*87.08*

Source: Calculated from Census of India, 1991, C-4 Series

Note: Male and female school attendance rates have been calculated as a per centage of male and female child population 5-14 years.

Another interesting fact is that for all the major states, school attendance rates for males are higher than for females, in rural as well as urban areas. This gender disadvantage in schooling is glaring in Bihar, Rajasthan and Uttar Pradesh where the difference between male and female school attendance is over ten per centage points. In rural areas Andhra Pradesh and Madhya Pradesh also show a similar disparity, in rural Rajasthan, the gender disadvantage is the maximum, with school attendance rates for girls as low as 18 per cent, as against 48 per cent for boys. In urban areas, gender disadvantage in schooling is most prominent in Rajasthan and Bihar.

Child Work-force Participation

The participation of children in the work-force shows a uniform pattern across all the states with the per centage of working children being highest in Andhra Pradesh at 9.45 per cent for males and 10.54 per cent for females.

Only in the case of Kerala the participation of children in the work-force shows a noticeably low figure of 0.32 per cent for males and 0.26 per cent for females (Table 5).

Another interesting fact is that the male child work-force participation is higher than that of female children in the urban areas across all states. One possible explanation for this could be the migration of male children seeking work from the rural to urban areas. The female child may not enjoy similar mobility.

Table 5: Child Work-force Participation Rates (5-14 Years) -Major States, 1991

	Total		*Rural*		*Urban*	
	Male	*Female*	*Male*	*Female*	*Male*	*Female*
INDIA						
Andhra Pradesh	9.45	10.54	11.43	13.58	3.96	2.18
Karnataka	8.90	8.71	10.70	11.34	4.59	2.38
Madhya Pradesh	7.64	8.56	9.19	10.66	2.25	\21
Assam	6.80	4.07	7.19	4.20	2.96	2.82
Orissa	6.30	5.43	6.87	6.03	2.54	1.26
West Bengal	5.58	2.68	6.55	3.10	2.42	1.29
Rajasthan	5.19	7.88	6.00	9.75	2.20	1.11
Gujarat	5.08	5.45	6.40	7.81	2.48	0.77
Punjab	4.97	0.86	5.91	1.07	2.69	0.35
Uttar Pradesh	4.94	2.49	5.31	2.82	3.65	0.81
Maharashtra	4.89	6.63	6.51	9.86	2.10	0.96
Bihar	4.76	2.94	5.29	3.26	2.37	0.67
Arunachal Pradesh	4.63	6.74	4.95	7.38	2.42	2.11
Tamil Nadu	4.57	5.11	5.26	6.63	3.15	2.02
Haryana	3.18	1.81	3.59	2.24	1.80	0.39
Kerala	*0.64*	*0.52*	*0.67*	*0.54*	*0.54*	*0.46*

Source: Calculated from Census of India, 1991, B2 Series

Note: Male and female child work-force participation rates have been calculated as a per centage of male and female child population (5-14 years) respectively

Data for Himachal Pradesh for the B2 Series was not available at the time of preparation of this report. Thus, it does not include child labour figures for Himachal Pradesh.

Unaccounted Children

Unaccounted children form the residual category of children in the 5-14 age-group who are neither at work, nor attending school. States which show poor performance in school attendance at the elementary level could either have high proportion of children participating in the work process or high proportion of unaccounted children.

The Census data reveal that states with low school attendance rates, such as Bihar, Uttar Pradesh and Rajasthan, have the highest proportion of "unaccounted children", but do not have very high rates of work-force participation by children. This could be because of variations in the definition of work. It is possible that many of these unaccounted children are engaged in domestic work, or work in cottage industries etc., which goes unreported by the Census.

Table 6: "*Unaccounted Children*" (5-14 years) - Major States, 1991

(per cent)

State	*Total*		*Rural*		*Urban*	
	Male	*Female*	*Male*	*Female*	*Male*	*Female*
INDIA	39.00	51.97	42.16	57.14	28.98	35.73
Bihar	52.44	71.22	55.05	75.03	34.39	45.33-
Uttar Pradesh	50.63	69.66	52.41	73.82	43.13	52,88
Arunachal Pradesh	49.60	57.45	51.87	59.85	33.92	40.03
West Bengal	44.77	55.14	48.31	59.80	33.25	39.69
Assam	43.61	52.65	45.13	54.75	28.79	32.17
Rajasthan	43.22	67.04	46.38	72.89	31.61	45.79
Madhya Pradesh	39.76	53.87	43.22	59.07	27.80	35.89
Orissa	36.90	51.52	38.19	53.62	28.44	36.94
Andhra Pradesh	34.74	47.55	37.60	52.26	26.81	34.65
Gujarat	31.97	42.58	32.95	45.52	30.04	36.72
Haryana	31.09	45.44	32.99	49.86	24.72	30.84
Punjab	30.17	40.07	31.09	43.54	27.96	31.76
Karnataka	29.64	40.60	31.91	44.84	17.50	24.42
Maharashtra	26.74	33.91	28.90	37.65	23.02	27.37
Tamil Nadu	22.18	28.85	23.34	31.48	19.78	23.53
Himachal Pradesh	21.00	27.40	21.53	28.22	14.87	17.05
Kerala	*13.89*	*13.96*	*14.39*	*14.45*	*12.38*	*12.48*

Source: Calculated from Census of India, 1991, C-4 Series

Note: Proportions of male and female unaccounted children have been calculated as a per centage of male and female child population, 5-14 years, respectively.

Himachal Pradesh and Kerala, with high rates of school attendance, have the lowest proportion of' nowhere' children. From the school attendance figures (Table 6), it is observed that school attendance is higher amongst boys than girls. This corroborates the presence of a higher proportion of unaccounted female children compared to their male counterparts.

District Level Analysis

To be able to get a better picture of participation in education at the elementary level and work-force participation by children we go on further to study district level data for the major states. The three levels of analysis carried out include:

- For the 17 major states, district level data was collated and ranked to arrive at the worst 100 and best 50 districts in terms of participation in schooling and work by children in the 5-14 age-group.

- To further understand the socio-economic factors that could possibly explain low rates of school attendance and high rates of work-force participation by children in the 5-14 age-group, four parameters in the worst 10 districts have been considered. These include adult (15+) female literacy rate, adult (15+) female work-force participation rate, proportion of scheduled caste and tribal population in the district.
- Scatter diagrams for a few associations have been carried out for the complete set of districts for the major states to study the relationship between:
  (a) school attendance (total) and adult literacy rate;
  (b) female school attendance and adult female literacy rate; and
  (c) female child labour and adult female work-force participation rate.

School Attendance at the District Level

Ranking of the worst 100 districts by school attendance rates (total) in the 5-14 age- group brings out that Bihar, Madhya Pradesh, Uttar Pradesh and Rajasthan are the four states where districts with low rates of school attendance are concentrated. These vary from as low as 17 per hundred children in Kishanganj district of Bihar to 38 per hundred children in East Kameng district of Arunachal Pradesh (Appendix 1). School attendance rates in urban areas are Higher than those in rural areas by about 10 per centage points. Urbah areas reap the advantages of better schooling infrastructure, and also probably socio-cultural advancements, which could be the reason for the existence of such a disparity (Appendix 2).

Appendix 1: School Attendance Rate (per cent) (5-14 Years)

WORST 100 Districts -Ranked by Total School Attendance Rate (pre cent) Census 1991

Rank	*State*	*District*	*Per cent School Attendance*		
		Worst 100 Districts	*Total*	*Male*	*Female*
1.	BIH	KISHANGANJ	17.85	24.23	11.50
2.	BIH	ARARIA	20.72	27.01	13.92
3.	UP	BUDAUN	20.99	27.25	12.79
4.	UP	RAMPUR	21.60	27.33	14.88
5.	MP	JHABUA	21.64	27.79	15.17
6.	UP	BAHRAICH	23.43	31.19	13.73
7.	BIH	MADHEPURA	23.55	30.24	15.61
8.	BIH	PURNIA	23.96	29.73	17.54
9.	UP	SITAPUR	24.46	30.40	17.37

(Contd...)

10.	BIH	SAHARSA	24.51	32.26	15.21
11.	UP	MORADABAD	24.52	30.41	17.77
12.	BIH	KATIHAR	24.54	31.03	17.48
13.	UP	KHERI	25.27	32.72	16.44
14.	BIH	SAHIBGANJ	25.36	30.29	19.99
15.	BfH	SITAMARHI	25.38	32.15	17.04
16.	BIH	PURBA CHAMPARAN	25.39	32.76	16.60
17.	RAJ	BANSWARA	25.57	34.26	16.49
18.	RAJ	BARMER	25.69	38.79	10.75
19.	UP	GONDA	25.92	34.35	15.72
20.	UP	PILIBHIT	26.54	33.99	17.73
21.	UP	BAREILLY	26.71	32.59	19.72
22.	BIH	PASHCHIM CHAMPARAN	27.02	34.95	17.79
23.	UP	SHAHJAHANPUR	27.03	34.06	18.47
24.	UP	MAHARAJGANJ	27.27	39.02	14.14
25.	UP	SIDDHARTHNAGAR	27.37	37.05	16.11
26.	RAJ	JALOR	28.29	44.95	9.49
27.	BIH	PALAMU	28.29	37.03	18.77
28.	UP	BARABANKI	28.46	35.34	20.54
29.	OR.	KORAPUT	28.50	35.66	21.09
30.	BIH	KHAGARIA	28.51	34.99	20.59
31.	UP	LALITPUR	29.00	37.63	18.78
32.	WB	MALDAH	29.16	32.70	25.40
33.	UP	SONBHADRA	30.01	37.46	21.53
34.	TN	DUMKA	30.12	71.26	63.01
35.	UP	HARDOI	30.51	38.23	20.83
36.	UP	BASTI	30.83	40.38	20.29
37.	WB	WESTDINAJPUR	30.88	34.16	27.46
38.	MP	BASTAR	30.98	36.55	25.33
39.	WB	MURSHIDABAD	31.12	33.50	28.61
40.	BIH	MADHUBANI	31.28	40.96	20.16
41.	UP	BANDA	31.67	41.94	19.11
42.	BIH	DARBHANGA	31.84	39.38	22.84
43.	BIH	GODDA	31.93	40.07	22.92
44.	MP	SHIVPURI	32.08	41.11	21.41
45.	ARP	TAWANG	32.37	37.74	27.19
46.	RAJ	DUNGARPUR	32.52	37.63	22.16
47.	ARP	TIRAP	32.71	39.78	24.79
48.	RAJ	JHALAWAR	32.76	44.10	19.90
49.	MP	SIDHI	32.90	44.36	20.46
50.	RAJ	DHUBRI	32.97	46.46	19.24
51.	AP	MEHBUBNAGAR	32.99	40.57	24.96
52.	BIH	MUZAFFARPUR	33.01	39.11	25.83
53.	BIH	GOPALGANJ	33.14	43.59	21.47
54.	MP	GUNA	33.17	41.82	23.13
55.	BIH	BEGUSARAI	33.17	39.13	26.08

(*Contd...*)

56.	RAJ	JAISALMER	33.25	47.57	16.12
57.	RAJ	BUNDI	33.53	45.52	19.62
58.	UP	MIRZAPUR	33.59	42.44	23.34
59.	BIH	BHAGALPUR	33.67	39.87	26.29
60.	BIH	DEOGHAR	33.69	43.67	22.58
61.	BIH	SAMASTIPUR	33.71	41.11	25.05
62.	MP	WEST NIMAR	34.17	39.05	28.98
63.	AS	KOKRAJHAR	34.23	37.41	30.98
64.	KAR	RAICHUR	34.25	41.95	26.33
65.	BIH	NAWADA	34.45	43.90	23.92
66.	BIH	GIRIDIH	34.58	45.52	22.75
67.	BIH	GAYA	34.79	42.76	25.82
68.	RAJ	BHILWARA	34.81	47.76	20.93
69.	OR	DHOLPUR	34.82	56.27	43.65
70.	UP	ETAH	34.83	42.60	24.83
71.	RAJ	NAGAUR	34.94	50.04	18.18
72.	UP	BIJNOR	35.11	42.35	26.74
73.	OR	KALAHANDI	35.28	46.18	24.66
74.	MP	PANNA	35.34	41.56	28,39
75.	BIH	MUNGER	35.40	43.11	26,19
76.	RAJ	CHURU	35.66	48.51	21.65
77.	RAJ	CHITTAURGARH	35.92	48.60	22.37
78.	RAJ	SAWAI MADHOPUR	35.97	49.99	18.74
79.	MP	RAJGARH	36.07	46.78	24.37
80.	HP	HAMIRPUR	36.39	83.98	82.44
81.	UP	UNNAO	36.55	44.03	27.98
82.	MP	DHAR	36.68	61.34	43,62
83.	UP	GORAKHPUR	36.77	45.78	26..S9
84.	RAJ	TONK	36.79	52.21	19,99
85.	UP	DEORIA	36.94	47.86	25.12
86.	WB	KOCH BIHAR	36.96	39.50	34.29
87.	UP	AGRA	36.97	44.17	28.57
88.	UP	ALLAHABAD	37.06	46.76	26.02
89.	WB	JALPAIGURI	37.23	41.76	32.45
90.	BIH	SIWAN	37.29	48.22	25.60
91.	UP	SAHARANPUR	37.35	43.84	29.76
92.	BIH	HAZARIBAG	37.44	47.40	26.66
93.	UP	ALIGARH	37.46	44.81	28.69
94.	UP	GHAZIPUR	47.37	46.71	27.38
95.	UP	JAUNPUR	37.54	48.06	26.09
96.	RAJ	UDAIPUR	37.29	49.28	25.28
97.	RAJ	BIKANER	37.62	47.32	27.05
98.	UP	FARRUKHABAD	37.68	42.53	31.90
99.	ARP	EAST KAMENG	37.75	48.53	25.87
100.	AP	MEDAK	37.84	46.15	28.97

Source: Calculated from the Census of India, 1991, C-4 Tables - "Population (Ages 5-19) by single years of age, school, attendance and economic activity."

Appendix 2: Rural & Urban School Attendance Rates (per cent) (5-14 Years) Census 1991

Worst 100 District - Rural Areas				*Worst 100 District - Urban Areas*			
Rank	***State***	***Worst 100 District***	***Rural***	***Rank***	***State***	***District***	***Urban***
I	BIH	KISHANGANJ	15.34	I	UP	RAMPUR	34.58
2	UP	RAMPUR	17.10	2	UP	BUDAUN	34.58
3	MP	JHABUA	17.82	3	UP	BIJNOR	38,02
4	UP	BADUAN	17.91	4	UP	MORADABAD	38.87
5	BIH	ARARIA	19.09	5	UP	PILIBHIT	39.02
6	UP	MORADABAD	19.11	6	UP	BAREILLY	39.33
7	UP	BAREILLY	20.55	7	Ar.P	EAST KAMENG	39.99
8	BIH	PURNIA	21.21	8	BIH	KISHANGAN.I	40.75
9	BIH	KATIHAR	21.47	9	UP	HARDOI	41.58
10	UP	SITAPUR	21.76	10	UP	BARABANKI	41.86
11	UP	BAHRAICH	21.77	II	UP	SHAHJAHANPUR	41.93
12	RAJ	BANSWARA	22.11	12	UP	FARRUKHABAD	41.99
13	BIH	MATHEPURA	22.23	13	UP	AGRA	42.80
14	RAJ	BARMER	22.46	14	UP	BAHRAICH	42.82
15	UP	KHERI	22.68	15	UP	VARANASI	42.91
16	BIH	SAHIBGANJ	22.90	16	UP	SITAPUR	43.69
17	BIH	SAHARSA	22.90	17	BIH	MADHEPURA	43.83
18	UP	SHAHJANPUR	23.01	18	BIH	ARARIA	45.25
19	UP	PILIBHIT	23.75	19	UP	SIDDHARTHNAGAR	45.40
20	UP	SONBHADRA	23.76	20	BIH	SAHARSA	45.71
21	BIH	SITAMARHI	23.88	21	UP	ETAH	45.73

(Contd...)

22	BIH	PURBA CHAMPARAN	23.93	22	UP	KHERI	46.01
23	UP	GONDA	23.99	23	UP	BASTI	46.09
24	OR	KORAPUT	24.04	24	BIH	KHAGARIA	46.39
25	BIH	PASCHIM CHAMPARAN	24.17	25	UP	JALAUN	46.44
26	UP	LALITPUR	24.18	26	UP	ALIGARH	46.44
27	RAJ	BIKANER	24.95	27	BIH	GOPALGANJ	46.47
28	UP	MAHARAJGANJ	25.92	28	UP	BULANDSHAHR	46.62
29	WB	WEST DINAJPUR	26.24	29	RN	DHOLPUR	46.71
30	MP	SHIVPURI	26.53	30	RN	NAGAUR	47.02
31	RAJ	JAOR	26.66	31	UP	MEERUT	47.19
32	UP	SIDDHARTH NAGAR	26.67	32	BIH	BEGUSARAI	47.97
33	UP	BARABANKI	27.01	33	UP	MUZAFFARNAGAR	47.99
34	RAJ	JHALAWAR	27.02	34	UP	AZAMGARH	48.10
35	BIH	PALAMU	27.07	35	UP	Cl AW AH	48. LI
36	WB	MALDAH	27.29	36	WB	MURSHIDABAD	48.30
37	BIH	KHAGARIA	27.41	37	UP	JAUNPUR	48.44
38	MP	GUNA	27.45	38	UP	MIRZAPUR	48.60
39	RAJ	JODHPUR	27.86	39	UP	FIROZABAD	48.7]
40	MP	BASTAR	28.11	40	UP	MATHURA	48.71
41	RAJ	JAISALMER	28.18	41	UP	FAIZABAD	48.97
42	RAJ	BUMDI	28.21	42	BIH	PURBACHAMPARAN	49.25
43	BIH	DUMKA	28.22	43	UP	GONDA	49.27
44	Ar.P	TIRAP	28.50	44	BIH	PASHCHIMCHAMPARAN	49.56
45	AP	MEHBUBNAGAR	28.74	45	RAJ	SIKAR	50.09
46	UP	BANDA	28.77	46	BIH	SITAMARHJ	50.42
47	RAJ	BHILWARA	28.98	47	UP	RAE BARELI	50.78
48	UP	HARDOI	28.99	48	UP	UNNAO	50.93

(Contd...)

49	WB	MURSHIDABAD	29.35	49	UP	BALLIA	50.94
50	BIH	DEOGHAR	29.36	50	RAJ	JALOR	50.95
51	KT	RAICHUR	29.51	51	BIH	MADHUBANI	5 1.09
52	BIH	DARBHANGA	29.52	52	RAJ	CHURU	51.20
53	AS	DHUBRI	29.65	53	UP	KANPUR(DEHAT)	51.44
54	UP	BASTI	29.78	54	BIH	PALAMU	51.62
55	RAJ	CHURU	29.83	55	BIH	SIWAN	51.64
56	RAJ	DUNGARPUR	30.13	56	UP	MAU	51.78
57	MP	WEST NIMAR	30.13	57	RAJ	SAWAIMADHOPUR	51.83
58	BIH	GIRIDIH	30.21	58	UP	SAHARANPUR	51.86
59	RAJ	CHITTAURGARH	30.25	59	UP	HAMIRPUR	52.11
60	BIH	MADHUBANI	30.50	60	UP	BANDA	52.15
61	BIH	MUZAFFARPUR	30.67	61	UP	MAHARAJGANJ	52.24
62	BIH	BHAGALPUR	30.81	62	BIH	VAISHALI	52.24
63	RAJ	UDAIPUR	30.82	63	MP	TIKAMGARH	52.25
64	MP	SIDHI	31.02	64	WB	BIRBHUM	52.54
65	BIH	GAYA	31.07	65	BIH	NALANDA	52.63
66	BIH	GODDA	31.09	66	BIH	NAWADA	52.66
67	UP	MIRZAPUR	31.17	67	KT	RAICHUR	52.79
68	MP	RAJGARH	31.47	68	RAJ	JHUNJHUNUN	53.08
69	MP	RAJGARH	31.47	69	BIH	ROHTAS	53.15
70	BIH	BEGUSARAI	31.55	70	BIH	MUNGER	53,35
71	UP	ALLAHABAD	31.83	71	RN	TONK	53.79
72	MP	PANNA	31.88	72	UP	MAINPURI	53.92
73	BIH	MUNGER	31.93	73	UP	PRATAPGARH	53.95
74	MP	RATLAM	31.98	74	UP	FATEHPUR	53.97
75	AP	KURNOOL	32.04	75	Ar.P	WEST KAMENG	54.02

(*Contd...*)

76	BIH	HAZARIBAG	32.26	76	UP	GHAZIABAD	54.07
77	BIH	GOPALGANJ	32.35	77	BIH	SARAN	54.65
78	BIH	SAMASTIPUR	32.42	78	BIH	JEHANABAD	54.65
79	RAJ	DHOLPUR	32.43	79	BIH	BHAGALPUR	54.95
80	UP	SAHARANPUR	32.45	80	BIH	PURNIA	55.07
81	RAJ	SIROHI	32.45	81	UP	GORAKHPUR	55.09
82	KT	GULBARGA	32.51	82	BIH	BHOJPUR	55.30
83	UP	ETAH	32.54	83	UP	DEORIA	55.61
84	AS	KOKRAJHAR	32.56	84	AP	KURNOOL	55.71
85	RAJ	NAGAUR	32.70	85	Ar.P	LOWERSUBANSIRI	55.96
86	RAJ	TONK	32.70	86	BIH	DARBHANGA	56.42
87	UP	GORAKHPUR	32.76	87	UP	GHAZIPUR	56.69
88	AP	MEDAK	32.96	88	WB	SOUTH TWENTY FOUR PARGANAS	56.79
89	BIH	NAWADA	33.06	89	BIH	KATIHAR	56.81
90	MP	DHAR	33.11	90	BIH	SAHIBGANJ	57.00
91	UP	HAMIRPUR	33.11	91	UP	NAINITAL	57.09
92	MP	SURGUJA	33.17	92	WB	JALPAIGURI	57.48
93	MP	SURGUJA	33.17	93	WB	PURULIYA	57.49
94	RAJ	SAWAIMADHOPUR	33.27	94	UP	JHANSI	57.50
95	UP	AGRA	33.30	95	G.I	BANAS KANTHA	57.57
96	OR	KALAHANDI	33.52	96	RAJ	BARMER	57.59
97	WB	JALPAIGURI	33.85	97	MP	GUNA	57.73
98	MP	CHHATARPUR	33.86	98	AS	GOALPARA	57,81
99	UP	LUCKNOW	33.91	99	BIH	MUZAFFARPUR	57.83
100	UP	BIJNOR	34.11	100	RAJ	PALI	57.95

Source: Calculated from the Census of India, 1991, C-4 Table - "population (ages 5-19) by single years of age, school, attendance and economic activity".

Of the worst 10 districts in terms of school attendance rates, five are located in Bihar, four in Uttar Pradesh and one in Madhya Pradesh (Table 7). Even in the worst 10 districts, male school attendance is higher than female school attendance by about 7 per centage points.

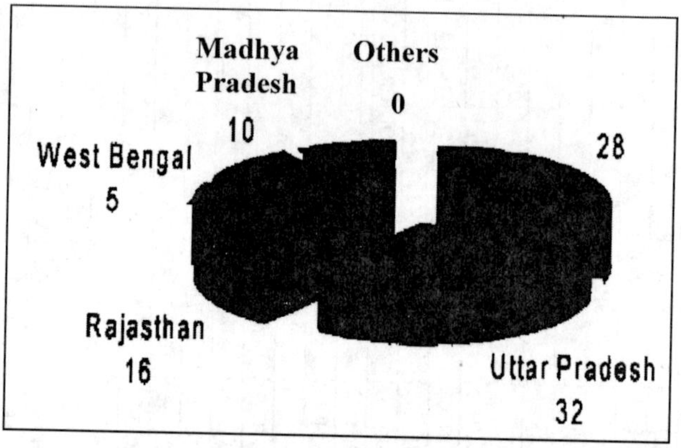

Figure 2: Distribution of Worst 100 Districts for Total School Attendance, 1991

In all the worst ten districts, where school attendance is very low, adult female literacy is also low (Table 7). Kishanganj, which has the lowest rate of school attendance (17.85 per cent), also has the lowest adult female literacy rate (11.5 per cent). It can be expected that an educated mother values education of her child more and has also a say in intra-household decision making process about whether children should be at school or at work. In the above districts, adult female literacy, which can be taken as a proxy for parental education, is very low and thus we also find correspondingly low rates of school attendance at the elementary level.

Work force participation by adult females can be an important factor influencing school attendance by children. Increased rates of work force participation by women could increase their bargaining power within the family. This could in turn increase their voice in the decision making process of the household including whether the children should be attending school or not. In the worst 10 districts under consideration, except for Jhabua, all the other districts show work force participation rates of adult women at less than 40 per cent, with Badaun, Rampur and Sitapur showing work force participation rates by adult women of less than 10 per cent. Another line of argument can be that in districts where the adult female work force participation rates are reasonably high, but school attendance rates are low, children are required to stay at home and tend to domestic work and siblings. This may be what is happening in the case of Jhabua, for instance, which shows low school

TABLE 7: School Attendance Rate (Total) ¯ Worst 10 Districts, 1991 (mapped across four parameters)

DISTRICT	*STATE*	*SCHOOL ATTENDANCE RATE (PER CENT)*			*ADULT FEMALE LITERACY RATE PER CENT)*	*ADULT FEMALE WORK-FORCE PARTICIPATION RATE (PER CENT)*	*SC POP. PER CENT**	*ST POP. PER CENT**
		TOTAL	*MALE*	*FEMALE*				
KISHANGANJ	BI	17.85	24.23	11.50	7.18	11.04	6.6	3.34
A RAN A	BI	20.72	27.01	13.92	10.8	25.78	3.7	1.29
BUDUAN	UP	20.99	27.25	12.79	10.64	5.99	17.3	0.0
RAMPUR	UP	21.60	27.33	14.88	12.93	9.32	13.0	0.0
JHABUA	MP	21.64	27.79	15.17	8.80	79.74	3.1	85.7
BAHRAICH	UP	23.43	31.19	13.73	8.36	27.18	16.46	0.34
MADHEPURA	BI	23.55	30.24	15.61	11.1	35.98	16.3	1.0
PURNIA	BI	23.96	29.73	17.54	13.47	29.33	12.5	4.4
SITAPUR	UP	24.46	30.40	17.37	13.87	7.28	32.2	0.01
SAHARSA	BI	25.51	32.26	15.21	11.53	36.94	15.5	0.3

* Taken as a proportion of district population

Source: Calculated from the Census of India 1991.

attendance rates (21.64 per cent) but has an adult female work force participation rate at 80 per cent (Table 7).

Caste and tribal status can also act as deterrent to a child's access to primary/elementary education. Lack of exposure and access to education could lead to low levels of school attendance by children belonging to these social groups. In Table 7 above, we see that in districts such as Jhabua (MP) and Sitapur (UP), the proportion of SC/ST population is high. This could explain the low rates of school attendance by children in these districts.

Comparison of school attendance rates for boys and girls in the worst 100 districts shows a clear disadvantage that the girl child faces in participation in the schooling process. The school attendance rates for girls in the worst 100 districts are well below the school attendance rates for boys. School attendance by the female child is the worst in Jalor district of Rajasthan (9 per hundred girls attend school as compared to 45 per hundred boys) (Appendix 1).

In India, the lack of importance for female education can be linked to deep- rooted aspects of gender relations. In rural areas particularly, three such links are observed (Dreze and Saran 1994). First, the gender division of labour reduces the perceived benefits of female education. A majority of the female children, more so in the rural areas, are expected to engage in activities such as domestic work, child rearing and family labour in agriculture. Given such expectations by their families, about their adult life, educating females seems a pointless exercise to their parents. Secondly, the norms of patri-local residence and village exogamy, prevalent in many parts of India, undermine any incentives of the family in educating the girl child as the final benefits of it would accrue to the family she eventually marries into. Finally, the persistent presence of the dowry system also makes educating the girl child a liability as it now becomes difficult to find a groom of similar or more qualifications than her.

Child Work Force Participation at the District Level

Work force participation rates for children, when ranked by the worst 100 districts bring out that Andhra Pradesh, Karnataka, Madhya Pradesh and

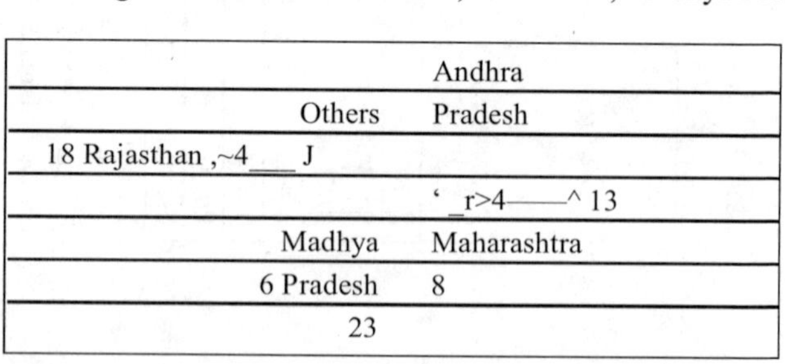

Figure 3: Distribution of Worst 100 Districts for Total Child Labour, 1991

Rajasthan have a large number of districts where child labour is concentrated (Appendix 4). Work force participation in the worst 100 districts varies from 25 children per 100 children in Jhabua to 8 children per hundred in Akola district of Maharashtra. For child work force participation rates, the difference between the male and female child is not much, approximately one per centage point.

Appendix 3: School Attendance Rate (per cent) - Total Census 1991

Rank	*State*	*District*	*Per Cent Of School Attendance*		
		Best 50 District	*Total*	*Male*	*Female*
1.	KER	ERNAKULAM	89.67	89.81	89.52
2.	KER	PATHANAMTHIl lA	88.72	88.72	88.72
3.	KER	ALAPPUZHA	88.66	88.27	89.06
4.	KER	KOriAYAM	88.40	88.13	88.66
5.	KER	THRISSUR	88.10	87.87	88.32
6.	KER	KOLLAM	86.98	86.49	87.48
7.	KER	KOZHIKODE	85.55	85.24	85.87
8.	KER	KANNUR	85.34	85.44	85.23
9.	KER	TRIVANDRUM	85.13	84.97	85.29
10.	KER	PALAKKAD	83.93	84.50	83.36
11.	UP	HAMIRPUR	83.22	46.04	24.53
12.	KER	IDUKKI	83.15	83.35	82.96
13.	TN	KANNIYAKUMARI	82.20	82.25	82.14
14.	KER	MALAPPURAM	81.97	81.90	82.03
15.	HP	BILASPUR	80.92	83.81	77.87
16.	KER	WAYANAD	80.61	80.65	80.56
17.	KER	KASARAGOD	79.72	80.80	78.65
18.	TN	MADRAS	78.58	71.04	68.07
19.	HP	KANGRA	78.28	80.53	75.96
20.	MAH	GREATER BOMBAY	76.53	77.79	75.17
21.	MAH	SINDHUDURG	76.40	77.58	75.16
22.	TN	NILGIRI	75.94	77.04	74.86
23.	HP	UNA	75.85	78.05	73.52
24.	PUNJ	JALANDHAR	74.53	75.11	73.88
25.	HP	MANDI	74.43	79.14	69.60
26.	KAR	DAKSHIN KANNAD	74.33	77.60	71.07
27.	TN	THANJAVUR	73.68	76.60	70.68
28.	HP	KINNAUR	73.54	76.52	70.46
29.	TN	CHIDAMBARANAR	73.31	75.94	70.56
30.	HP	SHIMLA	73.07	76.81	69.18
31.	TN	PASUMPON THEVAR THIRUMAGAN	72.96	77.15	68.62
32.	HAR	REWARI	72.85	76.35	68.92
33.	MAH	PUNE	72.66	75.95	69.19
34.	PUNJ	HOS'HIARPUR	72.64	73.76	71.41
35.	TN	CHENGAI-ANNA	72.58	76.10	68.89

(Contd...)

36.	MAH	NAGPUR	72.12	72.64	71.57
37.	KAR	BANGALORE	72.10	73.65	70.53
38.	MAH	SATARA	71.74	76.26	66.91
39.	MAH	KOLHAPUR	71.67	49.31	20.09
40.	MAH	WARDHA	71.61	71.42	71.80
41.	TN	PUDUKKOTTAI	71.58	77.04	65.98
42.	TN	MADURAI	71.44	74.87	67.82
43.	HP	SOLAN	71.44	75.85	66.75
44.	TN	TIRUNELVELI KATTABOMMAN	71.40	75.61	66.99
45.	TN	COIMBATORE	71.22	73.42	68.99
46.	MAH	BHANDARA	70.84	73.01	68.60
47.	MAH	SANGLI	70.30	72.75	67.71
48.	TN	TIRUCHCHIRAPPALLI	70.17	74.26	65.86
49.	TN	NORTH ARCOT-AMBEDKER	69.81	73.14	66.47
50.	TN	RAMANATHAPURAM	69.72	73.67	65.73

Source: Calculated from the Census of India, 1991, C-4 Tables - "Population (ages 5-19) by single years of age, school, attendance and economic activity."

Appendix 4: Child Work Force Participation Rates (per cent) (5-14 Years)

Census 1991

Rank	*State*	*District*	*CHLAB Per cent*		
		Worst 100 Districts	*Total*	*Male*	*Female*
1.	MP	JHABUA	25.52	23.38	27.77
2.	MP	BASTAR	17.68	16.29	19.09
3.	KAR	BELLARY	15.81	14.83	16.83
4.	AP	MAHBUBNAGAR	14.64	14.00	15.32
5.	AP	KURNOOL	14.05	13.10	15.07
6.	MP	BETUL	13.84	13.28	14.40
7.	KAR	RAICHUR	13.81	13.40	14.24
8.	OR	KORAPUT	12.69	13.14	12.23
9.	MP	WEST NIMAR	12.64	12.24	13.07
10.	AP	VIZIANAGARAM	12.55	12.27	12.84
11.	OR	KALAHANDI	12.54	14.45	10.68
12.	MP	RATLAM	12.14	11.13	13.2!
13.	AP	GUNTUR	11.95	10.39	13.60
14.	AP	KARIMNAGAR	11.74	8.24	15.38
15.	AP	KHAMMAM	11.41	10.90	11.96
16.	MP	DHAR	11.35	10.06	12.71
17.	BIH	GUMLA	1 1.34	10.80	11.88
18.	AP	NIZAMABAD	11.33	9.30	13.47
19.	KAR	GULBARGA	11.26	11.75	10.76
20.	MP	RAJNANDGAON	11.24	8.55	14.03
21.	AP	ANANTPUR	11.20	10.78	11.64
22.	MP	RAJGARH	11.19	10.69	11.73

(Contd...)

23.	MP	SURGUJA	11.13	10.73	11.55
24.	MAH	NANDED	11.,08	9.46	12.83
25.	AP	MEDAK	10.93	10.36	11.53
26.	AP	SRIKAKULAM	10.78	9.58	12.04
27.	MP	SEONI	10.74	10.09	11.40
28.	KAR	TUMKUR	10.70	10.09	11,32
29.	MP	EAST NIMAR	10.63	10.40	10.89
30.	KAR	DHARWAD	10.61	10.42	10.82
31.	ARP	TAWANG	10.60	9.78	11.40
32.	AP	PRAKASAM	10.54	8.50	12.72
33.	MP	CHHINDWARA	10.46	10.00	10.94
34.	KAR	KOLAR	10.44	9.67	1 1.21
35.	MAH	JALNA	10.42	8 19	12.82
36.	AP	WARANGAL	10.40	8.81	12.08
37.	MP	MANDLA	10.33	8.33	12.45
38.	MAH	PARBHANI	10.16	8.43	12.05
39.	AP	NALGONDA	10.10	9.03	11.22
40.	RAJ	JHALAWAR	10.07	7.85	9.31
41.	RAJ	BARMER	10.00	7.75	12.56
42.	KAR	CHITRADURGA	9.97	9.62	10.33
43.	RAJ	BANSWARA	9.93	8.05	11.90
44.	MAH	GADCHIROLI	9.90	8.48	11.36
45.	AP	ADILABAD	9.87	8.61	11.20
46.	AP	WEST GODAVARI	9.83	11.07	8.57
47.	MP	RAIGARH	9.75	9.19	10.31
48.	RAJ	CHITTAURGARH	9.73	7.61	11.99
49.	MAH	BID	9.56	7.63	11.66
50.	AS	DHEMAJI	9.56	8.54	10.60
51.	KAR	BIJAPUR	9.52	9.20	9.86
52.	OR	PHULABANI	9.49	8.30	10.69
53.	RAJ	BHILWARA	9.47	7.53	11.55
54.	MP	MANDSAUR	9.28	7.33	11.30
55.	MAH	YAVATMAL	9.22	7.49	11.05
56.	AP	KRISHNA	9.21	9.06	9.37
57.	AP	NELLORE	9.13	8.68	9.59
58.	MAH	DHULE	9.02	8.13	9.97
59.	BIH	KISHANGANJ	9.01	15.80	2.26
60.	AP	VISHAKHAPATNAM	8.94	8.69	9.20
61.	MAH	BULDANA	8.91	6.29	11.69
62.	TN	DINDIGUL-QUAID-E-MILLETH	8.89	5.96	6.81
63.	KAR	MANDYA	8.74	9.84	7.65
64.	KAR	BANGALORE RURAL	8.58	8.71	8.46
65.	TN	PERIYAR	8.55	8.18	8.95
66.	RAJ	JHUNJHUNUN	8.54	2.89	5.61
67.	RAJ	CHURU	8.52	6.60	10.63
68.	OR	BALANGIR	8.52	9.87	7.15

(Contd...)

69.	MP	SIDHI	8.50	7.61	9.46
70.	MP	CHHATARPUR	8.48	9.30	7.51
71.	GUJ	BHAVNAGAR	8.43	9.18	7.62
72.	KAR	BELGAUM	8.39	8.39	8.39
73.	MP	SHAJAPUR	8.37	8.29	8.47
74.	UP	BANDA	8.32	7.96	8.76
75.	GUJ	PANCH MAHALS	8.32	5.70	11.01
76.	AP	CHiriOOR	8.30	7.73	8.93
77.	HAR	HASSAN	8.30	8.06	8.53
78.	KAR	HASSAN	8.30	8.06	8.53
79.	OR	GANJAM	8.09	7.97	8.21
80.	TN	DHARMAPURI	8.09	7.88	8.30
81.	MP	SHIVPURI	7.97	8.44	7.40
82.	GUJ	THE DANGS	7.95	6.60	9.44
83.	MP	SHAHDOL	7 94	'7.55	8.35
84.	RAJ	DUNGARPUR	7.93	6.27	9.66
85.	MP	PANNA	7.92	8.40	7.39
86.	BIH	DUMKA	7.86	7.63	8.10
87.	AP	CUDAPPAH	7.85	6.77	9.02
88.	ARP	CUDDAPAH	7.85	6.77	9.02
89.	WB	MALDAH	7.84	9.50	6.07
90.	AP	RANGAREDDI	7.78	9.19	7.35
91.	MP	TIKAMGARH	7.75	8.24	7.18
92.	OR	SAMBALPUR	7.75	7.58	7.92
93.	RAJ	TONK	7.69	6.35	9.15
94.	RAJ	SIROHI	7.68	6.03	7.49
95.	ARP	CHANGLANG	7.65	6.22	9.17
96.	GUJ	BAN AS KANTHA	7.62	9.23	8.05
97.	KAR	MYSORE	7.60	9.83	5.35
98.	WB	WEST DINAJPUR	7.59	11.30	3.73
99.	MP	RAIPUR	7.58	6.59	8.60
100.	RAJ	AJMER	7.57	5.76	9.60

Source: Calculated from the Census of India, 1991, B(l) Series - "Main workers, marginal workers, non-workers and those non-workers seeking/available for work classified by age and sex.

When we narrow down our attention to the worst 10 districts, it is found that four districts are in Madhya Pradesh, three in Andhra Pradesh, and one each in Karnataka and Orissa (Table 8). In all these 10 worst performing districts, work force participation by the children lies in the range 25 to 12 per hundred children. What is interesting is that there is not much difference between male and female child work force participation rates in these districts.

Parental literacy, as proxied by adult literacy here, can be expected to have a negative relationship with child labour. Educated parents, and more so, an educated mother can be expected to know the importance of basic education and thus send her children to school provided the intra-familial decision making process is within her control. All the districts listed in the worst 10 listed above for child labour show adult female literacy rates of less than 25 per cent i.e., less than a fourth of women in these districts are literate, with adult female literacy rates as low as 9 per cent in Jhabua (MP) and 10 per cent in Koraput (Orissa) (Table 8). Low rates of adult female literacy in these districts could be contributing towards the high rates of work force participation by children here.

Table 8: Child Work Force Participation Rate - Worst 10 Districts, 1991 (Mapped Across Four Parameters)

District		*Child Work Force Participation Rate (per cent)*			*Adult Female Literacy Rate (per cent)*	*Adult Female Work Force Participation Rate (per cent)*	*SC&ST Population per cent*	
		Total	*Male*	*Female*			*SC*	*ST*
Jhabua	MP	25.52	23.38	27.77	8.80	79.74	3.06	86
Bastar	MP	17.68	16.29	19.09	10.74	71.82	5.9	67
Bellary	Kar	15.81	14.83	16.83	25.62	53.28	19.3	8.8
Mehbubnagar	AP	14.64	14.00	15.32	12.42	68.09	17.6	7.4
Kumool	AP	14.05	13.10	15.07	20.03	56.00	17.4	2
Betul	MP	13.84	13.28	14.40	25.38	61.71	10.8	38
Raichur	Kar	13.81	13.40	14.24	16.85	53.04	17.2	7.8
Koraput	Or	12.69	13.14	12.23	9.88	55.58	15.0	54
WestNimar	MP	12.64	12.24	13.07	17.17	61.62	9.76	46.2
Vizanagaram	AP	12.55	12.27	12.84	15.95	58.39	10.44	9.0

Source: Taken as a proportion of district population Calculated from the Census of India 1991.

In the above 10 districts, where child work force participation rates are high, adult female work force participation rates are also high. Although one would expect *a priori* that work force participation by women would give them higher bargaining power in the household, thus enabling them to keep children out of the work force and in school, it has also been shown that higher work force participation by women leads to higher rates of child work force participation by male and female children (Jayachandran 1997). Since ail of the worst 10 districts listed above show reasonably high rates of adult female work force participation, alongwith high rates of male child labour, this suggests a complementarity between the two. The children could be accompanying the mother to work, for instance, and complementing her activities at the work place, for example, doing small finishing jobs at the tailor shop where the mother works, plucking leaves in tea plantations for a lower wage etc. Common demand factors and fewer restrictions on the gender division of labour in certain regions, both for adults and children, could be the possible reason for such a complementarity.

Social factors such as caste and tribal status could lead towards higher rates of work force participation by children. In these categories of households, poor economic conditions could lead to children having to participate in the work process and contribute towards the family income. Table 8 shows that in

Bellarv, Mehbubnagar, Raichur and Kurnool, close to a fifth of the district population belongs to the scheduled caste category. Jhabua, Bastar, Koraput, West Nimar and Betul show high proportion of tribal population, Jhabua having 86 per cent of the district population as tribals. The prevalence of such proportions of scheduled caste and tribal population in these districts could be another reason for the high rates of work force participation by children in these districts.

The worst 100 districts, where female child work force participation rates are high, are concentrated in the states of Andhra Pradesh, Madhya Pradesh, Rajasthan, Maharashtra and Karnataka (Appendix 4). Female child work force participation rates vary from 23 per hundred in Jhabua to 10 per hundred in Ajmer in Rajasthan. It needs to be pointed out here that in the definition of work adopted by the Census, domestic work is not included. This leads to enormous under-reporting of work by children in general and female children in particular as the latter are involved in domestic work in larger proportions. Any productive work on the family fields is included in the enumeration of workers, and here one could expect male children to be employed in larger proportions so that they get counted as part of the work process.

"Unaccounted Children" in the Worst Districts

Given the above discussed patterns in school attendance and child work force participation in the worst 100 districts of the country, it becomes necessary to put focus on the large pool of unaccounted children in the country.

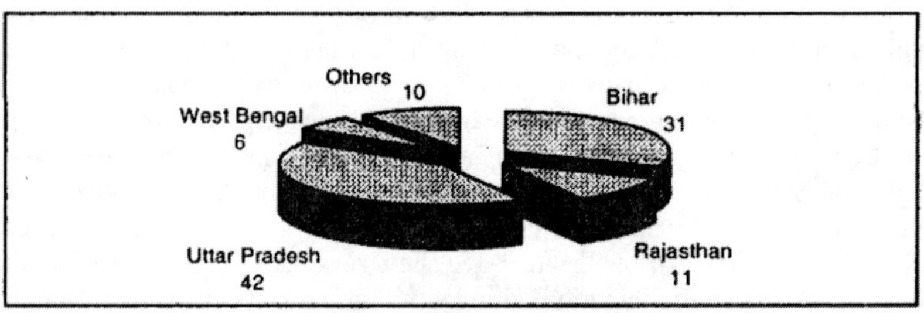

Figure 4: Distribution of the Worst 100 Districts for "Unaccounted Children" (Male & Female, 5-14 years), 1991

Districts with the highest per centage of "unaccounted children" are concentrated in Uttar Pradesh, Bihar and Rajasthan (Appendix 7). These are also the states where school attendance rates are low. This is an important insight for policy formulations because it implies that school attendance and child work force participation are not two sides of the same coin. It is thus not true that if children are not attending school, they must be at work, because there exists this large pool of unaccounted children as well which needs to be explained. At the same time, the high proportions of unaccounted children could be because of the Census' definition of work which does not include, for example, domestic work, children employed in cottage industries, children employed as domestic help for the middle class, children working in wayside stalls, etc. Policy efforts aimed at reducing child labour and enhancing school attendance at the elementary level need to take this into account.

TABLE 9: "Unaccounted Children"(Male+Female), Worst 10 Districts, 1991

	State	*District*	*Percentage of "Unaccounted Children" (Males+Females)*
1.	Uttar Pradesh	Badaun	74.18
2.	Bihar	Kishanganj	73.21
3.	Uttar Pradesh	Rampur	72.88
4.	Bihar	Araria	72.79
5.	Uttar Pradesh	Moradabad	71.55
6.	Uttar Pradesh	Sitapur	71.46
7.	Bihar	Sitamarhi	71.41
8.	Bihar	Purba Champaran	71.16
9.	Uttar Pradesh	Kheri	70.30
10.	Uttar Pradesh	Pilibhit	70.00

Source: Calculated from the Census of India, 1991.

Analysis of Best 50 districts

The best performing districts on school attendance, for male and female children, are concentrated in Kerala, Tamil Nadu, Himachal Pradesh and Maharashtra (Appendix 3). These states also exhibit high adult literacy rates for males and females. Since these districts show the highest rates of school attendance, one would expect that the per centage of child work force participation and 'nowhere' children would be the lowest for these districts. The figures derived from the Census data, for child labour and unaccounted children confirms this *a priori* expectation.

Attention needs to be drawn to the fact that in the 50 best performing districts for total school attendance, with the exception of Garhwal, no district in the worst performing states figures among the best performers in total school attendance. In Uttar Pradesh, which has a large number of the worst performing districts in school attendance, there are also districts such as Tehri Garhwal, Uttar Kashi, Dehradun, Pithoragarh, Garhwal and Almora which are among the best performers in urban school attendance. These are also areas where the adult female work force participation rate is relatively high. Kerala has the lowest rates of child labour and all its districts constitute the top bracket of the best 50 list (Appendix 6). High adult literacy rates here contribute to low rates of child labour.

Appendix 5: Child Labour (5-14 Years, %) in Rural and Urban Areas Census 1991

Worst 100 district - rural areas				*Worst 100 district - urban areas*			
Rank	***State***	***District***	***Rural***	***Rank***	***State***	***District***	***Urban***
1.	MP	**JHABUA**	27.32	1.	KAR	BANGALORERURAL	6.89
2.	KAR	BELLARY	19.37	2.	TN	KAMARAJAR	6.59
3.	MP	BASTAR	18.79	3.	KAR	BELLARY	6.59
4.	AP	KURNOOL	17.19	4.	TN	SALEM	6.49
5.	MP	BETUL	16.79	5.	MAH	GADCHIROLI	6.40
6.	MP	RATLAM	16.47	6.	BIH	MADHEPURA	5.58
7.	KAR	RAICHUR	16.13	7.	WB	MURSHIDABAD	5.49
8.	AP	MEHBUBNAGAR	16.01	8.	AP	KURNOOL	5.12
9.	AP	GUNTUR	14.87	9.	AP	WEST GODAVARI	4.83
10.	AP	VIZIANAGARAM	14.40	10.	UP	JALAUN	4.81
11.	AP	KARIMNAGAR	14.27	11.	KAR	RAICHUR	4.73
12.	MP	WEST NIMAR	14.16	12.	AS	DHEMA.II	4.71
13.	OR	KORAPUT	14.00	13.	AP	GUNTUR	4.71
14.	KAR	GULBARGA	13.99	14.	AP	SRIKAKULAM	4.65
15.	KAR	DHARWAD	13.81	15.	TN	PERIYAR	4.56
16.	AP	KHAMMAM	13.77	16.	AS	KAMRUP	4.50
17.	MP	EAST NIMAR	13.66	17.	MP	JHABUA	4.44
18.	AP	VISHAKHA-PATNAM	13.63	18.	KAR	DHARWAD	4.27
19.	AP	NIZAMABAD	13.51	19.	KAR	TUMKUR	4.16
20.	MAH	NANDED	13.29	20.	AS	GOALPARA	4.13
21.	AP	ANATPUR	13.28	21.	AP	MAHBUBNAGAR	4.12
22.	OR	KALAHANDI	13.21	22.	AP	ANANTPUR	4.12
23.	MP	RAJGARH	12.91	23.	KAR	CHITRADURGA	3.93
24.	MP	CHHINDWARA	12.87	24.	AS	GOLAGHAT	3.90
25.	MP	RAJNANDGAON	12.85	25.	AP	NELLORE	3.89
26.	MP	SURGUJA	12.72	26.	AP	KRISHNA	3.86
27.	MAH	PARBHANI	12.62	27.	TN	COIMBATORE	3.86
28.	MP	DHAR	12.52	28.	AP	PRAKASAM	3.81
29.	KAR	KOLAR	12.50	29.	AP	VIZIANAGARAM	3.80
30.	AP	MEDAK	12.43	30.	UP	AZAMGARH	3.79
31.	AP	ADILABADAB	12.39	31.	UP	RAMPUR	3.74
32.	AP	WARANGAL	12.32	32.	ARP	WEST KAMENG	3.72
33.	AP	RANGAREDDI	12.23	33.	KAR	MANDYA	3.69
34.	AP	KRISHNA	12.16	34.	UP	BAHRAICH	3.64
35.	KAR	CHITRADURGA	12.14	35.	MP	TIKAMGARH	3.56
36.	MAH	JALNA	12.11	36.	KAR	KOLAR	3.5?
37.	KAR	TUMKUR	11.96	37.	AS	SONITPUR	3.50
38.	AP	PRAKASAM	11.79	38.	UP	VARANASI	3.47
39.	BIH	GUMLA	11.75	39.	AP	CUDDAPAH	3.46
40.	AP	SRIKAKULAM	11.63	40.	TN	DHARMAPURI	3.44
41.	MP	SEONI	11.61	41.	UP	ALMORA	3,41
42.	RAJ	AJMER	11.44	42.	UP	MUZAFFARNAGAR	3.35
43.	KAR	BIJAPUR	11.43	43.	KAR	DAKSHINAKANNADA	3.33
44.	RAJ	CHIHAURGARH	11.28	44.	AP	EAST GODAVARI	3.29

(Contd...)

45.	MAH	BID	11.26	45.	IN	TIRUNELVELI KATTABOMMAN	3.26
46.	RAJ	BHILWARA	11.22	46.	IIAR	GURGAON	3.24
47.	MP	MANDSAUR	11.18	47.	AP	NIZAMABAD	3.2)
48.	AP	NALGONDA	11.17	48.	UP	BASTI	3.21
49.	MP	MANDLA	11.12	49.	UP	MORADABAD	3.20
50.	AP	WEST GODAVARI	11.11	50.	AS	NALBARI	3.19
51.	GUJ	BHAVNAGAR	11.07	51.	MAH	NANDED	3.17
52.	RAJ	CHURU	11.04	52.	KAR	KODAGU	3.17
53.	MAH	DHULE	10.92	53.	UP	FARRUKHABAD	3.16
54.	RAJ	BARMER	10.82	54.	BIH	KISHANGANJ	3.15
55.	MAH	YAVATMAL	10.78	55.	MP	WESTNIMAR	3.14
56.	AP	NELLORE	10.65	56.	BIH	PASHCHIMCHAMPARAN	3.14
57.	RAJ	BANSWARA	10.64	57.	KAR	BANGALORE	3.13
58.	ARP	TAWANG	10.60	58.	KAR	BIJAPUR	3.11
59.	RAJ	JALOR	10.59	59.	AP	KARIMNAGAR	3.11
60.	MAH	BULDANA	10.56	60.	GUJ	BHAVNAGAR	3.10
61.	MP	RAIGARH	10.55	61.	UP	BARABANKI	3.09
62.	TN	KAMARAJAR	10,17	62.	RAJ	TONK	3.06
63.	KAR	BELGAUM	10.10	63.	BIH	GUMLA	3.03
64.	RAJ	BIKANER	10.05	64.	UP	BANDA	3.01
65.	TN	PERIYAR	9.97	65.	OR	KALAHANDI	3.00
66.	UP	NAINITAL	9.95	66.	KAR	MYSORE	3.00
67.	OR	PHULABANI	9.94	67.	HAR	HASSAN	2.98
68.	MAH	AMRAVATI	9.94	68.	KAR	HASSAN	2.98
69.	RAJ	JHALAWAR	9.85	69.	ARP	East SIAng	2.96
70.	MP	SHAHDOL	9.84	70.	AS	SIBSAGAR	2.95
71.	MAH	AKOLA	9.80	71.	AP	CHITTOOR	2.91
72.	MP	CHHATARPUR	9.78	72.	UP	BULANDSHAHR	2.89
73.	KAR	MANDYA	9.72	73.	KAR	CHIKMAGALUR	2.86
74.	MP	UJJAIN	9.70	74.	UP	BUDAUN	2.86
75.	BIH	KISHANGANJ	9.66	75.	UP	MIRZAPUR	2.86
76.	AS	DHEMAJI	9.64	76.	KAR	SHIMOGA	2.84
77.	MP	SHAJAPUR	9.62	77.	UP	SHAHJAHANPUR	2,81
78.	AP	CHITTOR	9.58	78.	MP	RAJGARH	2.80
79.	BIH	RANCHI	9.56	79.	MP	DHAR	2,79
80.	MAH	NASHIK	9.51	80.	RAJ	JALOR	2.79
81.	KAR	HASSAN	9.42	81.	AS	MARIGAON	2.77
82.	KAR	HASSAN	9.42	82.	MP	CHHATARPUR	2.75
83.	KAR	MYSORE	9.40	83.	WB	JALPAIGURI	2.73
84.	MAH	AURANGABAD	9.29	84.	WB	KOCH BIHAR	2.72
85.	AP	CUDDAPAH	9.20	85.	AS	DARRANG	2,72
86.	OR	BALANGIR	9.17	86.	GUJ	SURAT	2.71
87.	MP	SHIVPURI	9.10	87.	MAH	SOLAPUR	2.70
88.	UP	BANDA	9.07	88.	RAJ	PALI	2.69
89.	GUJ	VADODARA	8.99	89.	TN	MADURAI	2.67
90.	OR	GANJAM	8.99	90.	BIH	SAHARSA	2.66
91.	OR	SAMBALPUR	8.97	91.	GUJ	AMRELI	2.66
92.	KAR	BANGALORE RURAL	8.97	92.	UP	MAU	2.63

(*Contd...*)

93	MP	SIDHI	8.95	93	AS	BONGAIGAON	2.63
94	GUJ	PANCH MAHALS	8.94	94	OR	GANJAM	2,62
95	RAJ	SIROHI	8.90	95	UP	BIJNOR	2.61
96	RAJ	TONK	8.81	96	UP	SAHARANPUR	2.59
97	GUJ	THE DANGS	8.80	97	MP	MANDSAUR	2.59
98	MP	RAIPUR	8.75	98	UP	BAREILLY	2.58
99	MP	PANNA	8.75	99	AS	LAKHIMPUR	2.53
100	BIH	PASHCHIMI SINGHBHUM	8.66	100	MP	RAIPUR	2.53

Source: Calculated from the Census of India, 1991, B(l) Series - "Main workers, marginal workers, non-workers and those non-workers seeking/available for work classified by age and sex.

Appendix 6: Child Labour (Per cent) (5-14 Years) Census 1991

Rank	*State*	*District*	*Per cent School Attendance*		
		Best 50 Districts	*Total*	*Male*	*Female*
1	KER	KOZHIKODE	0.29	0.36	0.20
2.	KER	KANNUR	0.31	0.29	0.33
3.	KER	ALAPPUZHA	0.32	0.29	0.35
4.	KER	PATHANAMTHITTA	0.34	0.42	0.25
5.	KER	KOI lAYAM	0,36	0.47	0.25
6.	KER	MALAPPURAM	0.37	0.49	0.23
7.	KER	KOLLAM	0.53	0.63	0.43
8.	KER	ERNAKULAM	0.63	0.82	0.43
9.	KER	TRIVANDRUM	0.66	0.69	0.62
10.	KER	IDUKKI	0.66	0.68	0.65
11.	KER	THRISSUR	0.76	0.92	0.61
12.	HAR	GURGAON	0.82	2.74	2.89
13.	KER	PALAKKAD	1.11	1.15	1.06
14.	KER	WAYANAD	1.12	1.18	1.06
15.	HAR	REWARI	1.12	1.08	1.17
16.	PUNJ	GURDASPUR	1.19	3.21	0.48
17.	UP	KANPUR (NAGAR)	1.24	2,11	0.24
18.	OR	CUTTACK	1.24	1.83	0.62
19.	TN	NILGIRI	1.25	1.27	1.22
20.	HAR	MAHENDRAGARH	1.25	1.20	2.01
21.	KER	KASARAGOD	1.26	0.87	1.65
22.	BIH	DHANBAD	1.26	1.63	0.86
23.	TN	KAMARAJAR	1.33	6.92	10.97
24.	MAH	GREATER BOMBAY	1.38	1.93	0.78
25.	PUNJ	RUPNAGAR	1.39	2.09	0.60
26.	TN	KANNIYAKUMARI	1.41	1.54	1.13
27.	GUJ	GANDHINAGAR	1.44	1.44	1.44
28.	UP	MAINPURI	1.59	2.64	0.29
29.	HAR	AMBALA	1.60	2.58	0.51
30.	HAR	YAMUNANAGAR	1.63	2.61	0.54

(Contd...)

31.	HAR	ROHTAK	1.66	1.99	1.29
32.	HAR	SONIPAT	1.69	2.02	1,30
33.	MP	BHIND	1.69	2.64	0,46
34.	PUNJ	HOSHIARPUR	1.72	1.74	0.57
35.	HAR	FARIDABAD	1,75	2.05	1.40
36.	PUNJ	KAPURTHALA	1.77	3.72	1.27
37.	BIH	BHOJPUR	1,78	2.45	0.97
38.	UP	ETAWAH	1.81	3.13	0.26
39.	BIH	SARAN	1.83	2.80	0.75
40.	AP	HYDERABAD	1.89	2.96	0,77
41.	PUNJ	GANG AN AGAR	1.94	7.43	6.18
42.	OR	BALESHWAR	2.01	2.90	1.10
43.	HAR	KURUKSHETRA	2.06	3.25	0.69
44.	UP	GORAKHPUR	2.07	2.42	1.68
45.	UP	KANPUR (DEHAT)	2.14	3.42	0.70
46.	BIH	SIWAN	2.15	3.02	1.23
47.	UP	FIROZABAD	2.16	3.58	0.38
48.	BIH	JEHANABAD	2.21	2.59	1.79
49.	BIH	AURANGABAD	2.22	2.76	1.62
50.	WB	HAORA	2.24	3.73	0.71

Source: Calculated from the Census of India, 1991, B(l) Series - "Main workers, marginal workers, non-workers and those non-workers seeking/available for work classified by age and sex.

Appendix 7: Unaccounted Children (Per cent) (5-14 Years)

Worst 100 Districts - Ranked by Percentage of Unaccounted Children Census 1991

Rank	*State*	*District*	*Per cent Unaccounted Children*		
		Worst 100 Districts	*Total*	*Male*	*Female*
1.	UP	BUDAUN	74.18	64.86	86.38
2.	BIH	KISHANGANJ	73.21	60.10	86.25
3.	UP	RAMPUR	72.88	63.75	83.59
4.	BIH	ARARIA	72.79	63.69	82,67
5.	UP	MORADABAD	71.55	63 13	81.20
6.	UP	SITAPUR	71.46	62.71	81.90
7.	BIH	SITAMARHI	71.41	62.66	82,20
8.	BIH	PURBA CHAMPARAN	71.16	61.99	82.08
9.	UP	KHERI	70.30	59.68	82,91
10.	UP	PILIBHIT	70.00	60.37	81.39
11.	UP	BAHRAICH	69.77	59.43	82,69
12.	UP	BAREILLY	69.70	61.39	79.58
13.	BIH	SAHARSA	69.59	61.24	79.60
14.	BIH	PURNIA	69.27	61.07	78.38
15.	BIH	KATIHAR	69.20	60.02	79.21
16.	BIH	MADHEPURA	69.18	61.32	78,50
17.	UP	SHAHJAHANPUR	68.98	59.14	80.96
18.	UP	GONDA	68.55	58.33	80.90

(Contd...)

19	UP	SIDDHARTHNAGAR	68.05	57.53	80.29
20	BIH	KHAGARIA	67.98	60.51	77.10
21	BIH	PASHCHIM CHAMPARAN	67.94	58.60	78.89
22	BIH	SAHIBGANJ	67.77	63.07	72.89
23	UP	MAHARAJGANJ	67.63	55.42	81.27
24	UP	BARABANKI	67.12	58.40	77.17
25	BIH	PALAMU	66.41	57.00	76.67
26	UP	LALITPUR	66.36	57.71	76.60
27	UP	HARDOI	65.98	56.17	78.29
28	UP	BASTI	65.86	55.64	77.15
29	BIH	MADHUBANI	65.36	54.76	77.54
30	BIH	DARBHANGA	65,08	56.20	75.65
31	RAJ	BANSWARA	64.88	58.22	71.85
32	RAJ	BARMER	64.76	54.16	76.86
33	BIH	GOPALGANJ	64.57	53.09	77.40
34	BIH	MUZAFFARPUR	64.11	56.39	73.21
35	BIH	BEGUSARAI	63.88	56.64	72,49
36	BIH	SAMASTIPUR	63.81	55.20	73.89
37	UP	SONBHADRA	63.31	55.63	72,05
38	WB	MALDAH	63.14	57.96	68.67
39	BIH	GODDA	62.92	54.54	72.21
40	BIH	BHAGALPUR	62.55	55.62	70.78
41	WB	MURSHIDABAD	62.54	58,17	67.14
42	RAJ	JALOR	62.51	48.37	78.47
43	BIH	GIRIDIH	62.25	51.24	74.17
44	BIH	NAWADA	62.13	52.11	73.30
45	BIH	DUMKA	62.11	54.85	69.80
46	RAJ	DHOLPUR	62.04	49.32	79.06
47	RAJ	JAISALMER	62.03	48.51	78.18
48	UP	ETAH	61.97	52.80	73,78
49	UP	BIJNOR	61.90	52.78	72,45
50	BIH	GAYA	61.88	53.29	71.55
51	Ar.P	TIRAP	61.73	57.09	66.94
52	WB	WEST DINAJPUR	61.66	54.74	68,86
53	MP	GUNA	61.64	52.15	72,64
54	BIH	DEOGHAR	61.60	50.75	73.67
55	UP	MIRZAPUR	61.44	51.43	73.03
56	AS	DHUBRI	61,31	53.63	69.38
57	UP	GORAKHPUR	61.22	51.89	71.45
58	BIH	MUNGER	60.90	52.56	70.85
59	UP	AGRA	60.65	51.95	70.81
60	BIH	SIWAN	60.65	48.90	73.20
61	UP	BANDA	60.34	50.53	72.32
62	MP	SHIVPURI	60.20	50.83	71.26
63	UP	GHAZIPUR	60.14	50.74	70.39
64	UP	JAUNPUR	60.14	49.38	71.85
65	RAJ	BUNDI	60.12	48.45	73.64

(Contd...)

66	RAJ	DUNGARPUR	59.85	50.75	69.34
67	BIH	SARAN	59.85	49.08	71.94
68	UP	UNNAO	59.85	50.98	70.01
69	UP	FARRUKHABAD	59.44	53.18	66.89
70	UP	DEORIA	59.38	48.19	71.48
71	UP	ALIGARH	59.35	51.27	68.99
72	RAJ	SAWAI MADHOPUR	59.31	46.67	74.84
73	UP	HAMIRPUR	59.28	49.44	71.38
74	MP	SIDHI	59.03	48.60	70.36
75	UP	ALLAHABAD	58.98	49.08	70.24
76	OR	KORAPUT	58.93	51.38	66.74
77	RAJ	JHALAWAR	58.88	48,28	70.89
78	AS	KOKRAJHAR	58.83	53.68	64,09
79	RAJ	NAGAUR	58.82	45.71	73.38
80	BIH	HAZARIBAG	58.82	48.57	69.90
81	UP	SAHARANPUR	58.73	49.85	69.09
82	UP	AZAMGARH	58.61	48.31	69.74
83	BIH	VAISHALI	58.28	48.72	69.47
34	WB	KOCH BIHAR	58.22	52.88	63.82
85	WB	JALPAIGURI	58.07	52.08	64.38
86	UP	SULTANPUR	57.89	47.21	69.97
87	UP	FAIZABAD	57.85	49.00	67.50
88	UP	BULANDSHAHR	57.65	47.60	69.54
89	WB	BIRBHUM	57.47	50.79	64.50
90	UP	BALLIA	57.46	48.67	67.75
91	UP	RAE BARELI	57.45	47.95	67.95
92	UP	PRATAPGARH	57.43	46.64	69.57
93	Ar. P.	TAWANG	57.27	52.87	61.52
94	MP	PANNA	57.04	50.44	64.43
95	UP	VARANASI	57.03	47.52	67.73
96	BIH	BHOJPUR	56.96	46.15	69.98
97	UP	MATHURA	56.92	44.94	71.80
98	AS	BARPETA	56.46	50.52	62.68
99	UP	FIROZABAD	56.30	.47.97	66.70
100	RAJ	JODHPUR	56.23	45.38	68.44

Source: Calculated from the Census of India, 1991, C-4 Tables - "Population (ages 5-19) by single years of age, school, attendance and economic activity."

Some Associations - Scatter Diagrams

To study the relationship between child labour and school attendance on the one hand, and the other four parameters viz., adult female literacy, adult female work force participation, caste and tribal proportions in the district on the other, scatter diagrams were made for the complete set of districts, for the major states. Meaningful associations that emerged are presented below.

Appendix 8: Unaccounted Children in Rural & Urban Areas (Per cent) (5-14 Years) Census 1991

Worst 100 Districts - Rural Areas				*Worst 100 Districts - Urban Areas*			
Rank	***State***	***District***	***Rural***	***Rank***	***State***	***District***	***Urban***
1.	UP	BUDAUN	76.80	1	UP	BUDAUN	62.60
2.	UP	RAMPUR	76.74	2	UP	RAMPUR	61.76
3.	UP	MORADABAD	76.66	3	UP	BIJNOR	59.41
4.	UP	BAREILL Y	75.31	4	UP	PILIBHIT	58.70
5.	BIH	KISHANGANJ	75.08	5	UP	BAREILL Y	58.19
6.	BIH	ARARIA	74.15	6	UP	MORADABAD	58.01
7.	UP	SITAPUR	73.86	7	BIH	KISHANGANJ	56.14
8.	BIH	SITAMARHI	72.85	8	UP	HARDOI	55.98
9.	UP	SHAHJAHANPUR	72.67	9	UP	SHAHJAHANPUR	55.30
10.	UP	KHERI	72.61	10	UP	BARABANKI	55.20
11.	BIH	PURBA CHAMPARAN	72.55	11	UP	AGRA	54.98
12.	UP	PILIBHIT	72.53	12	UP	FARRUKHABAD	54.89
13.	BIH	KATIHAR	71.83	13	UP	SITAPUR	54.36
14.	BIH	PURNIA	71.63	14	UP	BAHRAICH	53.69
15.	UP	BAHRAICH	71.15	15	UP	VARANASI	53.67
16.	BIH	SAHARSA	70.95	16	UP	SIDDHARTHNAGAR	53.34
17.	UP	LALITPUR	70.58	17	BIH	ARARIA	52.47
18.	BIH	MADHEPURA	70.38	18	BIH	GOPALGAN.I	52.06
19.	UP	GONDA	70.20	19	UP	ETAH	52.02
20.	BIH	PASHCHIM CHAMPARAN	70.18	20	RAJ	DHOLPUR	51.94
21.	BIH	SAHIBGANJ	69.76	21	UP	KHERI	51.91
22.	BIH	KHAGARIA	68.98	22	BIH	KHAGARIA	51.72
23.	UP	MAHARAJGANJ	68.80	23	BIH	SAHARSA	51.65
24.	UP	SONBHADRA	68.64	24	UP	AL1GARH	51.42
25.	UP	SIDDHARTH NAGAR	68.62	25	RAJ	NAGAUR	51.15
26.	UP	BARABANKI	68.41	26	UP	BASTI	50.98
27.	RAJ	BANSWARA	67.64	27	UP	BULANDSHAHR	50.78
28.	BIH	PALAMU	67.42	28	UP	MEERUT	50.67
29.	UP	HARDOI	67.35	29	BIH	MADHEPURA	50.64
30.	RAJ	BARMER	67.20	30	BIH	BEGUSARAI	50.42
31.	BIH	DARBHANGA	67.20	31	UP	JAUNPUR	50.26
32.	UP	BASTI	66.88	32	UP	ETAWAH	50.23
33.	MP	GUNA	66.53	33	UP	FAIZABAD	49.40
34.	RAJ	JAISALMER	66.46	34	UP.	MATHURA	49.30
35.	BIH	MUZAFFARPUR	66.37	35	UP	JALAUN	48.86
36.	BIH	GIRIDIH	66.23	36	UP	MUZAFFARNAGAR	48.69
37.	BIH	MADHUBANI	66.07	37	UP	GONDA	48.61
38.	WB	WEST D1NAJPUR	65.55	38	UP	MIRZAPUR	48.60
39.	Ar.P	TIRAP	65.51	39	UP	AZAMGARH	48.48

(Contd...)

40.	RAJ	BIKANER	65.51	40.	BIH	PURBA CHAMPARAN	48.35
41.	BIH	DEOGHAR	65.44	41.	RAJ	SIKAR	48.33
42.	BIH	BEGUSARA1	65.35	42.	UP	RAE BARE LI	47.63
43.	BIH	GAYA	65.32	43.	Bill	SITAMARIII	47.5.3
44.	BIH	GOPALGANJ	65.31	44.	Bill	PASHCHIM CHAMPARAN	47.51
45.	RAJ	JODHPUR	65.30	45.	Bill	MADHUBANI	47.44
46.	BIH	BHAGALPUR	65.17	46.	UP	BALLIA	47.41
47.	BIH	SAMASTIPUR	65.05	47.	BIH	PALAMU	47.18
48.	UP	GORAKHPUR	65.05	48.	RAJ	CHURU	47.05
49.	WB	MALDAH	64.65	49.	UP	UNNAO	46.84
50.	MP	SHIVPURI	64.64	50.	RAJ	JALOR	46.62
51.	RAJ	BUNDI	64.56	51.	RAJ	SAWAI MADHOPUR	46.60
52.	UP	AGRA	64.22	52.	UP	KANPUR(DEHAT)	46.60
53.	AS	DHUBRI	64.19	53.	WB	MURSHIDABAD	46.56
54.	WB	MURSHIDABAD	64.18	54.	Bill	SIWAN	46.54
55.	RAJ	DHOLPUR	64.07	55.	BIH	VAISHAL1	46.36
56.	UP	ETAH	64.07	56.	UP	HAMIRPUR	46.23
57.	BIH	MUNGER	63.97	57.	BIH	NAWADA	46.20
58.	BIH	GODDA	63.66	58.	UP	MAIIARAJGANJ	45.95
59.	RAJ	JALOR	63.65	59.	UP	MAU	45.70
60.	UP	ALLAHABAD	63.64	60.	Bill	NALANDA	45.65
61.	BIH	DUMKA	63.64	61.	UP	SAHARANPUR	45.65
62.	UP	MIRZAPUR	63.51	62.	RAJ	JHUNJHUNUN	45.54
63.	BIH	HAZARIBAG	63.42	63.	BIH	ROHTAS	45.47
64.	BIH	NAWADA	63.34	64.	WB	B1RBHUM	45.46
65.	RAJ	JHALAWAR	63.33	65.	UP	MANIPURI	45.27
66.	UP	SAHARANPUR	63.14	66.	UP	BANDA	45.09
67.	UP	BI.INOR	62.75	67.	Bill	MUNGER	45.00
68.	UP	LUCKNOW	62.58	68.	UP	FATEHPUR	44.57
69.	UP	BANDA	62.49	69.	Bill	JEHANABAD	44.56
70.	OR	KORAPUT	62.10	70.	MP	TIKAMGARH	44.48
71.	UP	ALIGARH	62.04	71.	UP	PRATAPGARH	44.25
72.	UP	HAMIRPUR	62.00	72.	UP	GHAZIABAD	44.09
73.	UP	UNNAO	61.94	73.	BIH	SARAN	44.09
74.	RAJ	DUNGARPUR	61.79	74.	UP	GORAKHPUR	43.71
75.	UP	GHAZIPUR	61.58	75.	BIH	BHOJPUR	43.57
76.	RAJ	UDAIPUR	61.50	76.	RAJ	TONK	43.34
77.	RAJ	SAWAI MADHOPUR	61.47	77.	BIH	BHAGALPUR	42.98
78.	BIH	SIWAN	61.38	78.	UP	DEORIA	42.72
79.	BIH	SARAN	61.33	79.	KT	RAICHUR	42.64
80.	WB	JALPAIGURI	61.11	80.	BIH	DARBHANGA	42.58
81.	UP	HARDWAR	60.99	81.	UP	FIROZABAD	42.56
82.	UP	JAUNPUR	60.87	82.	BIH	PURNIA	42.49
83.	UP	DEORIA	60.71	83.	Ar.P	WEST KAMENG	42.49
84.	UP	FARRUKHABAD	60.49	84.	UP	GHAZ1PUR	42.39

(Contd...)

85.	MP	SIDHI	60.46	85.	BIH	SAHIBGANJ	42.15
86.	RAJ	NAGAUR	60.25	86.	Ar.P	LOWE R SUBANSIRI	41.93
87	AS	KOKRAJHAR	60.22	87	WB	SOUTH TWENTY FOUR PARGANAS	41.76
88	RAJ	BHILWARA	60.05	88	WB	PURULIYA	41.21
89	MP	PANNA	59.70	89	GJ	BANAS KANTHA	41.14
90	RAJ	CHURU	59.61	90	BIH	AURANGABAD	41.07
91	WB	KOCH BIHAR	59.57	91	UP	NA1NITAL	40.91
92	UP	BULANDSHAHR	59.46	92	UP	JHANSI	40.87
93	UP	AZAMGARH	59.41	93	RAJ	BARMER	40.64
94	RAJ	SIROHI	59.17	94	MP	GUNA	40.61
95	RAJ	KOTA	59.15	95	WB	BARDDHAMAN	40.59
96	UP	MATHURA	59.14	96	RAJ	BHARATPUR	40.39
97	BIH	VAISHALI	59.12	97	BIH	MUZAFFARPUR	40.22
98	UP	FIROZABAD	59.02	98	MP	DATIA	40.14
99	RAJ	CHITTAURGARH	58.99	99	UP	LALITPUR	39.92
100	UP	JHANSI	58.94	100	BIH	GIRIDIH	39.84

Source: Calculated from the Census of India, 1991, C-4 Tables - "Population (ages 5-19) by single years of age, school, attendance and economic activity."

Appendix 9: Unaccounted Children (Per cent) (5-14 Years) Census 1991

Rank	***State***	***District***	***Per cent Unaccounted Children***		
		Best 50 Districts	***Total***	***Male***	***Female***
1.	KER	ERNAKULAM	9.72	9.39	10.06
2.	KER	pathanamThu l A	11.01	10.94	11.08
3.	KER	ALAPPUZHA	11.05	11.45	10.63
4.	KER	THRISSUR	11.16	11.23	11.09
5.	KER	KOTTAYAM	11.25	11.41	11.10
6.	KER	KOLLAM	12.51	12.90	12.11
7.	KER	KOZHIKODE	14.18	14.41	13.94
8.	KER	TRIVANDRUM	14,25	14.38	14.11
9.	KER	KANNUR	14.37	14.29	14.46
10.	KER	PALAKKAD	15.01	14.40	15.63
11.	HP	HAMIRPUR	15.78	15.24	16.34
12.	KER	IDUKKI	16.23	16.03	16.43
13.	IN	KANNIYAKUMARI	16.47	16.22	16.74
14.	HP	BILASPUR	16.79	14.79	18.90
15.	KER	MALAPPURAM	17.69	17.63	17.74
16.	KER	WAYANAD	18.36	18,26	18.46
17.	KER	KASARAGOD	19.07	18.40	19.74
18.	TN	MADRAS	20.02	18.75	21.34
19.	HP	KANGRA	20.69	18.62	22.84
20.	KT	DAKSHIN KANNAD	21.28	19.62	22.94

(*Contd...*)

21.	MAH	SINDHUDURG	21.48	21.08	21.90
22	HP	MANDI	22.12	18.94	25.37
23	MAH	GREA'I'ER BOMBAY	22.24	20.46	24.17
24	TN	CHIDAMBARANAR	22.46	20.65	24.36
25	TN	TIRUNELVELIKATTA-BOMMAN	22.77	20.48	25.17
26	HP	UNA	22.79	20.69	25.02
27	TN	NILGIRI	22.83	21.68	23.94
28	HP	SHIMLA	22.98	20.53	25.53
29	TN	COIMBATORE	22.98	20.68	25.32
30	HP	KINNAUR	23.41	21.29	25.61
31	TN	PASUMPON THEVAR THIRUMAGAN	23.46	20.06	26.98
32	IN	MADURAI	23.63	20.65	26.77
33	TN	KAMARA.IAR	23.69	21.10	26.41
34	TN	THANJAVUR	23.76	20.59	27.01
35	PJ	JALANDHAR	23.87	22.20	25.74
36	TN	PUDUKKO'FTAI	24.06	19.41	28.82
37	TN	CHENGAI-ANNA	24.12	20.65	27.75
38	K'T	BANGALORE	24.31	21,65	27.00
39	MAH	PUNE	24.37	21.91	26.96
40	MAH	SATARA	24.42	21.17	27.89
41	JP	LAHUL AND SPITI	24.71	22.88	26.54
42	MAH	WARDHA	24.84	25.19	24.48
43	HP	SOLAN	25.12	21.66	28.81
44	TN	TIRUCHCHIRAPPALLI	25.25	21.71	28.97
45	MAH	NAGPUR	25.33	24.88	25.80
46	MAH	BHANDARA	25.59	24.12	27.10
47	TN	RAMAN ATHAPURAM	25.82	22.22	29.47
48	MAH	SANGLI	25.88	23.96	27.91
49	TN	NORTH ARCOT-AMBEDKER	25.91	22.45	29.38
50	HAR	REWARI	26.22	22.72	30.15

Source: Calculated from the Census of India, 1991, C-4 Tables - "Population (ages 5-19) by single years of age, school, attendance and economic activity

School Attendance and Adult Female Literacy

To study whether there exists any meaningful relationship between school attendance by children at the elementary *level* and adult female literacy, the former was plotted against the latter for the complete set of districts for the major states. Figure 5 shows that the scatter exhibits a positive relationship between school attendance by children and adult female literacy. At higher literacy rates for adult females, school attendance rates at the elementary level are also higher. Thus, it can be inferred that educated parents are more concerned about education of their children and this leads to higher rates of school attendance.

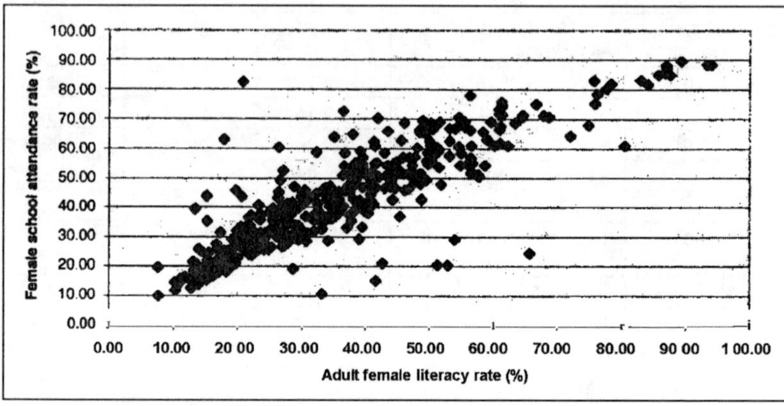

Figure 6: Relationship between Female School Attendance Rate (5-14 yrs) and Adult Female Literacy Rate, 1991

Figure 6 shows the plot between school attendance by the female child and adult female literacy. This is also a positive sloping scatter which implies that at higher levels of adult female literacy, school attendance by the girl child is also high. This is an important implication for efforts aimed at reducing the disadvantage that the girl child faces in access to education. An educated mother can be expected to better appreciate the benefits of schooling and be more inclined towards sending the girl child to school. Also, with some bargaining power, they may be able to influence the household decision making process about sending the girl child to school.

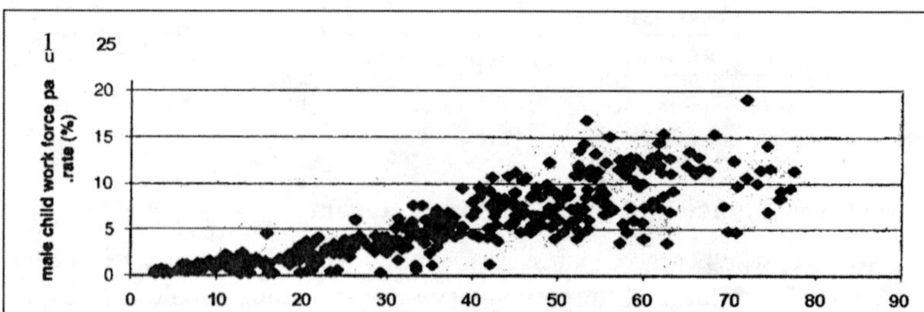

Source: Calculated from the Census of India, 1991, B-Series

Figure 7: Relationship between Female Child Labour (5-14 yrs, per cent) and Adult Female Work Force Participation Rate, 1991

Female Child Labour and Adult Female Work Force Participation Rate

The scatter diagram for child labour and adult female work force participation also shows a positive relationship. In Figure 7, relationship between female child labour and adult female work force participation rates is presented. The plot shows that at higher rates of work force participation by adult women, female children also exhibit high rates of participation in work. The complementarity between the two could be one possible reason for such a relationship. To be able to better understand the mechanics behind such a relationship, a study into the labour market conditions, the prevailing wage rate etc., may be separately called for.

Main Findings

- Approximately 50 per cent of the child population (5-14 years) in India attends school, about 5 per cent work and the remaining 45 per cent are unaccounted children
- At the State level, Bihar, Rajasthan and Uttar Pradesh have school attendance rates of less than 40 per cent.

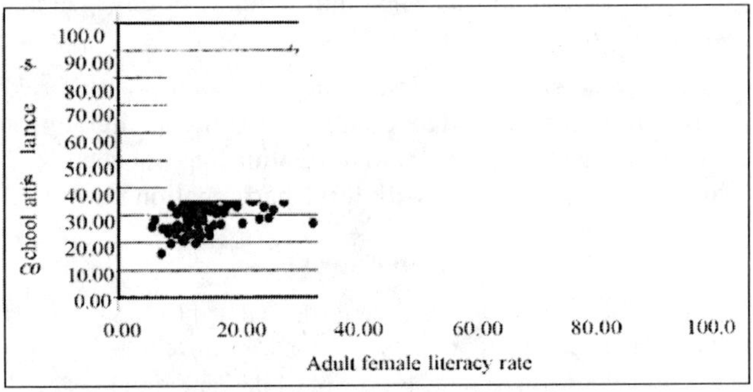

Figure 5: Relationship between Adult (15+) Female Literacy Rate and School Attendance (Total, 5-14 years), 1991

- Across States, school attendance rates for males are higher than those for females and school attendance rates in urban areas are greater than those in rural areas.
- Child work participation rates in the states of Karnataka and Andhra Pradesh are nearly twice the All-India average.
- Child labour in Kerala is remarkably low, at one-tenth the All-India average. States which are doing badly in school attendance are not among the worst performers in child labour. States like Bihar, Uttar Pradesh, Arunachal Pradesh and Rajasthan have high concentration of "unaccounted children."

- The districts with the lowest rates of school attendance also have the lowest rates of adult female literacy.
- The districts with the highest rates of child labour have high rates of adult female work force participation implying a complementarity between the two. Unaccounted children are in high proportions in states where school attendance is low implying that school attendance and child labour need not be two faces of the same coin. This has important implications for policy formulations aimed at reducing child labour and enhancing school attendance at the elementary level. As compared with 1981 (Jayachandran 1997), school attendance rates in 1991 are greater, showing an improvement over the decade 1981-1991.
- Child work force participation rates, analysed at the district level, show that incidence of child labour is more a function of availability of work opportunities for children. The worst 100 districts for child labour are concentrated in Andhra Pradesh, Karnataka and Madhya Pradesh, rather than in Uttar Pradesh and Bihar, as in the former, there exist more work opportunities for children (work as defined by the Census). In Uttar Pradesh and Bihar, there are higher proportions of unaccounted children who might actually be engaged in domestic work but go unreported by the Census.
- Scatter plots show that firstly, there exists a positive relationship between school attendance and adult female literacy rates, and secondly, there exists a positive relationship between female child labour and adult female work force participation rates.

References

Aggarwal, Y and Shibou, S (1994): "Educating Scheduled Castes - A Study of Inter-district and Inter- Caste Differentials", NIEPA, New Delhi

Chaudhuri, D. P. (1996): "A Dynamic Profile of Child Labour in India, 1951-1991", ILO, New Delhi

Colclough, C. (1993): "Educating All the Children: Strategies for Primary Schooling in the South". Oxford, Clarendon Press

Dreze, J and Saran, M (1993); "Primary Education and Economic Development in China and India: Overview and Two Case Studies".

Dreze, J and Sen, A K (1995): "Basic Education as a Political Issue" *Journal of Educational Planning and Administration,* Vol. IX, No. 1, January 1995, p. 1-2

Dreze, J and Sen A K, (eds.): "Indian Development - Selected Regional Perspectives", New Delhi, Oxford University Press.

Dreze. J and Sen A K, (1995): "India - Economic Development and Social Opportunity", New Delhi, Oxford University Press.

Government of India (1991): Census of India, 1991, Bll-Series, C-II and C-IV Series.

Government of India (1993): Education for All: The Indian Scene, New Delhi, Ministry of Human Resource Development.

Government of India (1996): Selected Educational Statistics 1996, New Delhi, Ministry of Human Resource Development.

Haq, Mahbub Ul and Haq, K (1998): Human Development in South Asia - The Education Challenge, OUP.

International Labour Organisation (1993): Bulletin of Labour Statistics.

Jayachandran, U (1997): 'The Determinants of Primary Education in India" M. Phil. Thesis, Department of Economics, Delhi School of Economics.

Psacharopoulos, G and Woodhall, M (1991): "Education for Development - An Analysis of Investment Choices", A World Bank Publication.

Tan, Jee-Peng and Mingat, A (1992): "Education in Asia - A Comparative Study of Cost and Financing", *World Bank Regional and Sectoral Studies.*

United Nations Development Programme, 1996: Human Development Report, 1996, New York, Oxford University Press.

Weiner, M (1991): "The Child and the State in India", Oxford University Press.

World Bank (1997): "Primary Education in India", New Delhi, Allied Publishers.

15

WOMEN'S EDUCATION AND EMPOWERMENT IN RURAL AREAS – A CASE STUDY OF WEST BENGAL, INDIA

RAKHEE BANERJEE, PRADIP KUMAR SAHU AND SANTIRANJAN PAL

Abstract

Starting with the global documents on women education and empowerment, this paper makes an attempt to examine rural and urban women in West Bengal, particularly with respect to the availability of educational opportunities and empowerment. All the results were on the basis of a 10 per cent sampling of households in selected villages classified according to soil-agro-climatic zones of West Bengal.

Introduction

Globally women comprise more than 40% of the agricultural workforce - a pattern that is found in all FAO regions and it is also expanding. The migration has pulled males out of rural occupations and rural communities to a far greater degree than rural women. Moreover, women tend to work in low productive jobs more often than men, especially those who remain in the agricultural sector (Mehra and Gammage, 1999). Women in male-headed households also generally have the prime responsibility of food production while men commonly concentrate on cash crops. Women's roles in food production frequently go beyond providing labour and encompass organizing the production process, recruiting additional labour and hiring mechanized services, as well as storing, selling and controlling the use of crops. In other words, they are "own account farmers" (Ismail Serageldin, 2000).

In spite of such services in agricultural field women have very unequal access to and control over rural land and associated resources (water, woody plants, fishery resources, etc) (Brown & Das Chowdhury, 2002). The probable reasons may be: (i) food production by itself is a long-term enterprise and requires physical and legal security for agricultural producers whether they are men or women, and (ii) effective resource use also requires fair and secure access to basic infrastructures and services that underpin effective land-use and improved agricultural technologies.

There are many new pressures affecting traditional arrangements related to women and land that need to be understood and resolved at the family, community and national levels. To summarize, some of the greatest aspects include:

- **Changing socio-economic conditions,** such as increased population, new types of employment and growing cash economy; migration to urban and peri-urban areas; incorporation and/or replacement of traditional and religious institutions and local government structures; divorce; and changes in inheritance patterns.
- **Environmental degradation and resource shortages** caused by the decreasing supply of land and other natural resources for specific purposes, in absolute and relative (person/land ratio) terms, and by the growing competition among land users. There are in reality two separate issues, which are often interlinked, but not necessarily related to cause and effect. It is a question again of the institutional arrangement controlling access to agricultural technology necessary to find sustainable land-use practices.
- **Education and economic opportunities** for women, which open up a wider range of choices and therefore a wider variety of needs, situations etc. (e.g. financing for small business).
- **Migrant labour and rural migration** changing the *de facto* status of household members remaining on the land and their family and community relationships, usually putting increased responsibility on women and the aged without increased decision-making power.

So undoubtedly, women form an increasingly important segment of the local and national economy in addition to providing primary family maintenance (ECOSOC, 1999). It has also been shown (World Food Summit, 1996) that women tend to reinvest more resources in the family unit than men and this reinvestment is the building block for nutrition, health, education and effective poverty alleviation. Indeed, in both developed and developing countries have shown that the success rate of rural as well as urban small businesses started by women is significantly higher than for those started by men (ILO,1999).

In rural Bengal, labour force participation of women was 10 per cent according to the Labour Force Survey of 1985/86. But in 1989 when the Labour Force Survey included activities – as threshing, food processing and poultry rearing, the economic activity rate went up to 63 per cent (UN, 1995).

Now education is an endowment that enables a woman to use the skill and knowledge to obtain the entitlements. Furthermore, considerable emphasis has been placed in the literature on education (Roy and Tisdell, 2000), primary education being the key to the success of women's empowerment process. To know the impact of education on women, we need to have an understanding of the position of women in the Indian setting first. Table 1 gives certain self-revealing demographic statistics of women in India.

Table 1: Trend in Female Population, Dependency Ratio and Literacy Rate

Year	*Female Population (million)*	*Sex Ratio*	*Dependency Ratio*	*Literacy Rate (Per cent)*
1971	213	941	887	13.0
1981	264	930	939	18.7
1991	331	933	812	24.8
2001	407	929	NA	39.29

Source: Census of India Report 1991, 2001 and Agricultural Research Data Book, 1999.

The worldwide status of female literacy can be visualized from Table 2.

Table 2: Literacy Status in Nine Most Populous Countries

Country	*Total Non-Literate Population 15+ Age (millions) Literacy*	*Rate 15+ (Per cent)*		
		Total	*Male*	*Female*
Mexico	6.52	91	92	90
Indonesia	15.10	90	94	87
Brazil	17.36	89	88	89
China	87.01	91	95	87
India	268.42	61	73	48
Egypt	14.21	71	83	59
Pakistan	48.81	50	63	36
Bangladesh	52.53	43	52	33

Source: Education for All – Global Monitoring Report – 2007.

The table shows that India has the highest not literate population of 15+ ages and per centage of women literate is distinctly lower than the males and it is only 48 per cent.

Table 3: Indicators of Human Development in India and Important Asian Countries (2007-2008)

Country	*Life Expectancy at Birth (years)*	*Infant Mortality Rate (per '000 births)*	*Adult Literacy Rate (Per cent)*
India	68.59	55	61.0
China	72.88	23	90.9
Korea	79.10	4.1	NA
Thailand	72.55	10.6	92.6

Source: CIA World Fact Book, 2008; UNDP Report, 2007/2008.

It is also assumed that in developing countries where the ratio of rural population to total population is higher, the per centage of illiterate rural women will be proportionately higher (FAO, 1999). Education along with food and shelter should be accorded high priority by the governments of the third world countries and subsequent expansion in education should narrow the gap considerably. Education would not only serve as a vehicle for the economic independence of the individual but would be a harbinger of social change, assuming a special role in breaking economic and caste barriers. The Directive Principles of the Indian Constitution enshrine the objective of free compulsory education for all children till the age of fourteen. There has been an improvement in the literacy rate as well as other indicators of human development over time, but in comparison with some of the other Asian economies like South Korea, Thailand and China, it fades into insignificance (Table 3). But even within India, we find wide disparity in human development profiles across states. Thus, it is important to look at the role of the state in improving the level of education. (Pradhan and Singh, 2000).

Institutional changes and a large-scale programmes of rural electrification in the 1980s and early 1990s were followed by accelerated agricultural production; the rate of growth of agricultural production in West Bengal was the highest among the 17 most populous states of India from the 1980s through the mid-1990s (Rawal et. al, 1998 & Saha et. al, 1994).

The proportion of girls enrolled both at primary and upper primary levels continue to be lower than the gross enrolment of boys. From Table 4, it is found that in West Bengal the enrolment of boys in primary level is 112.92 per cent, while it is 111.27 per cent in the case of girls in the year 2004-05. In India, the per centage of enrolment for boys and girls are 111.41 and 105.48 per cent, respectively. But the picture is not at all satisfactory as we move towards the upper primary level. In India 74.84 per cent boys and 65.76 per cent of girls are enrolled in upper primary level, while in West Bengal these per centages are 69.43 and 63.31, respectively (Educational Statistics, Ministry of HRD, Govt. of India, 1998-99, 2004-05)).

Again Table 5 shows the proportion of literates in West Bengal has been higher than the corresponding figure for India at every post-Independence Census after 1961.

Table 4: Gross Enrolment Ratio in Classes I-V and VI-VIII for West Bengal and India (1998-99 & 2004-2005)

States	*Year*	*Primary Classes (I-V)*			*Upper Primary Classes (VI-VIII)*		
		Boys	*Girls*	*Total*	*Boys*	*Girls*	*Total*
West Bengal	1998-1999	99.2	87.01	98.1	56.99	43.60	50.50
	2004-2005	112.92	111.27	112.11	69.43	63.31	66.46
India	1998-1999	96.86	82.85	94.85	65.27	49.08	57.58
	2004-2005	111.41	105.48	108.56	74.84	65.76	70.51

Source: Selected Educational Statistics, Ministry of HRD, Govt. of India (1998-99, 2004-05).

Table 5: Literate Persons as Percentage of All Persons in West Bengal and India (1951-2001)

Year	*Males*		*Females*	
	West Bengal	*India*	*West Bengal*	*India*
1951	30.9	25.0	11.5	12.9
1961	40.3	34.3	17.0	12.9
1971	42.8	39.5	22.4	18.7
1981	50.7	46.7	30.3	24.9
1991	56.6	52.7	38.4	32.1
2001	77.58	75.96	60.22	54.28

Source: Census of India, various volumes.

Literacy rates, unequal across the sexes, also continue to be steeply unequal across castes and communities. Data in Table 6 indicate that although Dalits (Scheduled Castes persons) require improvement educationally, from 1971 onwards, literacy among Dalits in West Bengal has remained better compared to the Indian average for Dalits.

Table 6: Literate Dalit Persons as Percent of All Persons in West Bengal and India (1961-2001)

Year	*Males*		*Females*	
	West Bengal	*India*	*West Bengal*	*India*
1961	10.4	17.0	0.6	3.3
1971	25.5	22.3	9.2	6.4
1981	34.3	30.9	13.7	10.8
1991	44.4	40.2	23.3	19.0
2001	60.5	48.5	36.9	32.0

Source: Census of India, various volumes.

Adivasi (Scheduled Tribes persons) in West Bengal, however, and Adivasi women in particular, lag behind Adivasi women in other states in respect of literacy (Table 7).

Table 7: Literate Adivasi Persons as Percent of All Persons in West Bengal and India (1961-2001)

Year	*Males*		*Females*	
	West Bengal	*India*	*West Bengal*	*India*
1961	14.4	13.8	1.8	3.2
1971	14.5	17.6	3.0	4.9
1981	21.2	24.5	5.0	8.0
1991	32.3	32.5	12.0	14.5
2001	47.4	29.6	29.2	18.2

Source: Census of India, various volumes.

Thus, keeping in mind the above-mentioned worldwide as well as within country and state level information, the present study conceives the following assumptions about the importance of women education:

(i) Women education is one of the essential instruments for lower mortality at birth, higher life expectancy.

(ii) The education of women is an equally relevant factor in the country's economic growth as it has direct bearings on individual health and child nourishment.

(iii) The participation of women in decision-making process concerning their own lives can create new opportunities for social change, especially for an effective family planning.

(iv) Women education is one of the essential instruments for better population.

The Platform of Actions set up by the Fourth World Conference on Women (1995) stressed the need for enhancing women's skills, knowledge and access to such information for proper utilization of resources towards overall development of the family, a micro unit of the society. This was also stressed by the Director-General, FAO, 1999 that women's education was absolutely necessary for overall development of the society as women contributed to two-thirds of the world's work-hours, produced 50 per cent of world's food supplies, account for 60 per cent of the work- force in the global market.

Female education bears one of the strongest and most consistent negative relationships to fertility. Women, who obtain secondary and higher education, marry later and increase in the age of marriage has a pronounced effect on a country's fertility rate (Birdsall, 1977). Worldwide study shows that 1/4th of the households are headed by women and in other one-third of the households 50 per cent of the total earnings are contributed by females (Fourth

World Conference on Women, 1995). It is estimated that the money value of the invisible non-monetized contribution of women towards the family is 25 to 39 per cent of the Gross National Product in developing countries (ILO, 1996) and to be around $11 trillion or almost 50 per cent more than the officially estimated figure of $23 trillion of global output (Shiv Kumar, 1996). Despite the services rendered by women in the family and work place, they make up for nearly 70 per cent of the world's poor and more than 65 per cent of the illiterates (UNDP, HDR, 1995). Investigation (Jain, 1985) of three villages in West Bengal and Rajasthan, covering 127 households over 12 months, found that women in the age groups 19-34, 34-44 and 44-70 spend longer hours than men in a variety of activities. Therefore keeping in mind the above facts, the present study incorporates the adult females i.e. females attaining 18 years of age or married.

West Bengal is one of the important eastern states of India, having population around 100 millions, ruled by the Left Front government for over the last 33 years. According to Ramachandran, Swaminathan and Rawal (2003), the leading development achievements of this government have been in the countryside, where there have been two major institutional changes: land reforms and the establishment of three tier local government. In spite of this claim for radical change in the development of the state, from Table 5 it is clear that no extraordinary changes have taken place for the state; rather it is the general picture of the country as a whole.

In West Bengal, information related to the status of women in which education is playing a vital role, is very sparse and scare. The generational change in education level of women and its effect on influencing the family planning and development is also having lots of importance. Thus, the present study aims at critically examining the status of women education in West Bengal to get an idea about the variation of education level of women across the state. As a varied range of agro-climatic conditions, and the life, rituals, culture etc., characterize the state of West Bengal, it is worthwhile to study the state by dividing it into different agro-climatic zones.

Materials and Method

West Bengal is characterized by widely varying eco-geographical regions. It has got places like Darjeeling, Kalimpong etc. at its north at an altitude of round about 2000 metres from the mean sea level, and places like Sagardweep, Nayachar, Mousuni etc. surrounded by the Bay of Bengal. In between is the vast area, enriched by the alluvial soils of the river Ganges. A part of the state is also characterized by dry and hot weather and red and laterite soil. Thus varied climatic and agricultural conditions have resulted in the variations in socio-economic, cultural, rituals of the people of the state. As a result, the state has mainly been divided into six agro-climatic zones, namely the hill zone, the terrai zone, the coastal zone, the old alluvial zone, the new alluvial zone, and the red-laterite zone. Thus, any study relating to the people of West Bengal has to be compartmentalized into six parts so as to capture the true picture of each and every zone in detail.

The present study purposively selected two villages from each zone as guided by the above factors. For each village, details of households were collected from the respective gram panchayats (lowest level of the three tier local government). Altogether 3008 families were covered in 12 selected villages spread over the six agro-climatic zones of West Bengal. According to our sampling scheme we decided to have 300 sample units. Hence, the weightage to be given while fixing the number of households to be selected randomly from each village is w= n/N = 300/ 3008 = 0.0997. Households were selected following simple random sampling without replacement (SRSWOR) method. To overcome the problem of misreporting and /or non-response, the study opted for adding 10 per cent more households from each village for the survey purpose. Kesia and Chakedabad are the two selected villages from the red-laterite zone of West Bengal which have low number of households. It was decided to go in for complete enumeration and for the same reason more than 80 per cent households were taken up from the village Kodalia. The details of sampling are presented in Table 8.

Table 8: Sampling Frame

Zone	*District*	*Village*	*Total Number of Households*	*Selected Households*	*No. of Females*
Coastal-Saline	24 Parganas (S)	Nimpith	350	40	68
		Taldihi	300	40	42
New Alluvial	Nadia	Chandamari	400	50	68
		Shikarpur	150	20	24
		Kodalia	54	25	54
		Kanagarh	104	20	24
Red-Laterite	West Midnapur	Kesia	33	30	68
	Purulia	Chakedabad	29	28	47
Terai	Jalpaiguri	Banarhata	240	30	52
		Matigara	198	25	52
Hill	Darjeeling	Kalimpong	550	65	54
		Sukiapokhri	600	75	102
Total			**3008**	**450**	**672**

It is necessary to have an idea about the characteristics of the family related data, such as land holdings, number of family members (both adult and children), their ages, education and occupational standards, monthly income and expenditure patterns etc. The descriptive statistics (mean, median, standard error, skewness, kurtosis) on each and every parameter has been calculated based on the above mentioned parameters.

Variables taken for describing the village characteristics are:

1. Land holdings (ha)/family	11. Total monthly family income
2. No. of family members	12. Monthly food expenditure/family
3. No. of adult male/family	13. Monthly education expenditure/family
4. No. of adult female/family	14. Monthly clothing expenditure/family
5. No. of male child/family	15. Monthly medical expenditure/family
6. No. of female child/family	16. Monthly cultivation expenditure/family
7. Avg. education of adult male	17. Monthly miscellaneous expenditure / family
8. Avg. education of adult female	18. Monthly total expenditure/family
9. Avg. education of male child	19. Monthly savings/family
10. Avg. education of female child	20. Monthly income of adult female/family

As has been mentioned already, there exist wide regional variations with respect to climatic conditions, geographic terrains, occupations, livelihood and above all the people of West Bengal. The present study is based on primary information collected from two selected villages in each agro-climatic zone resulting from a random sample of 450 households. Education standard of the married women are categorized into seven groups, viz. illiterate-0, up to class IV-1, V to class X-2, XI & XII-3, graduate-4, postgraduate-5 and above post graduation-6. Similarly, depending upon the type of occupation they are categorized into six groups, viz. housekeeping-1, agriculture works-2, business-3, service-4, hired labour-5, student-6. The nature of each and every factor under consideration is described with the help of different statistical measures, like arithmetic mean, standard error, etc. Empowerment quotient (X1) for married women is worked out by considering their intensity of involvement in different decision making processes of family affairs (like family finance, savings, selling and purchasing of farm output/input etc.), family expenses (like education, cultivation, healthcare, marriages of near relatives, etc.) etc.

Variables taken for the women empowerment study are given below:

1. Present Age (yrs)- X_2	11. Family Food Expenditure Rs)/ Month- X_{12}
2. Education standard - X_3	12. Family education expenditure (Rs) / month-X_{13}
3. Occupation standard -X_4	13. Family clothing expenditure (Rs) / month- X_{14}
4. Female income (Rs) / month -X_5	14. Family medical expenditure (Rs) / month- X_{15}
5. Age at marriage(yrs) - X_6	15. Family cultivation expenditure (Rs) / month-X_{16}
6. First bearing age (yrs)- X_7	16. Family others expenditure (Rs) / month- X_{17}
7. Number of children - X_8	17. Total expenditure (Rs) / month- X_{18}
8. Number of birth -X_9	18. Family savings (Rs) /month - X_{19}
9. Family members -X_{10} 10. Total monthly family income (Rs)-X_{11}	19. Media exposure and social involvement -X_{20}, which takes into consideration the exposure of women to print, audio, audio-visual media, involvement in socio-political and economic activities

As education has been taken as one of the major indictors for women empowerment, women development vis-à-vis development of society, a section is devoted to the study of variations in women education in the different agro-climatic zones of West Bengal and combining the information from all the six zones. For this purpose the correlation analysis, analysis of variance, has been used as the statistical tools. Before proceeding for the analysis, the data on the educational standard of present generation married women of has been divided under three different age groups. The first group includes women who are below 30 years of age. The second group comprises women aged between 30-45 years, and the third group comprises women aged above 45 years.

Education index is one of the important indices to compare education at different levels. This index is also one of the three indices on which the human development index has been built by UNDP. It is based on the literacy index (LI) and the combined gross enrolment index (CGEI) for primary, secondary and tertiary schools. In calculating the education index, two-third weight has been given to the literacy index and one-third weight to the school enrolment index.

If x = literacy index (LI) and y = school enrolment index (CGEI)

$$\text{Then Equation Index (EI)} = \left[x \times \frac{2}{3}\right] + \left[y \times \frac{2}{3}\right]$$

For the present study, education index has been calculated at village level for both males and females separately. A comparative study has been done on males and females with the help of analysis of variance for identifying the existence of zonal variation in this respect.

Findings and Discussion

Village Characteristics

Appendix 1 gives the descriptive statistics of the selected parameters of every village. A graphical representation has also been provided in Appendix 2.

In village Kanagarh, most of the households are those of small farmers, dominated by male income earners, with an average family size of 5 and having Madhyamik standard of education. Negative and positive skewness respectively for number of male and female children indicate that most of the families have higher number of male children than female children. The distribution of education for female child is more positively skewed and less flattened as the value of kurtosis is nearly half of that of the male child. This implies that the spread of education among female children is better than that in the male children. The positively skewed distribution of average monthly income

Appendix 1: Descriptive Statistics of Variables

A. Village Kanagarh in Old Alluvial Zone

	1	2	3	4	5	6	7	8	9	10	11	12	13	14	15	16	17	18	19	20
Mean	3.32	5.20	1.15	1.20	1.65	1.20	1.88	1.93	1.64	1.60	10395.00	2038.95	2214.06	1344.00	1448.93	1819.58	520.28	9385.79	1009.22	2271.43
Std Error	0.68	0.30	0.08	0.09	0.20	0.19	0.13	0.12	0.18	0.17	1376.22	278.73	297.58	247.41	199.51	245.85	72.19	1240.51	141.05	359.04
Media	2.08	5.00	1.00	1.00	2.00	1.00	2.00	2.00	1.00	1.25	7500.00	1537.50	1635.00	1050.00	1044.25	1247.00	379.25	6847.50	734.25	2000.00
Kurtosis	-0.04	-0.63	2.78	0.70	-0.34	-0.36	0.58	0.60	-1.36	-0.68	-0.64	0.00	-0.46	3.27	0.24	0.03	0.33	-0.65	0.31	0.84
Skewness	1.14	0.35	2.12	1.62	-0.25	0.19	0.05	0.05	0.55	0.82	1.06	1.16	1.11	1.84	1.24	1.22	1.25	1.05	1.29	1.04

B. Village Kodalia in Old Alluvial Zone

	1	2	3	4	5	6	7	8	9	10	11	12	13	14	15	16	17	18	19	20
Mean	2.40	7.96	2.68	2.04	1.40	1.80	1.47	0.72	1.20	0.88	5300.00	2688.00	318.00	276.00	238.00	662.00	218.00	4400.00	900.00	1946.15
Std Error	0.53	0.68	0.21	0.20	0.22	0.26	0.26	0.21	0.16	0.12	694.53	283.69	47.51	33.68	28.33	188.09	29.56	546.24	273.85	535.37
Median	2.50	7.00	3.00	2.00	1.00	2.00	1.00	0.00	1.00	1.00	3900.00	2500.00	250.00	250.00	200.00	0.00	150.00	3400.00	500.00	1200.00
Kurtosis	-1.17	-0.35	-0.37	-0.44	-0.27	0.13	5.82	5.37	0.08	-0.25	0.68	0.69	1.96	1.67	-0.40	0.14	0.98	1.27	17.73	3.19
Skewness	0.54	0.60	0.04	0.17	0.66	0.63	2.13	2.04	0.24	-0.15	1.12	0.81	1.45	1.33	0.90	1.17	1.34	1.14	3.97	1.80

C. Village Shikarpur in New Alluvial Zone

	1	2	3	4	5	6	7	8	9	10	11	12	13	14	15	16	17	18	19	20
Mean	2.00	4.04	1.08	1.12	0.96	0.88	1.86	1.88	1.71	1.86	8600.00	1821.01	1072.78	1170.44	925.46	2478.96	521.52	7990.18	609.82	1977.78
Std Error	0.32	0.16	0.06	0.07	0.14	0.15	0.14	0.15	0.13	0.15	809.73	168.23	103.25	110.88	89.01	235.45	61.29	758.17	68.20	180.11
Median	1.32	4.00	1.00	1.00	1.00	1.00	2.00	2.00	2.00	2.00	8500.00	1853.00	1037.00	1147.50	892.50	2465.00	425.00	7820.00	576.00	2000.00
Kurtosis	-0.16	-1.35	9.64	4.56	-0.61	1.90	-0.90	-1.12	-0.42	-0.42	0.33	-0.01	0.72	0.43	0.67	0.70	2.77	0.46	1.24	1.93
Skewness	0.97	-0.07	3.30	2.49	0.05	0.90	0.15	0.20	0.21	0.01	0.76	0.64	0.90	0.80	0.88	0.79	1.59	0.80	0.96	0.06

D. Village Chandamari in New Alluvial Zone

	1	*2*	*3*	*4*	*5*	*6*	*7*	*8*	*9*	*10*	*11*	*12*	*13*	*14*	*15*	*16*	*17*	*18*	*19*	*20*
Mean	0.93	7.02	2.44	2.12	1.28	1.58	2.15	1.66	1.37	0.96	6173.81	1917.36	698.64	841.07	322.55	1531.19	341.40	5573.02	600.79	2265.00
Std Error	0.07	0.53	0.19	0.16	0.16	0.21	0.25	0.23	0.14	0.09	687.37	208.38	90.58	101.01	36.76	169.12	34.96	615.13	87.29	439.27
Median	0.86	6.50	3.00	2.00	1.00	1.00	1.67	1.00	1.00	1.00	5550.00	1560.00	496.00	695.00	280.00	1387.50	300.00	4884.00	484.00	1550.00
Kurtosis	0.11	0.11	-0.54	-0.79	-0.01	0.05	-0.74	-0.95	-0.10	0.44	9.40	4.34	6.50	11.94	6.88	10.30	7.32	8.37	9.49	-5.74
Skewness	0.91	0.91	0.15	0.57	0.71	0.79	0.53	0.60	0.21	-0.27	2.55	1.96	2.18	2.93	2.28	2.68	2.22	2.42	2.52	2.12

E. Village Kesia

	1	*2*	*3*	*4*	*5*	*6*	*7*	*8*	*9*	*10*	*11*	*12*	*13*	*14*	*15*	*16*	*17*	*18*	*19*	*20*
Mean	0.52	7.24	2.85	2.06	1.24	1.09	0.96	0.70	0.93	0.85	2313.64	897.77	153.29	267.36	373.15	425.42	115.33	2232.33	81.31	706.25
Std Error	0.06	0.41	0.25	0.18	0.20	0.13	0.09	0.09	0.09	0.07	172.17	64.22	11.67	33.24	31.41	34.65	12.36	165.23	7.37	81.76
Median	0.40	7.00	3.00	2.00	1.00	1.00	1.00	1.00	1.00	1.00	2100.00	870.00	130.00	230.00	342.00	400.00	96.00	2026.50	73.50	700.00
Kurtosis	1.44	4.02	0.08	0.72	2.19	0.36	1.12	-0.59	2.72	2.33	2.53	1.49	1.38	6.69	2.11	2.20	8.41	2.54	1.71	-0.99
Skewness	1.46	1.92	0.48	1.05	1.21	0.39	-0.52	-0.21	-0.64	-2.04	1.53	1.01	1.15	2.23	1.41	1.45	2.56	1.52	1.32	0.28

F. Village Chakedabad

	1	*2*	*3*	*4*	*5*	*6*	*7*	*8*	*9*	*10*	*11*	*12*	*13*	*14*	*15*	*16*	*17*	*18*	*19*	*20*
Mean	1.91	6.14	2.36	1.68	1.18	0.96	0.83	0.54	1.11	0.81	1147.86	409.88	138.11	40.00	59.07	161.75	75.99	884.80	263.06	340.00
Std Error	0.21	0.48	0.21	0.12	0.18	0.17	0.11	0.10	0.06	0.10	115.10	39.35	13.87	3.75	5.58	12.38	8.92	77.19	41.19	47.61
Median	1.91	6.00	2.00	2.00	1.00	1.00	1.00	1.00	1.00	1.00	1115.00	390.25	133.80	36.75	58.00	143.50	78.05	848.50	296.50	275.00
Kurtosis	-1.20	4.29	2.68	-0.53	2.23	0.22	-0.50	-2.14	5.68	0.32	0.11	0.23	0.14	-0.19	0.28	-0.96	-0.31	0.33	-0.73	-1.19
Skewness	0.00	1.36	1.21	0.29	1.32	0.77	-0.12	-0.15	2.53	-1.40	0.77	0.75	0.71	0.77	0.72	0.32	0.53	0.72	0.49	0.73

	1	2	3	4	5	6	7	8	9	10	11	12	13	14	15	16	17	18	19	20
G. Village Nimpith																				
Mean	0.28	5.58	2.21	1.65	0.95	1.08	3.10	2.51	1.46	1.08	6005.00	3005.00	296.25	340.00	286.75	902.50	276.25	5106.75	898.25	2420.00
Std Error	0.05	0.44	0.20	0.15	0.14	0.19	0.23	0.24	0.14	0.10	485.44	184.74	35.60	26.38	25.32	136.23	34.67	369.19	180.79	422.62
Median	0.26	5.00	2.00	1.00	1.00	1.00	3.58	3.00	1.33	1.00	5550.00	3000.00	200.00	325.00	250.00	1000.00	225.00	4875.00	500.00	1550.00
Kurtosis	-0.43	2.68	-0.62	0.72	0.30	2.57	-0.69	-1.16	0.16	0.91	4.40	-0.22	7.01	5.07	3.71	0.05	25.91	1.25	9.22	6.17
Skewness	0.78	1.60	0.64	0.95	0.82	1.60	-0.55	-0.19	0.24	0.02	1.66	0.37	2.44	1.42	1.71	0.76	4.68	1.08	2.57	2.15
H. Village Taldihi																				
	1	2	3	4	5	6	7	8	9	10	11	12	13	14	15	16	17	18	19	20
Mean	2.17	4.65	1.08	1.05	1.65	0.90	1.69	1.51	1.66	1.43	7802.50	1599.51	1388.85	741.24	951.91	2106.68	639.81	7427.98	374.52	1952.38
Std Error	0.27	0.15	0.07	0.03	0.13	0.12	0.10	0.08	0.10	0.12	619.91	127.08	110.34	58.89	75.63	167.38	50.83	590.15	29.76	141.69
Median	1.60	4.50	1.00	1.00	2.00	1.00	2.00	1.75	1.50	1.00	6550.00	1342.75	1165.90	622.25	799.10	1768.50	537.10	6235.60	314.40	2000.00
Kurtosis	0.72	-0.32	13.14	17.29	0.70	-0.12	3.82	-2.08	-0.08	0.35	2.54	2.54	2.54	2.54	2.54	2.54	2.54	2.54	2.54	-1.47
Skewness	1.24	0.40	2.78	4.29	0.74	0.52	1.02	-0.05	0.91	0.29	1.62	1.62	1.62	1.62	1.62	1.62	1.62	1.62	1.62	0.21
I. Village Kalimpong																				
	1	2	3	4	5	6	7	8	9	10	11	12	13	14	15	16	17	18	19	20
Mean	0.20	8.28	2.68	2.16	1.54	1.96	1.85	1.57	1.52	1.29	10688.04	3098.92	2107.24	1447.24	1672.16	1646.80	1599.28	9972.36	715.68	3975.00
Std Error	0.03	0.69	0.21	0.19	0.22	0.25	0.25	0.19	0.14	0.09	1100.55	277.31	240.85	164.85	221.70	171.08	152.69	1034.01	75.15	579.82
Median	0.26	7.00	3.00	2.00	1.00	2.00	1.59	1.50	1.00	1.00	10401.00	3150.00	2060.00	1545.00	1404.00	1650.00	1545.00	9765.00	686.00	3100.00
Kurtosis	-0.80	-0.56	-0.37	-0.77	-0.21	0.22	5.79	3.10	-0.38	1.36	2.76	-0.01	4.19	0.81	5.86	3.81	1.00	2.86	0.14	0.64
Skewness	0.23	0.65	0.04	0.30	0.59	0.65	2.33	1.12	0.85	1.45	1.28	0.50	1.58	0.91	2.21	1.41	1.04	1.31	0.77	1.07

J. Village Sukiapokhri

	1	2	3	4	5	6	7	8	9	10	11	12	13	14	15	16	17	18	19	20
Mean	1.23	6.85	2.11	1.89	1.46	1.75	2.18	1.76	1.35	1.33	9894.46	2630.07	1747.43	1886.94	1169.80	713.16	1829.70	9304.10	590.36	4031.82
StdError	0.17	0.42	0.14	0.11	0.14	0.15	0.15	0.10	0.09	0.07	674.94	181.87	122.78	160.95	97.84	115.20	139.63	642.99	56.39	379.34
Median	0.53	6.50	2.00	2.00	1.00	1.50	2.00	2.00	1.00	1.00	9650.00	2519.00	1597.50	1708.00	1050.00	131.00	1650.00	9080.50	449.75	3500.00
Kurto sis	-0.77	0.22	-0.16	-0.59	3.85	1.02	2.15	3.10	0.35	0.01	3.93	2.18	0.46	6.86	2.51	-0.70	8.12	4.53	1.90	4.19
Skewness	0.82	0.93	0.59	0.44	1.63	1.00	1.31	0.50	0.96	0.42	1.36	1.09	0.79	1.96	1.52	0.88	2.16	1.47	1.38	1.77

K. Village Banarhata

	1	2	3	4	5	6	7	8	9	10	11	12	13	14	15	16	17	18	19	20
Mean	2.05	5.93	1.70	1.73	1.44	1.63	2.44	1.92	1.24	1.39	9836.67	2366.37	1594.67	2311.80	898.83	60.68	2082.07	9314.42	522.25	4336.00
Std Error	0.21	0.49	0.14	0.13	0.17	0.18	0.15	0.08	0.12	0.12	1010.88	252.46	165.64	241.30	101.85	7.19	219.32	970.90	85.55	553.71
Median	2.05	5.00	2.00	2.00	1.00	1.00	2.00	2.00	1.00	1.00	8750.00	2187.50	1395.00	2100.00	806.00	48.75	1925.00	8443.75	367.50	3500.00
Kurtosis	-1.20	1.45	-0.96	-0.77	11.72	0.87	-0.30	0.94	1.25	-0.42	5.20	5.81	2.41	5.68	6.31	0.65	6.26	5.63	3.43	4.82
Skewness	0.00	1.25	0.57	0.41	3.09	1.28	0.48	-0.31	1.09	-0.18	1.76	1.90	1.32	1.86	2.05	1.18	1.97	1.85	1.93	2.05

L. Village Matigara

	1	2	3	4	5	6	7	8	9	10	11	12	13	14	15	16	17	18	19	20
Mean	6.65	5.93	1.70	1.73	1.44	1.63	2.17	1.90	1.50	1.55	9836.67	2384.32	1589.22	2322.80	911.50	62.58	2099.40	9369.82	466.85	1806.67
Std. Error	0.43	0.34	0.10	0.09	0.12	0.13	0.14	0.13	0.13	0.10	708.71	180.52	115.21	171.57	73.44	5.70	157.44	696.51	73.02	219.00
Median	5.50	5.00	2.00	2.00	1.00	1.00	2.00	2.00	1.00	2.00	8750.00	2125.00	1325.00	2100.00	785.00	52.50	1880.00	8202.50	387.00	1900.00
Kurto sis	0.14	1.22	-0.98	-0.81	10.41	0.65	-0.20	0.71	-0.24	-0.16	4.66	4.56	2.29	4.66	4.67	1.22	4.82	4.37	2.29	-1.65
Skewness	0.94	1.22	0.55	0.40	2.99	1.24	-0.12	-0.10	0.78	0.11	1.72	1.73	1.35	1.74	1.80	1.35	1.78	1.70	1.50	0.09

M. Summary of the Family Particular for Different Zones

OAZ	XI	X2	X3	X4	X5	X6	X7	X8	X9	X10	X11	X12	X13	X14	X15	X16	X17	X18	X19	X20
Mean	2.81	6.73	2.00	1.67	1.51	1.53	1.65	1.26	1.39	1.19	7564.44	2399.53	1160.69	750.67	776.19	1176.48	352.34	6615.90	948.54	2060.00
SE	0.42	0.45	0.17	0.13	0.15	0.17	0.16	0.16	0.12	0.11	809.53	204.11	194.56	135.99	126.93	172.74	42.16	724.74	163.13	364.94
Median	2.24	6.00	2.00	1.00	1.00	1.00	1.67	1.25	1.00	1.00	6000.00	2000.00	700.00	450.00	500.00	1110.00	280.00	5490.00	667.50	1750.00
Kurtosis	-0.24	1.10	-0.39	0.31	-0.48	0.86	6.26	0.35	-0.32	0.54	1.36	0.34	2.07	7.92	2.81	0.35	2.76	1.74	21.41	3.34
Skewness	0.87	1.21	0.80	0.92	0.31	0.83	1.78	0.50	0.27	0.52	1.42	0.92	1.68	2.65	1.81	0.96	1.72	1.53	4.09	1.66
NAZ																				
Mean	2.16	6.73	2.00	1.64	1.15	1.24	2.19	1.83	1.37	1.16	6710.00	1522.50	1003.30	580.56	606.19	1759.11	388.84	5860.50	849.50	840.00
SE	0.28	0.45	0.14	0.11	0.12	0.14	0.16	0.14	0.10	0.07	540.38	130.10	86.00	66.77	53.55	148.07	34.15	496.29	69.63	138.14
Median	1.09	6.00	2.00	1.00	1.00	1.00	2.00	2.00	1.33	1.00	5800.00	1304.00	898.00	372.00	480.00	1470.00	317.50	4966.00	720.00	0.00
Kurtosis	2.68	1.10	-0.33	0.29	0.45	1.35	0.01	-0.46	-0.26	0.48	4.36	7.25	9.63	2.37	2.41	3.17	3.42	3.85	3.23	0.95
Skewness	1.80	1.21	0.84	0.99	0.82	1.23	0.68	0.53	-0.10	0.05	1.72	2.11	2.42	1.67	1.55	1.60	1.71	1.69	1.64	1.30
R&L																				
Mean	0.58	6.78	2.62	1.91	1.24	1.02	0.93	0.62	1.01	0.83	1801.90	670.70	147.17	164.51	230.83	295.07	101.57	1609.85	192.04	311.36
SE	0.05	0.34	0.18	0.12	0.14	0.11	0.08	0.07	0.05	0.06	133.39	51.73	8.87	24.42	27.74	28.35	8.09	136.05	20.95	56.24
Median	0.40	6.50	2.00	2.00	1.00	1.00	1.00	1.00	1.00	1.00	1550.00	567.00	130.30	90.00	171.00	248.25	91.00	1455.75	126.00	250.00
Kurtosis	0.37	3.15	0.52	1.80	1.99	0.16	-0.40	-1.17	7.24	1.51	2.60	1.44	0.59	7.11	1.35	2.07	10.09	2.21	1.23	0.35
Skewness	1.13	1.36	0.78	1.21	1.21	0.59	-0.05	-0.13	-0.02	-1.86	1.33	1.10	0.85	2.26	1.23	1.34	2.51	1.32	1.36	1.14
Coastal																				
Mean	1.23	5.11	1.63	1.35	1.30	0.99	2.38	1.96	1.55	1.24	6903.75	2302.26	842.55	540.62	619.33	1504.59	458.03	6267.37	636.39	1774.60
SE	0.17	0.24	0.12	0.09	0.10	0.11	0.14	0.14	0.08	0.08	404.04	136.61	84.24	39.21	54.50	126.82	36.78	369.68	95.68	126.03
Median	0.64	5.00	1.00	1.00	1.00	1.00	2.00	2.00	1.50	1.00	6000.00	2000.00	800.50	451.25	524.50	1363.50	373.10	5413.20	340.80	1550.00
Kurtosis	3.39	6.93	1.39	4.08	0.07	3.12	-0.73	-0.31	0.53	0.44	3.27	-0.09	2.55	4.04	3.23	1.83	3.53	3.78	19.37	-0.22
Skewness	1.93	2.28	1.48	1.92	0.52	1.51	0.57	0.59	0.53	0.31	1.66	0.80	1.50	1.79	1.65	1.03	1.82	1.72	3.76	0.23

Terai																				
Mean	1.17	5.91	1.69	1.73	1.47	1.61	2.42	1.92	1.24	1.37	9854.55	2362.40	1608.18	2311.64	892.91	61.82	2078.55	9315.49	539.05	2327.27
SE	0.16	0.36	0.10	0.09	0.13	0.13	0.11	0.07	0.10	0.09	754.22	188.36	123.95	179.99	75.97	5.41	163.51	724.25	64.72	239.01
Median	0.84	5.00	2.00	2.00	1.00	1.00	2.00	2.00	1.00	1.00	8500.00	2125.00	1350.00	2040.00	762.00	45.00	1870.00	8202.50	367.50	3500.00
Kurtosis	12.79	1.46	-0.95	-0.78	9.57	0.88	-0.39	0.40	2.29	-0.20	4.76	5.38	2.02	5.24	5.93	0.26	5.83	5.19	2.53	-1.42
Skewness	3.28	1.30	0.57	0.40	2.90	1.31	0.39	-0.17	1.39	0.25	1.79	1.94	1.31	1.89	2.10	1.10	2.01	1.88	1.78	-0.40
Hill																				
Mean	1.08	7.48	2.36	2.02	1.52	1.85	2.02	1.63	1.42	1.31	10441.45	2860.25	1931.27	1765.06	1408.79	1096.86	1783.87	9791.14	650.31	4044.44
SE	0.09	0.28	0.09	0.07	0.09	0.10	0.09	0.07	0.06	0.04	456.26	119.20	92.08	93.80	82.78	84.33	82.16	432.44	34.48	242.84
Median	0.53	7.00	2.00	2.00	1.00	2.00	2.00	1.88	1.00	1.00	10400.00	2725.00	1746.50	1650.00	1193.00	900.00	1650.00	9660.00	525.00	3500.00
Kurtosis	0.04	-0.27	-0.62	-0.69	1.58	0.27	3.36	2.44	-0.24	0.26	2.96	0.94	3.33	7.22	5.94	0.91	7.67	3.26	0.72	2.39
Skewness	1.06	0.77	0.29	0.41	1.10	0.68	1.67	0.60	0.87	0.89	1.41	0.92	1.46	2.00	2.17	0.87	2.11	1.48	1.05	1.50

Appendix 2: Descriptive Statistics and Selected Variables on Women's Employment

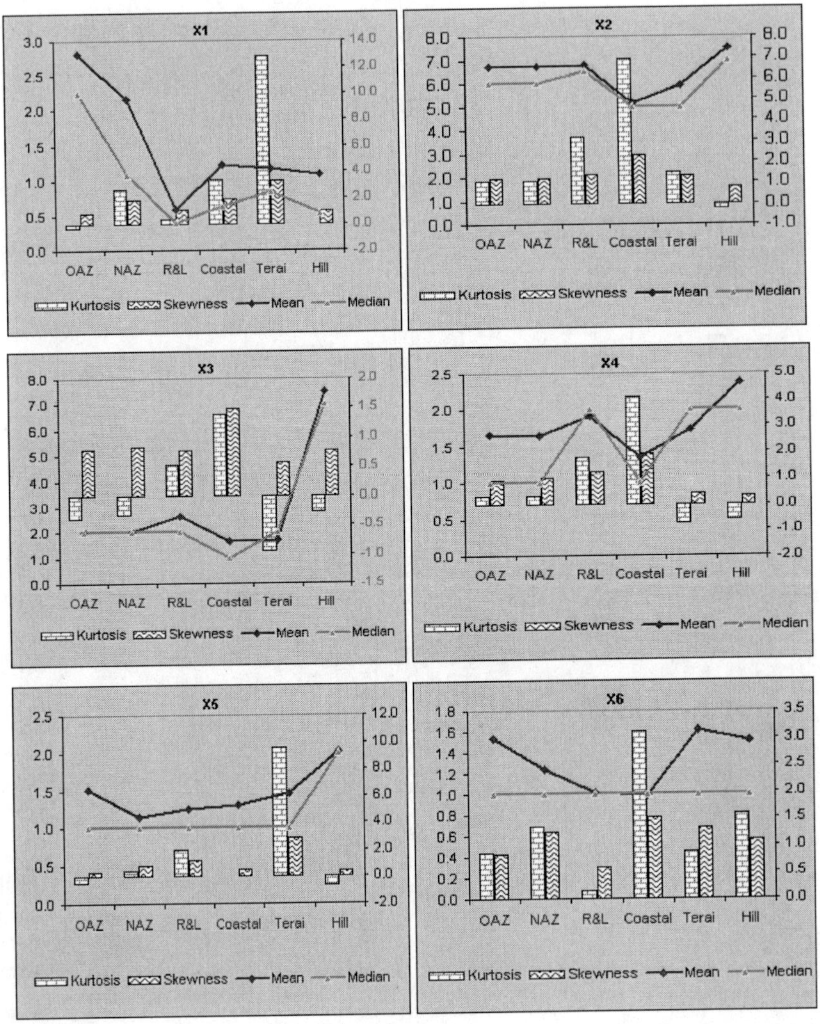

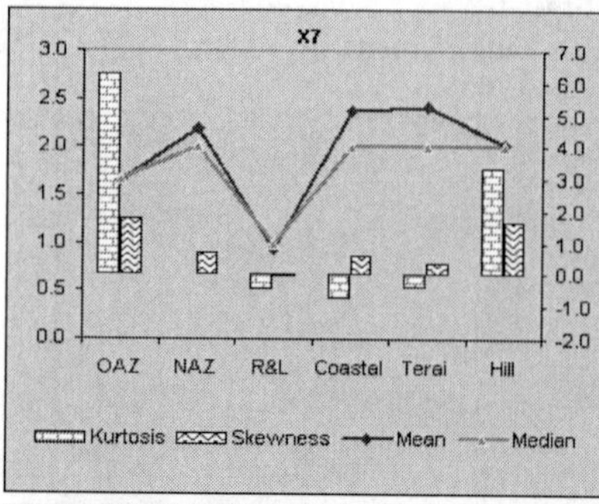
X7
OAZ NAZ R&L Coastal Terai Hill
Kurtosis Skewness Mean Median

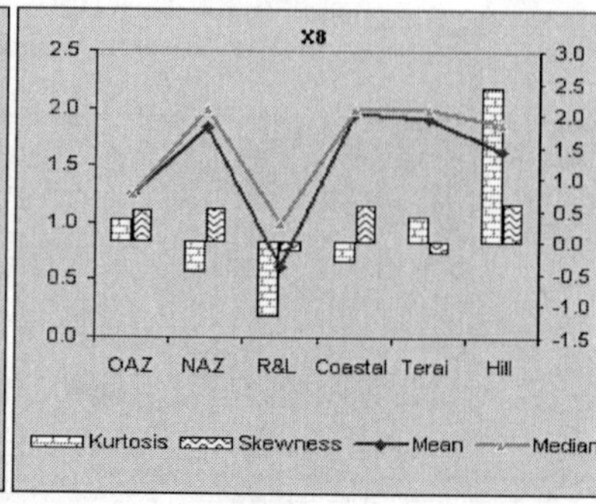
X8
OAZ NAZ R&L Coastal Terai Hill
Kurtosis Skewness Mean Median

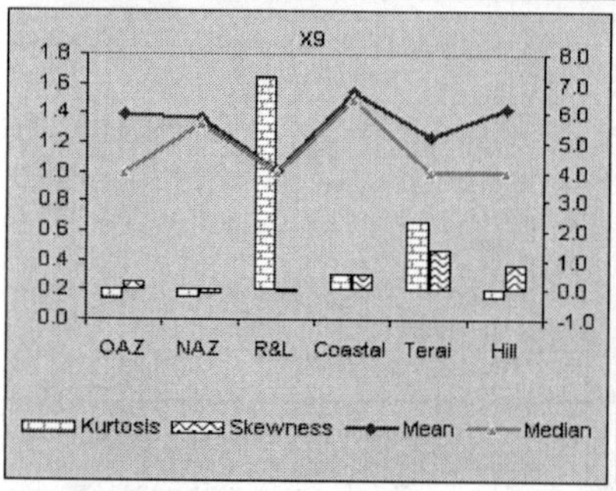
X9
OAZ NAZ R&L Coastal Terai Hill
Kurtosis Skewness Mean Median

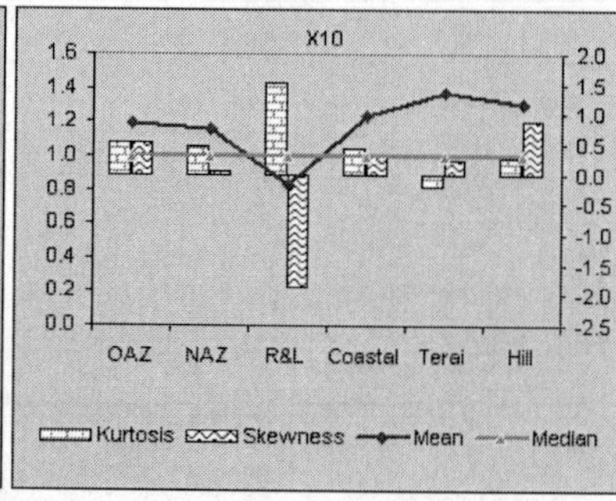
X10
OAZ NAZ R&L Coastal Terai Hill
Kurtosis Skewness Mean Median

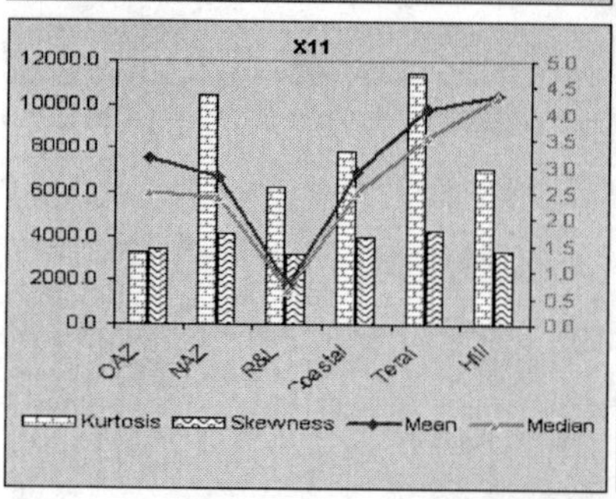
X11
OAZ NAZ R&L Coastal Terai Hill
Kurtosis Skewness Mean Median

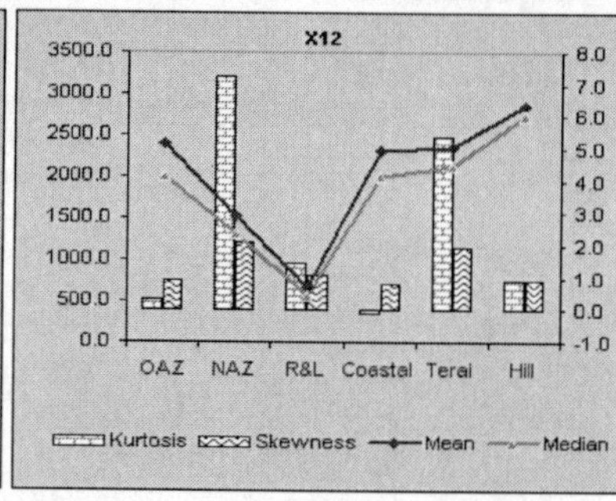
X12
OAZ NAZ R&L Coastal Terai Hill
Kurtosis Skewness Mean Median

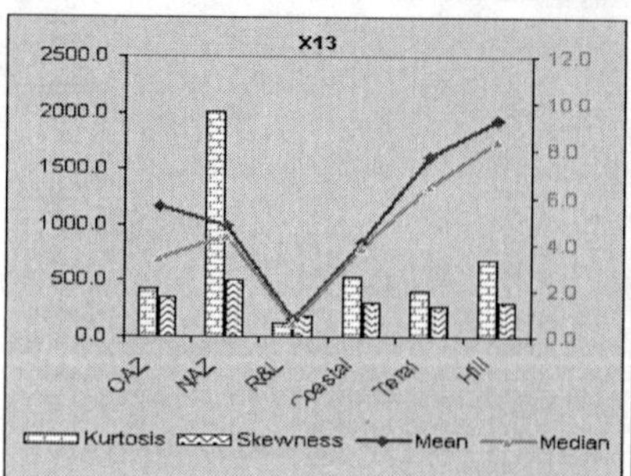
X13
OAZ NAZ R&L Coastal Terai Hill
Kurtosis Skewness Mean Median

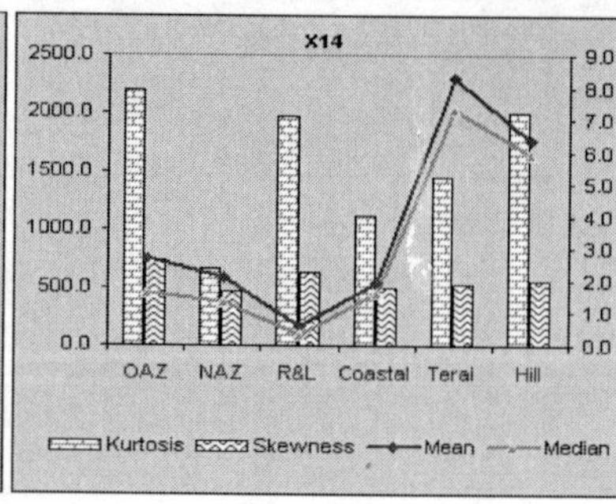
X14
OAZ NAZ R&L Coastal Terai Hill
Kurtosis Skewness Mean Median

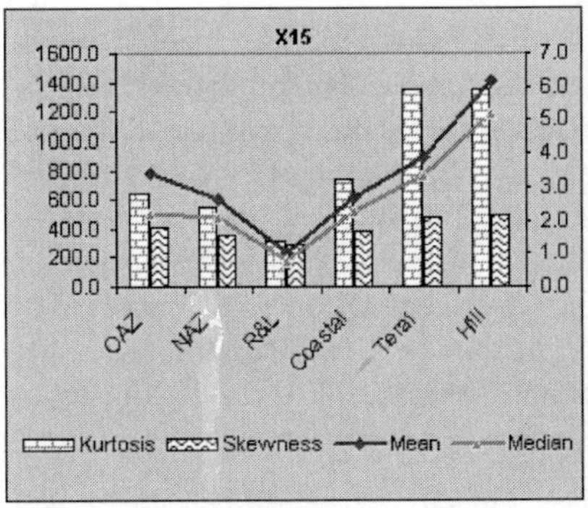
X15
1600.0
1400.0
1200.0
1000.0
800.0
600.0
400.0
200.0
0.0
7.0
6.0
5.0
4.0
3.0
2.0
1.0
0.0
OAZ
NAZ
R&L
Coastal
Terai
Hill
Kurtosis
Skewness
Mean
Median

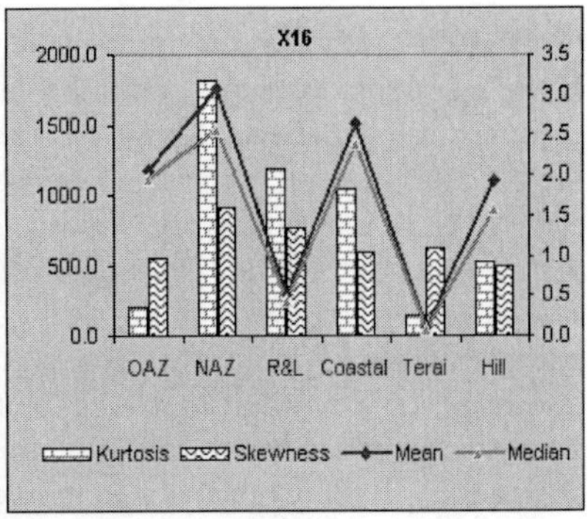
X16
2000.0
1500.0
1000.0
500.0
0.0
3.5
3.0
2.5
2.0
1.5
1.0
0.5
0.0
OAZ
NAZ
R&L
Coastal
Terai
Hill
Kurtosis
Skewness
Mean
Median

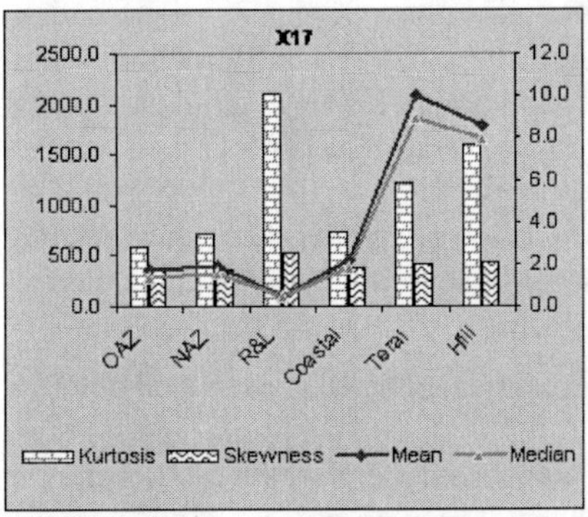
X17
2500.0
2000.0
1500.0
1000.0
500.0
0.0
12.0
10.0
8.0
6.0
4.0
2.0
0.0
OAZ
NAZ
R&L
Coastal
Terai
Hill
Kurtosis
Skewness
Mean
Median

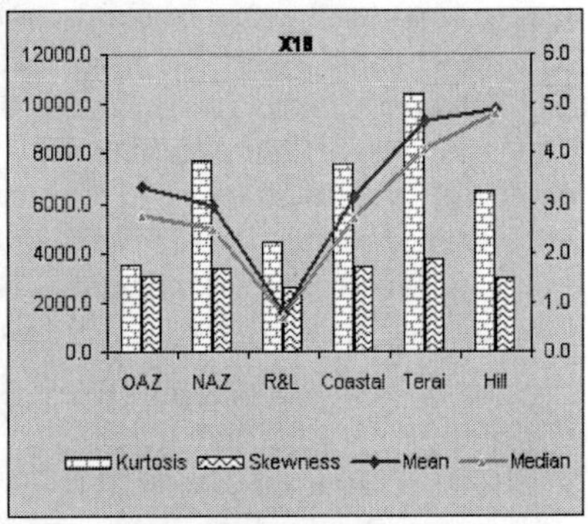
X18
12000.0
10000.0
8000.0
6000.0
4000.0
2000.0
0.0
6.0
5.0
4.0
3.0
2.0
1.0
0.0
OAZ
NAZ
R&L
Coastal
Terai
Hill
Kurtosis
Skewness
Mean
Median

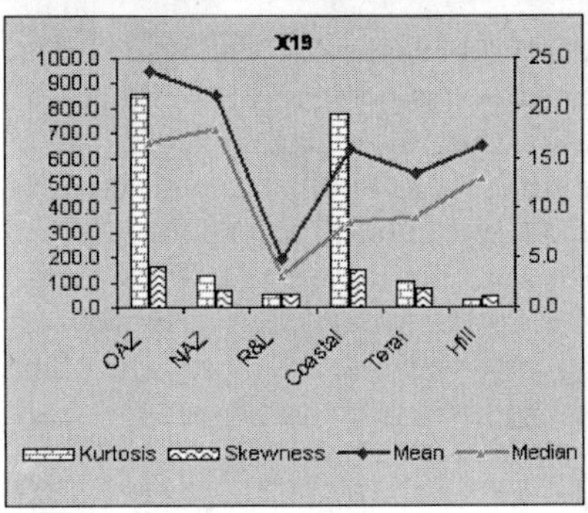
X19
1000.0
900.0
800.0
700.0
600.0
500.0
400.0
300.0
200.0
100.0
0.0
25.0
20.0
15.0
10.0
5.0
0.0
OAZ
NAZ
R&L
Coastal
Terai
Hill
Kurtosis
Skewness
Mean
Median

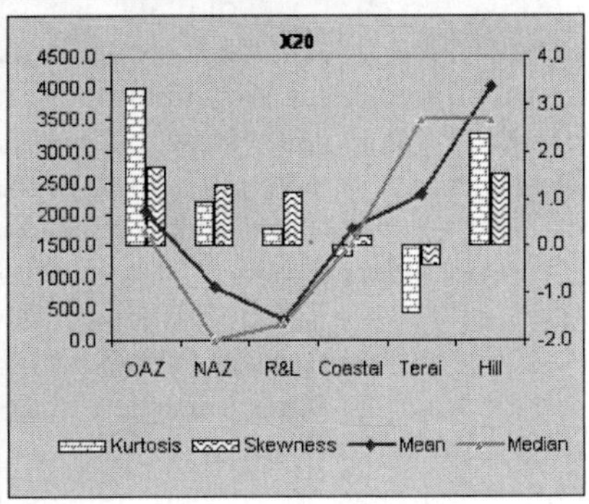
X20
4500.0
4000.0
3500.0
3000.0
2500.0
2000.0
1500.0
1000.0
500.0
0.0
4.0
3.0
2.0
1.0
0.0
-1.0
-2.0
OAZ
NAZ
R&L
Coastal
Terai
Hill
Kurtosis
Skewness
Mean
Median

(Rs 10395/-) indicates that most of the families belong to lower income group. In the selected households, only in 7 families, females are found to have some income varying between Rs 1200.00 and Rs 4000.00. In village Kodalia, from the old alluvial zone, the mean land holding is 2.40 hec/family with standard error of 0.53 and positively skewed. Leptokurtic shape of the land holding distribution curve tells that there are more number of landless households. The average family size is around 8 and the average education standard of adult males and male children is significantly more than their female counterparts. The adult males have around Madhyamik level of education, whereas the education standard of adult females is distributed with positive skewness and platykurtic shape in between the range of illiteracy and more than graduation. In case of children, the males have higher level education than the females as per the mean value. The average family income is Rs 5300.00/month. In this village, among the 25 households, in 16 families, women are found to have their own income, with an average Rs.1946.15/month. The curve is platykurtic shaped and positively skewed, which implies that majority of the women population of this village have lower income. Though education level is not at all satisfactory but the economic solvency is inversely related to the education standard for the adult women.

For the village Shikarpur (from new alluvial zone) the mean land holding of this village is 2 ha. and there is variability in this distribution. The average family size is four. In case of average adult males/family, the distribution is positively skewed and of platykurtic shape. The average education standard of males, females and the male and female children is nearly Madhyamik. The distribution of education in all these four cases is positively skewed and of platykurtic shape indicating that population with lower education standard is more. The average family income of the village is Rs 8600.00 and the curve is of positively skewed platykurtic shaped. Only 9 families among the selected 25 householders of village Shikarpur have women income earner. The average level of female monthly income is Rs 1977.78 and positively skewed distribution reveals that women earning lower income are more. The other village from the same zone (new alluvial zone) is village Chandamari. Here the total number of interviewed households is 50. In this village, along with cultivation there are service holders, and business-oriented people. Among the 42 households, in 20 households women are having their own earnings. The interviewed households have some variability in their income and depending on this difference, the different expenditure shares have high peak in their distribution curve. The average education standard of the adult males is above the secondary standard of education. Adult females have nearly Madhyamik standard. The male child education standard is more than primary level, whereas girl child is on just primary level. The female income/month on an average is Rs 2265.00.

From the red–laerite zone two villages i.e. Kesia and Chakedabad were selected. In village Kesia the number of households interviewed is 33. The maximum personal land holding is 1.58 hectare and the variability ranges from 0.20 ha. to 1.58 ha. On the other side, the mean total monthly income is Rs 2313.64. The villagers are not high-income earners and the frequency of lower income earners is more compared to high income earners, whose earnings range between Rs 900.00 (min. value) and Rs 5100.00 (max. value). Among the 33 households, in 16 households women are engaged in income earning jobs. But there is great variability in the distribution ranging between Rs 250.00-Rs.1300.00. In the village, family literacy as well as families having just primary standard of education were identified. The average education standard of adult male per family is better than their female counter parts. In village Chakedabad, the main occupation of the villagers is daily labour. The village, though have some cultivable land but due to lack of irrigation and other infrastructural facilities cultivation has no prominent effect on the economic status of the village. The parental generation has only the knowledge of writing their own name whereas in the second generation the male children are in relatively better position. The average family size of this village is 6 with an average family income of Rs 1147.86. The positive value of skewness indicates that lower income families are more in number. The average female income is Rs 340.00 and it varies from Rs.150.00 and Rs.550.00.

In the coastal zone, one of the selected villages is village Nimpith. The mean land holding of the village is 0.28 hac. The education standard of males is more than higher secondary level and the females on an average have nearly H.S. level education. The male child's education standard is nearly madhyamik level and that of female child education is primary level. The monthly average family income is Rs 6005.00 and various heads of expenditure reveal that as the family income grows up, the expenses on education, medical, savings etc. will increase. But the consumption of food, cultivation expenditure has no such variations. The adult female's monthly income (per family) is Rs 2420.00 and in 20 households among the 40 selected households income earner females are found and their income distribution shows high peak with positive skewness. For village Taldihi the average land holding is 2.17 hac./family. The male child's education standard (1.662) is relatively higher than the education standard of the girl child. The total average family monthly income is Rs 7802.50 and the adult female's monthly income is Rs 952.38. The positively skewed distribution of the curve indicates that the majority of the female earners are having almost the average level of income.

Village Kalimpong was selected from the hill zone where a total of 25 households were surveyed. The average land holding of this village is 0.20 hac./family and the distribution is positively skewed with 0.03 standard error. The village has an average of 8 members per family where the number of adult males and girls is relatively high. Average male education standard is nearly of secondary level (1.85) and positively skewed leptokurtic shape of the distribution curve indicates that a small per centage of the adult males have more education. A similar trend has been noticed for adult female's education standard (1.57). Average male child's and female child's education standard on an average is 1.52 and 1.29, respectively and the distribution is positively skewed, indicating a uniform flow though female child's education level is comparatively less than male child's. The average monthly family income of this village is Rs 10688.04 and the expenditure patterns are positively skewed, and the education, medical and cultivation expenditure has leptokurtic shape of distribution. This implies that families with high income, which is less in number, are able to spend on these above mentioned heads of expenditure. For village Sukiapokhri, the average land holding is 1.23 hac./family. The area is purely in hilly region. The inhabitants are mainly engaged in business such as transportation, hotel, grocery, export-import business etc. There are some service holders also, mainly in military and army, forest and tourism departments. The average number of family members is about 7. The education standard of the adult male is relatively higher than the adult female but in case of male and female children, virtually there is no significant difference. In this village more than 80% of the households have women bread earners. Family-wise, average total monthly income is Rs 9894.46, and high peakedness of the distribution implies that the income of all the households is not showing a stable flow. In case of adult female's monthly income (family-wise), there is some unstable flow with kurtosis value of 4.19, which means there is a small number of females who have more income and the majority has lower levels of income.

In village Banarhata, the average land holding per family is 2.05 hac. The distribution of female education is negatively skewed, indicating that the majority of the female population of this village has less than average level of education. The female child's education standards like their mothers, is also negatively skewed. The average total family income is Rs 9836.67 and the expenditures are positively skewed; and except the education and cultivation expenditure all the other heads are of leptokurtic shape. This indicates that higher income relates to higher expenditure and the per centage of families following this pattern is less. The average female income per month is Rs 4336.00 and this income is also positively skewed and leptokurtic shaped and nearly 75 per cent houses have female income earners. In village Matigara, the average land holding is 6.650 hac./family. Though average education standard is higher for adult males (2.17) than their female counterparts (1.90), but in the case of male children (1.50) and female children (1.55), it is of the same level (Table 9L). The total average monthly income is Rs 9836.67 and the value of kurtosis (4.659) indicates that the family income and the family expenditure pattern have some asymmetry. Male child's and female's child average education standard is in parity i.e. they are significantly positively related with each other.

Zonal Characteristics

Reflection of the village characteristics is noticed in zonal behaviour also. If landholding be one of the indicators of socio-economic conditions of the people then there could be three zonal groups: (a) the old and new alluvial zones with more than two hectares of land per family; (b) coastal, terai and hill zones with an average land holding of one hectare or more; and (c) the red and laterite zone, with an average land holding of only 0.58 hectare per family. Highest number of family members is recorded in hill zone (7.48) compared to around 6.7 in old alluvial zone, new alluvial zone and red and laterite zone. The lowest number of family members is recorded in coastal and terai zones. As far as standard of education is concerned, the overall standard of education is not at all satisfactory, with highest education score being 2.42 in terai zone and 1.96 in coastal and saline zone for adult males and females respectively. Clearly the red and laterite zone is lagging behind the other zones (Table 10, Appendix 1). The average monthly income per family varies between Rs 6700.00 and Rs 10440.00, excepting the red and laterite zone, where it is only Rs 1800.00 per month. Average monthly adult female income per family also follows the same pattern; maximum of Rs 4000.00 per family is recorded in hill zone followed by Rs 2300.00 in terai zone. This is because of the fact that in these two zones, females are mostly engaged in tea and orange plantations. The lowest family female income recorded is for laterite zone. This income pattern is also found in family expenditure pattern. The people of red and laterite zone could spend only Rs1600.00 per month for a family size of 6.7 against 4-5 times in other zones with an appreciable difference in average family sizes. Thus, there are variations in all aspects of our consideration among the zones of West Bengal, and particularly the people of red and laterite zone are not only socio-economically week but also are living below the subsistence level. By and large, it is clear from the study that after 32 years of Left Front Governance, the people of West Bengal are not at all living at the satisfactory level.

Women Empowerment and Empowerment Related Factors

Table 9 gives the summary of empowerment and empowerment related factors in different zones of West Bengal. From this table it is revealed that in the coastal-saline zone the level of empowerment (X1=35.27) and female education standard (X3=1.97) are significantly higher compared to the other five zones. Whereas in the hill zone, women are having 3.33 occupations standard (X4), the terai zone shows higher (Rs.2136.00 per month) female income (X5). This may be due to the fact that the opportunity of working in the tea gardens and ancillary work against remuneration is more in the terai zone compared to other zones. It is also noteworthy that the average female age at marriage (X6) and at first exposure to childbirth is higher in the hilly and terai zones that have higher income and occupation opportunities for

Table 9: Averages of the Family and Demographic Particulars of the Married Females of Present Generation in Different Zones of West Bengal

Zone	X_1	X_2	X_3	X_4	X_5	X_6	X_7	X_8	X_9	X_{10}
Z_1	31.31	30.62	1.09	2.06	637.18	15.91	17.51	1.68	1.96	7.90
Z_2	34.82	32.25	1.57	2.12	810.87	17.32	18.34	1.49	1.98	6.80
Z_3	30.77	30.16	0.59	2.24	130.87	15.90	17.50	1.37	1.77	7.44
Z_4	35.27	32.63	1.97	2.06	786.36	18.08	19.14	1.80	2.07	5.88
Z_5	35.06	31.02	1.91	2.31	2136.36	19.98	21.57	1.63	1.78	7.08
Z_6	34.71	31.77	1.66	3.33	1739.81	20.03	23.24	2.10	2.34	9.06
Levelof Sig.	*	*	**	*	*	**	*	*	*	**
Zone	X11	X12	X13	X14	X15	X16	X17	X18	X19	X20
Z_1	7617.95	2794.49	964.62	458.08	702.72	1305.51	350..92	6576.33	1041.62	11.67
Z_2	7579.35	1723.01	1144.11	630.91	675.52	1976.09	442..32	6591.96	987.39	11.07
Z_3	1989.65	756.29	134.91	163.70	292.74	351.90	94.54	1794.07	195.58	6.93
Z_4	7413.64	2744.21	800.92	532.88	582.90	1565.65	446.23	6672.79	740.84	11.43
Z_5	11585.95	2859.84	1914.75	2793.37	1091.88	72.28	2520.12	11252.24	626.27	8.00
Z_6	10787.06	2954.17	1990.59	1886.65	1411.54	1075.11	1851.29	10128.45	658.61	9.89
Level of Sig.	**	*	**	*	**	**	*	*	*	*

Note 1 Z_1= Old Alluvial Zone, Z_2=New Alluvial Zone, Z_3= Red Laterite Zone, Z_4= Coastal Zone, Z_5=Terrai Zone, Z_6=Hill Zone

Note 2 * =Significant at 5% level, ** = Significant at 1% level

Note 3 The factors X_1=Empowerment quotient, X_2=Present age (yrs), X_3=Education standard, X_4=Occupation standard, X_5=Female income (Rs)/month, X_6=Age at Marriage (yrs), X_7=Age at first birth(yrs), X_8=Number of children, X_9=Number of births, X_{10}= Number of family members, X_{11}=Total monthly family income (Rs), X_{12}=Family food expenditure (Rs)/month, X_{13}=Family education expenditure (Rs)/month, X_{14}=Family clothing expenditure (Rs)/month, X_{15}=Family medical expenditure (Rs)/month, X_{16}=Family cultivation expenditure (Rs)/month, X_{17}=Family others expenditure (Rs)/month, X_{18}=Total expenditure (Rs)/month, X_{19}=Family savings (Rs)/month, X_{20}=Media exposure and social attachment.

females respectively. Therefore, one can expect association between the female economic solvency and timely/delayed marriage. In the context of media exposure and social involvement (X20), coastal-saline, new alluvial and old alluvial zones show better values compared to other three zones. Therefore, it can be concluded that education standard (X3), media exposure and social involvement (X20) have a relationship in coastal-saline and old alluvial zones, whereas financial and demographic features are showing linkages in the hill and terai zones (Fig. 1).

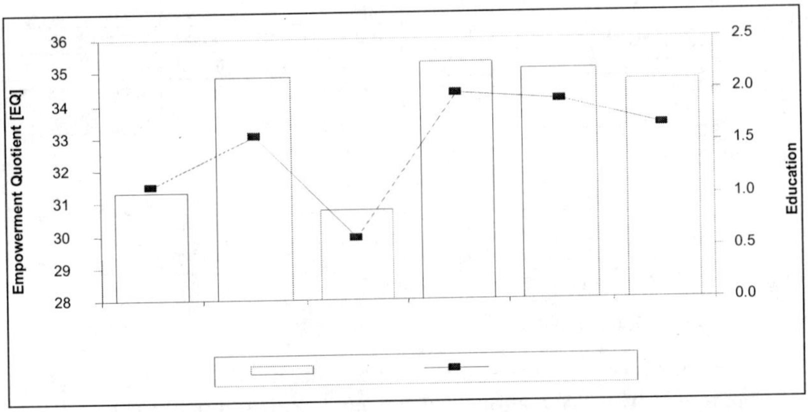

Figure 1: Women Empowerment vis-à-vis Standard of Education in Different Zones

Association of Education with Female Demographic Features

Table 10 depicts the liner association of education with number of children and number of births for married women. The relationship between number of births and number of children was also calculated at the village, zonal and state level.

Table 10: Degree of Linear Association between Education, Number of Children and Number of Births

A. Village Level

Item	*Kanagarh*	*Kodalia*	*Shikarpur*	*Chandamari*	*Kesia*	*Chakedabad*
Education x Number of Children	-0.733*	0.673*	0.854*	-0.783*	-0.018	-0.766*
Education x Number of Births	-0.848*	0.068	0.837*	-0.108	-0.063	0.264
Number of Births x Number of Children	0.872*	-0.142	0.823*	-0.007	0.725*	-0.191

Item	*Nimpith*	*Taldihi*	*Kalimpong*	*Sukiapokhri*	*Banarhata*	*Matigara*
Education x Number of Children	-0.798*	-0.760	-0.730*	-0.056	-0.754*	0.474*
Education x Number of Births	-0.731*	-0.678*	-0.734*	-0.052	0.742*	-0.721*
Number of Births x Number of Children	0.912*	0.902*	0.893*	0.922*	0.694*	-0.446*

B. Zonal Level

Item	*Old Alluvial Zone*	*New Alluvial Zone*	*Red - Laterite Zone*	*Coastal Zone*	*Hill Zone*	*Terai Zone*
Education x Number of Children	0.360*	-0.403*	-0.278*	-0.718*	-0.339*	-0.052
Education x Number of Births	0.194	0.121	0.069	-0.622*	-0.354*	-0.018
Number of Births x Number of Children	0.200	0.334*	0.332*	0.927*	0.911*	0.518*

C. State Level

Item	*West Bengal*
Education x Number of Children	-0.897*
Education x Number of Births	-0.774*
Number of Births x Number of Children	0.897*

*Significant at p=0.05

The study reveals that in 7 villages out of 12 there exist negative correlations between education level and number of children. But not all these villages show the same pattern of relation between number of births and education level. Only 5 out of the 7 villages show negative pattern. In village Matigara, the negative relation between the number of births and the number of children has been observed. Here the child birth and survival rate is inversely related. In case of zonal analysis, it has been found that except old alluvial zone and terai zone all the other zones have negative correlation between the education standard and number of children. Again in the context of relationship between number of births and education attainment only coastal and hill zones are showing significant negative correlation. Combining all the villages, the educational standard and number of children per female and number of births per female are highly negatively correlated, whereas there is high positive correlation between the number of births and number of children.

Zonal Study of Variation in Education Standard of Adult Women of Present Generation at Different Age Groups

Education has been taken as one of the major indictors for women empowerment, women development vis-à-vis development of society. Here, the variation in women education over the zones and the state as a whole has been analysed with the help of ANOVA. Before proceeding for the analysis, the whole data of education standard of the married women of present generation has been divided into three different age groups. The first group comprises the women who are below 30 years of age. The second group is for the women aged between 30-45 years and the third group comprises the women aged more than 45 years of age.

If one considers the standard of education among the adult women of most recent generation (i.e. the age group of 30 years), one can find that there has been general improvement in all the zones except the other two groups. The women of red and laterite zone are poorly educated, with average standard of education being only around primary and below. Maximum of 2.07 education score is recorded in terai zone followed by 1.973 in hill zone, 1.881 in coastal and saline zone. But one thing is very clear from Table 11 that for all the groups for all the regions, the standard of education of the adult and/or married females is not at all satisfactory (Fig. 2).

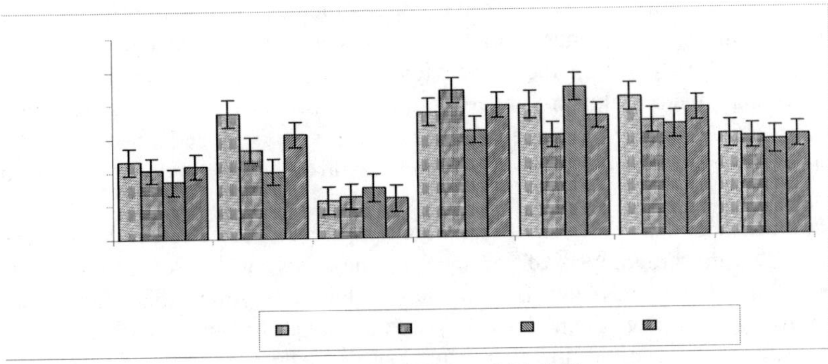

Figure 2: Education Status of Adult Women

Table 11: Zonal Analysis of Variance of Education Standard of the Women of Present Generation

Zone	*Average Level of Education*			*Group Comparison* (z)		
	Gr-1: 30 yrs	*Gr-2: 30-45 yrs*	*Gr-3: >45 yrs*	*Gr-1 vs Gr-2*	*Gr-1 vs Gr-3*	*Gr-2 vs Gr-3*
OAZ (zone 1)	1.162 (43)	1.036 (35)	0.857 (7)	0.150 0.301	0.286 0.240	0.136 0.589
NAZ (zone 2)	1.869 (46)	1.333 (36)	1.000 (10)	0.539 0.000	0.787 0.068	0.248 0.572
R-L Zone (zone 3)	0.560 (75)	0.625 (30)	0.750 (8)	0.066 0.583	0.198 0.356	0.132 0.560
Coastal (zone 4)	1.881 (59)	2.195 (41)	1.6 (10)	0.393 0.156	0.161 0.728	0.554 0.245
Hill (zone 5)	1.973 (74)	1.521 (67)	2.230 (13)	0.196 0.174	0.515 0.000	0.710 0.000
Terai (zone 6)	2.078 (64)	1.728 (48)	1.667 (6)	0.353 0.000	0.414 0.261	0.061 0.869

Note: Figures in the parenthesis are the number of respondents.
Underlined figures are the respective probability levels.
(z) : values shown in the comparison are the respective mean values.

Overall Study of Variation in Educational Standard of Adult Women of Present Generation at Different Age Groups at State Level (Combining all the Villages)

The result of analysis of variance for different age groups is described in Table 12. Total 672 adult females of present generation comprised the selected sample. Among them 361 belong to the age group one (<30 years of age), 257 belong to age group two (30-45 years), and 54 women group three i.e. above 45 years of age. As per the descriptive statistics, the average education standard of these three groups is 1.526, 1.478 and 1.425 respectively. Neither of these groups reaches the secondary standard of education, nor do they have any significant difference between their educational levels. In group comparison, only group one and group two have significant difference at 0.07% level; the other two combinations such as group two & three, and group one & three have no such differences. The old alluvial zone has just above primary level of education (1.089) whereas in the new alluvial zone, the standard is slightly high i.e. 1.565, which means the level is more than primary but below secondary. In coastal-saline and terai zones the standards are almost secondary level, 1.973 and 1.909 respectively. The hill zone is placed below the terai and coastal-saline zones but higher than the old and new alluvial zone with an average of 1.679. The real matter of concern is the education level of red-laterite zone, which is not at all satisfactory (0.591), i.e. far below the primary level. From the analysis of variance a zone-wise comparison of education standards has been made. In this study, it has been found that old alluvial significantly differs from all the other five zones. The new alluvial zone has significant differences with other zones, except the terrain zone. The red-laterite zone, i.e. 3rd zone, differs with all other zones at 0.001% level of significance. The coastal-saline zone (zone 4) has no difference with zone 6 only, and terai zone has significant difference with only new alluvial zone that has been mentioned earlier. The hill zone i.e. zone 6, significantly differs from other four zones, except the coastal-saline zone. Statistical tests (group comparison, Table 14) also reject the assumption of significant improvement in level of education among different age groups of adult females.

Table 12: Analysis of Variance of Education Standard of the Women of Present Generation in Different Zones, West Bengal: New ANOVA

Average Level of Education			*Group Comparison* [(z)]		
Gr-1: < 30 yrs	*Gr-2: 30-45 yrs*	*Gr-3: > 45 yrs*	*Gr-1 vs Gr-2*	*Gr-1vs Gr-3*	*Gr-2 vs Gr-3*
1.526 (361)	1.478 (257)	1.425 (54)	0.146 0.071	0.142 0.321	0.003 0.981

Zonal Comparison

Zone-1 vs. Zone-2	Zone-2 vs. Zone-3	Zone-3 vs. Zone-5
1.496 0.001	0.996 0.001	1.114 0.000
Zone-1 vs. Zone-3	Zone-2 vs. Zone-4	Zone-3 vs. Zone-6
0.513 0.000	0.402 0.000	1.336 0.000
Zone-1 vs. Zone-4	Zone-2 vs. Zone-5	Zone-4 vs. Zone-5
0.885 0.000	0.118 0.000	0.284 0.777
Zone-1 vs. Zone-5	Zone-2 vs. Zone-6	Zone-4 vs. Zone-6
0.601 0.000	0.340 0.000	0.062 0.000
Zone-1 vs. Zone-6	Zone-3 vs. Zone-4	Zone-5 vs. Zone-6
0.823 0.001	1.398 0.000	0.222 0.000

Note: Figures in the parenthesis are the number of respondents.
Underlined figures are the respective probability levels.
(z): values shown in the comparison are the respective mean values.
Zone-1: Old Alluvial zone, Zone-2: New Alluvial zone, Zone-3: Red and Laterite zone, Zone-4: Coastal and Saline zone, Zone-5: Hill zone, Zone-6: Terai zone

A nation/country progresses with the progress of the mothers of the country. Educated and empowered mothers are the building blocks of any progressive nation but that type of picture is not at all found in the state of West Bengal, in spite of political stability.

Zonal Variations of Education Index of Males and Females

The education index, following the procedure as mentioned earlier, has been calculated for each village for males and females, separately. Exercises have also been taken up at zonal and combining all the zones, to get a picture of the male-female education indices. Two-way analysis of variance has been conducted to examine the inter-zonal variations in education indices and the result of analysis of variance has been depicted in Table 13.

Table 13: Analysis of Variance of Education Index of the Males and Females at Different Zones

Zone/State	*Male Education Index*	*Female Education Index*	*Gender Comparison*(z)
Old Alluvial (Z1)	0.772	0.618	
New Alluvial (Z2)	0.792	0.636	
Red-Laterite (Z3)	0.690	0.457	
Coastal-Saline (Z4)	0.764	0.621	0.167 (*)
Terai (Z5)	0.787	0.620	
Hill (Z6)	0.765	0.634	
West Bengal	0.762	0.594	

Zonal Comparison$^{(z)}$

Zone 1 vs. Zone 2	Zone 2 vs. Zone 3	Zone 3 vs. Zone 5
0.019 (NS)	0.141 (*)	0.121 (*)
Zone 1 vs. Zone 3	Zone 2 vs. Zone 4	Zone 3 vs. Zone 6
0.121 (*)	0.022 (NS)	0.125 (*)
Zone 1 vs. Zone 4	Zone 2 vs. Zone 5	Zone 4 vs. Zone 5
0.004 (NS)	0.019 (NS)	0.002 (NS)
Zone 1 vs. Zone 5	Zone 2 vs. Zone 6	Zone 4 vs. Zone 6
0.000 (NS)	0.015 (NS)	0.007 (NS)
Zone 1 vs. Zone 6	Zone 3 vs. Zone 4	Zone 5 vs. Zone 6
0.004 (NS)	0.119 (*)	0.004 (NS)

(*) : Significant at 5% level
(NS) : Non-significant at 5% level
z : Values shown in comparison are the respective mean differences.

The analysis reveals that there exists significant difference between the male and female education indices. Generally the male education index is higher than the female education index. Maximum male education index (0.792) has been found in the new alluvial zone followed by the terrai zone (0.787). The maximum (0.636) female education index is found in the new alluvial zone, followed by the hill zone (0.634). Lowest male (0.690) and female (0.457) education indices are found in red-laterite zone. Among the different zones under consideration, red-laterite zone is found to have significantly low education index compared to any other zones of West Bengal. Over all 0.762 and 0.594 male and female education indices respectively are recorded, combining all the zones of the state of West Bengal.

Conclusion

From the overall study of women in six different zones of West Bengal, even after 60 years of independence of India, it is clear that:

1. Inspite of appreciable improvement in educational level it, has failed to attain a respectable level; it is not desirable to have average level of education around Madhyamik or below.
2. There have been variations in education indices not only among the zones of West Bengal but also between males and females of the state. For a state governed by the leftist for so many years this may be due to improper formulation of policy or failure to provide equal opportunity to both males and females.
3. Education is inversely related with number of children. In a country like India, where population pressure seems to be a major problem, education should have been given top priority or educational policies should have been implemented in such a way as to have an immediate impact on population besides other fields.

4. Higher education of women is directly related with higher women empowerment which envisages higher economic independence of women also. As it is evident from the study that among the six zones, the women of the hill zone and terai zone are not only having higher education but also are having higher income by virtue of the working opportunities in tea gardens etc., compared to their counterparts in other zones. Therefore, higher education opportunities, coupled with greater job opportunities, are also needed for proper development.
5. There exists regional disparities with respect to overall development of the society as evident from the wide range of variations in socio-economic indicators like possession of wealth like land, education at all levels (males, females children), family income, female income, women empowerment indicators etc. In a state which has been politically stabile for so many years, it was expected that the regional development should have taken place at equal pace all through the state. Most probably, region specific policy decision and its implementation, utilizing the local resources with active participation of local people, are required to be geared up still.
6. The study of all the socio-economic and other indicators indicate that red and laterite zone is lagging behind all other zones. The people of this zone are educationally poor, they have low income, low land holding etc. As a result, a family of around seven members is to manage with mere Rs 1600.00 for whole month to survive. If we look into the zone, one can see that this is the most disturbed zone of the state at present, may be improper development of the people is one of the reasons for such disturbances. Thus, the right policy followed by effective implementation strategy and with better empowered women providing a significant force for the development, better West Bengal could have been realized.

References

Anonymous (1991, 2001): *Census Reports of India*. Govt. of India.

Anonymous (1993): *World Education Report*. UNESCO

Anonymous (1995): *Women's Education and Fertility Behavior*. Department of Economics and Social Information and Policy Analysis, Population Division. United Nations, New York.

Anonymous (1996): Statistics and Gender – *Agricultural Censuses: Orientations for a Revision of Concepts and Methodology*. FAO, Rome.

Anonymous (1996): UNDP Human Development Report, 1996.

Anonymous (1996): World of Work, International Labour Organization.

Anonymous (1998-99): *Selected Educational Statistics*. Ministry of HRD, Govt. of India.

Anonymous (1999): Economic Imbalance – Poverty and Abundance, *Economic and Social Council,* 1999. Department of Public Information / Media Division UN.

Anonymous (1999): Filling the Data Gap – Gender-sensitive Statistics for Agricultural Development. Economic and Social Development Department, FAO Corporate Document Repository.

http://www.fao.org/docrep/x2785e/X2785e08.htm

Anonymous (1999): Innovations in Labor Statistics. *International Labors Review*, ILO, 138 (1).

Anonymous (2004-05): *Selected Educational Statistics*. Ministry of HRD, Govt. of India.

Anonymous (2007): *Education for All – Global Monitoring Report* – 2007

Anonymous (2008): United Nations Development Programme Report, 2007/2008. UNDP

Anonymous (1995): Fourth World Conference on Women. Action for Equality, Development and Peace. Beijing, 4-15 September. *Country Report*, Department of Child and Women, Government of India.

Birdsall Nancy (1977): Analytical Approaches to the Relationship of Population Growth and Development. *Population and Development Review*, Vol. 3, No. 1/ 2 Mar; Jun., 1977), pp. 63-102.

Brown Jennifer and Das Choudhury, Sujata (2002): Women's Land Rights in West Bengal: A Field Study. Rural Development Institute. ISSN 1071-7099.

CIA World Fact Book (2008): URL:http//en.wikipedia.org/wiki/CIA_World_ Factbook.

Ismail Serageldin (2000): Food Security – Daunting Research Tasks. *The Hindu*: Survey of Indian Agriculture.

Jain Devaki (1985): *Tyranny of the Household: Investigative Essays on Women's Work (Women in Poverty)*. Amazon Books.

Mehra, R. and S. Gammage (1999): Trends, Countertrends and gaps in women's employment. World Development Report, 27 (3): 533-50.

Pradhan, K Basant and Singh, Shalabh Kumar (2000): *Policy Reforms and Financing of Elementary Education in India*. A Study of the Quality of Service and Outcome. National Council of Applied Economic Research. New Delhi.

Ramachandran V.K., Madhura Swaminathan, Vikas Rawal (2003): Barriers To Expansion of Mass Literacy and Primary Schooling in West Bengal. A Study Based on Primary Data from Selected Villages. *Working Paper No. 345*. This paper is part of a larger study on primary education in West Bengal by UNICEF. (URL: http//www.cds.edu).

Rawal, Vikas and Madhura Swaminathan (1998): Changing Trajectories – Agricultural Growth in West Bengal, 1950 to 1996, *Economic and Political Weekly*; 33(40); Oct 3-9; pp. 2595-2602.

Roy, K. C. and C.A. Tisdell (2000): Institutional Impediments Entitlement Exchange and Women's Empowerment in Rural India – The Case of Access to Education, Social Economies, Policy and Development. *Working Paper No. 5*. Brisbane School of Economies, The University of Queensland.

Saha, Anamitra and Madhura Swaminathan (1994): Agricultural Growth in West Bengal in the 1980s: A Disaggregation by Districts and Crops. *Economic and Political Weekly;* 29 (13); Mar 26. pp: A2–A11.

Shiva Kumar, A K. (1996): UNDP's Gender-Related Development Index – A Computation for Indian States. *Economic & Political Weekly*; 31 (14); pp. 887-95.

16

NON-MARKET BENEFITS OF WOMEN'S EDUCATION

— MADHUSUDAN RAJ*

Abstract

This paper analyses the non-market benefits of women's education by using data of 300, 25+ age women from Surat city. These non-market benefits of education are extremely important from the human development perspective, but are by and large ignored by the economists so far. Women's education is of more importance because they spend most of their time in home outside market place, and thus they are more likely recipient of these benefits. Seen from this angle, and looking at the kind of responsibility of handling the whole family, women have their education and its non-market benefits are of immense importance for the household as well as the society. The results are mixed having major policy implications.

Introduction

Education is one of the important factors which enable human progress. It not only helps individuals in achieving economic prosperity but also in acquiring more satisfaction and happiness from their life. It teaches everyone how to be a good human and advance morally and materialistically. This is the reason why education is considered as the most essential part of growth and development policies around the world. Not only the developing countries are implementing policies to improve the educational standards of their population[1], but even developed countries like United States of America (USA) are worried about the falling educational standards of native population, and hence American federal government has started the educational programs like 'No Child Left Behind'. Education benefits individuals and the economy in many ways. Economists have classified education's benefits in two broad categories,

(a) Market benefits; and

(b) Non-Market benefits.

The market benefits of education are well documented in the economic literature (Psacharopoulos, 1973, 1985, 1994; Psacharopoulos & Patrinos, 2002). At micro level education increases individual's labour market earnings by increasing his/her marginal productivity, which results because of more accumulation of human capital which in turn is a result of more education. At macro level education affects, both directly and indirectly, the economic growth of the country. But this well documented benefit of education ignores the non-market benefits. Non-market benefits are far more important than the market benefits. This is because they are the real manifestation of overall improvement in the quality of life. Human development is reflected in the form of overall freedom, good health, knowledge, improvement in standard of living of people, improvement in political freedom, a secure life, a healthy environment and forests, wildlife, air and water, lesser crimes, protection of basic human rights etc. All these aspects of human development are also non-market benefits of education.

Economists, until recently, have largely ignored most of these non-market benefits of education. The present day estimates of benefits of education are grossly under-estimated because they exclude these very important non-market benefits. Once we take into account these benefits, the rate of return to investment in education improves dramatically. So far, in India there are very few available studies which try to capture the market and non-market benefits of education. In India the estimates of market rates of returns to investment in education are hard to find. And the relationship between education and these market benefits is also not very well explored. On the other hand, studies of non-market benefits of education have so far focused their attention on areas like education's effect on fertility rate of women, parental education's effect on child's education, health etc. But apart from this, there is very little attempt to measure the other non-market benefits of education like effects on health of spouse, crime reduction, increased savings behaviour, consumer choice efficiency, increased civic sense, increased environmental awareness, increased charitable activities, increased social cohesion etc.

India is a progressing economy and has all potentiality to achieve higher development levels. It is pertinent to study market and non-market benefits of education in India because education is one of the chief factors which is going to help India in achieving the developmental goals.

A Catalogue of Non-Market Benefits of Education

Table 1 below gives a detailed description of the different non-market benefits of education, which have been identified so far by the researchers[2]. As we can see, the range of outcomes span from very specific private benefits to some widespread social benefits as well as some benefits having a mixed private and social nature. The major impact of education is felt inside the household in the form of better quality of child's health and education, better quality of husband's health and some impact on spouse's labour market earning and better health of the individual possessor of education. A brief discussion on these benefits follows:

Table 1: Catalogue of Non-Market Benefits of Education[3]

Outcome Category	*Economic Nature*
Intra-family productivity	Private; some external effects; market and non-market effects.
Child quality: level of education and cognitive development	Private; some external effect; market and non-market effects
Child quality: health	Private: some external effects
Child quality: fertility	Private; some external effects
Own health	Private: modest external effects (Note: Some of the own health benefits from education will be captured in increased earnings)
Consumer choice efficiency	Private; some external effects; non-market effects
Labour market search efficiency	Private; non-market effects
Marital choice efficiency	Private; non-market effects
Attainment of desired family size	Private
Charitable giving	Private and public; non-market effects
Savings	Private; some external effects
Technological change	Public
Social cohesion	Public
Self-reliance or economic independence	Private and public
Crime reduction	Public

(i) Intra-family productivity: the evidences[4] suggest that there is a positive relationship between wives' schooling level and husbands' labour market earnings. This impact is likely to be stronger in the entrepreneurial families. This impact can work directly or indirectly. It is likely that wives are directly involved in the decision making process in husband's labour market work and thus through their education they help husband in taking better labour market decision. Indirectly by keeping a peaceful environment in home, by taking care of husband's health, and by providing moral support to husband, educated wives can impact husband's labour market performance.

(ii) Child quality (education and health): the evidences here reveal a positive relationship between parents' education and children's education (cognitive development) and health. Both mothers' and father's education is important in this regard but from empirical evidences it seems that mother's education weighs little heavier than father's education. Educated mother will directly involve herself into her children's education, she will provide nutritious food to her kids, and she will also have a better health related knowledge, which will help her in keeping her child healthy. Apart from parents, even grandparents' education has some influence over their grandchildren's education. This is likely to be the case in urban areas where both parents are working and thus kids are spending most of their time with grandparents. Neighbours also have some impact on child's education. This is known as 'the neighbourhood effect'. Studies have indicated that this effect operates through the socio-economic composition of the schools.

(iii) Own health: there is considerable amount of evidences which suggests that one's own schooling positively affects his/her health, increases person's life expectancy, lowers the prevalence of severe mental illnesses and improves the ability to deal with the stressful events. All these effects are enhanced as the person ages. This is because in old age the frequency of illnesses is likely to be high and during such precarious time education will be very helpful for the person in fighting with those illnesses.

(iv) Consumer choice efficiency: research work shows that educated people are efficient consumers. They waste little resource like time, money while shopping. There are little chances of them being cheated by the sellers.

(v) Labour market search efficiency: educated people are efficient with regard to labour market search for the job too. Educated people know different sources of information regarding job openings like online job portals, employment exchanges, etc. They are also likely to migrate to distant places for the jobs without any hesitation. This is because most of the time, they have already migrated longer distance for their education itself. It is also seen that the labour market turnover is considerably low for the educated women.

(vi) Marital choice efficiency: there is also some evidence that with increased level of schooling, people tend to sort their partners much more efficiently in the marriage market. The incidence of *assortative mating* is seen more widely amongst educated people. All these reduce the cost of marriage considerably for educated people.

(vii) Attainment of desired family size: the use of contraceptive measures by the educated people reduces their family size. With education, the evidences show that, women fertility rate declines. This effect works in two different ways. One, the increasing opportunity cost of having more children for the working women[5] and second, the increased desire of the educated mother to concentrate the family resources on a single child.

(viii) Charitable giving: evidences suggest that educated people are also likely to donate more of their time and money to different charitable activities like voluntary work, Non-Governmental Organisation (NGO) membership etc.

(ix) Increased saving: more schooling is also associated with higher savings[6]. Educated persons are likely to have higher earning which is sufficient for their present consumption needs. The leftover income is thus saved for the future.

(x) Technological change: technological change, both invention of new techniques as well as its usage, has a direct link with education. Research and Development activities are education intensive. It takes lot of skilled manpower for developing new technologies. With this, the diffusion of technology also requires a skilled labour force.

(xi) Social cohesion: one of the very important non-market benefits of education is that it encourages social cohesion. The evidences suggest that with increased education people show a tendency of not resorting on violence during the period of protests. They are also likely to oppose the repression of government. Education enables individuals in making informed political decisions. Education also improves trustworthy relationships between individual members of the society. It makes them more aware of the benefits of voluntary peaceful cooperation.

(xii) Independence: evidences also show that educated people are more self-reliant. Studies show that during their prime working years, educated people are less likely to rely on various social security schemes like unemployment insurance, subsidies from the government, widow-pensions, etc.

(xiii) Crime reduction: education also has some profound impact on crime reduction. By increasing person's opportunity cost of involvement in criminal activity it reduces the incidence of crime.

All the above discussed non-market benefits are likely to accrue more to women. The reason behind this is that women are, on an average, likely to spend more time out of labour market and in home, taking care of the family[7]. This way they spend substantial amount of their time in non-market activities in home and thus, they are likely to be the greater recipient of these non-market benefits. This way women's education is a very important factor for a household as well as for the society as a whole. Because all women don't participate directly in the labour market and thus don't produce any tangible output, the conventional measures like Gross Domestic Product (GDP) will not reflect importance of women in the household as well as society. If we take into account the contribution of women in household development and economic development from the non-market benefits perspective then only we can truly realize and account for the importance of women and their education. The catalogue of non-market benefits suggests that the benefits of women's education far exceed the market benefits. The quote below has captured the true essence of importance of women and their education. For example, as Mortensen (1957) observed – *You can hand out condoms, drop bombs, build roads, or put in electricity, but until the girls are educated, a society won't change."*

Methodology

This section discusses the different ways in which education is thought to be a cause of different non-market benefits.

Until the early 1960s, economists largely ignored the economic analysis of these non- market benefits of education. But as they became aware about the importance of these benefits, they started to think about actually how to measure these benefits and how to establish a causal relationship between education and the different non-market benefits. The theoretical foundation to this work was provided by Gary S. Becker (1965, 1976) and Lancaster (1966). Becker developed the Theory of Allocation of Time. In his theory, he introduced the idea that individuals not only work as producer in the market place but they also act as producer in a non-market place. Individuals working as producer produce their fundamental objects of choice, called commodities, in the non-market sector using inputs of market goods and services and their own time. Education is quite likely to influence the efficiency of these production processes (Grossman, 2005). Robert T. Michael (1973) by using Becker's earlier work, developed theoretical tools to study the effect of education on non-market returns by using the concept of household production function. Michael showed how individuals combine their education with other market commodities and their non- market time to produce different commodities like education, health of their children etc., which contribute to their utility function. A quote from Michael,

> ....The theory employs the concept of household production functions as developed in Becker's important article on the allocation of time (Becker 1965). The household is viewed as a small multiproduct firm in which its members' non-market time is combined with purchased market goods and services to produce commodities. The household consumes all of its own production of these commodities, and it is from these commodities that the household derives its utility (Michael, 1973, p. 307).

The rationale behind this theoretical work is that the knowledge (human capital) that a person has acquired through education is embedded within himself and accompanies him wherever he goes; to the labour market where money earnings are produced, to the doctor where health is produced, to the bedroom where sexual satisfaction and perhaps children are produced, to plays and movies where entertainment is produced, and to the tennis court and ski-slope where exercise and recreation are produced. If knowledge and traits acquired through schooling influence decision made at work, they are just as likely to influence decisions made at non-work places like cigarette smoking, type of food to eat, type of contraceptive technique to use, the portion of income to save etc. All these returns to education are at the non-work, i.e., non-market places[8].

Mathematically we can represent the theoretical model of the household production function as[9]:

$$Z=z(Y,(1-\mu)H) \qquad (1)$$

Here, the Z_i's are the final satisfactions produced; (1-μ), the fraction of time that is non-market; H^{β}, the stock of human capital measured by the educational attainment within the household; and $H^{\hat{a}}$, the average education level in the community representing external effects on households. And Y stands for all goods purchased in the market as measured by per capita GNP.

The *direct effects* of education, now on each non-market outcome, are the effects of (1-μ)H on Z in Eq. (1). Specifically, they are the partial derivatives of the Z_i's, the various types of non-market outcomes, with respect to (1-μ)H.

According to the positivist methodological approach it is needed that the above cited theory of household production function be tested against the empirical data to make it more acceptable. Economists have developed different empirical techniques to capture the non-market benefits of education. I now discuss these techniques in brief[10].

Empirical studies use mostly the behavioural categorical non-experimental data of cross section of people to study the non-market benefits of education. The theoretical model developed above is the main apparatus of this empirical work. They extend the mathematical model into an econometric model by using different specifications to control different situations and then try to fit the data to that model of household production function. The major technique being employed is the regression analysis. Depending on the type of data, the researcher uses Ordinary Least Square (OLS), Logit, Logistic, and Probit regression models to estimate the parameters of education. Because of estimation difficulties, many researchers have used different techniques like (Stacey and Behrman 2000 pp. 36-51).

(a) Instrumental variables,

(b) Fixed effect models[11] etc.

to study the causal link between education and its non market benefits. The basic model used to capture the causal link between education and its non market benefits is given (Allison, 2005, p. 22) as:

$$H_{ihc} = H(E_{ihc}, I^{h}_{ihc}, F^{h}_{hc}, C^{h}_{c}, I^{hu}_{ihc}, F^{hu}_{hc}, C^{hu}_{c}, X^{hu}_{ihc}, e^{h}_{ihc}) \quad (2)$$

Where,

E_{ihc} is Education,

H_{ihc} outcome of interest on which education has an impact (in this case it is health),

I^{h}_{ihc} is a vector of observed predetermined individual characteristics (e.g., gender),

F^{h}_{hc} is a vector of observed predetermined family (household) characteristics that contribute to the learning environment that the individual *i* experiences,

C^{h}_{c} is a vector of observed predetermined community characteristics that affect child education,

I^{hu}_{ihc} is a vector of unobserved predetermined individual characteristics that affect education (e.g., innate ability),

F^{hu}_{hc} is a vector of unobserved predetermined family (household), characteristic that affect education (e.g., intellectual atmosphere),

C^{hu}_{c} is a vector of unobserved predetermined community characteristics that affect education (e.g., general intellectual atmosphere, expected returns on investing in education given technology and structure of local community),

X^{hu}_{ihc} is a vector of unobserved resources allocated by the household that affect individual *i*'s education (e.g., parental time and reading material);

e^{h}_{ihc} is a stochastic disturbance term,

Subscript *i* refers to the ith individual,

Subscript *h* refers to the household (family) of the ith individual ,

Subscript *c* refers to the community of the ith individual,

Superscript *u* means unobserved in the data (though observed by decision makers in the processes being investigated), and

Superscript *h* means that the variables are defined for health.

There are two major ways in which these benefits flow from education. First way is called *the informational efficiency* and the second way is called *the allocative efficiency.* It is hypothesised that an educated person is likely to have a better access to different kinds of information which is necessary to take decision. For example, an educated job seeker is more likely to know different sources from where he can obtain job information e.g., online job portals, newspaper postings etc. Due to having better information, an educated person can take a better decision which will result into enhanced benefits for that person. This process is likely to be absent in the case of a less educated person. Education also increases efficiency in allocating resources to achieve different ends. An educated person is better equipped with knowledge of different means for achieving different ends which he is seeking. For example, suppose better health is the end sought-after, then an educated person knows different means of achieving better health like nutritious diet, exercise, mental peace etc. And accordingly s/he will allocate these means to achieve better health.

So far in India, no major attempt has been made by any researcher to measure the above discussed non-market benefits of education, especially women's education. The literature[12] suggests that so far Indian researchers have mainly explored the link between women's education and her fertility rate, child's education, infant mortality rate etc. To fill this research gap, the present work has tried to capture the relationship between women's education and the above cited various non-market benefits. This study used a non-random sample of 300 women of 25+ age[13] who are selected from a random cluster sample of four different zones of Surat city[14]. A structured questionnaire was used to elicit the information regarding various variables of education, non-market benefits and various control variables. For measuring women's education, two different variables were used viz. number of years of education and different levels of education (a nominal qualitative variable). To isolate the impact of education on non-market benefits, various control variables were used viz. respondent's mother's education, her age, family annual income (before and after marriage), family size (before marriage), community related variables like the locality where respondent was living and average education level of the neighbourhood of the respondent while they were studying etc. The questions were designed mainly to know the behaviouristic pattern and education's impact on that behaviour. This way we can study the household production function where individuals are using their education combined with different market commodities and their time to produce the non-market commodities. To analyze and study the relationship between education and various non-market benefits, different regression techniques were used. Where dependent variables were qualitative, dichotomous type (like YES or NO), logistic regression was used and where the data were quantitative, multivariate regression was used. Cross-tabulations were used as a preliminary device to gauge the correlation between different variables. The study used the following empirical model to study the relationship between education and non-market benefits:

$$O = \alpha + \beta_1 S_r + \beta_2 A_r + \beta_3 S_{rm} + \beta_4 SL_r + \beta_5 FS_r + \beta_6 I_r + \varepsilon \quad (3)$$

Where,

O = Outcome variable such as respondent's child's schooling status,

Sr = Years of schooling of the respondent,

Ar = Age of the respondent,

Srm = Level of schooling of respondent's mother,

SLr = Respondent's schooling locality environment as measured by average educational level of that locality,

FSr = Family size of the respondent,

Ir = Annual family income of the respondent (before and after marriage); and

ε = Stochastic disturbance term.

The collected data were fitted to the above given empirical model and the various results were studied. The following section discusses the empirical findings of this study.

Findings of the Study

Table 2 below presents the combined[15] results of logistic regression and Ordinary Least Square (OLS) regression together. It presents the relationship between all non-market benefits variables (qualitative dichotomous as well as quantitative) and education as measured by respondent's *total number of years of schooling* while controlling for family background variable as measured by mother's education and family size, community variable as measured by community's average education level, the income variable as measured by family's total annual income when the respondents were studying and in present time, and their age to control for experience. Now the main results in detail.

Women's Education and Own Health

The major variable for measuring women's health in this study was her body mass index (BMI). Other variables being used were: the days spent in hospital before one month of the survey date and frequency of doing exercise as well as other behaviour such as eating habits, smoking and drinking habit, and health related knowledge.

The results suggest that the impact of education on women's health is mixed. The non-market health benefit is present in the study in the form of health related knowledge, but is missing when we consider the body mass index and regular exercise as the measure of women's health. That means, as the number of years of education increases there is no perceptible effect of this increase in education on the body mass index and knowledge of health.

Women's Education and Child and Husband's Health

To measure child's health, this study used his/her body mass index as a major variable. The results of correlation analysis suggest rather a weak and statistically insignificant relationship between women's education and her child's health. The results of regression analysis, where control variables are introduced into the model, give similar results as the correlation analysis. Increased years of education have no impact on child's health as measured by the above mentioned variables.

Table 2: Education and Non-market Benefits: Empirical Results

Dependent non-market benefit variable (Y_d)	*β coefficient*	*Wald statistics OR t-statistics*	*ρ value (significance)*	*Exp (β) (Odds ratio)*
BMI	-.074	-.841	.401	
Child BMI	-.181	-1.322	.188	
Husband Weight	.177	.941	.348	
Fertility	-.041	-.928	.354	
Child Schooling	.283	8.793	.003	1.327
Child Year Education	.324	4.290	.000	
Job	.225	14.265	.000	1.252
Bank Account Status	.183	9.898	.002	1.201
Economic Independence	.117	3.715	.054	1.124
Product Price	.165	3.906	.048	1.179
Reading Instruction	.307	15.973	.000	1.359
Time Donation	.015	.035	.851	1.015
Money Donation	-.104	2.024	.155	.901
Court Marriage	-.085	1.092	.296	.918
Dowry	-.129	3.667	.055	.879
Fasting	-.172	7.427	.006	.842
God Belief	-.168	1.958	.162	.845
Superstition	-.012	.056	.813	.988
Political Knowledge	.198	9.653	.002	1.219
Voting	.023	.219	.640	1.024
Environment	.365	23.023	.000	1.440
Traffic Knowledge	.241	10.858	.001	1.273
Railway Queue	.036	.473	.492	1.036
Spitting	-.052	.142	.706	.950

The relationship was found to be significant when children's food habits were studied. It was found that women respondents were giving healthy food to their children and possibly through that were affecting their health. Husband's weight was the major variable for measuring husband's health. The correlation analysis between wife's education and her husband's health shows a weak but positive relationship. That is, as wife's education increases, husband's weight also increases, quiet contrary to what is being expected according to theories where there should be a negative relationship between these two variables. This relationship is statistically significant. The regression analysis showed similar results with no separate impact of women's education on their husband's weight.

To measure the impact of wife's education on her husband's health, this study also used two more categorical variables, namely, how much impact wife's education has on husband's smoking and alcohol drinking habit. It is expected that educated women are more successful in keeping their husbands away from smoking and drinking. This will have direct impact on husband's health. But the result of logistic regression showed no such relationship.

Overall results suggested that the non-market benefit of women's education in the form of child's healthy diet is present in the study but it is absent from child's body mass index perspective. The non-market benefit in the form of husband's good health, as measured by his weight and smoking and alcohol drinking habit, is also missing. More research work is required to understand these relationships further.

Women's Education and Fertility Rate[16]

The celebrated negative relationship between women's education and her fertility rate is not present in this study. Although the sign of the relationship was negative as expected but it is statistically insignificant. The logistic regression model showed that women's education level has a statistically significant and positive impact on her knowledge of various methods of family planning. As the number of years of education increased the knowledge of family planning methods also increased.

Overall, we can say that women's education can be one important factor in reducing her fertility rate through her increased knowledge regarding various birth control measures. Educated women are likely to have fewer children when they know more about various family planning methods which ultimately help them in stopping the *unwanted* pregnancies.

Women's Education and Child's Schooling

Child's schooling was measured by using variables such as his/her schooling status as measured by his/her going to school or completing school or dropping out of school, and his/her number of years of schooling.

The cross-tabulation between child's schooling status and mother's education level showed a statistically significant positive relationship. It was found that educated mother's children have either successfully completed all levels of education or were presently going to school. On the other side, uneducated mothers' children have mostly dropped out of the school. Logistic regression model also showed similar results between these two variables when the model is controlled for other variables. Educated mother's child has higher probability of finishing his/her school compared to uneducated mother's children.

The regression model also showed a positive and statistically significant relationship between mother's years of schooling and her child's years of schooling. As mother's education increases by one year, children's education increases by three months. This clearly suggests that the non-market benefits of women's education in form of higher schooling for her children is strong and present in the study. Educated mothers do have educated children.

Women's Education and Saving Behaviour

Saving behaviour was measured by using categorical variables viz. saving status (do they save money or not) and their status of bank account holding. The logistic regression model of this relationship is statistically significant and showing a positive impact of education level on both the predicted variables. This suggests that educated women are having high probabilities of having a bank account and more likely to save than their uneducated women counterpart.

Women's Education and Economic and Social Independence

To measure the economic independence this study used different variables like women's labour force participation rate, the mode of bank account, and a direct behavioural variable of perception about their overall economic freedom. The logistic regression model showed a positive and statistically significant impact of women's education on their labour market participation. Educated women were participating more in labour market compared to uneducated women. Educated women were also having a higher probability of keeping a single mode bank account[17].

Based on these two results I expected women to be more economically independent overall. But their answer on the question of their feeling about overall economic freedom contradicts the previous finding. The logistic regression model showed an insignificant effect of education on women's overall economic freedom. Even well educated women felt that they don't enjoy higher economic freedom in their homes. The dependency of women makes them vulnerable. Economic freedom is a prerequisite for all other kinds of freedom and when women don't have economic freedom, they are likely to lose their other freedoms too.

Once the economic independence is lost by women, other freedoms which women wish for are hard to come by. This is reflected in the analysis of social independence variable. Women were asked whether they need to take someone's permission before going out to attend any social function. The results suggest that even educated women had to take permission for attending social functions.

Women's Education and Consumer Choice Efficiency

To measure women's consumer choice efficiency, this study used two major variables.

1. Knowledge of product prices and food availability places; and
2. Habit of reading manufacturing date and expiry date instruction on package while shopping.

The logistic regression showed that educated women are having higher probability of reading the instructions on the packet vis-à-vis uneducated women. But they were unaware about the product prices and place of food availability.

Overall results suggest that when it is a matter of information regarding various aspects of shopping, education has no real impact on that behaviour. But once the women are on the shopping place, education does start to show its impact in a way that more educated women tend to check manufacturing and expiry date more than uneducated women.

Women's Education and Charitable Activity

Charitable activity was measured by using two variables. One variable measured their status of voluntary work (donation of time), and another measured their donation of money to some charitable institutions like Non-Governmental Organisations (NGOs).

The result suggests that women's level of education had no statistically significant impact on both the predicted variables of voluntary work and donation of money. The non-market benefit of women's education in form of charitable activity is not present in this study.

Women's Education and Marital Choice Efficiency

To measure the marital choice efficiency, this study used three different variables.

(a) Choice of doing a court marriage, which will save financial resources and time;

(b) Status of dowry i.e., whether her parents gave dowry or not? The presence of dowry shows inefficiency; and

(c) Total cost of marriage which again will reflect the efficient choice in marriage.

The results showed that women's education has no statistically significant impact on dowry and court marriage decision. On the contrary, educated women were giving more dowries in their marriages.

The regression analysis between women's education and their total marriage cost also shows no impact of women's education. This suggests that even educated women were spending more financial resources on their marriages.

Overall, there was no evidence of non-market benefit of women's education in the form of their marital choice efficiency[18].

Women's Education and Superstitious, Religious and Social Beliefs

To measure the superstitious behaviour of women respondents the study used the behavioural variable of their action when they see a cat crossing their road (if they stopped that shows belief in superstition and vice versa), to measure their religious behaviour it used frequency of going to temple/mosque/church etc., (regular visits suggesting religious beliefs), and to measure their social custom beliefs it used variable of frequency of fasting (regular fasting showing social beliefs).

The results suggest:

- Regarding fasting, education does have a statistically significant negative impact. The probability is high for educated women of not doing fast for various social and cultural traditional purposes like for a long life of her husband[19].
- Education has no impact on religious beliefs[20]. The parameter estimate B was statistically insignificant suggesting even educated women go regularly to temple/mosque/church etc., to worship God.
- The impact of education on women's superstitious beliefs is also not statistically significant. This again suggests educated women's belief in such superstitious beliefs.

All these results show that education still has to make big in roads to make people more scientific or logical. The non-market benefit of scientific critical thinking doesn't exist in this study.

Women's Education and Political Awareness

Political awareness is necessary to keep an eye on what is going on in the political sphere of the country. An alert citizenry can keep total control on rogue governments and notorious politicians from doing whatever they wish to. If educated and aware about the politics, then people can forever remove the State rulers when they see it fit to do. This way people around the world can protect their liberty. To measure the political awareness, this study used two categorical variables, namely, knowledge regarding different election types and the name of present prime minister of India. I used the voting frequency to see whether respondents were actively participating in the political process or not. The results suggest the following:

- Regarding their knowledge of various types of election, women's education has a positive and statistically significant impact. Probability was high that educated women would know more about various types of election vis-à-vis uneducated women.
- The odds were also high for educated women to know more about the prime minister of India.
- This knowledge of various political issues amongst educated women is not resulting into more voting in election. Odds ratio suggested that the level of education has no impact on voting[21].

Overall, the non-market benefit of women's education in the form of political awareness is high amongst educated women compared to uneducated women, but majority of them were not voting in elections because of some logical reasons which future studies need to find out.

Women's Education and Environmental Awareness

Global warming and climate change are big debatable issues of the present time. The debate is predominantly of a political nature rather than scientific. However, clean and healthy environment is desirable[22]. No one wants to live in a pollution ridden world. To measure the environmental awareness, this study used two variables namely, women's knowledge of the problem of global warming and local environmental problems of Surat city.

The regression model showed impact of level of education on women's awareness regarding environmental issues. Similar results were found regarding knowledge of different environmental problems of Surat city.

Women's Education and Civic Sense

Civic sense of people reflects the maturity and character of the country. It shows how civilized the society is. This study used, as measure of civic sense, three variables, namely, respondent's traffic knowledge, their implementation of these rules on road, and whether they stand in queue at railways station and their behaviour of spitting in public places. The logistic regression showed the following results:

- Educated women are more knowledgeable about various traffic rules i.e., as the number of years of education increases the knowledge of traffic rules also increases;
- Educated women are also implementing traffic rules on road;
- But when it comes to standing in a queue at railway station during testing situations, even educated women were breaking the queues frequently; and
- Similar results were found between women's education and their spitting habit. Most educated women were having this habit.

Overall results suggest that the relationship between women's education and their civic sense is very weak and only exists in their traffic sense. As the level of education increases, the study didn't see any perceptible difference in civic behaviour of women respondents. Education is not making these women civilized. This shows a failure of education system. The non-market benefit of education in form of higher civic sense is missing in this study.

Conclusion and Policy Implications

If we see the total picture of different non-market benefits of women's education, then the results are mixed. Increased years of education improved women's own and her family's health to some extent; it had an impact on her children's cognitive development. It increased savings rate and through that it did show an impact on long run economic progress of the family as well as of the economy at large. It improved the consumer efficiency to some extent. Educated women were also politically aware in context of measured variables and they also had basic awareness of various environmental issues.

On the other hand, women's education is failing in giving them their desired freedom. Educated women are also not very generous in terms of charitable activity. Education is proving to be quite ineffective in inducing women to make efficient marital choices. Superstitious, religious and social beliefs are still firmly gripping even the educated women. Education also has no perceptible influence on making women of this study more civic.

Education's impact is felt to some extent in the household but it is failing to have any big impact on larger issues like women's freedom, civic sense, blind beliefs etc. These results show that there is something wrong with the education system of the country. Education is not resulting into overall development of a girl child[23]. The vast resources which the country is spending on girl's education are going waste if it is not resulting into overall development of a girl child. There are many causes of this failure. The main causal factor is the present schooling system. Social and cultural environment of the country is also responsible for this. But, because schooling system is expected to change the societal structure, and instead of doing that it is only reinforcing the prevalent system so, ultimately schooling system is the main factor responsible for this problem.

At school level, I personally see the kind of education schooling system provides to our children as a fundamental problem. The way school promotes rote learning and its sole concentration on examination is truly problematic. The brainless process of classroom provides no stimulus to a child for learning new things. Instead of instilling and improving the critical faculties of children, classroom processes frequently try to kill those faculties. Suppressing child's curiosity is the major act of large number of teachers and even many parents. Textbooks are packed with useless information instead of concrete methods of acquiring knowledge. Schools fail to teach our children how to learn things. *Learning to learn* is the basic skill one needs to be an independent thinker and a good human being. The compulsory schooling system is a *weapon of mass instruction* (Gatto, 2009); it is *dumbing down* the children (Gatto, 1992).

Our society need to reintroduce the holistic concept of education into the schooling system. Education should promote and develop critical thinking of students. Schools should give them basic tools of acquiring and using knowledge effectively. Education should teach everyone how to live life fully. It should equip them with all the required skills so that they can face their life and its various problems successfully. Making education just geared towards job market creates problem for individuals and overall progress of the society.

Education will also make societal structure more conducive for girls. The task of changing this environment is herculean. It requires lot of patience and constant effort on part of people who understand the need for change. Societal institutions must protect the fundamental private property rights of women and everyone else. Institutions must see to it that no woman is coerced to do things against her will. If any individual woman is forced to do things against her will and if she raises her voice against that then she must get justice from the judicial institutions. Women themselves are required to work for their betterment by becoming aware about their *natural rights*. This requires lot of courage on the part of women and I know not many will attempt it. But changes come from the actions of small number of courageous people.

Education will help women in protecting their natural rights. It will make them independent from all sorts of unwanted dependencies. Educated women are the backbone of any society and its progress. To end with an important quote:

> *"Educate a boy, and you educate an individual. Educate a girl, and you educate a community: African proverb via Greg Mortensen"* - (Greg & Relin, 2007)

References

Allison, P. D. (2005): Fixed Effects Regression Methods for Longitudinal Data Using SAS. North Carolina, USA: SAS Publishing.

Becker, G. S. (1965): A Theory of Allocation of Time. *The Economic Journal, 75*(299), 493-517.

________ (1976): The Economic Approach to Human Behavior. Chicago: University of Chicago Press.

Gatto, J. T. (1992): Dumbing us Down : the Hidden Curriculum of Compulsory Schooling. Philadelphia: New Society Publishers.

________(2009): Weapons of Mass Instruction : A Schoolteacher's Journey Through the Dark World of Compulsory Schooling. Gabriola Island, BC: New Society Publishers.

Greg, M., & Relin, D. O. (2007): Three Cups of Tea: One Man's Mission to Promote Peace . . . One School at a Time. New York. Penguine Books.

Grossman, M. (2005): Education and Non-Market Outcomes. *NBER Working Paper No: 11582*.

Hirway, I. (2009). Mainstreaming Time Use Surveys in National Statistical System in India. *Economic and Political Weekly, XLIV* (49), 56-65.

Hirway, I., & Antonopoulos, R. (Eds.) (2010): Unpaid Work and the Economy: Gender, Time Use and Poverty. Palgrave MacMillan

Lancaster, K. J. (1966): A New Approach to Consumer Theory. *Journal of Political Economy, 74*, 132-157.

McMahon, W. W. (2000): The Impact of Human Capital on Non-Market Outcomes and Feedbacks on Economic Development. *OECD*.

________(2002): Education and Development: Measuring the Social Benefits. New York: Oxford University Press.

Michael, R. T. (1973): Education in Non-market Production. *The Journal of Political Economy, 81*(2), 306-327.

Psacharopoulos, G. (1973): Returns to Education: An International Comparison. Amsterdam: Elsevier.

________(1985): Returns to Education: A Further International Update and Implications. *Journal of Human Resources,* 20(4), 583-604.

________(1994): Returns to Investment in Education: A Global Update. *World Development,* 22(9), 1325-1343.

Psacharopoulos, G., & Patrinos, A. H. (2002): Returns to Investment in Education: A Further Update. *The World Bank Policy Research Working Paper 2881*.

Raj, M. (2009): Non-Market Benefits of Women's Education : An Evidence from the Surat City (Unpublished thesis). Surat.

Stacey, N., & Behrman, J. R. (2000): The Social Benefits of Education. Michigan: The University of Michigan Press.

Wolfe, B. L., & Haveman, R. H. (2002): Social and Nonmarket Benefits from Education in an Advanced Economy. Paper presented at the Federal Reserve Bank of Boston Conference Series. [Proceedings], Boston.

Notes

1. For examp'e India has started the nationwide programme of Sarva Siksha Abhiyan (SSA) to raise the educational standards of her population. Similarly, many developing and underdeveloped countries of the world have adopted the Millennium Development Goals (MDGs), in which achieving the universal elementary education is one of the important goals.
2. For the empirical evidences of non-market benefits of education please refer to Grossman (2005); McMahon (2002); Stacey & Behrman (2000); Wolfe & Haveman (2002).
3. Taken from Wolfe & Haveman (2002) with modifications.
4. For evidence of this benefit and also for other discussed benefits in this section please see, (Wolfe & Haveman) (2002).

5. In today's costly inflationary and high tax economies where increasing income is necessary to maintain the otherwise falling standard of living, wives will also have to work. Single earner family is a phenomenon of past.
6. It is important to stress here the absolute necessity of savings for the future progress of the economy. Without saving and investment, capital accumulation will become impossible, which in turn will retard the long run economic growth. The economy where saving and investment are lower than consumption is a retrogressing economy and where they are higher is a progressing economy. Education, thus, by playing a role in increasing the habits of savings, enhances long run economic growth.
7. According to ILO, the labour force participation rate (LFPR) of Indian women aged 25 to 54 in year 2008 was 43.1 percent compared to 96.3 percent for their male counterparts. For further evidence of this pattern of division of labour for Indian women see the results of NSSO's Time Use Survey 1998-99 (available online here - http://www.mospi.nic.in/stat_act_t5_2.htm, accessed on 20th December, 2009). For some interesting analysis of this time use survey please refer to, (Hirway, 2009; Hirway & Antonopoulos, 2010).
8. Taken from Grossman (2005) with some modifications.
9. The following discussion is taken from McMahon (2000).
10. For a full discussion of these techniques and various other conceptual and measurement issues involved in capturing the non-market benefits of education see Stacey & Behrman (2000), pp. 17-67).
11. To know more about the fixed effect model, please refer to Allison (2005).
12. To see this literature please refer to Raj (2009).
13. The rationale for selecting only 25+ age women is that 25+ age women have normally finished their education and are thus already using their education in producing non-market benefits in their households.
14. Because of the unavailability of sampling frame the sample of women could not be selected randomly. Four zones of Surat city were selected randomly through lottery method and from those zones respondents were selected by going to field directly. Because of the non-random nature of the sample the external validity of my research is weak.
15. These results include only major dependent non-market benefits variable and the independent education variable with which their relationship is being studied. Because of space constraints all the variables are not included here.
16. How many children to have is the decision of individual parents. If a family can support more children on their own then there is nothing wrong in having them.
17. According to me, sharing a bank account with husband shows a likely economic dependency, although not necessarily. A joint bank account can also be the result of mutual consent between husband and wife.
18. All these results may just reflect the fact that marriage is seen as a once in a lifetime event in individual's life in India and is also an opportunity to show the social status so people spend lavishly in marriages. I see no problem with this behaviour as long as individuals are facing consequences of their decision and not passing such cost on other individuals in society.

19. There is no logic here as how by remaining hungry a wife can increase longevity of her husband. If she wants to increase his life then, as research shows, she has to take care of his physical and mental health directly. She has to give him nutritious food, has to take control over her risky health habits and need to give her mentally healing emotional support throughout her life. This is true for all husbands too. In a married life husband and wife both are partners of everything. So the responsibility lies on both to take care of each other. I wonder why husbands don't do such fasting for long life of their wives, even if it just doesn't work!
20. Believing in God is harmless as long as it does not involve retardation of one's development as a good human being. If such beliefs are retarding mental growth and thinking power of an individual then I see it as a major problem.
21. Given the low voting turn out ratio all over the country, it will be very important to study the causes of such low turnout. There must be a logical reason behind people not voting. I think people are so fade up with the overall political atmosphere of the country that they are refraining from voting. Probably they just don't want to be ruled.
22. But environmental extremism is very dangerous. Trading-off the standard of living and lives of people for green environment and few animal species etc., is never a good option to choose.
23. And same may be true for boys too who are also the product of this same education system.

END NOTE

– *RATNA M. SUDARSHAN AND J. B. G. TILAK*

This volume represents a modest effort of the editors to articulate the 'collective mind' of gender and education research in India. Taking a selection of sixteen research articles, the majority of which were published in the Journal of Educational Planning and Administration, as a guide to the gender issues that have been addressed by education researchers in India, an attempt is made to draw a picture on the contemporary research on gender issues in education.

What emerges from the volume? The intersecting nature of disadvantage, calling for attention simultaneously to gender, caste, class, location, emerges as an insight. Some research has been done on the interaction between culture and economics in explaining educational outcomes suggesting that culture alone does not explain gendered educational outcomes and economic factors have a strong often underestimated influence. One area that is insufficiently studied is that of wider impacts of education in social and political spaces. Overall, the papers suggest that education continues to be both a way of sustaining some structures of inequality, as well as being part of change processes particularly when seen together with work opportunities. That there are different findings on the extent to which education can be 'empowering' could indicate differences in the context, and many more empirical studies may be needed before any clear associations could be drawn or pathways of empowerment through education be better understood.

In concluding, five main points can be made.

First, the several studies re-affirm the view that context makes a difference. As M.N. Srinivas put it in a lecture on the changing position of Indian women, 'generalization is pretty nearly impossible because of the existence of considerable variation between regions, between rural and urban areas, between classes, and finally between different religions, ethnic and caste groups. While in certain contexts the Indian sub-continent is a single cultural region, in many others it is heuristically more rewarding to look upon it as a congeries of micro-regions, differences between which are crucial.' (Srinivas 1977: 222). Thirty years later, this comment still appears to be as relevant as it was earlier. Velaskar's study of the interaction between caste, class and patriarchy in explaining educational access of dalits in Maharashtra is an example of articulating such 'micro regions'. A good illustration of the differences that exist between regions or groups, is seen in the finding that women usually marry men who are better educated (as in Lakshamanasamy's paper) but another study tells us that among Muslims a substantial segment of girls may marry less well educated men (as in Husain). These and other papers seem to make a good case for field work based micro studies that can throw light on the complex realities of gender and education.

Second, there appears to be no substantial empirical work or at least none presented in JEPA that tries to understand the ways in which schools contribute to the construction of gendered identities, including the ways in which educational failure can lead to aggressive masculinity or passive acceptance. While the third gender is now a recognized category in schools, adolescent sexuality is still rarely addressed within schools. As R. W. Connell pointed out, 'Schools do not simply adapt to a natural masculinity among boys or femininity among girls. They are agents in the matter, constructing particular forms of gender and negotiating relations between them' (Connell 1989). How this plays out in different contexts in India is an unexplored area.

Third, many more cross- sectoral studies are needed. The linkages between education and other sectors need to be better understood in order to identify the wider impacts of education. In particular, the interactions between gender, education and work; gender, education and political participation; and gender, education and decision making within the home, have been noted and yet inadequately studied. Several papers draw attention to the better performance of girls in some situations and the higher dropout of boys in order to join the workforce. However, reasons why better (or worse) school performance does not often translate into any noticeable change in post-schooling norms and behaviours are less explored. The question of how education interacts with underlying and persistent structures of gender inequality needs more attention. Most studies limit the studies of wider impacts to inter-generational effects - adult female literacy/ education has been found by many researchers to be an effective tool to increase girls' access to education. Different outcomes have been noted, for example, education can increase women's own earnings and work opportunities, and hence improve bargaining power and control over decision making according to some research, but can also be a way of strengthening assortative marriages and maintaining conventional roles. The possibility of adverse effects of women's work on girl child education has been hinted at in one paper.

Fourth, there is the question of method. Over the years, more data has become available encouraging greater data-based research. Analysis of national data throws up interesting and important patterns; but for deeper understanding of the social change processes that are closely linked to education, it becomes necessary to examine regional and social group-wise differences, and incorporate qualitative and ethnographic information. Perhaps as a result of editorial policy, it can be noted that there is a clear emphasis on quantitative methods in general in JEPA, with most articles using quantitative analysis to explore issues, including gender issues. Of the articles included here, only one empirical study can properly be described as based on qualitative analysis, and one is a historical study. Quantitative analysis can be more effectively used to explore gender issues, if there is adequate contextualization, a clear framing of the gender issues being explored, and innovative methods of analysis used. Without this, quantitative methods run the danger of leading to a focus on only that which can be easily measured, which especially in the context of gender leads to only partial analysis of the issues. As the popular quotation goes, 'Not everything that counts can be counted, and not everything that can be counted, counts'.[1] Well-contextualized econometric analysis and analytical frameworks for non-linear relationships would better represent the complexity of the gender equality and education issue. Alternatively, a stronger combination of qualitative and quantitative research methods would be needed.

And finally, a dialogue between researchers either in the context of a particular social group, or a particular part of the country, would add depth to what is known, and allow better generalization of the relationships between education and gender equality. Given the wide variations by location and social group, many more empirical studies are needed across the country, but at the same time moving away from stand-alone studies to efforts at synthesizing across studies done in a particular part of the country, for a particular social group, or for social groups within a region. A quick scan of the bibliographic references in each article suggests that there are no texts on gender and education in India that have been repeatedly cited or used to frame the different studies. Each article draws thus on a somewhat different background reading. While data sources used are similar in most cases, and some of the econometric techniques used are similar, the understanding of gender issues in education does not necessarily draw upon common texts and sociological studies. Although each author may build upon their previous work, it does not appear that different authors have referred to or built upon each other's work. None of the articles appears to have stimulated discussion within the pages of the journal and there is little evidence of a body of work emerging around key themes that may have emerged. Of course, this may be a problem with social science research in general: in a research note PunitaGovil points out that 'There has long been a pessimistic feeling that progress in the field of social sciences is not as orderly as of 'harder' sciences. The most recent work of 'harder' sciences seems to build upon the older work of those sciences, while the most recent work of social sciences seems to be 'starting from scratch''

(Govil 2004: 240). The 'stand-alone' nature of the articles reviewed here certainly limits the possible impact on subsequent research or policy formulation.

References

Govil, Punita, 2004, Educational research and policy making: the Indian scene, JEPA Vol XVIII, no 2, pp 235-242.

Connell, R.W. 1989, 'Cool guys, swots and wimps: the interplay of masculinity and education', *Oxford Review of Education*, Vol 15, no 3, pp 291-303

Srinivas, M.N. 1977The Changing Position of Indian Women. *Man*12:221–38.